Advanced
Visual Basic Techniques

Advanced
Visual Basic Techniques

Rod Stephens

WILEY COMPUTER PUBLISHING

John Wiley & Sons, Inc.
New York • Chichester • Weinheim • Brisbane • Singapore • Toronto

Publisher: Bob Ipsen
Senior Editor: Robert Elliott
Senior Managing Editor: Frank Grazioli
Electronic Products, Associate Editor: Michael Green
Text Design & Composition: Benchmark Productions, Inc., Boston, MA

Copyright © 1997 by Rod Stephens
Published by John Wiley & Sons Publishing, Inc.

Library of Congress Cataloging-in-Publication Data:
ISBN: 0-471-18881-6

Printed in the United States of America
10 9 8 7 6 5 4 3 2 1

Contents

Introduction

In recent years Visual Basic has revolutionized Windows programming. By handling many of the tedious details of Windows programming, Visual Basic allows developers to focus on more application-specific tasks.

Despite the fact that Visual Basic handles the more mundane Windows programming details, few books cover sophisticated programming methods. Books that do mention advanced concepts do so only briefly, and they often demonstrate complicated techniques with over-simplified examples. For instance, the "Scribble" application for drawing a simple freehand picture using the mouse is often used to demonstrate such concepts as SDI and MDI interfaces, saving and loading data in files, common dialogs, drawing attributes, and even object-oriented data structures. The Scribble application may teach important lessons, but it provides little help in solving real-world problems because very few real applications call for freehand drawing. The reader is left to decide how to apply the lessons learned to solve real programming problems.

By providing complete solutions to realistic problems, *Advanced Visual Basic Techniques* goes farther than other Visual Basic texts. A book can stretch artificial examples like Scribble only so far. It would be difficult to extend Scribble to reasonably demonstrate client/server architectures, storage of bitmaps for database applications, and Web browsing. By giving separate solutions to a variety of realistic problems, *Advanced Visual Basic Techniques* can explain all of these techniques within meaningful contexts.

Advanced Visual Basic Techniques bridges the gap between programming technique and real-world applications. It provides working solutions to a selection of realistic problems that you might actually want to solve, and, in the course of explaining the solutions, it demonstrates advanced programming concepts that you will find in few other Visual Basic programming books.

What You Will Gain

This book and its compact disk will provide you with the following:

- An in-depth introduction to advanced application programming techniques. After reading the book and studying the applications, you will be able to incorporate sophisticated capabilities into your Visual Basic projects.
- Complete, ready-to-run applications that solve real-world problems. You can use these applications as they are written, or you can customize them to meet your specific needs.

If you are not already an experienced Visual Basic application developer, you will be one by the time you have studied all the sample applications. Armed with an arsenal of powerful implementation techniques, you will be prepared to attack the most complex development problems.

Intended Audience

This book covers intermediate and advanced Visual Basic application programming topics. It does not teach the Visual Basic language itself. If you have a good understanding of the fundamentals of Visual Basic, you are ready for the applications and advanced techniques in this book. If you do not know how to place controls on a form, write an event handler to respond to a command button's Click event, or run a Visual Basic program, you might want to brush up on the basics a bit before proceeding.

Even if you have not yet completely mastered Visual Basic, you will be able to understand and run the applications. With occasional references to your Visual Basic manuals, you will be able to modify the examples to build similar applications of your own. By the time you have finished exploring all of the examples, you will have become an experienced Visual Basic application developer.

How to Use This Book

You might take a couple of different approaches to using this book. Naturally, you can read the book from front to back, studying each chapter in turn. This will give you a broad introduction to many powerful application implementation techniques. You will then be able to incorporate those techniques into your own Visual Basic applications.

A second approach is to pick a chapter that describes an application similar to one you want to build. Then you can study that chapter and modify the application to suit your particular needs. If you want to conduct a survey using a Web page, for example, you could move immediately to Chapter 18. The WebSurvey application described there provides a framework you can use to conduct your survey. With a few modifications you will be running your survey in no time.

The later section "How this Book Is Organized" describes each of the sample applications so that you can find the one that best fits your particular needs. Each chapter begins with a description of the application explained in that chapter. Each also includes a "Key Techniques" section listing the main concepts and programming methods described in that chapter.

A third strategy for using *Advanced Visual Basic Techniques* is to select a technique or concept you would like to use in your applications. You can then learn more about that technique by studying the corresponding sample applications. For example, you might want to add a recent file list to your drawing application. The ExpenseReporter application described in Chapters 1 and 2 uses a recent file list. By reading the appropriate sections in Chapter 1, you can learn how to add this feature to your application.

Finally, each of the applications described in this book was selected for its easy usability. You will probably find at least one or two that you can use as they are written. For example, the PropertySetter, Aligner, Scroller, and AddInMaker applications described in Chapters 4 through 7 are handy tools that make Visual Basic programming easier. You can add these applications to the Add-Ins menu of your Visual Basic development environment and take advantage of their power even if you do not examine their code in detail.

How This Book Is Organized

The chapters presented later in the book are generally more "advanced" than those at the beginning. You may think the earlier chapters are less "state-of-the-art," but they are not necessarily less complicated or less difficult to understand. For example, Chapters 1 and 2 describe a single-document interface application. Putting all of the finishing touches on even a simple application can be quite difficult. It is no trivial task to give this application recent file lists, help, context-sensitive help, scrolling regions, printing, printer control, print previewing, field validations, and all of the other features needed by a professional-quality application.

The chapters are arranged so that they do not depend on your having read the earlier material. This means you can read the chapters in any order you like. The exception to this rule is Chapter 2, which continues the discussion of the ExpenseReporter application described in Chapter 1. Chapter 1 explains ExpenseReporter from the user's point of view. Although the concepts explained in Chapter 2 do not require that you understand all of Chapter 1, they will make more sense if you have read at least the beginning of Chapter 1.

Applications later in the book may use techniques described earlier without any explanation. For example, several applications provide some form of help, but help systems are described only in the first few chapters. When you are working with an application, if you come across a topic that was covered earlier, you can always go back to the previous chapters to learn more.

The chapters in *Advanced Visual Basic Techniques* are divided into five parts.

Part I—Application Basics

The applications described in these chapters cover basic techniques that are common in many Visual Basic applications. Some concepts, such as help and context-sensitive help, are essential for any successful application. Others, including object-oriented input and output, are useful in a wide variety of circumstances.

- **Chapter 1: ExpenseReporter—Part I.** ExpenseReporter is a single-document interface (SDI) program that allows the user to create, edit, and print a one-page expense report. Chapter 1 explains application fundamentals including scrolling areas, control arrangement, dynamic controls, field navigation, SDI issues, loading and saving files, menu design, and recent file lists.
- **Chapter 2: ExpenseReporter—Part II.** Chapter 2 continues the explanation of ExpenseReporter started in Chapter 1. It covers the more complicated topics of field- and form-level validation, printing, print preview, help, about dialogs, and splash screens.
- **Chapter 3: AppointmentBook.** This application allows the user to schedule and track appointments. When it is time for an appointment, the program presents a reminder. AppointmentBook shows how to work with bit masks, use the MVC paradigm to manage complex views of data, create rotated fonts, scroll large amounts of data, set alarms to wait until a specified time, and create non-rectangular forms.

Part II—Programming Tools

These applications implement useful programming tools. You can add them to your Visual Basic development environment's Add-Ins menu and use them to make routine programming tasks easier. In addition to providing you with helpful tools, these applications show how you can create other programming aids to automate mundane programming chores.

- **Chapter 4: PropertySetter.** This application allows a developer to view and modify the properties of many controls at the same time. For example, if a group of label controls is selected, Property-Setter can give them all the same name and place them in a control array. The chapter explains how to create, connect, and disconnect add-ins, access controls selected in the development environment, and set control properties.
- **Chapter 5: Aligner.** This add-in allows a developer to align controls on a Visual Basic form easily. Aligner can arrange controls in several ways including vertically, horizontally, and in grids. Aligner demonstrates how an add-in can reposition existing controls in a Visual Basic project.
- **Chapter 6: Scroller.** The Scroller add-in takes a group of selected controls and places them in a scrolling region. It shows how an add-in can create new controls, add them to a form, and place one control inside another. It also demonstrates how to create add-in submenus and how to add Visual Basic source code to a form.
- **Chapter 7: AddInMaker.** AddInMaker is an add-in that automates the creation of add-ins. It provides an interesting exercise in add-in creation. Once you understand an add-in that creates other add-ins, you will understand the topic thoroughly.

Part III—Databasics

Part III contains database applications that run on the same computer that holds the database. Using a database, your applications can easily manage large amounts of complex data. A database also allows multiple applications to use the same data in different ways without interfering with each other.

- **Chapter 8: PeopleWatcher.** This application is a corporate personnel system. It demonstrates how to use an outline control to display data, how to store bitmaps in an Access database, and how to manage user changes to data. It also shows how to present different users with different views of the data and how to determine which users should be allowed to modify specific data fields.
- **Chapter 9: Query.** The Query application allows the user to enter and execute SQL queries on a database. This chapter explains how an application can create, connect, and disconnect databases and process SQL statements. It also explains the most common SQL commands including SELECT, INSERT, UPDATE, and DELETE.
- **Chapter 10: PeopleWatcher Remote.** This application extends the PeopleWatcher application described in Chapter 8 across a network. By connecting the program to a database located elsewhere in the network, the application allows multiple users on different computers to use PeopleWatcher at the same time. This chapter explains how a program can connect directly to a database across a network and how it can use local tables attached to tables in a remote database.

Part IV—Client/Server Applications

Part IV includes client/server applications. In a client/server application, one program, the *server*, provides some sort of service for another application, the *client*. Client/server applications allow a system to distribute functionality across a network to provide features such as improved performance and centralized resource management.

- **Chapter 11: TimeSync.** TimeSync allows two computers to synchronize their clocks. This application has been kept fairly simple so that you can concentrate on the process of creating a client/server application rather than on application issues. This chapter describes the complicated process of creating, testing, and installing a simple client/server application.
- **Chapter 12: QueryServer.** This application uses client and server programs to generate standard reports. It shows how a centralized report server can make managing reports distributed across a network simple while minimizing network traffic.
- **Chapter 13: AsyncServer.** Normally a client application waits until a server finishes its processing tasks before continuing. AsyncServer shows how a client can continue processing while one or more servers run asynchronously. This allows the application to take full advantage of the network's distributed processing power.

Part V—ActiveX

ActiveX is a specification that describes how objects should interact with each other. Because Visual Basic 5 complies with the ActiveX standard, it allows a programmer to build new objects that were not possible before. These objects include controls created from other controls. The chapters in Part V explain how to create ActiveX controls that can be used in Visual Basic projects or applications written in other languages.

- **Chapter 14: The Alarm Control.** Visual Basic's Timer control is designed for triggering frequently occurring events. In contrast, the Alarm control schedules isolated events that occur relatively far in the future. This chapter shows how to create properties and events; initialize, save, and restore property values; delegate responsibilities to other controls; and use an ActiveX control in another application.
- **Chapter 15: The Bar Gauge Control.** The Bar Gauge control uses several techniques that are not needed by the Alarm control. The Bar Gauge demonstrates how to draw a control with a visible interface, manage mouse movement, and handle keyboard events.
- **Chapter 16: The Histogram Control.** ActiveX controls behave almost exactly as other controls behave. In particular, they can be used to create other ActiveX controls. The Histogram control uses a set of Bar Gauge controls to display a set of data values. This chapter shows how an ActiveX control can manage an array of other ActiveX controls, use a scroll bar to allow the user to scroll through data, support indexed properties, and raise indexed events.

Part VI—Spinning the Web

The World Wide Web allows millions of computer users to visit a multitude of different computers effortlessly. On those computers, visitors can find a practically limitless number of pages of multimedia information. The applications presented in Part VI deal with creating and manipulating Web pages in Visual Basic.

- **Chapter 17: ActiveX Controls on the Web.** This chapter explains how a Web page can display ActiveX controls. It describes special Web licensing issues, ensuring control safety, and the actual use of ActiveX controls in a Web page. It presents several examples including a WebLabel control that can be used to display and update labels on a Web page. It also explains how a control can load larger amounts of data, such as pictures, asynchronously from the server computer.
- **Chapter 18: WebSurvey.** This application allows a Web user to fill in a survey form and send the results to a remote program written in Visual Basic. That program can then process the results in any way necessary—for example, saving the results in a file. This chapter explains how to build a survey Web page, send data across the Web to a remote program, receive data at the remote program, and pack and unpack data so that it is not damaged during the process.
- **Chapter 19: SiteMapper.** The SiteMapper application starts at a Web address and visits all of the Web documents it can reach without leaving the original site. It shows how the various documents are related, and it lists the references to image files they contain. SiteMapper shows how a program can retrieve Web documents, parse URLs, expand partial URLs, and follow links to visit a Web site.

Approach

Most Windows programs are event-driven. The computer spends most of its time sitting around waiting for the user to do something that will send the program into action. When the user presses a command button, selects a menu item, or adjusts the value of a scroll bar, the program briefly awakens. It performs some task and then lapses back into hibernation to await the user's next command.

This sort of design makes an application responsive to the user's needs, but it can make the application design harder to explain. Simple diagrams such as flow charts cannot adequately represent the program's architecture. Because the application spends most of its time idle, there is little control flow to diagram. Other constructions, such as entity-relationship (ER) diagrams, can describe relationships among classes and certain other large-scale objects, but they do not explain how event-driven programs work.

It is probably more productive to think of a typical Windows program as a collection of user interface elements tied to underlying code. A form contains command button, menu, and list box controls. There is often little or no meaningful relationship among these controls. It makes no sense to think of one command button as a "child" of another. It also makes little sense to think of a menu item "passing control" to a list box. Generally, the user interacts with a control, and that control invokes some Visual Basic source code. It is the controls themselves and the underlying code that define the application's architecture.

The chapters that follow focus on the code behind the controls. Each chapter begins by explaining what its application does from the user's point of view. It then gives a list of the key techniques demonstrated by the underlying code behind the controls. The sections that follow describe those key concepts.

Note that the concepts do not always match one-to-one with the controls. For example, the ExpenseReporter application described in Chapter 1 contains many fields that contain numbers. This application uses field validation functions to ensure that the user enters only valid numeric values in those fields. In this case, a single set of field validation routines can manage user input for dozens of different text boxes.

An application's controls function independently, but the underlying key concepts are often coupled. For example, the functions that implement recent file lists are closely related to the subroutines that load, save, and create new files. Because there is no clear flow of control among these subroutines, you may need to read about them all to get a clear understanding of how they fit together.

This book describes only pieces of code that are particularly interesting or confusing. Control placement and source code that is straightforward are not described here. You can find the complete source code for every application on the accompanying compact disk. See the section "Using the Compact Disk" for instructions on loading the source code from the disk.

Equipment You Will Need

To run and modify the example applications, you need a computer that is reasonably able to run Visual Basic 5.0. A 486-based computer running Microsoft Windows 95 or Windows NT will work. You will also need a compact disk drive to load the programs from the accompanying compact disk.

The client/server applications described in Chapters 10 through 13 use more advanced networking and OLE server techniques that work only in the Visual Basic Enterprise Edition under Windows 95 and

Windows NT. The ActiveX applications presented in Chapters 14 through 19 use features introduced in Visual Basic 5.

If you do not have the Enterprise Edition, or if you are running an older version of Windows, some of these applications will not run as they are presented in the book. You can still read the chapters and learn valuable lessons about the application architectures. Using the fundamental architectures and some file management tricks, you can even implement similar applications without using OLE servers. This is a hard route to follow, however, and you may be better off if you upgrade your software and save yourself a lot of time and trouble.

All the applications on the CD, except the programs in Chapter 13, have been tested in Visual Basic 5.0 under Windows 95 and Windows NT. The programs explained in Chapters 1, 2, and 4 through 13 were also tested using 32-bit Visual Basic 4.0. Though the programs may look slightly different in the two environments, they will perform in roughly the same manner. The applications described in Chapters 3 and 14 through 19 use features introduced by Visual Basic 5.0 so they will not run with earlier versions of Visual Basic.

The applications will run at different speeds on different computers with different configurations, but they will all work. If you own a 200 megahertz Pentium with 64MB of memory, applications will run much faster than they would if you owned a 486-based computer with 8MB of memory. Both machines will be able to run the applications, but at different speeds. You will quickly learn the limits of your hardware.

Using the Compact Disk

The accompanying compact disk contains Visual Basic source code for all the applications described in the book. The files on the compact disk are separated by chapter. Code for the PeopleWatcher application described in Chapter 8, for example, is stored in the Ch8 subdirectory. Some chapter directories contain subdirectories that hold data or different programs described within the chapter.

You can load the example programs into the Visual Basic development environment using the Open Project command in the File menu. You can select the files directly from the compact disk, or you can copy them onto your hard disk first. Note that files on a compact disk are always marked read-only because you cannot save files to a compact disk. If you copy files onto your hard disk, the copies are also marked as read-only. If you want to modify these files, you must give yourself write permission for them: this is particularly important for database files because the database programs will not run if their databases cannot be accessed.

You can do this with the Windows Explorer. First, copy the files you want onto your hard disk. Then select the files and invoke the Properties command in the Explorer's File menu. Uncheck the Read Only check box and press the OK button. At this point, you can make changes to the copied application and save the changes to your hard disk. Do not worry about making careless changes to the copy and accidentally breaking the application. You can always restore the original versions from the compact disk.

Part One

Application Basics

Chapters 1, 2, and 3 demonstrate many important techniques that are required by any truly professional application. Many of these techniques are used throughout the rest of the book.

The first application, ExpenseReporter, allows the user to create, modify, and print trip-related expense reports using a single main form. In addition to features needed by any single-form application, ExpenseReporter implements a wide variety of sophisticated features—features such as recent file lists, printer setup, print previewing, and context-sensitive help give any application a polished look.

In fact, ExpenseReporter demonstrates so many techniques that they do not all fit in a single chapter. For that reason, ExpenseReporter is covered in both Chapter 1 and Chapter 2. Chapter 1 explains application fundamentals including scrolling areas, control arrangement, dynamic controls, field navigation, single document interface (SDI) issues, loading and saving files, menu design, and recent file lists. Chapter 2 discusses the more complicated topics of field- and form-level validation, printing, print preview, help, about dialogs, and splash screens.

Chapter 3 describes the AppointmentBook application, which allows the user to schedule and track appointments. When it is time for an appointment, the program presents a reminder. This application shows how to work with bit masks, use the model/view/controller (MVC) paradigm to manage complex views of data, preview key strokes, create rotated fonts, scroll large amounts of data, set alarms to wait until a specified time, and create nonrectangular forms.

Chapter 1

ExpenseReporter from a User's Point of View

ExpenseReporter lets the user edit and print trip-related expense reports. This application demonstrates many fundamental techniques used by most high-quality applications. Chapters 1 and 2 describe these techniques in detail.

The first section of this chapter, "Using ExpenseReporter," describes the ExpenseReporter application from the user's point-of-view. This section also describes data validation and other features of ExpenseReporter that may be less obvious to users.

The "Key Techniques" section briefly lists important programming methods used by ExpenseReporter and described in Chapter 1; the remaining sections of this chapter describe these techniques in detail. Chapter 2 completes the discussion of ExpenseReporter by describing some of its more advanced features, including the print and preview capabilities, field validation, and help.

Using ExpenseReporter

Before you read about how ExpenseReporter was designed and coded, take a few minutes to run the program and test some of its features. The section, "Using the Compact Disk," in the Introduction explains how you can load the program's source files from the compact disk. ExpenseReporter is contained in the Expense.VBP project in the Ch1 directory.

Figure 1.1 shows the running ExpenseReporter application. The following sections describe most of ExpenseReporter's features from the user's point-of-view.

Field Validations

ExpenseReporter validates the values entered in many of its fields. For example, ExpenseReporter assumes the user's name contains only letters, spaces, and periods as in John Q. Public. To help the user enter a correct value in this field, the program will not allow any other characters to be entered. If the user tries to enter an invalid character such as a number or an exclamation mark, the program beeps and ignores the character.

Similarly, ExpenseReporter assumes that department and project fields are numeric. The user can enter only digits in those fields.

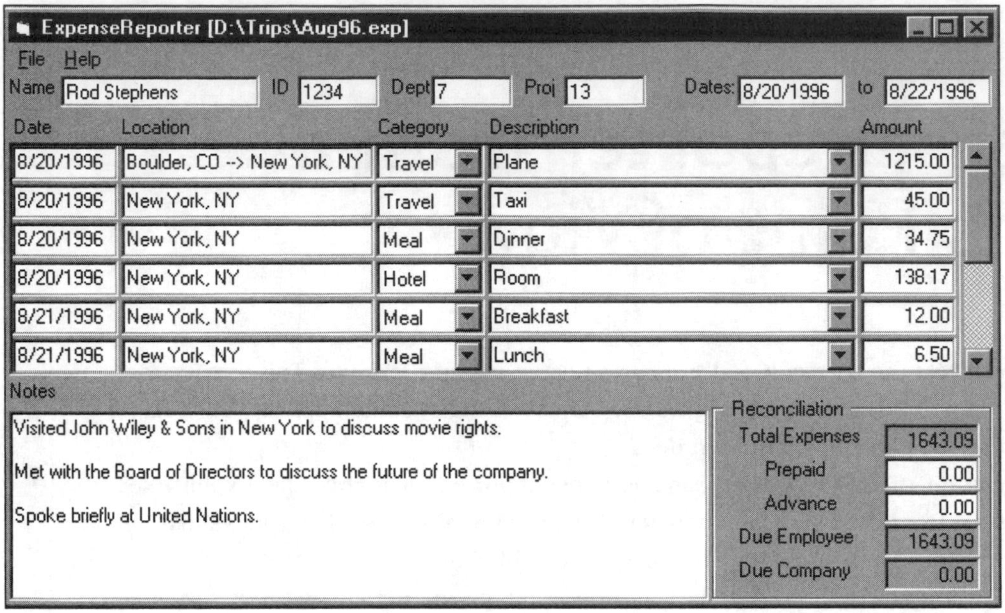

FIGURE 1.1 ExpenseReporter.

Understanding how the program handles date fields is a little trickier. The program must allow partial dates such as 1/22/ while the user is in the middle of entering a date value. This is not a valid date, but the program cannot tell ahead of time whether the user will enter more characters to make this a complete date.

ExpenseReporter does prevent the user from entering month numbers greater than 12 and day numbers greater than 31—those numbers are never valid in date fields. As the user types, however, the program does not verify that the complete date entered exists. For example, the user can enter **4/31/1997** even though April never has 31 days.

Only when the program is certain the user has finished entering data on the form does it verify that the entered dates exist. When the user selects the File menu's Print or Print Preview command, the program assumes the values entered are final. It then verifies that the dates exist and checks that the dates are complete rather than partial dates such as 1/22/. If a field contains an invalid value, the program presents a warning message and asks the user to correct the value.

The Category combo boxes in the expense rows contain a list of expense categories. These include Travel, Meal, Hotel, and Misc. The list also includes a blank option that is used in blank rows.

The values allowed by the Description combo boxes are related to the values selected in the corresponding Category box. For example, when an expense row's Category is Meal, its Description choices are Breakfast, Lunch, and Dinner. When a row's Category is Misc, its Description can be Gasoline, Parking, and Toll. When the user changes a Category value, the choices available for the corresponding

Description field are changed appropriately. The user can also type directly into the Description field if an expense does not fit one of the predefined descriptions.

When the user enters a value in any Amount field, ExpenseReporter automatically computes the total of all the expenses. It then subtracts any values entered in the Prepaid and Advance fields and displays the amount due to the employee or to the company.

Managing Controls

ExpenseReporter cannot know ahead of time how many expense rows the user will need. To be certain it provides enough, the program always ensures that there is at least one empty row. As soon as the user enters data into the last empty row, the program creates another. There is always a place to enter more expense information without forcing the user to ask for more rows using a menu item or command button.

If the user creates so many expense rows that they cannot all fit on the screen, a vertical scroll bar appears. The scroll bar allows the user to move through the data to see all of the expense rows. If the user resizes the form so all of the rows fit, the scroll bar disappears until it is needed again.

ExpenseReporter also enhances the standard Windows navigation features to allow the user to move more conveniently through the form's fields. When the input cursor is in a Date, Location, or Amount field, the user can press the up and down arrow keys to move to the previous or next expense row. If the user moves to a row that is not visible, the scrolling area adjusts so the user can see the row.

Print Preview and Printing

To see what an expense report would look like printed, the user can select the Print Preview command from the application's File menu. At that point ExpenseReporter performs form-level validations. If the user entered any invalid dates such as 4/31/1996 or if a date field contains a partial date such as 1/12/, the application presents a warning message. The program also warns the user if any required fields have been left blank. In ExpenseReporter the Name, ID, Dept, Proj, and start and stop dates are all required.

Before presenting the print preview screen, ExpenseReporter also performs one form-level validation to ensure that the form makes sense overall. The program calculates the total meal and miscellaneous expenses for each day. If any day's total exceeds the set per-diem allowance of $50, the program warns the user.

Finally, ExpenseReporter also reformats some of the fields. It extends dollar amounts that do not contain two digits after the decimal point. For example, the program converts 12 to 12.00. This alteration makes the amount columns line up nicely and produces a better-looking printout.

Finally, once the main expense form has passed all of the form-level validations, ExpenseReporter presents the print preview screen. Here the user can see approximately what the form will look like when printed. The user can view the form at large scale to see the parts of the printout in detail or at smaller scales to get an idea of how the printout will fit on the page.

Figure 1.2 shows the print preview screen displaying the expense report from Figure 1.1 at large scale. Because the printed form does not fit on the screen at this scale, scroll bars allow the user to view different parts of the form. Figure 1.3 shows the same form previewed at the smallest scale. Even though the text is unreadable, the display does show how the expense report will fit on the printed page.

The user can select the Print Setup command from the File menu to select a printer and specify printer properties. For instance, most printers can print in portrait (normal) or landscape (sideways) orientation. The Print Setup command allows the user to change the printer's orientation. If the user changes the printer's orientation, the change is immediately reflected on the print preview screen. Figure 1.4 shows a preview of the same expense report shown in Figure 1.3 but in landscape orientation.

Once satisfied with the expense report's appearance, the user can select the Print command from the File menu to send the report to the printer.

Managing Files

ExpenseReporter keeps track of the four files it has most recently accessed. It presents a list of those files near the bottom of its File menu. When the user opens an existing file or saves a new file to disk, this recent file list is updated. The user can select one of the recent file list entries to reload the corresponding file quickly.

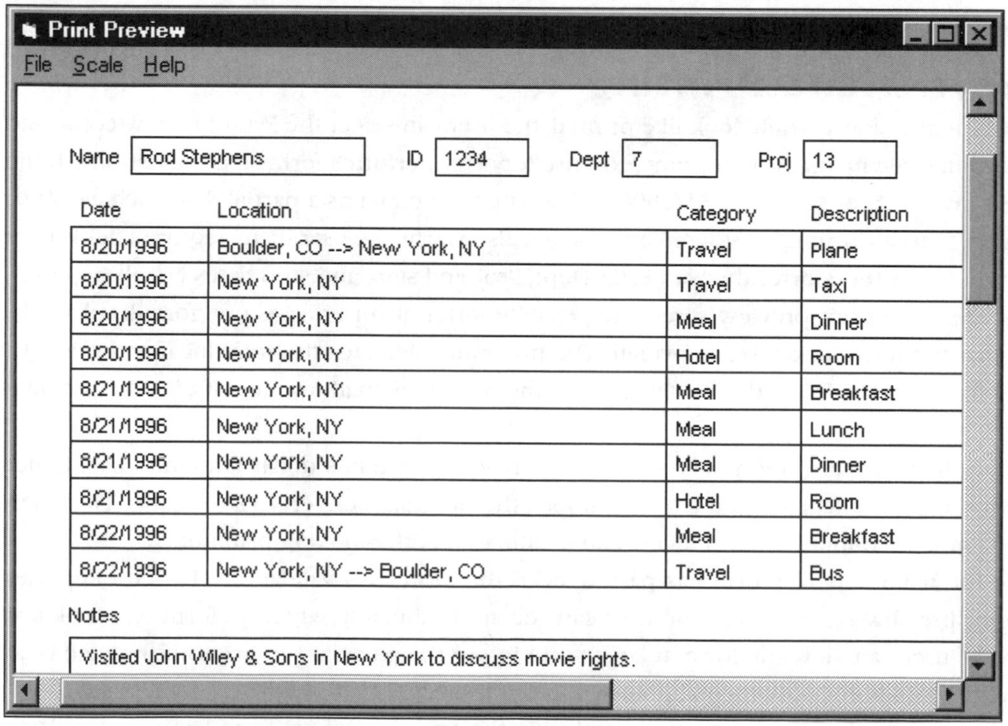

FIGURE 1.2 ExpenseReporter's print preview screen.

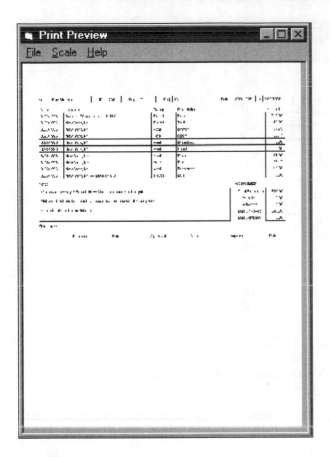

FIGURE 1.3 Print preview screen at small scale.

Help

ExpenseReporter's Help menu allows the user to view the help file's table of contents, search for help topics, see help about the current screen, or see an about dialog giving the program's copyright and version information.

The user can also place the cursor in any data field and press the F1 key to see context-sensitive help about that field. The help file supplied with ExpenseReporter is fairly small. Most production applications have far more extensive help systems.

Key Techniques

The rest of this chapter and Chapter 2 explain how ExpenseReporter was programmed. The following sections of this chapter describe key parts of the code—only those sections that are particularly interesting or confusing—in detail. Control placement and source code that is straightforward are not

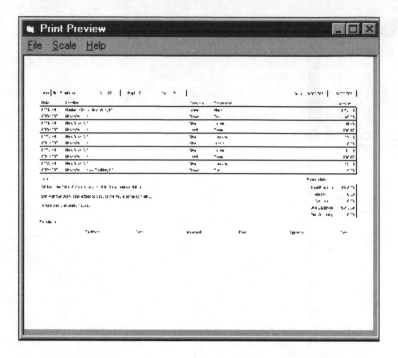

FIGURE 1.4 Print preview screen at small scale with landscape printer orientation.

described here. The complete source code for the application is on the accompanying compact disk. See the section "Using the Compact Disk" in the Introduction for instructions on loading the source code from the disk.

The following list introduces the key techniques described in the rest of this chapter. Many of the topics are closely related. For example, file names play important roles in saving files and in recent file lists. You may need to read several sections to see how all the pieces fit together.

- **Creating Scrolling Areas**. A scrolling area allows a program to display more data than will fit within the available space. This section explains how ExpenseReporter manages its scrolling region.
- **Arranging Controls**. Whenever the user resizes the expense report form, ExpenseReporter rearranges its controls to take full advantage of the form's new size. This section describes the Resize event handler that performs this rearrangement.
- **Creating Controls Dynamically**. ExpenseReporter adds new expense rows as they are needed so the user always has a fresh row for entering data. This section tells how ExpenseReporter manages these controls.
- **Enhancing Field Navigation**. When the input cursor lies within a Date, Location, or Amount field, the user can use the up and down arrow keys to move to the previous or next row. This section explains how ExpenseReporter provides this navigation feature.

- **Selecting a Document Interface**. Single and multiple document interfaces (SDIs and MDIs) both have strengths and weaknesses. This section lists some of the trade-offs and tells which one is better under different circumstances.

- **Managing SDI Documents**. A document management strategy ensures that documents modified by the user are properly saved. This section explains ExpenseReporter's document management strategy.

- **Loading and Saving Files**. Most applications load and save data. This section tells how ExpenseReporter loads and saves its data in files.

- **Designing Menus**. By using a standardized menu structure, an application can make it easier for users to learn its user interface. This section describes menus that are common to many Windows applications.

- **Providing Recent File Lists**. Providing a recent file list is simple but impressive. This section explains how ExpenseReporter's recent file list works.

Creating Scrolling Areas

By using a scrolling area, an application can allow the user to view more information than will fit on the screen at one time. Visual Basic does not provide a simple scrolling area control, but with a little work you can build a scrolling area using the tools Visual Basic does provide.

The idea is to place controls within a picture box next to vertical and horizontal scroll bars. When the user adjusts the scroll bars, the program changes the Left and Top properties of the controls to make them move within the picture box. Visual Basic automatically clips off controls that lie beyond the edges of the picture box.

It is even easier to move the inner controls if they are all placed inside a picture box within the outer picture box. Then only the inner picture box needs to be moved; all of the controls it contains will move with it.

In ExpenseReporter the outer picture box is named Viewport. It acts as a viewport into a large piece of scrolling data.

The inner picture box, named ScrollArea, contains the expense row controls for the Date, Location, Category, Description, and Amount fields.

Figure 1.5 shows the Viewport and ScrollArea controls schematically. The shaded portions of Scroll-Area are beyond the edges of Viewport so they are not visible.

To move the ScrollArea up within the Viewport, the program decreases the value of ScrollArea.Top. This moves the top of ScrollArea upward, and the controls within it come along for the ride. Similarly, when the program increases ScrollArea.Top, ScrollArea moves down within the Viewport.

To give the user control over the scrolling process, ExpenseReporter adds a vertical scroll bar next to Viewport. The program adjusts ScrollArea.Top in the scroll bar's Change and Scroll event handlers, as shown in the following code.

```
Private Sub ScrollBar_Change()
    ScrollArea.Top = -ScrollBar.Value
End Sub

Private Sub ScrollBar_Scroll()
    ScrollArea.Top = -ScrollBar.Value
End Sub
```

A scroll bar allows the user to select values that lie between those specified by its Min and Max properties. By default, these have the values 0 and 32,767. ExpenseReporter resets these properties so they control the ScrollArea properly.

When ScrollArea.Top is zero, the top of ScrollArea control lies at the top of Viewport. Increasing ScrollArea.Top moves ScrollArea down and exposes empty space at the top of the Viewport. To prevent the scroll bar from setting ScrollArea.Top to a value greater than zero and displaying this empty space, ExpenseReporter sets the scroll bar's Min property to 0.

Viewport's ScaleHeight property determines how much space is available within Viewport. If ScrollArea has height H and Viewport has a ScaleHeight value of S, then the farthest distance ExpenseReporter will ever need to move the top of ScrollArea is H – S. If the ScrollArea were moved farther, empty space would be displayed below the ScrollArea controls. To make the scroll bar move ScrollArea no farther

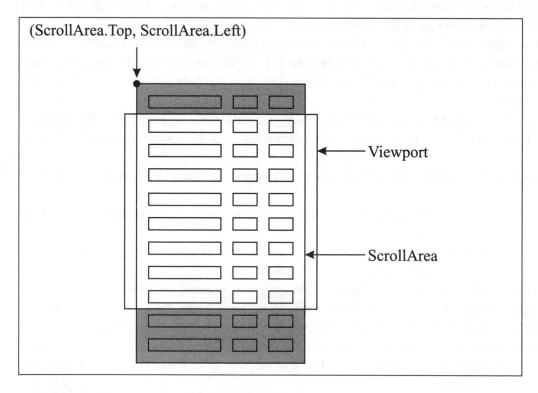

FIGURE 1.5 The Viewport and ScrollArea picture boxes.

than this, ExpenseReporter sets the scroll bar's Max property to ScrollArea.Height – Viewport.Scale-Height. Figure 1.6 schematically shows the situation when ScrollArea has been moved up as far as possible.

Scroll bars have two other properties that affect the user's control. The SmallChange property determines by what amount the scroll bar's value changes when the user presses the scroll bar's arrow buttons. This value should be small enough that most of the currently displayed fields are still visible after the ScrollArea is moved, but large enough to make some new fields become visible. ExpenseReporter sets this value to be the height of one row of expense fields. When the user presses one of the scroll bar arrows, one new row of fields becomes visible.

A scroll bar's LargeChange property determines by what amount the scroll bar's value changes when the user clicks on the scroll bar between the scroll bar's slider and its arrow buttons. When the user clicks in this area, most or all of the currently visible data should be moved out of view so that the Viewport shows mostly new data.

Some applications move the scrolling area by the full size of the viewport when the user triggers a LargeChange. Others move a large fraction of this distance (80 or 90 percent) so that some of the old information remains visible to give the user some continuity. This is particularly common with applications that display maps or pictures. ExpenseReporter moves the ScrollArea by the full height of the Viewport.

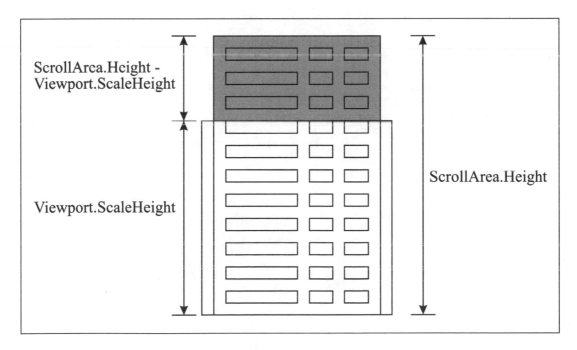

FIGURE 1.6 The ScrollArea moved up as far as possible.

When ExpenseReporter's form is resized, it may be large enough to display the entire ScrollArea. In that case the program does not need the scroll bar. ExpenseReporter hides the scroll bar by setting its Visible property to false. It then sets ScrollArea.Top to zero so ScrollArea is positioned at the top of the Viewport.

The ResetScrollbar subroutine that follows performs all of these calculations for ExpenseReporter. It determines whether the scroll bar is needed and hides it if it is not. Otherwise, it calculates the correct values for the scroll bar's Min, Max, SmallChange, and LargeChange properties.

```
Sub ResetScrollbar()
Dim space_needed As Integer
Dim space_available As Integer

    ' See how much room the loaded rows need.
    space_needed = ScrollArea.Height

    ' See how much space is available.
    space_available = Viewport.ScaleHeight

    ' If there is enough room without the scroll
    ' bar, do nothing. The scroll bar should
    ' already be hidden.
    If space_needed <= space_available Then
        If ScrollBar.Visible Then
            ScrollBar.Value = 0
            ScrollBar.Visible = False
        End If
        Exit Sub
    End If

    ' Reset the scroll bar values.
    '
    ' Min and Max are set so the top of the
    ' scrolling area should be at -Value.
    ScrollBar.Min = 0
    ScrollBar.Max = space_needed - space_available
        ' SmallChange scrolls by one row.
    ScrollBar.SmallChange = DateText(0).Height + GAP

    ' LargeChange scrolls by the viewport size.
    ScrollBar.LargeChange = space_available

    ' Show the scrollbar.
    If Not ScrollBar.Visible Then _
        ScrollBar.Visible = True
End Sub
```

Arranging Controls

Whenever the user resizes the expense report form, ExpenseReporter rearranges its controls to take full advantage of the form's new size. If the form becomes taller, it can display more expense rows. If the form becomes smaller, it can display fewer. The Form's Resize event handler performs the rearrangement.

Before going to all the bother of rearranging the form's controls, the Resize event handler checks the form's WindowState property. If the user has just minimized the form so that it appears as an icon in the taskbar, there is no point in rearranging the controls. Because none of the controls are visible anyway, there is no need to move them around.

The event handler also determines whether the form's height has changed since the last time the controls were rearranged. If the user has just changed the form's width, there is no need to rearrange the controls for this application. Also, if the user has just restored the form after minimizing it, the form's height is the same as it was when it was minimized. The form's height has not changed since the last time the controls were arranged, so they are still in their correct positions.

As the event handler positions the controls, it must be careful not to make any controls too small. In this case Viewport is resized to fill all of the vertical space available after subtracting room for the other controls. If the form is too small, this subtraction will yield a negative number. The application will crash if it tries to give Viewport a negative height. Also, if the application makes controls too small, they will look strange and be difficult or impossible for the user to understand. To prevent these problems, applications should always give controls no less than some reasonable minimum size.

The following code shows the Resize event handler for ExpenseReporter's main form. It ensures that the Viewport is always large enough to display at least one row of expenses. This approach does not allow the user to view much information at one time, but it is better than displaying a strange little scrolling area only a few pixels tall. And it is much better than allowing the application to crash.

```
Private Sub Form_Resize()
Static old_height As Single

Dim viewport_hgt As Single
Dim min_hgt As Single
Dim frame_offset As Single
Dim pos As Single
    ' If the form is being minimized, don't bother.
    If WindowState = vbMinimized Then Exit Sub

    ' If the form hasn't changed height since the
    ' last rearrangement, the controls are in the
    ' right places.
    If Height = old_height Then Exit Sub
    old_height = Height

    ' See how much space is available for the rows.
    viewport_hgt = ScaleHeight - Viewport.Top - _
```

```
            NotesText.Height - NotesLabel.Height - _
            2 * GAP

        ' Don't let it become too small.
        min_hgt = DateText(0).Height + 2 * GAP
        If viewport_hgt < min_hgt Then _
            viewport_hgt = min_hgt

        ' Set the viewport and scrollbar heights.
        Viewport.Height = viewport_hgt
        ScrollBar.Height = viewport_hgt

        ' Position the controls that lie below.
        frame_offset = ReconFrame.Top - NotesText.Top
        pos = Viewport.Top + Viewport.Height + GAP
        NotesLabel.Top = pos
        pos = pos + NotesLabel.Height + GAP
        NotesText.Top = pos
        ReconFrame.Top = pos + frame_offset

        ' Reset the scrollbar parameters.
        ResetScrollbar
End Sub
```

Creating Controls Dynamically

Using a ScrollArea control within a Viewport control, a program can implement scrolling regions in Visual Basic. Some applications can add all the required controls to the ScrollArea at design time. The ExpenseReporter application, however, does not know how many rows of expense fields it will need until run time.

ExpenseReporter adds a new expense row to the end of the ScrollArea whenever the user enters data in the row that is currently last. This step always gives the user a fresh row for entering data.

ExpenseReporter creates new controls at run time using control arrays. At design time, one control representing each column in the expense rows is placed on the expense form. The Index properties of these controls are set to 0. For example, the Date field on the left is represented by a text box named DateText. The application refers to the initial control, which has Index 0, as DateText(0). At design time, this control and the others with Index 0 can be seen within the ScrollArea in the Visual Basic development environment.

At run time the application can create other controls similar to these but with new indexes using the Load statement. The following code creates a new control named DateText(1).

```
Load DateText(1)
```

When the control is first created, it has most of the same property values as the original DateText(0). The new control's Visible property, however, is set to false. The application can reposition the control and make other changes before it makes the control appear by setting its Visible property to true.

The Load command creates new combo boxes without any list choices. After creating a new combo box, the program must add choices to it using the control's AddItem method. If the list for the new combo box should be the same as the list used by the control with index 0, the program can copy the list using code similar to the following:

```
For i = 0 To CategoryCombo(0).ListCount - 1
    CategoryCombo(Index).AddItem CategoryCombo(0).List(i)
Next i
```

When a program creates a new control using the Load statement, Visual Basic adds the control to the end of the form's tab order. Sometimes this may not be a very good position for the control. In ExpenseReporter it would be best if the new expense rows were adjacent to each other in the tab order. The user should be able to tab from the "to" date field to the first field in the first expense row. The tab key should then move the user through the expense rows in order. Tabbing out of the last expense field in the last row should place the input focus in the Prepaid field.

When a program creates a new control, it can change the control's tab order by setting its TabIndex property. The program sets this property to indicate the position in the tab order that the control should have. Controls with larger TabIndex values are bumped up one position to make room for the new control.

ExpenseReporter uses subroutine MakeRow to create a new row of expense fields. This routine creates the new fields and sets their TabIndex values so they lie at the proper position in the tab order. It then creates the list of choices for the new CategoryCombo control. Next it calls subroutine SetDescr-ComboChoices to initialize the choices available for the Description combo box based on the value initially selected in the Category combo box. It positions the new controls below the controls in the previous row and makes the ScrollArea control large enough to hold the new row. Finally, MakeRow calls ResetScrollbar to set the scroll bar's Min, Max, SmallChange, and LargeChange values based on the new size of ScrollArea.

```
Sub MakeRow(Index As Integer)
Dim top_value As Integer
Dim i As Integer
Dim prev_tab As Integer

    ' Load the controls.
    Load DateText(Index)
    Load LocationText(Index)
    Load CategoryCombo(Index)
    Load DescrCombo(Index)
    Load AmountText(Index)

    ' Set tab indexes for the new controls.
    prev_tab = AmountText(Index - 1).TabIndex
    DateText(Index).TabIndex = prev_tab + 1
    LocationText(Index).TabIndex = prev_tab + 2
    CategoryCombo(Index).TabIndex = prev_tab + 3
```

```
DescrCombo(Index).TabIndex = prev_tab + 4
AmountText(Index).TabIndex = prev_tab + 5

    ' Create the list values for the combos.
    For i = 0 To CategoryCombo(0).ListCount - 1
        CategoryCombo(Index).AddItem _
            CategoryCombo(0).List(i)
    Next i
    SetDescrComboChoices Index

    ' Blank the new controls.
    ClearRow Index

    ' Give the row the correct top.
    top_value = DateText(Index - 1).Top + _
                DateText(Index - 1).Height + GAP

    DateText(Index).Top = top_value
    LocationText(Index).Top = top_value
    CategoryCombo(Index).Top = top_value
    DescrCombo(Index).Top = top_value
    AmountText(Index).Top = top_value

    ' Make sure the scrolling area is big enough.
    ScrollArea.Height = DateText(Index).Top + _
                        DateText(Index).Height + GAP

    ' Display the controls.
    DateText(Index).Visible = True
    LocationText(Index).Visible = True
    CategoryCombo(Index).Visible = True
    DescrCombo(Index).Visible = True
    AmountText(Index).Visible = True

    ' Reset the scrollbar parameters.
    ResetScrollbar
End Sub
```

Enhancing Field Navigation

ExpenseReporter's scrolling area contains a set of controls arranged in rows and columns. This arrangement creates one new field navigation opportunity and one new challenge.

First, the challenge. Suppose the form contains some rows of controls that lie below the visible part of the scrolling area. If the user clicks on the last amount field and then presses the Tab key, the input focus moves to the Date field in the next row. That row is not visible because it lies below the bottom of the Viewport, so the user cannot see where the focus has gone.

ExpenseReporter makes the field show itself in the control's GotFocus event handler. When the input focus moves to the field, the GotFocus event handler checks the control's position in the ScrollArea to see if it is visible. If it is not, it adjusts the scroll bar's Value property to move the control into view.

The following GotFocus event handler for the expense Date field invokes subroutine CheckScrollingTop to ensure that the scrolling area displays a certain row. The GotFocus event handlers for the other expense fields are similar.

CheckScrollingTop determines the minimum and maximum values the scroll bar can have and still keep the row visible. If the scroll bar's current Value property is outside this range, the subroutine adjusts it.

```
Private Sub DateText_GotFocus(Index As Integer)
    CheckScrollingTop Index
End Sub

Sub CheckScrollingTop(Index As Integer)
Dim min_value As Single
Dim max_value As Single

    ' If there are no scroll bars, everything
    ' is visible.
    If Not ScrollBar.Visible Then Exit Sub

    max_value = DateText(Index).Top
    min_value = DateText(Index).Top + _
        DateText(Index).Height - _
        Viewport.ScaleHeight

    ' See if the row is off the top.
    If ScrollBar.Value > max_value Then _
        ScrollBar.Value = max_value

    ' See if the row is off the bottom.
    If ScrollBar.Value < min_value Then _
        ScrollBar.Value = min_value
End Sub
```

Arranging the expense controls in rows and columns creates a new navigation opportunity as well. Using the Tab key the user can move to the right through an expense row. Using Shift-Tab the user can move to the left in a row. ExpenseReporter uses code in the text box event handlers to allow the user to move up and down through the columns by using arrow keys.

In the text box's KeyUp event handler, ExpenseReporter checks to see if the key pressed is an up or down arrow. If the key is an up arrow and if this field is not in the first expense row, the program uses the SetFocus method to move the cursor to the row above. Similarly, if the key is a down arrow key and the field is not in the last expense row, the program uses SetFocus to move the cursor to the row below. When focus moves to the new field, that field's GotFocus event handler ensures that the scrolling area is positioned so the field is visible.

The following code shows the KeyUp event handler for the AmountText field. The KeyUp event handlers for the other fields are similar.

```
Private Sub AmountText_KeyUp(Index As Integer, KeyCode As Integer, Shift As Integer)
    If KeyCode = vbKeyDown And Index < MaxRow Then
```

```
        AmountText(Index + 1).SetFocus
    ElseIf KeyCode = vbKeyUp And Index > 0 Then
        AmountText(Index - 1).SetFocus
    End If
End Sub
```

The up and down arrow keys have special meaning for list and combo box controls. These keys move the value displayed by the control through the available choices. For example, suppose the choices available in a combo box are Travel and Meal. If the user selects Travel with the mouse and then presses the down arrow key, the control's value changes to Meal. If the user then press the up arrow key, the value changes back to Travel.

Because the arrow keys have special meanings for these controls, applications should not use a KeyUp event handler to change those meanings. That will prevent the user from moving up and down through these columns using the arrow keys, but it allows the combo boxes to keep their standard arrow key functionality.

Selecting a Document Interface

An application with a single document interface (SDI) allows the user to interact with only one document at a time. Microsoft Paint, which comes with Windows 95 and Windows NT, uses a single document interface. A Microsoft Paint user can open a file and edit the drawing it contains. To open a different file, the user must first close the one that is currently open. If the user tries to open a new file without closing the first file, the program closes it automatically. If changes have been made to the file, Paint asks if the user wants to save the changes before it closes the file, so it will not automatically lose any work the user has done. Figure 1.7 shows Microsoft Paint editing a simple drawing.

In contrast, an application with a multiple document interface (MDI) allows the user to interact with more than one file at one time. Microsoft Word uses a multiple document interface to allow a user to edit more than one file at once. The Window menu allows the user to switch quickly from one open file to another. The Split command in the Window menu creates two views of the same document. Figure 1.8 shows Word displaying two views of the same document.

Even though a multiple document interface gives the user more flexibility than a single document interface, MDI is not the best choice for all applications. Some tasks are fairly limited, and allowing the user to present multiple views of the same task may not be very helpful. In that case, the extra benefit given by an MDI is not worth the added complexity for the developer or for the user.

For example, Windows Explorer allows the user to perform a simple task: locating and executing files. If this application used a multiple document interface, the user could see multiple views of the files on more than one disk or computer at one time. In some cases, this might make it a bit easier to drag and drop files from one directory to another. It would, however, make the user interface quite a bit more complicated. By using the scroll bars it is only a little more difficult to perform this same operation using the SDI Explorer.

To perform operations that are difficult using Explorer's SDI interface, the user can start another copy of Explorer and drag files from one to the other. This approach gives the user the flexibility of an

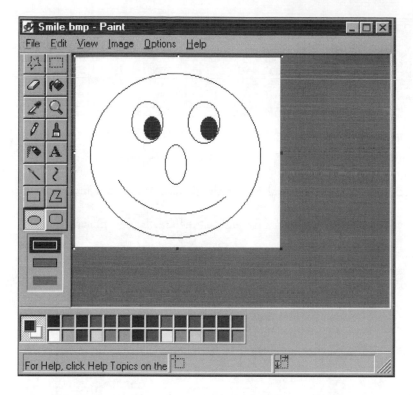

FIGURE 1.7 Microsoft Paint's single document interface.

MDI interface when it is really needed and avoids the extra complexity most of the time when SDI is powerful enough.

Because Explorer is a small, fast application, starting a second copy will not slow the user's computer significantly. Starting a second copy of a large application like Microsoft Word, on the other hand, could have a serious effect on the system's performance. For that reason it makes sense for Microsoft Word to use an MDI. Because a single copy of Word can display many documents, the user does not need to start another copy and possibly slow the entire system.

Notice that a "document" is not always what one traditionally thinks of as a document. As far as SDI and MDI are concerned, a "document" is the largest coherent unit that the user manipulates. For Paint and Word this unit is a file representing a picture or a printed document. For Windows Explorer a "document" is a view of the files on a computer.

The following lists summarize some of the things to consider when choosing between SDI and MDI for an application.

SDI is appropriate when the following conditions hold:

- The application is small and fast.
- The task the application performs is small and well defined, so MDI will not provide a large benefit.

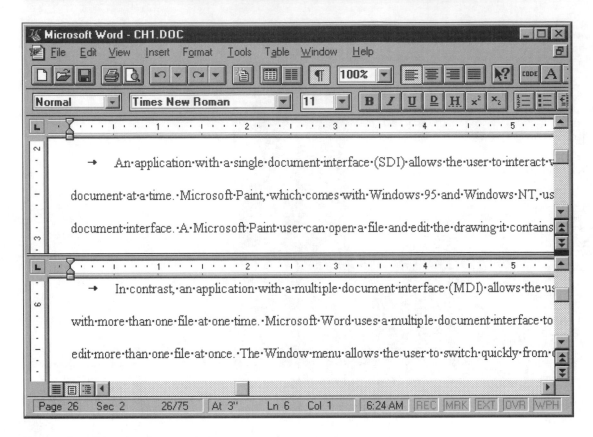

FIGURE 1.8 Microsoft Word displaying two views of a document.

MDI is appropriate when the following conditions hold:

- The application is large and slow to load.
- The user will often want to view or modify more than one document at one time.
- The application uses lots of different screens that would be hard to keep track of if they were not contained in an MDI.

Managing SDI Documents

Whether an application uses an SDI or an MDI, it must have a document management strategy. This strategy must ensure that documents modified by the user are properly saved. If the user wants to close a document or exit from the application, the program needs to make sure that each loaded document is safe. If a document has been modified since it was last saved, the application needs to give the user a chance to save the changes before continuing.

Setting DataModified

ExpenseReporter uses a Boolean variable DataModified to keep track of whether the currently loaded document has been modified since the last time it was saved. Because this is an SDI application, a single variable is sufficient. An MDI application would need one variable for each open file. DataModified is declared in the declarations section of ExpenseReporter's Expense.FRM module. The program changes the value of DataModified when certain events occur. When the user opens an existing file on disk, for example, the document contained in that file has not yet been modified so the program sets DataModified to false. Table 1.1 lists the events that make the program change the value of DataModified.

DataModified is fairly straightforward. It is true when there are pending changes to the document and false when there are no new changes to save. When the user successfully opens or saves a file, ExpenseReporter sets DataModified to false. The program uses Change events to set DataModified to true whenever the user changes data in a text box. For example, when the user types text into the Name field, the NameText_Change event handler executes code similar to the following:

```
Private Sub NameText_Change()
    DataModified = True
End Sub
```

IgnoreModify

In practice, using DataModified is not quite this simple. Occasionally the application needs to modify the controls that represent a document. This sort of modification does not represent a user-made change to the document. One example occurs when the user loads a file. When ExpenseReporter loads an existing expense report, it fills in all the text fields with values loaded from the file. This generates change events for every text box, but this does not mean the data has been modified. The file is simply being loaded, and initial values are being assigned to the fields.

ExpenseReporter prevents confusion in this case by resetting DataModified to false after it has loaded the document and filled in all of the fields. A trickier problem occurs when the program reformats data but does not change its value. For instance, before printing a report, ExpenseReporter

TABLE 1.1 Events That Change DataModified

Event	DataModified Becomes
The user creates a new file	False
The user opens an existing file	False
The user saves the file	False
The user changes the current document	True

makes sure that all dollar amount fields display two places beyond the decimal point. If the user enters "12.1" in the Prepaid field, ExpenseReporter changes the value to "12.10" before it prints the document. At this point the PrepaidText control's Change event handler will detect the change and set DataModified to true even though the field's value has not really changed. If the user opens an expense report, prints it, and then tries to exit from ExpenseReporter, the program will ask if it should save the changes. The user may rightfully be annoyed and confused because he or she has made no changes.

Even trickier problems can occur in control management code. Suppose the user loads an existing expense report and the first expense has Category value Meals. The values presented by the Description combo box depend on the value of an expense's Category. Because the program now knows the Category of this expense, it must update the list of Description choices, which will cause the Description combo box to receive a Change event even though the data has not actually changed.

A simple solution to these problems is to create a new Boolean variable IgnoreModify. Whenever the application needs to make a change that does not represent a user-made change to the document's data, it sets IgnoreModify to true. Change events then check this value to see if they should ignore the change or flag the document as modified. The following code shows the new Change event handler for the Name field.

```
Private Sub NameText_Change()
    If Not IgnoreModify Then DataModified = True
End Sub
```

After the program has made its nonmodifying changes, it must be sure to restore IgnoreModify to false. Otherwise, the program will never know if the document is later altered by the user.

This workaround can be particularly tricky if a routine that changes IgnoreModify is called by another routine that also sets IgnoreModify. The inner routine must not set IgnoreModify to false before it returns because the calling routine may still need the value to be true. If there is any doubt about whether one of these routines will be called by another, the routine should save the original value of IgnoreModify and restore it before returning. The SetDescrComboChoices subroutine that follows uses this technique to set the Description combo box choices based on an expense row's Category.

```
Sub SetDescrComboChoices(Index As Integer)
Dim txt As String
Dim old_ignore As Boolean

    old_ignore = IgnoreModify
    IgnoreModify = True

    ' Save the current DescrCombo value.
    txt = DescrCombo(Index).Text

    ' Remove the old choices.
    DescrCombo(Index).Clear
```

```
    ' Create the appropriate choices.
Select Case CategoryCombo(Index).Text
    Case "Travel"
        DescrCombo(Index).AddItem "Bus"
        DescrCombo(Index).AddItem "Car Mileage"
        DescrCombo(Index).AddItem "Car Rental"
        DescrCombo(Index).AddItem "Plane"
        DescrCombo(Index).AddItem "Taxi"
        DescrCombo(Index).AddItem "Train"
    Case "Meal"
        DescrCombo(Index).AddItem "Breakfast"
        DescrCombo(Index).AddItem "Lunch"
        DescrCombo(Index).AddItem "Dinner"
    Case "Hotel"
        DescrCombo(Index).AddItem "Room"
    Case Else
        DescrCombo(Index).AddItem "Gasoline"
        DescrCombo(Index).AddItem "Parking"
        DescrCombo(Index).AddItem "Toll"
End Select

    ' Restore the previously selected value.
    DescrCombo(Index).Text = txt

    ' Restore IgnoreModify.
    IgnoreModify = old_ignore
End Sub
```

One final way in which IgnoreModify can cause trouble occurs if a routine exits early. For whatever reason, a routine may finish early using an Exit Sub statement. A subroutine also might catch an error using an On Error GoTo statement and then error-handling code might execute an Exit Sub statement. In these cases, the subroutine must be certain it resets IgnoreModify to its previous value before exiting. It should always reset IgnoreModify before any Exit Sub statement and before the subroutine ends normally using End Sub.

An even trickier situation occurs if the routine is called by another subroutine that contains an On Error statement. If the inner routine generates an error, control will pass immediately back to the calling subroutine. The inner routine will not have the chance to reset IgnoreModify to its original value. To handle this situation the inner routine should use its On Error GoTo statement to catch errors. The error-handling code should reset IgnoreModify and then use the Err object's Raise method to raise the error again so the calling routine can handle it.

```
Sub ChangeField()
Dim old_ignore As Boolean

    old_ignore = IgnoreModify    ' Save IgnoreModify.
    IgnoreModify - True
    On Error GoTo ResetIgnore    ' Set the error trap.
```

```
    ' Modify field values, etc.
        :

    ' If all is well, the program gets here.
    IgnoreModify = old_ignore    ' Restore IgnoreModify.
    Exit Sub                     ' Exit Normally.

ResetIgnore:
    ' Error. Restore IgnoreModify and reraise the error.
    IgnoreModify = old_ignore
    Err.Raise Err.Number, Err.Source, Err.Description
End Sub
```

Using DataModified

When the user wants to close the document, open a new document, or exit the application, ExpenseReporter must decide if the document is safe. If DataModified is false, the data has not been changed since it was loaded or since the last time it was saved. In that case, the document is safe and ExpenseReporter can grant the user's request with no more trouble.

If DataModified is true, the application cannot immediately do the user's bidding without losing changes to the data. To prevent this, the program first asks the user if it should save the changes. ExpenseReporter gives the user three choices.

- Yes, save the data.
- No, discard the changes.
- Cancel the requested operation and resume editing the document.

To make managing all of this easier, ExpenseReporter uses the function DataSafe. This function returns true if the data is safe and false otherwise.

DataSafe begins by checking the value of DataModified. If DataModified is false, the data is safe and no more checking is required.

Next, if the document has been modified, DataSafe asks the user if the program should save the changes. The function takes the question it should ask the user as a parameter so the program can match the question to the situation. For example, when the user wants to exit, ExpenseReporter passes DataSafe the string, "Do you want to save the changes before exiting?"

If the user responds by clicking the Yes button, DataSafe invokes the SaveData function. This function, which is described later, attempts to save the document. It returns true if it succeeds and false otherwise. SaveData may fail if it encounters trouble writing the data file.

A less obvious problem can arise if the document is new. In that case, the application does not yet have a name for the document's data file, so SaveData asks the user to select a file for saving. If the user cancels the file selection dialog, the file will not be saved so SaveData will return false. In turn, DataSafe will return false so the original operation, such as closing the file or exiting ExpenseReporter, will be considered unsafe.

When DataSafe asks the user if the program should save the modified data, the user may click the No button. In that case the user wants to discard the changes so the data is considered safe. DataSafe returns true so the user can close the document, open a new file, or exit.

Finally, when DataSafe asks the user if it should save the data, the user may click the Cancel button. In that case, the user has decided not to close the current document. DataSafe returns false to indicate that the data is not safely saved. The application will not close the document, open a new document, or exit.

The following code shows how DataSafe works in detail.

```
Function DataSafe(prompt As String) As Boolean
Dim result As Integer

    If DataModified Then
        ' See if the user wants to save the data.
        result = MsgBox( _
            "The data has been modified. " & prompt, _
            vbYesNoCancel, "Data Modified")
        If result = vbYes Then
            ' The data is safe if the user
            ' successfully saves it.
            DataSafe = SaveData()
        ElseIf result = vbNo Then
            ' The user does not want to save the
            ' changes so the data is "safe."
            DataSafe = True
        Else
            ' The user canceled the exit operation.
            ' Set DataSafe false so QueryUnload
            ' cancels the unload.
            DataSafe = False
        End If
    Else
        ' The data has not been modified.
        DataSafe = True
    End If   ' End if the data has been modified.
End Function
```

The DataSafe function encapsulates the complicated process of deciding whether the application should continue with a file close, file open, or exit operation. This makes the routines that handle those operations much simpler.

For instance, ExpenseReporter uses the main form's QueryUnload event to decide when to exit. The QueryUnload event is generated whenever Visual Basic is about to unload the form. This includes when the user selects the Close command from the form's control box menu, as well as when the program executes an UNLOAD statement for the form. If the application's Exit command in the File menu ends the program using the UNLOAD statement rather than the End command, the QueryUnload event also occurs. This gives the application a single place to handle all the ways the user might attempt to exit the application.

The QueryUnload event handler has an integer parameter Cancel. If the subroutine sets Cancel to true, Visual Basic cancels the unload operation and the form remains loaded. The following code shows how the QueryUnload event for ExpenseReporter's main form uses DataSafe to decide whether to allow the user to exit. Because all of the complicated document-saving code is located in the DataSafe function, this subroutine can be quite simple.

```
Private Sub Form_QueryUnload(Cancel As Integer, UnloadMode As Integer)
    Cancel = (Not _
        DataSafe("Do you want to save the changes before exiting?"))
End Sub
```

Loading and Saving Files

Loading or saving a file is simple in itself. ExpenseReporter uses Visual Basic's INPUT statement to read data from a file and the **WRITE** statement to write data into a file. The functions FileInput and FileWrite read and write the data for a complete expense report.

It is important that these two functions remain exactly synchronized. If FileWrite saves a group of data items and FileInput attempts to read the items in a different order, FileInput will not read the same values that FileWrite saved. This can be a big problem if the data file formats change between different releases of the application.

One way to protect the applications from this sort of data format mismatch is to place a file type identifier at the beginning of the data files. FileWrite saves a string indicating the data format of the file. When FileInput reads this string, it decides if the format is one it recognizes. If not, it tells the user there is a problem and stops reading from the file before it loads all sorts of confusing half-information.

If an application has a long life span, different releases may require different file formats. In that case, later versions of FileInput can use the file identification string to select one of several different file-reading subroutines to read any of the different formats. FileWrite would save files in only the most recent format. This is similar to the way Visual Basic 4 can read Visual Basic 3 project files but saves them in the newer version 4 format.

The following code shows ExpenseReporter's FileWrite and FileInput functions. The constant FILE_IDENTIFIER is declared in the form's declarations section. The RowNotBlank function examines the controls in one expense row and returns true if any of them has a nonblank value.

In addition to loading the data file, the FileInput function performs a couple of other tasks to prepare the newly loaded file for use. It invokes the SortRows subroutine to arrange the expense rows so they are sorted by date. ExpenseReporter also sorts the rows before printing an expense report so the rows are printed in their most natural order. The application, however, does not reorder the rows as they are entered because that might distract and confuse the user.

FileInput also invokes the SetFileName subroutine. This simple routine saves the file name in the variable FileName for later use. It then resets the main form's caption so the user can see the name of the file in the form's banner. Finally, it invokes the AddRecentFile subroutine to add the file name to the recent file list. The recent file list is described later.

FileInput then invokes the ComputeTotals subroutine. This routine updates the expense report's total and amount due fields.

```
Const FILE_IDENTIFIER = "ExpenseReporter 1.0 data file"

Function FileWrite(fname As String) As Boolean
Dim fnum As Integer
Dim i As Integer
Dim num_rows As Integer

    ' Open the file.
    On Error GoTo WriteOpenError
    fnum = FreeFile()
    Open fname For Output As #fnum

    ' Write the data into the file.
    On Error GoTo WriteError

    Write #fnum, FILE_IDENTIFIER

    Write #fnum, NameText.Text, IDText.Text, _
        DeptText.Text, ProjText.Text, _
        FromDateText.Text, ToDateText.Text, _
        NotesText.Text, PrepaidText.Text, _
        AdvanceText.Text

    ' See how many rows are nonblank.
    num_rows = 0
    For i = 0 To MaxRow
        If RowNotBlank(i) Then _
            num_rows = num_rows + 1
    Next i

    ' Save the number of rows.
    Write #fnum, num_rows

    ' Save the nonblank rows.
    For i = 0 To MaxRow
        If RowNotBlank(i) Then
            Write #fnum, DateText(i).Text, _
                LocationText(i).Text, _
                CategoryCombo(i).ListIndex, _
                DescrCombo(i).Text, _
                AmountText(i).Text
        End If  ' End if the row is nonblank.
    Next i  ' End saving the nonblank rows.

    ' Close the file.
    Close #fnum

    ' Save the file name.
    SetFileName fname
```

```
    ' The data is now safe.
    DataModified = False

    FileWrite = True
    Exit Function

WriteOpenError:
    Beep
    MsgBox "Error opening file " & fname & ".", _
        vbOKOnly + vbExclamation, _
        "File Open Error"
    FileWrite = False
    Exit Function

WriteError:
    Beep
    MsgBox "Error writing to file " & fname & ".", _
        vbOKOnly + vbExclamation, _
        "File Write Error"
    Close #fnum
    FileWrite = False
    Exit Function
End Function

Function FileInput(fname As String) As Boolean
Dim fnum As Integer

Dim txt As String
Dim name_text As String
Dim id_text As String
Dim dept_text As String
Dim proj_text As String
Dim from_text As String
Dim to_text As String
Dim remarks_text As String
Dim prepaid_text As String
Dim advance_text As String
Dim date_text As String
Dim location_text As String
Dim category_num As Integer
Dim description_text As String
Dim amount_text As String
Dim num_rows As Integer
Dim i As Integer

    ' Open the file.
    On Error GoTo InputOpenError
    fnum = FreeFile()
    Open fname For Input As #fnum

    ' Read the data from the file.
    On Error GoTo InputError
```

```
' Read the file identifier string.
Input #fnum, txt
If txt <> FILE_IDENTIFIER Then
    Beep
    MsgBox "Unrecognized file format.", _
        vbOKOnly + vbExclamation, _
        "File Input Error"
    Close #fnum
    FileInput = True
    IgnoreModify = False
    Exit Function
End If

Input #fnum, name_text, id_text, dept_text, _
    proj_text, from_text, to_text, _
    remarks_text, prepaid_text, advance_text

IgnoreModify = True
NameText.Text = name_text
IDText.Text = id_text
DeptText.Text = dept_text
ProjText.Text = proj_text
FromDateText.Text = from_text
ToDateText.Text = to_text
NotesText.Text = remarks_text
PrepaidText.Text = prepaid_text
AdvanceText.Text = advance_text

' Create any extra rows that are needed.
Input #fnum, num_rows
For i = MaxRow + 1 To num_rows
    MakeRow i
Next i

' Blank any rows that were not just created.
For i = 0 To MaxRow
    ClearRow i
Next i
If MaxRow < num_rows Then MaxRow = num_rows

' Read the rows.
For i = 0 To num_rows - 1
    Input #fnum, date_text, location_text, _
        category_num, description_text, _
        amount_text
    DateText(i).Text = date_text
    LocationText(i).Text = location_text
    AmountText(i).Text = amount_text
    CategoryCombo(i).ListIndex = category_num
    DescrCombo(i).Text = description_text
Next i
```

```
    ' Sort the rows by date.
    SortRows

    IgnoreModify = False

    ' Close the file.
    Close #fnum

    ' Save the new file name.
    SetFileName fname

    ' Display the totals.
    ComputeTotals

    ' The data is safe for now.
    DataModified = False
    FileInput = False
    Exit Function

InputOpenError:
    Beep
    MsgBox "Error opening file " & fname & ".", _
        vbOKOnly + vbExclamation, _
        "File Open Error"
    FileInput = True
    IgnoreModify = False
    Exit Function

InputError:
    Beep
    MsgBox "Error reading data from file " & fname & ".", _
        vbOKOnly + vbExclamation, _
        "File Input Error"
    Close #fnum
    FileInput = True
    IgnoreModify = False
    Exit Function
End Function

Sub SetFileName(Name As String)
    FileName = Name
    Caption = "ExpenseReporter [" & FileName & "]"
    AddRecentFile Name
End Sub
```

SaveDataAs

The FileInput and FileWrite functions perform the actual job of reading and writing data. Other routines use those functions to implement the file management features that the user sees.

The SaveDataAs function allows the user to save the document into a new file. This function is invoked by the File menu's Save As command.

SaveDataAs begins by preparing the application's common dialog box FileDialog. It sets the dialog's flags that are appropriate when the user is selecting a file for saving. ExpenseReporter uses the flags listed in Table 1.2.

SaveDataAs then sets the initial file name to *.exp so the dialog will display files with a .exp extension. The function sets the dialog's CancelError property to true so the dialog will generate an error if the user presses the Cancel button. It uses the ON ERROR RESUME NEXT statement to catch the error.

SaveDataAs then presents the common dialog box so the user can select the file that should contain the data. When the dialog is finished, the function checks to see if an error was generated, indicating that the user pressed the Cancel button.

If the user did not cancel, the function sets the dialog's InitDir property to hold the directory that contains the file selected by the user. This will make the dialog begin the file selection process with that directory the next time the user selects a file.

There are a couple of other strategies for specifying the initial directory for file selection dialogs. Many applications never set the InitDir property. This makes the dialog begin in the application's default directory every time the user needs to select a file. This approach can be quite annoying. Generally a user will work with several files in the same directory, and forcing the user to relocate that directory each time the dialog appears is a waste of the user's time.

Some applications use separate directories for opening and saving files. This method is convenient if the user is likely to load files in one directory and save them in another. This particularly makes sense if the application supports many different file formats. When loading several files in one format and saving them in a different format, the user may want to load them all from one directory and save them in another.

Other applications keep track of different directories for files with different extensions. For example, CorelDRAW! keeps track of the last directories used for files with extensions .BMP, .CDR, .TIF, and many others. This is useful if the user keeps files of different types in different directories, something the user is likely to do when working with many file types.

TABLE 1.2 Common Dialog Flags Used by SaveDataAs

Flag	Meaning
cdlOFNOverwritePrompt	If the user selects an existing file, ask the user if the program should overwrite the file.
cdlOFNHideReadOnly	Do not display the Read Only check box on the dialog.
cdlOFNExplorer	Use the Windows Explorer file selection style.
cdlOFNLongNames	Allow long file names.

CorelDRAW! also remembers where these directories are each time the program starts. ExpenseReporter does not save the file search directory each time it selects a file, but it could easily support this feature using the Windows Registry, described later in this chapter.

After the user has selected a file, SaveDataAs invokes the FileWrite function to save the data.

```
Function SaveDataAs() As Boolean
    ' Prepare the file common dialog.
    FileDialog.Flags = cdlOFNOverwritePrompt + _
        cdlOFNHideReadOnly + cdlOFNExplorer + _
        cdlOFNLongNames

    FileDialog.FileName = "*.exp"
    FileDialog.CancelError = True

    ' Present the dialog.
    On Error Resume Next
    FileDialog.ShowSave

    ' If the user canceled, we're done.
    If Err.Number = cdlCancel Then Exit Function

    ' If there is some other error, say so.
    If Err.Number > 0 Then
        Beep
        MsgBox "Error %d reading file name. " & _
            Err.Description, _
            vbOKOnly + vbExclamation, "Error"
        Exit Function
    End If

    ' Resume normal error handling.
    On Error GoTo 0

    ' Save the directory for next time.
    FileDialog.InitDir = _
        Left$(FileDialog.FileName, _
            Len(FileDialog.FileName) - _
            Len(FileDialog.FileTitle))

    ' Save data to the indicated file.
    SaveDataAs = FileWrite(FileDialog.FileName)
End Function
```

SaveData

The SaveData function is much simpler than SaveDataAs. The SaveData function allows the user to save a document into the same file from which it was loaded. The application calls SaveData when the user selects the Save command from the File menu.

If the form variable FileName is blank, the document is new and does not yet have a file name. In that case, SaveData invokes function SaveDataAs so the user can decide where to save the new document.

Otherwise, if FileName is not blank, SaveData uses the FileWrite function to save the document into the file FileName.

```
Function SaveData() As Boolean
    ' If there is no file name, treat this as if
    ' the user had selected "Save As..."
    If FileName = "" Then
        SaveData = SaveDataAs()
    Else
        SaveData = FileWrite(FileName)
    End If
End Function
```

Some applications disable the File menu's Save command whenever there is no known file name for the document. When the user creates a new document, the application blanks the FileName variable and disables the Save command. When the user saves the data or loads an existing document, the application saves the file's name in FileName and enables the Save command.

Most Windows applications, including ExpenseReporter, do not bother to disable the Save command. They simply treat it the same way they treat the Save As command if the document does not yet have a file name.

Open

The File menu's Open command opens an existing document saved on disk. It begins by using the DataSafe routine to decide if it is safe to close the current document. If so, it uses a common dialog to allow the user to select a file, much as the Save As command does.

The dialog flags used for opening a file are slightly different from those used for saving data to a file. Because the application is not saving data, it does not need to worry about overwriting existing files so the cdlOFNOverwritePrompt is not necessary. Because the user wants to open an existing file, the flags include cdlOFNFileMustExist. This means the dialog does not allow the user to enter the name of a file that does not already exist. The flags used by ExpenseReporter to open a file are listed in Table 1.3.

Once the user has selected a file, the application uses the FileInput function to load the data. The following code shows the event handler that is triggered when the user selects the Open command from ExpenseReporter's File menu.

```
Private Sub mnuFileOpen_Click()
Dim status As Boolean

    ' See if the data is safe.
    If Not DataSafe("Do you want to save the changes?") _
        Then Exit Sub

    ' Prepare the file common dialog.
    FileDialog.Flags = cdlOFNFileMustExist + _
        cdlOFNHideReadOnly + cdlOFNExplorer + _
        cdlOFNLongNames
    FileDialog.FileName = "*.exp"
    FileDialog.CancelError = True
```

TABLE 1.3 Common Dialog Flags Used for Opening a File

Flag	Meaning
cdlOFNFileMustExist	The user cannot enter the name of a file that does not exist.
cdlOFNHideReadOnly	Do not display the Read Only check box on the dialog.
cdlOFNExplorer	Use the Windows Explorer file selection style.
cdlOFNLongNames	Allow long file names.

```
    ' Present the dialog.
    On Error Resume Next
    FileDialog.ShowOpen

    ' If the user canceled, we're done.
    If Err.Number = cdlCancel Then Exit Sub

    ' If there is some other error, say so.
    If Err.Number > 0 Then
        Beep
        MsgBox "Error %d reading file name. " & _
            Err.Description, _
            vbOKOnly + vbExclamation, "Error"
        Exit Sub
    End If

    ' Start waiting.
    WaitStart

    On Error GoTo FileOpenError

    ' Save the directory for next time.
    FileDialog.InitDir = _
        Left$(FileDialog.FileName, _
            Lcn(FileDialog.FileName) - _
            Len(FileDialog.FileTitle))

    ' Load the indicated file.
    status = FileInput(FileDialog.FileName)

FileOpenError:
    ' Do not leave the cursor as an hourglass.
    WaitEnd
End Sub
```

Files Specified in the Command Line

There is one other way the user can specify a file to open. Using Windows Explorer the user may double-click on an expense report data file. The first time this happens, Explorer will ask the user what application to use to open the file. If ExpenseReporter has been compiled into an executable, the user can use it to open the file. At this point, the user can tell Explorer to associate .EXP files with the ExpenseReporter application so ExpenseReporter will automatically run whenever a .EXP file is opened in the future.

When an application is started in this way, Windows Explorer passes the application the name of the file as a command-line argument. This gives the same result as if the user had typed the following command on an MS-DOS command line:

```
ExpenseReporter filename
```

In Visual Basic, the Command function returns the application's command-line arguments. The application can see if the arguments contain the name of a file and open the file if they do. ExpenseReporter uses the following code to do this in the Load event handler of its main form:

```
If Command <> "" Then status = FileInput(Command)
```

New

The New menu command blanks the existing document and begins a new one. Because the current document will be erased, ExpenseReporter uses the DataSafe function to decide if the data is safe before continuing.

Once it has determined that the current document is safe, the application resets controls and data structures so they represent a new document. These steps will vary from application to application. ExpenseReporter blanks most of its controls. It sets the values for the Prepaid and Advance fields to 0.00 because those values are the most common. It also calls the ComputeTotals subroutine so it displays the correct new totals, initially also 0.00 because there are no expenses on the form at this point.

An application should then use the SetFocus method for one of its controls to move the cursor to the control that the user will most likely want to modify first. For the ExpenseReporter application, the user will probably begin a new expense report by filling in the employee name. The program uses the following code to set the input focus to the Name field:

```
NameText.SetFocus
```

The program also blanks the variable FileName to indicate that the new document does not yet have an associated file name. Finally, it sets DataModified to false. If the user wanted to open an existing file or exit the application at this point, DataSafe would return true and the application would proceed without asking if the data should be saved. This is reasonable: The user does not need to save a blank document because creating a new one at any time is easy.

The following code shows the event handler that is triggered when the user selects the New command from ExpenseReporter's File menu.

```
Private Sub mnuFileNew_Click()
    ' See if the data is safe.
    If Not DataSafe("Do you want to save the changes?") _
        Then Exit Sub

    ' Start waiting.
    WaitStart

    ' Clear all the controls.
    ClearControls

    ' Prepaid and Advance are usually 0.00.
    PrepaidText.Text = "0.00"
    AdvanceText.Text = "0.00"

    ' Move the focus to the employee name field.
    NameText.SetFocus

    ' Blank the file name.
    SetFileName ""

    ' Display the zero totals.
    ComputeTotals

    ' Mark the data as not modified.
    DataModified = False

    ' End waiting.
    WaitEnd
End Sub
```

Designing Menus

Deciding what kinds of menu commands go where is fairly simple because most choices are restricted by custom. For instance, almost every Windows program in existence has a File menu at the left end of the menu bar. Some programs have no commands other than Exit in this menu. Custom dictates that the Exit command be placed at the bottom of the File menu, even though Exit really does not have much to do with files.

The following sections describe standard menu design principles. These rules are not absolutely perfect, and some applications do not follow the rules closely. If an application's menus are as standard as possible, however, users will feel more comfortable with the application and will not waste time hunting for common commands. Any experienced user will know to look for printing functions and the Exit command in the File menu.

Mnemonics and Accelerators

Main menus and many common menu commands have standard mnemonic and accelerator (shortcut) keys. For example, the mnemonic for the File menu is its first letter, F. If the user presses and releases the Alt key and then the F key, the File menu should appear. In Visual Basic a menu's mnemonic is determined by the letter proceeded by an ampersand (&) in the menu item's caption. For example, in Visual Basic's Menu Editor the caption for the File menu is displayed as &File. This makes the menu's mnemonic the letter F. Visual Basic will display the mnemonic letter underlined.

This special use of the ampersand character can be a problem if the program wants an ampersand to appear. For instance, menu items, labels, and command buttons display the text "John Wiley & Sons, Inc." as "John Wiley _Sons, Inc." To force one of these controls to display an ampersand, precede it with another ampersand, as in "John Wiley && Sons, Inc."

The commands within a menu should also have mnemonic letters. Usually this is the first letter in the command's name. If that letter is used by another command in the same menu, the first letter in another word in the command makes a good second choice. For instance, in most applications the Save command uses the letter S as a mnemonic, so the Save As command uses the letter A in the word As. If no first letters are available, the command should use the next letter in any word that has not yet been used by another command. If every letter in the command's name has been used, the mnemonics of the other commands should probably be changed to make a letter available.

Many commands have standard accelerators. For instance, Ctrl-P is the standard accelerator for printing. If the user presses Ctrl-P, the application should print the current document. In Visual Basic an application designer assigns an accelerator to a menu item by selecting from the Shortcut combo box list in the Menu Editor.

An application should not use Ctrl-C, Ctrl-X, or Ctrl-V as accelerators. These keys are the standard accelerators for the text copy, cut, and paste commands, respectively. Normally these commands work automatically in all the text boxes in a Visual Basic application without any extra coding on the developer's part. If they are used as menu command accelerators, they will not work as users expect for text boxes.

Menus That Present Dialogs

If a menu command presents a dialog box or message box, or if it requires other user input before it takes action, its caption should end with an ellipsis ... (three dots). This tells the user that the command will not execute immediately when it is selected. For instance, every application's Open command should have an ellipsis because the user must always select the file before it can be opened.

Commands with an ellipsis should always be safe. The user should always have a chance to cancel the command before any action takes place. Usually this is easy because the command presents a dialog box that can include a Cancel button. Encountering a dialog that does not allow the user to cancel can be a horrible experience. The user is forced to agree to unwanted actions while the program continues remorselessly to an unwanted result.

Separators

Many applications use separators to create visible breaks in long menus. The breaks should group related commands and move potentially dangerous commands away from less dangerous commands. For example, accidentally selecting the Exit command can be quite frustrating. Even if the application correctly ensures that the data is safe, forcing the user to restart the application is annoying and time consuming. To make it less likely that the user will accidentally select the Exit command, Exit is placed at the bottom of the File menu and set apart from other commands by a separator.

Many applications group the commands in the File menu in these categories.

- Creating, opening, or closing files
- Saving files
- Print preview, print setup, and printing
- Loading recent files (discussed later)
- Exiting

In Visual Basic a separator is created in the Menu Editor. A menu entry that has a single dash - as its caption is displayed as a separator. Even though the user cannot select the separator menu item, the item must have a menu name. Separators should have names such as mnuFileSep1, mnuFileSep2, mnuEditSep1, and so on, so that it is easy to tell what they are.

Some rare applications use a blank menu entry as a separator. In other words they create a menu item and leave its caption blank. This may cause some confusion because the user can select a blank menu item. To prevent this confusion applications should use separators with a dash for a caption instead.

Standard Menus

The following sections describe menus and commands that are fairly standard in Windows programming. If an application's menus are reasonably standard, users will feel more comfortable with the application and will not waste time hunting for common commands.

The Menus.VBP project in the Ch1 directory contains a form that includes most of the standard menu commands described in the following sections. You can use this form as a starting point for forms in your applications. Copy Menus.FRM into your project directory, and add it to your project. Then you can remove any menu commands that you do not need and enter functions to support the others.

File The File menu contains commands that deal with files. Loading and saving data to files certainly belong here. By tradition, document printing and print management commands also belong here. Commands that affect the application as a whole, such as Exit, also usually go in the File menu.

Figure 1.9 shows a File menu. The standard mnemonic for this menu is the letter F. Standard entries in the File menu are listed below. Accelerators are shown in parentheses after the menu names.

New (Ctrl-N). Closes the current document and creates a new document. If the current document has been modified, the application should give the user a chance to save it or to cancel the New operation.

Open (Ctrl-O). Uses a file selection dialog box to allow the user to select a file to open. Closes the current document the same way the New command does.

Close. Closes the current document. For an SDI application this command closes the current document, much as the New and Open commands do. It then removes all the controls that represent

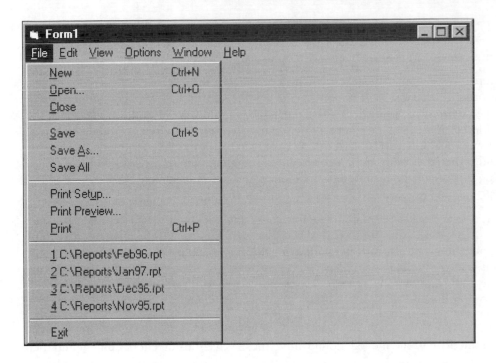

FIGURE 1.9 A File menu.

a document so that the form is blank and it is obvious that no document is loaded. Many SDI applications do not provide a Close command. A few applications use the Close command to close the entire application. The majority of applications do not, however, and that makes this a very bad idea. If the user is accustomed to the Close command being relatively harmless, changing its meaning to something as potentially dangerous as exiting the application could be disastrous.

Save (Ctrl-S). Saves the current document. If that document does not yet have an associated file name, this command is the same as Save As.

Save As (Ctrl-A). Uses a file selection dialog box to allow the user to enter the name of the file in which to save the data.

Save All. For MDI applications, saves all open documents. For any that do not yet have associated file names, the application uses a file selection dialog to allow the user to select a file name. This command should not be used in SDI applications.

Print Setup. Allows the user to perform printer setup functions including selection of the printer, page orientation, and selection of other printer-specific options. Printing-related commands are described in Chapter 2.

Print Preview. Displays an image of what the document would look like if it were printed.

Print (Ctrl-P). Prints the current document. Some applications present a dialog allowing the user to select a printer, specify the number of copies, and so forth. In this case, the command's caption should include an ellipsis because it presents a dialog. If the application provides a Print Setup command that allows the user to specify these options, this is not necessary. In that case, this command should immediately print the document with no dialog.

Recent file commands. These commands list the names of a few of the most recently accessed files. They are listed in order so that the most recently accessed file is listed first. While a document is loaded and has an associated file name, that document's file is listed first. Most applications list the four most recent files, though a few programs allow the user to configure the application to list more or fewer files. Some applications place the recent file list after the Exit command, but this is not standard. It hides the Exit command in the middle of the menu where the user will have a harder time finding it. Instead, the recent file list should be placed immediately before the Exit command. Recent file lists are explained further later in this chapter.

Exit. If the current document has been modified, this command asks the user if it should save the changes. After the document has been saved, or if the user wants to discard the changes, this command exits the application. The standard mnemonic for this command is the second character x, though some applications use the initial E. Since Ctrl-X is the standard accelerator for the text cut operation, an application should never use Ctrl-X as a shortcut for the Exit command. Making a potentially dangerous command such as Exit easier to invoke accidentally is a bad idea in any case.

Some applications use a Quit (Ctrl-Q) command to exit the application. Some even use Quit to mean "quit the application immediately" and the Exit command to mean "save the current document and then quit." These commands have gone out of style, so new applications should stick with the Exit command described previously. Creatively changing the meanings of common commands can cause nothing but headaches for both developers and users.

Edit The Edit menu contains commands that modify the current document. These include copy, paste, and undo. The Find (or Search) command does not modify the document, but the Replace command does. Because the two commands go together, Find and Replace belong in the Edit menu.

Figure 1.10 shows an Edit menu. The standard mnemonic for the Edit menu is the letter E. Standard entries in the Edit menu are listed below.

Undo (Ctrl-Z). Undoes the previous editing command. A program can implement undo in many ways. Some programs simply undo the previous command. Others then allow the user to activate a Redo command to undo the undo. Still other programs keep a long list of previous commands so the user can undo and redo many commands in the list. These methods give the user more flexibility, but they are harder to implement. Some programs use Alt-Backspace as the accelerator for undo.

Redo (Ctrl-Y). Repeats the command just undone using undo. Programs that use Alt-Backspace as the undo accelerator use Alt-Return as the redo accelerator.

Repeat (Ctrl-R). Repeats the previous command. For example, suppose a word processing application changes the formatting on a paragraph so it is indented. If the user then moves the cursor to the next paragraph and presses Ctrl-R, the application should indent that paragraph in a similar fashion. This can be a very useful command, but it can also be tricky to implement and, depending on the application, it can be hard for the user to understand.

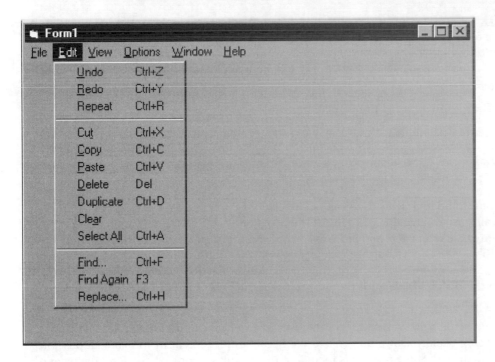

FIGURE 1.10 An Edit menu.

Cut (Ctrl-X). Copies the currently selected objects to the clipboard and removes them from the document. The Paste command can later retrieve the objects from the clipboard. Visual Basic text boxes and some other controls implement cut, copy, and paste with no extra work from the application developer. If an application deals only with text, these commands are not needed in the Edit menu. These commands are more important for graphic applications where the user might want to cut an object from one document and paste it into another. Some applications use Shift-Delete as the Cut accelerator.

Copy (Ctrl-C). Copies the currently selected objects to the clipboard and leaves them in the document. Applications that use Shift-Delete as the Cut accelerator use Ctrl-Ins as the Copy accelerator.

Paste (Ctrl-V). Retrieves whatever objects are available in the clipboard and inserts them into the current document. Applications that use Shift-Delete as the Cut accelerator use Shift-Ins as the Paste accelerator.

Delete (Delete). Removes the currently selected object from the document. Some programs call this command Clear. Visual Basic text boxes and other controls normally delete text when the user selects it and presses the Delete or Backspace key. If an application uses Delete as a menu accelerator, Visual Basic controls cannot perform their normal functions. This is similar to the way copy, cut, and paste do not work normally if an application uses Ctrl-C, Ctrl-X, and Ctrl-V as accelerators. For this reason, most applications should not use Delete as an accelerator.

Duplicate (Ctrl-D). Creates a copy of the currently selected objects and adds them to the document. This command is similar to copy followed by paste, though it does not leave a copy of the objects in the clipboard for later pasting. Because the user can use copy and paste, this command is necessary only in applications where it will probably be used frequently.

Select All (Ctrl-A). Selects all of the objects in the document. For example, the user could then copy them all to the clipboard using the Copy command.

Find (Ctrl-F). Presents a dialog that allows the user to enter text. The application then finds and highlights the text. Some programs use F3 for the accelerator. Many programs provide search options such as matching complete words only (so "act" does not match "reactor"), requiring an exact case match (so "fish" does not match "Fish"),and so on.

Find Again (F3). Finds and highlights the next occurrence of the text previously found by Find. Some programs call this command Find Again. If the program uses F3 as the Find accelerator, it cannot use F3 as an accelerator for the Find Next command. Most programs in this situation require the user to reopen the Find dialog. The dialog will contain the previously entered search value so the user can simply press the OK button or the return key to find the text again. Some applications keep the dialog visible until the user closes it, allowing the user to perform several searches in succession.

Replace (Ctrl-H). Presents a dialog that allows the user to enter text to be found and a replacement value. The dialog usually allows the user to verify each replacement or to make all possible replacements automatically. Some programs include replacement options on the Find dialog and do not have a separate Replace command. Some applications preserve the case of the replaced text. For example, while replacing "text" with "string," the program would replace "Text" with "String" and "TEXT" with "STRING."

View The View menu contains commands that change the user's view of the data without changing the actual data values. Commands may change the scale at which the data is viewed, the filter used to select the types of data displayed, or the ordering of the data.

Commands that determine which user interface components are present also belong in the View menu. For example, a command that allows the user to decide which toolbars are displayed belongs in this menu. Notice that there is some ambiguity here. One could also reasonably think of this sort of command as a configuration command that belongs in the Options menu, discussed in the next section.

Figure 1.11 shows a View menu. The standard mnemonic for this menu is V. Standard entries in the View menu are listed below.

Toolbar. Toggles toolbar display. The menu item's Checked property indicates whether the toolbar is displayed. Applications that have many toolbars can display a dialog that allows the user to select the toolbars that should be visible all at once. An application that does this should add an ellipsis to the end of the command name. Other applications provide separate commands for activating cach of thc toolbars individually. These commands are placed as submenu items cascading from the Toolbar command.

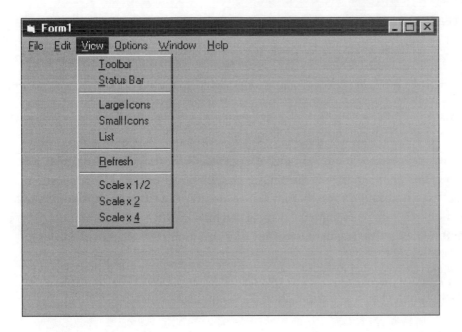

FIGURE 1.11 A View menu.

Status Bar. Toggles status bar display. The menu item's Checked property indicates whether the status bar is displayed.

Large Icons. Displays items as large icons.

Small Icons. Displays items as small icons.

List. Displays items in a list. This command makes sense only if the Large Icons and Small Icons commands are also present.

Refresh. Refreshes the display or reloads the data. This is useful if the data presented by the application changes and the application does not automatically refresh the display. For example, if a new file is added to a directory displayed by Windows Explorer, Explorer adds the file to the end of its display. If you invoke the Refresh command, Explorer rearranges the directory list according to its sorting criteria (alphabetical, by type, by size, and so on) and puts the new file in its proper position.

Scale. Changes the scale at which the document is displayed.

Options The Options menu contains commands that customize the application. There is some ambiguity about whether certain commands belong in the Options menu or elsewhere. Commands that determine which user interface components are visible (that is, toolbars) are often placed in the View menu. The Print Setup command is always placed in the File menu, even though it is more properly a configuration command.

As a rule of thumb, if a configuration command is complicated and the application saves the settings to use them the next time it is run, the command probably belongs in the Options menu. Commands that affect the inner workings of the application but do not change the visible interface almost surely belong here. For example, in a programming environment, commands to change compiler options would belong in the Options menu.

The standard mnemonic for the Options menu is O. Options menu entries are extremely application-specific so no commands are truly standard for the Options menu.

Window Although the Window menu is used only by MDI applications, it is described here for completeness. This menu contains commands that manipulate the windows in the MDI application. These commands allow the user to arrange the windows in various ways and to make one of the windows active. These functions are simple to implement using the MDI form's Arrange method.

Figure 1.12 shows a Window menu. The standard mnemonic for this menu is W. Standard entries in the Window menu are listed below.

Arrange Icons. Arranges the icons for any minimized child forms. An application can implement this command for the MDI form MyForm by simply using the following command:

```
MyForm.Arrange vbArrangeIcons
```

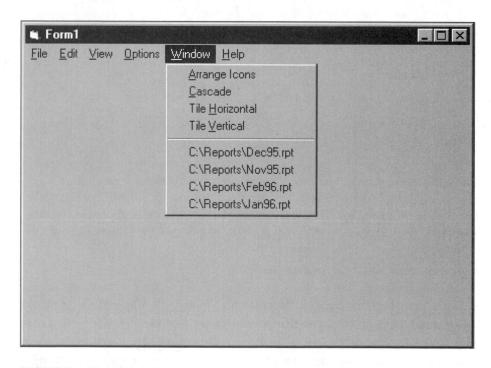

FIGURE 1.12 A Window menu.

Cascade. Arranges the nonminimized child forms so they overlap each other slightly. This makes it easy for the user to jump between windows quickly. An application can implement this command for the MDI form MyForm using the following command:

```
MyForm.Arrange vbCascade
```

Tile Horizontal. Arranges the nonminimized child forms horizontally so they do not overlap. If this would make the forms too small to be usable, the application should not provide this command. An application can implement this command for the MDI form MyForm with the following command:

```
MyForm.Arrange vbTileHorizontal
```

Tile Vertical. Arranges the nonminimized child forms vertically so they do not overlap. If this would make the forms too small to be usable, the application should not provide this command. An application can implement this command for the MDI form MyForm using the following command:

```
MyForm.Arrange vbTileVertical
```

Window list. If the Window menu's WindowList property is set to true, Visual Basic automatically adds a list of the MDI child windows to the menu. The list of children is separated from the other commands in the menu by a separator. When the user selects one of the children, it becomes the current window. The application does not need to do anything to implement this feature other than setting the menu's WindowList property to true.

Help The Help menu contains commands that give the user help. There are also a few other ways the user can obtain help. These methods are discussed in the section "Help" in Chapter 2.

Help commands are slightly different from other menu commands that use dialogs. The Print Setup command, for example, presents a modal dialog. The user cannot continue working with the application until the dialog is closed. Help, on the other hand, is displayed by a separate application. The user can click on the original application and resume working there without closing the help application. Even so, the name of each help command should end with an ellipsis so the user knows it presents a new form.

Figure 1.13 shows a Help menu. The standard mnemonic for this menu is H. Standard entries in the Help menu are listed below.

Contents (F1). Presents the application's help table of contents. In many applications F1 displays context-sensitive help on whichever control currently has the input focus. A form's ActiveControl property indicates which control has the focus.

Search For Help On. Allows the user to search the application's help file.

Index. Presents the application's help index. This is a list of keywords much like the index in a book. In some help systems, buttons allow the user to jump to entries starting with a letter of the

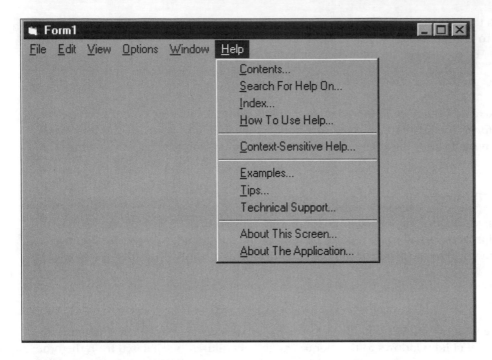

FIGURE 1.13 A Help menu.

alphabet. The keywords should be marked as hypertext links so the user can jump to a topic by clicking on a keyword. This is not a searchable index, as is the one presented by the Search For Help On command.

How To Use Help. Presents help on using help. Many applications do not provide this command, assuming that most users know how to use help. This command is very easy to provide, however, so there is no reason to omit it.

Context-Sensitive Help. Initiates context-sensitive help. This command changes the cursor to a question mark. When the user clicks on a user interface element, the application presents help for that element. For example, the user might click on a text field to find out more about the data in that field.

Examples. Presents application-specific examples.

Tips. Presents short, application-specific usage hints and tips.

Technical Support. Explains how to obtain technical support for the application.

About This Screen. Provides help for the current screen. The word "screen" should be replaced with the name of the current screen, as in "About The Expense Screen."

About The Application. The word "application" should be replaced by the application's name, as in "About ExpenseReporter." Almost every Windows program has an About command at the bottom of the Help menu. This command presents a dialog that gives the name and version number of the application. It often contains brief copyright information and sometimes tells who is the registered owner of the application. Many applications also include system information. Some list the amount of free disk space, others show memory usage, and still others provide a button that opens another application that tells all about the system. This information has nothing to do with the application so it should not be here.

Special Menus Many applications have special needs that can be met only with nonstandard menus. For example, word processing applications have many commands that change the formatting of text. For that reason, it makes sense to create a nonstandard Format menu rather than cramming these commands into an existing menu. These custom menus are usually placed to the right of all of the standard menus except the Help menu. The Help menu should always be the rightmost menu.

Some applications include nonstandard commands in relevant standard menus. A word processing application could place a command to capitalize all of the words in a paragraph in the Edit menu because this command is related to editing. An application, however, should not include unrelated commands in a standard menu. It would be confusing to place this same command in the File or Help menu. If a group of commands does not fit within a standard menu, the application should create a new menu where the command will make more sense.

Providing Recent File Lists

Many applications present a list of the most recently loaded files in the File menu. Figure 1.14 shows a File menu with four recently loaded files listed above the Exit command. If the user selects one of these files, the program loads it.

Displaying a recent file list is fairly easy in Visual Basic. ExpenseReporter uses several subroutines to manage its recent file list. UpdateRecentFileMenu displays the recent file names in File menu items. SaveRecentFiles and LoadRecentFiles save and load the recent file list from the system Registry. This allows ExpenseReporter to maintain the recent file list when the user quits and restarts the application. Subroutine AddRecentFile adds a new file to the recent file list when it is created or opened. RemoveRecentFile removes a file from the list if the file cannot be found. These routines, and the menu items that display the list, are described in the following sections.

File List Menu Items

Some applications place the recent file list below the Exit command. Most, however, place the list as shown in Figure 1.14—immediately above Exit with separators between the list and the other commands in the File menu. Most applications save the four most recent file names though a few, including Microsoft Word, allow you to specify the number of files listed.

Most applications also begin the recent file entries with a number (1, 2, 3, or 4) that is used as the file's mnemonic. For example, in Figure 1.14 the first recent file entry begins with 1. The 1 is underlined to indicate that it is a mnemonic.

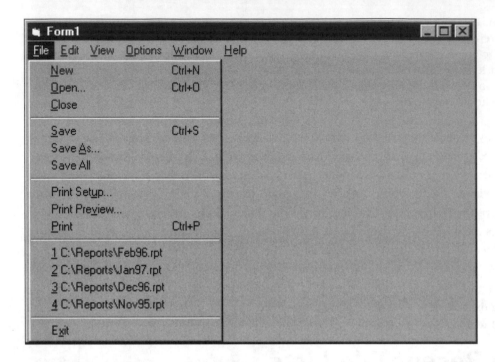

FIGURE I.14 A File menu with a recent file list.

ExpenseReporter uses five menu items in its File menu to display the recent file list. The first four all have the name mnuFileList. They have indexes 1, 2, 3, and 4. Their captions do not matter because ExpenseReporter changes their captions at run time anyway.

The fifth File menu item is a separator between the mnuFileList items and the Exit command. This separator is named mnuFileListSep.

ExpenseReporter defines an array of strings named RecentFile in the main form's declarations section. This array holds the names of the four most recently accessed files.

```
' The four most recently loaded files.
Dim RecentFile(1 To 4) As String
```

UpdateRecentFileMenu

Subroutine UpdateRecentFileMenu displays the File menu's entries for the recent file names. First it checks to see if any of the file names are nonblank. If all of the names are blank, it sets the Visible property to false for the menu separator mnuFileListSep and all of the recent file menu entries mnuFileList. Otherwise, it makes the separator visible.

UpdateRecentFileMenu then examines each of the recent file names. For any that are nonblank, it makes the corresponding menu entry visible and sets that entry's Caption property. It uses the entry's index as a mnemonic for the command. The subroutine hides any entries that correspond to blank file names.

```
Sub UpdateRecentFileMenu()
Dim i As Integer

    ' If there are no recent file entries, hide
    ' the menu entries and separator and exit.
    If RecentFile(1) = "" Then
        For i = 1 To 4
            If mnuFileList(i).Visible Then _
                mnuFileList(i).Visible = False
        Next i
        If mnuFileListSep.Visible Then _
            mnuFileListSep.Visible = False
        Exit Sub
    End If

    ' Since there is at least one entry, show the
    ' recent file list separator.
    If Not mnuFileListSep.Visible Then _
        mnuFileListSep.Visible = True

    ' Show the non-blank entries.
    For i = 1 To 4
        If RecentFile(i) <> "" Then
            ' Show this non-blank entry.
            mnuFileList(i).Caption = _
                "&" & Format$(i) & " " & RecentFile(i)
            If Not mnuFileList(i).Visible Then _
                mnuFileList(i).Visible = True
        Else
            ' Hide this blank entry.
            If mnuFileList(i).Visible Then _
                mnuFileList(i).Visible = False
        End If
    Next i
End Sub
```

When the user selects one of the recent file menu entries, ExpenseReporter opens the corresponding file. The menu entries' event handlers first make sure the currently loaded data is safe. If so, it calls the FileInput function to load the selected recent file.

```
Private Sub mnuFileList_Click(Index As Integer)
    ' See if the data is safe.
    If Not DataSafe("Do you want to save the changes?") _
        Then Exit Sub

    ' Load the recent file.
    If FileInput(RecentFile(Index)) Then _
        RemoveRecentFile Index
End Sub
```

SaveRecentFiles

The recent file list should be a permanent part of the user's system. Each time the user starts the application, the File menu should list the four files that were most recently used the last time the application ran. In Windows 95 and Windows NT, this sort of permanent information is stored in the Windows Registry. Visual Basic provides some very simple functions for saving and retrieving Registry entries.

The SaveSetting subroutine saves a value in the Registry. SaveSetting takes as parameters the name of the application, the section within the application where the value should be stored, the name of the data item, and the item's value. The following code saves the value C:\8_20_97.exp for the File1 item in the RecentFiles section of the ExpenseReporter application:

```
SaveSetting "ExpenseReporter", "RecentFiles", "File1", _
    "C:\8_20_97.exp"
```

Experienced Registry users can use the REGEDIT program that comes with Windows 95 and Windows NT to examine and modify the Registry. The entry created by the previous code would be located in HKEY_CURRENT_USER\Software\VB and VBA Program Settings\ExpenseReporter\RecentFiles\File1.

Users who are not familiar with the Registry should not fool around with REGEDIT. Looking at entries can do no harm, but modifying entries can seriously damage the operating system. A system with a badly corrupted Registry may be unable to boot.

ExpenseReporter uses SaveSetting to save the names of the four most recently used files in the Registry. It saves the files every time one of the files changes rather than before exiting so the list will be up to date even if the application crashes or the computer halts unexpectedly.

```
Sub SaveRecentFiles()
Dim i As Integer
Dim key As String

    For i = 1 To 4
        key = "File" & Format$(i)
        SaveSetting APPNAME, "RecentFiles", key, RecentFile(i)
    Next i
End Sub
```

LoadRecentFiles

When the application starts, it must reload the recent file list saved to the Registry by subroutine SaveRecentFiles. The GetSetting function returns the value of an entry in the Registry. This routine takes as parameters the name of the application, the section within the application where the value is stored, the name of the data item, and a default value to return if the value is not found.

ExpenseReporter uses the LoadRecentFiles subroutine to retrieve the recent file list when it first starts. As it reads the files it arranges them so that nonblank entries come first in the list. After it has loaded the list, it calls subroutine UpdateRecentFileMenu to fill in the recent file entries in the File menu.

```
Sub LoadRecentFiles()
Dim i As Integer
```

```
Dim pos As Integer
Dim key As String

    pos = 1
    For i = 1 To 4
        key = "File" & Format$(i)
        RecentFile(pos) = GetSetting(APPNAME, "RecentFiles", key, "")
        If RecentFile(pos) <> "" Then pos = pos + 1
    Next i

    ' Blank any that were not loaded.
    For i = pos To 4
        RecentFile(i) = ""
    Next i

    ' Update the File menu's list.
    UpdateRecentFileMenu
End Sub
```

AddRecentFile

ExpenseReporter uses subroutine AddRecentFile to add a file name to the recent file list when the file is opened or created. If the name is already in the list, this routine just moves the name to the first position. If the name is not already in the list, it puts it in the number one position and bumps the other names down one spot, discarding the last name in the list. After it has rearranged the list, AddRecentFile calls subroutines UpdateRecentFileMenu and SaveRecentFiles to update the File menu and save the new file list in the Registry.

```
Sub AddRecentFile(ByVal fname As String)
Dim i As Integer
Dim j As Integer

    ' Don't save empty file names.
    If fname = "" Then Exit Sub

    ' See if the file is already in the list.
    For i = 1 To 3
        If fname = RecentFile(i) Then Exit For
    Next i

    ' Move the other files down one position.
    For j = i To 2 Step -1
        RecentFile(j) = RecentFile(j - 1)
    Next j

    ' Add this file to the top.
    RecentFile(1) - fname

    ' Update the File menu's list.
    UpdateRecentFileMenu
```

```
    ' Update the Registry.
    SaveRecentFiles
End Sub
```

RemoveRecentFile

Subroutine RemoveRecentFile takes a file name out of the recent file list, moving the other files up one position so the nonblank entries are at the top of the list. ExpenseReporter invokes RemoveRecentFile if it tries to open a file and fails.

For example, suppose the user selects the first recent file from the File menu but that file has been deleted. The program will fail to open the file. Because the program will be unable to open the file in the future, it removes the file from the list so that the user will not try to open it again later.

```
Sub RemoveRecentFile(Index As Integer)
Dim i As Integer

    For i = Index To 3
        RecentFile(i) = RecentFile(i + 1)
    Next i
    RecentFile(4) = ""

    ' Update the File menu's list.
    UpdateRecentFileMenu

    ' Update the Registry.
    SaveRecentFiles
End Sub
```

Summary

This chapter explains fundamental programming topics that are in some sense localized within the application. Creating scrolling regions, loading data files, and building recent file lists do not require complicated interactions among different parts of the application.

Chapter 2 covers topics that are harder to localize. For example, form validations may require an application to compare the values in many of its text fields. Printing, help, and about dialogs relate more to the external system than to the application itself. Chapter 2 completes the discussion of the ExpenseReporter by discussing these more global issues.

Building the ExpenseReporter

Chapter 1 described ExpenseReporter from the user's point-of-view and explained some of the important programming methods used to build the application. This chapter continues the discussion of the methods used to build ExpenseReporter.

The next section, "Key Techniques," briefly describes the topics covered in this chapter. The sections that follow describe these techniques in detail.

Key Techniques

The following list briefly introduces the key techniques described in the rest of this chapter:

- **Providing Feedback**. When a user interacts with an application, the application should provide prompt, appropriate feedback. This section explains how an application can use feedback to appear responsive while letting the user know it is working correctly.
- **Validating Data**. An application should protect itself from the user's entering invalid data. This section explains how ExpenseReporter allows the user to enter only appropriate data in its fields.
- **Validating Forms**. Some validations cannot occur until the user has finished entering data. This describes ExpenseReporter's form-level validations.
- **Printing**. Printing is one of the most complicated subjects in Visual Basic programming. This section shows how ExpenseReporter uses the Printer object to provide high-resolution printouts.
- **Print Previewing**. Allowing the user to preview a document before printing it makes an application appear more professional. This section describes methods an application can use to simplify print previewing.
- **Printing with a Dialog**. Some applications allow the user to specify the number of copies to be printed or the range of pages to be printed. This section explains how an application can provide a dialog to allow the user to select these options while printing.

- **Providing Printer Setup**. A high-quality application that provides printing features should also allow the user to select the printer and specify its properties. This section shows how an application can invoke the standard printer setup dialog.
- **Providing Help**. Every application must provide help. This section tells how to build and use a help file.
- **Providing Context-Sensitive Help**. Context-sensitive help allows the user to obtain information about specific parts of an application's user interface. This section explains how a program can provide this feature.
- **Displaying About Dialogs and Splash Screens**. Although easy to implement, about dialogs and splash screens make applications appear more professional. This section tells how a program can display these forms with little effort.

Providing Feedback

When a user interacts with an application, the application should provide immediate feedback so the user knows the program is working correctly. Feedback also makes the application appear more responsive because the user receives feedback when a task begins rather than only when it ends.

Many interactions between a user and an application provide their own feedback. When a user adjusts ExpenseReporter's vertical scroll bar, the expense rows that are visible change. When the user types into a text box, the text is immediately visible. ExpenseReporter goes to some lengths to ensure that the text box that has the input focus is always visible. Otherwise, the feedback is lost, and the user has little confidence that the application is behaving correctly.

Other operations do not provide feedback on their own. When an application prints a file, there is no feedback unless the application intentionally provides it. A user who does not know the print operation is in progress may press Ctrl-P several times and start several print jobs.

The easiest way to indicate that a long operation is in progress is to change the application's mouse cursor to an hourglass. A Visual Basic application can do this using the WaitStart subroutine shown in the following code. The WaitEnd routine restores the cursor to its default shape.

```
Sub WaitStart()
    MousePointer = vbHourglass
    Refresh
End Sub

Sub WaitEnd()
    MousePointer = vbDefault
End Sub
```

WaitStart and WaitEnd work only for the current form. If an application displays more than one form, it must change the cursors for each form separately. An application can use the following version of WaitStart and WaitEnd to change the cursors for every loaded form.

```
Sub WaitStart()
Dim frm As Form
```

```
    For Each frm In Forms
        frm.MousePointer = vbHourglass
    Next frm
    Refresh
End Sub

Sub WaitEnd()
Dim frm As Form

    For Each frm In Forms
        frm.MousePointer = vbDefault
    Next frm
End Sub
```

An application must be certain to call WaitEnd every time it calls WaitStart. If a subroutine invokes WaitStart and then exits before it calls WaitEnd, the cursor will remain an hourglass. This can be particularly tricky if a routine that uses an On Error statement invokes a subroutine that uses WaitStart. If the second routine generates an error, control returns immediately to the outer routine's error-handling code without giving the subroutine a chance to call WaitEnd.

To prevent this problem from occurring, the inner subroutine should also use an On Error GoTo statement. Its error-handling code should call WaitEnd and then use the Err object's Raise method to pass the original error up to the calling routine.

When an application performs very short operations, WaitStart and WaitEnd may not work. If the operation is too quick, the user will not be able to see the hourglass cursor. One solution is to use a timer control to make the program delay a short while before calling WaitEnd. This may seem like a waste of the user's time. If the delay is only half a second or even a full second, the user loses very little time and has gained important feedback.

An even better solution is to present feedback in a visible but unobtrusive form. If the application has a status bar, it can place a message there. For example, when the user saves a file, the application can make the status bar say "File saved." This method works only if the status bar message changes frequently. If the message bar still says "File saved" the next time the user saves a file, the user will not be able to tell that a new message has appeared.

One way to guarantee that status bar messages change frequently is to use a timer control. After presenting the "File saved" message, the application can activate a timer that blanks the message in two or three seconds.

Another visible indication for file saving uses the form's caption. When no file is associated with the data displayed by ExpenseReporter, the program's caption reads "ExpenseReporter [ ]." If the user loads the data in the file C:\1_1_97.EXP, the caption becomes "ExpenseReporter [C:\1_1_97.EXP]." When the user modifies the data, the program adds an asterisk, as in "ExpenseReporter * [C:\1_1_97.EXP]." After the user saves the changes, the program removes the asterisk. These techniques allow the user to determine quickly the name of the data file loaded and whether any unsaved changes have been made.

Validating Data

Another important type of feedback an application can give the user is field validation. For example, the application can prevent the user from entering letters in a numeric text field. If the user tries to enter a letter, the application beeps and then discards the character. This signal tells the user that the character is not allowed.

By presenting this feedback as soon as the user types an invalid character, the application prevents problems later. If the user successfully entered a letter into this field, the program would later be unable to convert the text into a number. At that point the application would be forced to tell the user that the input is invalid and the user would need to enter a new value. By this time, the user would probably have left this field and moved on to other things. To enter a new value, the user would need to shift context mentally, reexamine the old field, figure out why the current value is invalid, and enter a new value. The user may even need to refer to notes that were readily available earlier. It is much easier on the user if the program refuses the incorrect data in the first place.

There are times when invalidating the user's input and beeping is very annoying. If the field requires an obscure pattern of characters, the user may become frustrated trying to figure out what to enter. In this case it is essential that the application provide help that explains the field's format. The best way to do this is by using context-sensitive help. The user can press F1 to activate the context-sensitive help for the field and learn exactly what value is required.

Field validation is also frustrating if it prevents the user from leaving the field. A program could use a field's LostFocus event handler to check the field's value. If the value was invalid, the program could beep and use the SetFocus method to move the input focus back to the field. If the user cannot figure out what form of input the field requires, the program could trap the user there forever. Even a user who knows what kind of input is required will sometimes want to move on and come back to fill the field in later. To make this possible, applications should not use SetFocus in LostFocus event handlers.

Visual Basic itself provides very little support for field validation. You can set a text field's MaxLength property to indicate how many characters the user can enter, but many fields require more sophisticated validation.

ExpenseReporter uses several different types of field validations that all follow a similar pattern. Each field's KeyDown and KeyPress event handlers invoke routines in the Visual Basic module Fields.BAS. These routines determine whether the new key will make the field's value invalid. If so, the routine beeps and discards the key.

For example, ExpenseReporter's AdvanceText field allows the user to enter only a dollar amount. The following code shows this field's KeyDown and KeyPress event handlers.

```
Private Sub AdvanceText_KeyDown(KeyCode As Integer, Shift As Integer)
    ValidateMoney_KeyDown AdvanceText, KeyCode
End Sub
```

```
Private Sub AdvanceText_KeyPress(KeyAscii As Integer)
    ValidateMoney_KeyPress AdvanceText, KeyAscii
End Sub
```

The ValidateMoney_KeyDown subroutine checks to see if the user pressed the Delete key. If so, it invokes the same ValidateMoney_KeyPress routine called by the field's KeyPress event handler. ValidateMoney_KeyDown ignores all keys except the Delete key because those keys are handled by the KeyPress event handler.

```
Public Sub ValidateMoney_KeyDown(ctl As TextBox, key As Integer)
Dim newkey As Integer

    ' Only bother for vbKeyDelete. All others are
    ' handled in the KeyPress event handler.
    If key = vbKeyDelete Then
        newkey = KEY_DELETE
        ValidateMoney_KeyPress ctl, newkey

        ' If the routine rejected newkey, reject
        ' the original key.
        If newkey = 0 Then key = 0
    End If
End Sub
```

ValidateMoney_KeyPress first uses the function NewValue to determine the new value the field will have if the key is allowed. It then uses function ValidMoney to decide if the result is in a valid dollar format.

```
Public Sub ValidateMoney_KeyPress(ctl As TextBox, key As Integer)
Dim txt As String

    txt = NewValue(ctl, key)
    If Not ValidMoney(txt) Then
        Beep
        key = 0
    End If
End Sub
```

The NewValue function must deal with several possibilities. The new key might be an ordinary keyboard key such as A or 7. The new key might be a special key such as Delete or Backspace. It could even be an unusual key like Ctrl-V, which copies the current clipboard selection into the field.

When the user presses a key, the new text will replace whatever text is currently highlighted in the field. The highlighted text begins at the position given by the field's SelStart property and is SelLength characters long. If no text is highlighted, the new text is inserted at the location given by SelStart.

Notice how the following code uses the Clipboard object's GetText function to decide what text to insert if the user pressed Ctrl-V.

```
Public Function NewValue(ctl As TextBox, key As Integer) As String
Dim txt As String
Dim start As Integer
```

```
Dim length As Integer
Dim length3 As Integer
Dim txt1 As String
Dim txt2 As String
Dim txt3 As String

    txt = ctl.Text

    If (key < KEY_MIN Or key > KEY_MAX) And _
        key <> KEY_CTL_V And _
        key <> KEY_CTL_X And _
        key <> KEY_DELETE And _
        key <> vbKeyReturn And _
        key <> vbKeyBack _
    Then
        ' It's an unknown nonvisible key like ^C.
        ' Assume it will not change the text.
        NewValue = txt
        Exit Function
    End If

    start = ctl.SelStart
    length = ctl.SelLength

    ' Calculate the first part of the new text.
    If start < 1 Then
        txt1 = ""
    Else
        txt1 = Left$(txt, start)
    End If

    ' Calculate the third part of the new text.
    length3 = Len(txt) - start - length
    If length3 < 1 Then
        txt3 = ""
    Else
        txt3 = Right$(txt, length3)
    End If

    ' Calculate the middle part of the new text.
    If key = KEY_CTL_V Then
        txt2 = Clipboard.GetText()
    ElseIf key = KEY_CTL_X Then
        ' Delete the selected text.
        txt2 = ""
    ElseIf key = KEY_DELETE Then
        If length = 0 And txt3 <> "" Then
            ' Delete the character after the
            ' insertion point.
            txt3 = Right$(txt3, Len(txt3) - 1)
        Else
            txt2 = ""
```

```
        End If
    ElseIf key = vbKeyBack Then
        If length = 0 And txt1 <> "" Then
            ' Delete the character before the
            ' insertion point.
            txt1 = Left$(txt1, Len(txt1) - 1)
        Else
            txt2 = ""
        End If
    Else
        ' It's a return or printable character.
        txt2 = Chr$(key)
    End If

    NewValue = txt1 & txt2 & txt3
End Function
```

ExpenseReporter's last function used to validate monetary fields is ValidMoney. This function determines whether the new text contains a numeric value with at most two digits after the decimal point. Because the application cannot tell whether the user has finished typing at this point, the routine cannot require that the field contain exactly two digits. In other words, the function must accept the values "12.34," "12.3," "12.," and "12." Allowing prefixes of valid strings is also important for date fields where "1/1/97," "1/1/," and even "1" must all be allowed initially.

```
Public Function ValidateMoney(ctl As TextBox, msg As String) As Boolean
Dim txt As String
Dim bad As Boolean
Dim pos As Integer

    ' Assume the field is valid.
    bad = False

    txt = ctl.Text
    If txt = "" Then
        ' Allow "".
    ElseIf Not IsNumeric(txt) Then
        bad = True
    Else
        pos = InStr(txt, ".")
        If pos = 0 Then
            ' Not found. Add ".00"
            ctl.Text = ctl.Text & ".00"
        ElseIf pos < Len(txt) - 2 Then
            ' Too many digits after the decimal.
            bad = True
        ElseIf pos = Len(txt) - 1 Then
            ctl.Text = ctl.Text & "0"
        ElseIf pos = Len(txt) Then
            ctl.Text = ctl.Text & "00"
        End If
    End If
```

```
    If bad Then _
        PresentMessage ctl, msg, vbOKOnly, _
            "Invalid Monetary Format"

    ValidateMoney = bad
End Function
```

Module Fields.BAS contains other functions for validating fields that allow only letters, digits, and dates.

Note that a program can set the value of a text field while bypassing keystroke validations. Field validations will not prevent an application from setting a numeric text field's value to "ABC." This lapse can sometimes cause problems. When the input focus reaches such a field, nothing the user can type will make the input valid. Even placing the input focus at the end of the field and pressing the Backspace key will not work because "AB" is also invalid. The only way the user can fix the value is to select it all and delete it with the Backspace or Delete key. To prevent this sort of confusion, an application should take care not to place invalid values in validated fields.

Validating Forms

Some validations cannot be performed as the user is typing into fields. An application may require that one field have a larger value than another. Another field may be required but only if a second is not blank. These sorts of constraints require form-level validations.

Deciding when to perform form validation can be difficult. Generally, the application should validate a form before another application might look at it—that usually means just before the form is saved in a database or file. In some applications the user may want to save a form that is not fully filled in and finish later. In that case, validating the form before it is saved may inconvenience the user.

The final output of the ExpenseReporter application is a printed form, so this program validates the form before printing or print previewing. It also performs some field formatting tasks when it validates the form and when it loads data from a file. For example, if a dollar amount does not include two digits after the decimal point, the application adds them. The value "12" becomes "12.00."

ExpenseReporter's ValidForm function performs form validations. ValidForm uses the BlankRequired function to verify that the user has entered values in all required fields. It uses functions ValidateDigits, ValidateDate, and ValidateMoney to verify that the data values have correct formats. Date field validations must allow the user to type values such as "1/1/" and "1," but those values are not allowed at form validation time.

ValidForm also computes the total meal and miscellaneous expenses for each day. If any total exceeds the per diem of $50.00, the program notifies the user and concludes the form is invalid.

```
Function ValidForm() As Boolean
Const PER_DIEM = 50       ' Max meals plus misc per day.

Dim i As Integer
Dim date_text As String
Dim total As Single
```

```
' If we fail we leave early.
ValidForm = False

If BlankRequired(NameText, _
    "Please enter the employee name.") _
    Then Exit Function

If BlankRequired(IDText, _
    "Please enter the employee ID.") _
    Then Exit Function
If ValidateDigits(IDText, _
    "The employee ID must contain only digits 0 - 9.")
    Then Exit Function

If BlankRequired(DeptText, _
    "Please enter the department number.") _
    Then Exit Function
If ValidateDigits(DeptText, _
    "The department number must contain only digits 0 - 9.") _
    Then Exit Function

If BlankRequired(ProjText, _
    "Please enter the project number.") _
    Then Exit Function
If ValidateDigits(ProjText, _
    "The project number must contain only digits 0 - 9.") _
    Then Exit Function

If BlankRequired(FromDateText, _
    "Please enter the trip start date.") _
    Then Exit Function
If ValidateDate(FromDateText, _
    "The trip start date does not have a valid date format.") _
    Then Exit Function

If BlankRequired(ToDateText, _
    "Please enter the trip end date.") _
    Then Exit Function
If ValidateDate(ToDateText, _
    "The trip end date does not have a valid date format.") _
    Then Exit Function

' Validate the nonblank rows of data.
For i = 0 To MaxRow
    If RowNotBlank(i) Then
        If BlankRequired(DateText(i),
            "Date is required for non-blank expense rows.") _
            Then Exit Function
        If ValidateDate(DateText(i), _
            "This row's date does not have a valid date format.") _
            Then Exit Function
```

```
        If BlankRequired(LocationText(i), _
            "Location is required for non-blank expense rows.") _
            Then Exit Function

        If BlankRequired(CategoryCombo(i), _
            "Category is required for non-blank expense rows.") _
            Then Exit Function

        If BlankRequired(DescrCombo(i), _
            "A description is required for non-blank expense rows.") _
            Then Exit Function

        If BlankRequired(AmountText(i), _
            "An amount is required for non-blank expense rows.") _
            Then Exit Function
        If ValidateMoney(AmountText(i), _
            "Please enter a valid monetary value for the prepaid amount.") _
            Then Exit Function
    End If
Next i

' Make sure prepaid and advance are filled in.
If BlankRequired(PrepaidText, _
    "Please enter the prepaid amount.") _
    Then Exit Function
If ValidateMoney(PrepaidText, _
    "Please enter a valid monetary value for the prepaid amount.") _
    Then Exit Function

If BlankRequired(AdvanceText, _
    "Please enter the advance amount.") _
    Then Exit Function
If ValidateMoney(AdvanceText, _
    "Please enter a valid monetary value for the advance amount.") _
    Then Exit Function

' Sort the rows by date.
SortRows

' Check that meal and misc totals for each day
' do not exceed the per diem.
date_text = ""
total = 0
For i = 0 To MaxRow
    If RowNotBlank(i) Then
        ' See if this is a new day.
        If DateText(i) <> date_text Then
            If total > PER_DIEM Then
                Beep
                MsgBox "Total meals plus miscellaneous expenses on " & _
                    date_text & " is $" & _
```

```
                            Format$(total, "0.00") & _
                            ". This exceeds the allowed per diem of $" & _
                            Format$(PER_DIEM, "0.00") & "."
                    Exit Function
                End If

                date_text = DateText(i)
                total = 0
            End If

            If CategoryCombo(i).Text = "Meal" Or _
                CategoryCombo(i).Text = "Misc" _
                Then _
                    total = total + CSng(AmountText(i).Text)
        End If
    Next i

    If total > PER_DIEM Then
        Beep
        MsgBox "Total meals plus miscellaneous expenses on " & _
            date_text & " is $" & _
            Format$(total, "0.00") & _
            ". This exceeds the allowed per diem of $" & _
            Format$(PER_DIEM, "0.00") & "."
        Exit Function
    End If

    ValidForm = True
End Function
```

Output-Only Text Boxes

Every part of a user interface provides some sort of feedback to the user. The shape, arrangement, border style, and color of objects on the screen give the user important clues to the objects' use. For example, gray objects are not editable, but white objects are. Label controls have gray backgrounds to indicate that the user is not expected to enter data in them. Text boxes have white backgrounds to indicate that user input is expected.

Applications should provide similar clues where possible. If an application changes the background colors of objects, it should do so consistently. If the application's text boxes and labels are randomly assigned all the colors of the rainbow, users will have a hard time deciding where they should enter data and where they should not.

ExpenseReporter provides additional clues for output-only text boxes. The expense total field and the fields that display the amounts due to the company and employee have a special meaning. Unlike most labels, the values of these fields change frequently. Unlike text boxes, the user cannot enter data into these fields.

ExpenseReporter sets these fields apart by making them output-only text boxes. These are normal text boxes with the Locked property set to true. Setting Locked to true prevents the user from editing the fields. The background colors of the text boxes are set to gray so it is obvious to the user that the fields are not editable.

A side benefit to using text boxes for these fields rather than label controls is that this allows the user to select text in the controls. The text can then be copied to the clipboard by pressing Ctrl-C so that it can later be pasted into other controls. For these small fields this benefit is minor. Cutting and pasting the results of a long report, however, could be quite useful.

Formatting Text

Right-justifying dollar amounts makes them easier to read and understand. Figure 2.1 shows two columns of numbers. The values on the left do not have the same number of digits after the decimal point and are aligned on the left. The numbers on the right all have two digits after the decimal point and are right-justified. Notice how much easier it is to find the largest dollar amounts in the list on the right.

Visual Basic's text box controls have an Alignment property that can be set to vbRightJustify to make a field right-justified. If several of these fields are aligned on their right edges, their text will be aligned in a column.

Unfortunately Visual Basic ignores the Alignment property unless the control's MultiLine property is also set to true. To make a single line text box that is right-justified, an application can set the control's Alignment property to vbRightJustify and its MultiLine property to true. Then any carriage return characters the user enters can be discarded in the control's KeyPress event handler, thereby ensuring that the input remains visible on a single line.

The application must also consider characters added to the field by cutting and pasting. The application cannot allow the user to copy text containing a carriage return to the clipboard and then paste it into the right-justified field. ExpenseReporter's money fields use this technique to remain right-justified. The money validation routine ValidMoney explicitly disallows carriage return keys.

Printing

Printing is one of the most complex issues in application programming. Different types of printers provide hundreds of features. Writing routines that take full advantage of a printer's capabilities can be as challenging as building the rest of the application.

Visual Basic's PrintForm method allows an application to provide a simple printing function easily. When the application invokes a form's PrintForm method, Visual Basic sends a bitmap image of the form to the current printer.

```
123.1         123.10
6.53            6.53
2165         2165.00
17.16          17.16
4               4.00
```

FIGURE 2.1 Dollar amounts that are right-justified are easier to read.

ExpenseReporter's File menu contains a PrintForm command for experimentation purposes, but that command's Visible property is set to false. It can be made visible by setting its Visible property to true using the Menu Editor.

The PrintForm method has the advantage of requiring almost no programming, but it has some big disadvantages as well.

PrintForm creates a bitmap image of the form using the screen's resolution. A typical screen has a fairly low resolution—less than 100 pixels per inch. Most printers have a much higher resolution—typically 300 or more dots per inch. When a low-resolution image is printed on a high-resolution printer, the result is somewhat less than satisfying. Screen pixels appear as square blocks on the printout, making lines appear abnormally jagged. Text is often ugly and hard to read. Figure 2.2 shows text printed at low and high resolutions.

The PrintForm method also attempts to reproduce form colors. In particular, it tries to use the printer's capabilities to make a typical form's background appear gray. Unfortunately, this tends to make the form look spotted. It can also make text, particularly label controls, nearly impossible to read.

A potentially more important problem occurs for forms that have controls in scrolling regions. Because PrintForm displays an exact image of whatever is visible on the form, controls that are scrolled out of the visible area are not printed.

The PrintForm method has its problems, but it is extremely easy to use. For that reason it is very convenient during the early stages of application development. When the project is closer to completion and control arrangements are fairly stable, PrintForm can be replaced with the more advanced printing techniques described in the following sections.

The Printer Object

A Visual Basic application prints high-resolution output using the Printer object. This object represents the system's default printer. The Printer object supports many of the same properties and methods supported by forms and picture boxes. For example, all three of these objects have a Line method that draws lines and boxes. An application could use the following code to draw a one-inch square box on

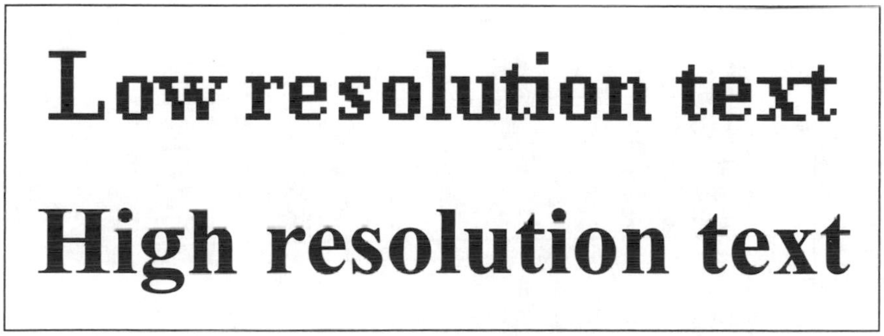

Low resolution text

High resolution text

FIGURE 2.2 Text printed at low and high resolutions.

the Printer object, two inches from the upper left corner. Note that the printer measures distances in twips and that there are 1440 twips in an inch.

```
Printer.Line (2 * 1440, 2 * 1440)-Step(1440, 1440), , B
```

Printers, forms, and picture boxes also have Circle, PaintPicture, Print, PSet, TextHeight, and Text-Width methods. Using these methods an application can create high-resolution output for the printer.

The Printer object has a few additional methods that forms and picture boxes do not:

- **NewPage** tells the printer that the program is finished sending output to be drawn on the current page and that the Printer object should begin a new one.
- **EndDoc** tells Visual Basic that the program is done creating the document and that it should be sent to the physical printer for printing.
- **KillDoc** cancels the current print job. An application should end each print session with either EndDoc or KillDoc.

ExpenseReporter uses several printer support subroutines. The PrintString subroutine displays text on a picture box or printer object. It takes parameters that specify such things as the text string to be printed, its placement, and the width and height of an optional box to draw around the text. When it is finished, PrintString advances the variables holding the string's position by specified amounts so that the program is ready to output the next string.

```
Sub PrintString(obj As Object, txt As String, cur_x As Single, _
    cur_y As Single, x_off As Single, y_off As Single, _
    ByVal wid As Single, hgt As Single, alignment As Integer, _
    x_add As Single, y_add As Single)

    If wid <= 0 Then wid = obj.TextWidth(txt)

    ' Draw the box if desired.
    If hgt > 0 Then _
        obj.Line (cur_x, cur_y)-Step(wid, hgt), , B

    Select Case alignment
        Case vbCenter
            obj.CurrentX = cur_x + (wid - _
                obj.TextWidth(txt)) / 2
        Case vbLeftJustify
            obj.CurrentX = cur_x + x_off
        Case vbRightJustify
            obj.CurrentX = cur_x + wid - _
                obj.TextWidth(txt) - x_off
    End Select

    ' Draw the text.
    obj.CurrentY = cur_y + y_off
    obj.Print txt;
```

```
            cur_x = cur_x + x_add
            cur_y = cur_y + y_add
End Sub
```

The PrintMultiline subroutine displays a text string that might span multiple lines. It uses the Get-Token function to break out pieces of the text that are separated by pairs of carriage returns and line feeds.

```
Sub PrintMultiline(obj As Object, txt As String, cur_x As Single, _
    cur_y As Single, y_off As Single, x_off As Single, line_hgt)
Dim got_token As Boolean
Dim max_x As Single
Dim txt_line As String

    cur_x = cur_x + x_off
    max_x = cur_x
    cur_y = cur_y + y_off

    got_token = GetToken(txt, vbCrLf, txt_line)
    Do While got_token
        obj.CurrentX = cur_x
        obj.CurrentY = cur_y
        obj.Print txt_line;
        If max_x < obj.CurrentX Then _
            max_x = obj.CurrentX
        cur_y = cur_y + line_hgt
        got_token = GetToken("", vbCrLf, txt_line)
    Loop
    cur_x = max_x
End Sub


Public Function GetToken(txt As String, delim As String, _
    token As String) As Boolean
Static the_text As String
Dim pos As Integer

    If txt <> "" Then the_text = txt
    pos = InStr(the_text, delim)
    If pos <> 0 Then
        GetToken = True
        token = Left$(the_text, pos - 1)
        the_text = Mid$(the_text, pos + Len(delim))
    Else
        GetToken = (the_text <> "")
        token = the_text
        the_text = ""
    End If
End Function
```

Using these routines, ExpenseReporter displays an expense report on a picture box or on the Printer object. The PrintDocument routine that accomplishes this is quite long and not tremendously interesting.

Most of the code deals with creating a nice arrangement of text and lines. You can examine the code on the compact disk if you want to see the details. A few parts of this subroutine, however, are worth special attention.

All output created by PrintDocument is specified in the Printer object's units. If the application uses PrintDocument to send output to a picture box, the picture box must be sized and scaled so its coordinates match those of the printer. This is explained in more detail in the following section, "Print Previewing."

The following code, for example, uses the Printer object's ScaleLeft, ScaleTop, ScaleWidth, and ScaleHeight properties to determine where the output's margins should be. Printing routines would make sure their output remained within the calculated margins.

```
' Set margins to 1/2 inch on the sides and
' 1 inch at the top and bottom.
left_margin = Printer.ScaleLeft + 1440 * 0.5
right_margin = Printer.ScaleLeft + _
    Printer.ScaleWidth - 1440 * 0.5
top_margin = Printer.ScaleTop + 1440 * 1
bottom_margin = Printer.ScaleTop + _
    Printer.ScaleHeight - 1440 * 1
```

Before ExpenseReporter's PrintDocument subroutine creates any output, it sets the font of the printer or picture box to 8 point Arial. It sets several other font characteristics to be certain the Printer object uses the correct font.

```
obj.Font.Bold = False
obj.Font.Italic = False
obj.Font.Name = "Arial"
obj.Font.Strikethrough = False
obj.Font.Underline = False
obj.Font.Size = 8
```

By default, picture boxes use a system-defined font such as MS Sans Serif. This font is shipped with Windows and is very likely to be present on any user's computer. Unfortunately, this font is unlikely to be found on a user's physical printer. By specifying a font like Arial or Times Roman, fonts that are common on printers, PrintDocument increases the chances that output to the printer will look like output to a picture box. This is important because it means the printed output will look as much like the previewed output as possible.

ExpenseReporter uses the PrintDocument function, as shown in the following code. Notice that this subroutine performs form validations before it invokes PrintDocument.

```
Private Sub mnuFilePrint_Click()
Dim form_valid As Boolean

    ' Make sure the fields are valid.
    ' Ignore modifications made by ValidForm.
    IgnoreModify = True
    form_valid = ValidForm()
```

```
IgnoreModify - False
If Not form_valid Then Exit Sub

    ' Start waiting.
    WaitStart

    ' Print to the printer.
    PrintDocument Printer

    ' Close the document.
    Printer.EndDoc

    ' End waiting.
    WaitEnd
End Sub
```

Figure 2.3 shows printed output produced by the PrintDocument subroutine.

Print Previewing

A print preview feature allows the user to see how a printed document will look before it is printed. Figure 2.4 shows ExpenseReporter's print preview screen.

At first one might think implementing a Print Preview command would be quite difficult. It seems reasonable that building a Print Preview command should be at least as hard as actually printing the document. In reality, it takes only a little more work to add print preview capabilities to an application that provides high-resolution printed output. Because this feature makes an application appear more professional, the extra work is well worth the effort.

The document printing routines described in the previous section, PrintString, PrintMultiline, and PrintDocument, all take as their first parameter an object. This parameter is the object to which the routine should send its output. ExpenseReporter uses the following line of code to pass the Printer object into the PrintDocument subroutine so that it can create a printout.

```
PrintDocument Printer
```

To create a print preview, the program passes PrintDocument a picture box instead of the Printer object. PrintDocument sends an image of the printout to the picture box instead of the physical printer. The program uses that picture box to give the user a preview of the printout. The basic idea is simple, though a few details require a bit of work.

Many SDI applications present a print preview on the same form where they display the program's data. The application hides the controls on the main form and makes new controls visible to display the preview. In this case, the application also needs to rearrange menu items to provide scaling and other commands that are appropriate for print previewing. All this makes coding the main form a bit confusing. ExpenseReporter takes a different approach.

ExpenseReporter displays print previews in a separate form that is quite simple. It contains its own menus appropriate for a print preview. It holds two picture boxes and two scroll bars that implement a scrolling area much like the one on the main ExpenseReporter form. Finally, the preview

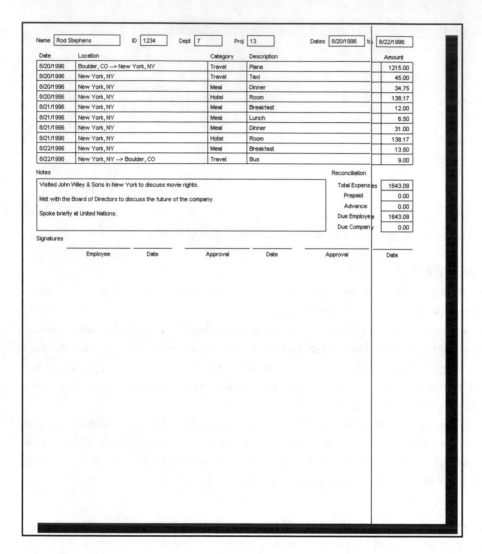

| Name | Rod Stephens | | ID | 1234 | Dept | 7 | Proj | 13 | | Dates | 8/20/1996 | to | 8/22/1996 |

Date	Location	Category	Description	Amount
8/20/1996	Boulder, CO ---> New York, NY	Travel	Plane	1215.00
8/20/1996	New York, NY	Travel	Taxi	45.00
8/20/1996	New York, NY	Meal	Dinner	34.75
8/20/1996	New York, NY	Hotel	Room	138.17
8/21/1996	New York, NY	Meal	Breakfast	12.00
8/21/1996	New York, NY	Meal	Lunch	6.50
8/21/1996	New York, NY	Meal	Dinner	31.00
8/21/1996	New York, NY	Hotel	Room	138.17
8/22/1996	New York, NY	Meal	Breakfast	13.50
8/22/1996	New York, NY ---> Boulder, CO	Travel	Bus	9.00

Notes

Visited John Wiley & Sons in New York to discuss movie rights.

Met with the Board of Directors to discuss the future of the company.

Spoke briefly at United Nations.

Reconciliation

Total Expenses	1643.09
Prepaid	0.00
Advance	0.00
Due Employee	1643.09
Due Company	0.00

Signatures

| Employee | Date | Approval | Date | Approval | Date |

FIGURE 2.3 Printed output from ExpenseReporter.

screen contains a hidden picture box to hold the initial preview image. This picture box will be passed into the PrintDocument routine so PrintDocument will build its image of the printout there.

When the print preview screen is created, its Load event handler calls subroutine MakePreview. MakePreview resizes and scales the hidden picture box so that its dimensions match those of the Printer object. It then uses the PrintDocument subroutine to draw an image of the printout in the hidden picture box. Once this picture has been created, it does not need to be created again while the preview

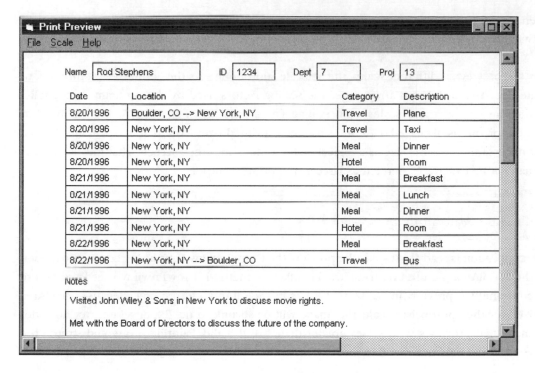

FIGURE 2.4 ExpenseReporter's print preview screen.

screen is loaded. Commands in the Scale menu display the image at different scales on a visible picture box, but the hidden picture remains unchanged.

```
Sub MakePreview()
    ' Start from scratch.
    HiddenPicture.Cls

    ' Give the hidden picture the right size for
    ' the printer.
    HiddenPicture.Width = Printer.Width
    HiddenPicture.Height = Printer.Height

    ' Set the hidden picture's scale factors.
    HiddenPicture.ScaleLeft = Printer.ScaleLeft
    HiddenPicture.ScaleTop = Printer.ScaleTop
    HiddenPicture.ScaleWidth = Printer.ScaleWidth
    HiddenPicture.ScaleHeight = Printer.ScaleHeight

    ' Print to the hidden picture.
    ExpenseForm.PrintDocument HiddenPicture
End Sub
```

The screen displays print previews at several different scales. At the largest scale the user can read the text that will be printed. The smallest scale gives an overview showing how the printed material fits on the page.

To display the preview at different scales, the SetScale subroutine sets the ScrollArea picture box to an appropriate size. The ScaleValue array stores the scaling factors used by the program. ExpenseReporter displays previews at three scales with scaling factors 1.0, 0.75, and 0.375. For example, at medium scale the picture is displayed 0.75 times its logical printed size. Note that a logical inch on the printer is not necessarily the same size as a logical inch on the computer's screen. That means the preview image may not be exactly 75 percent as large as the printed output.

```
' Resize the scroll area.
wid = Printer.Width * ScaleValue(PreviewScale)
hgt = Printer.Height * ScaleValue(PreviewScale)
ScrollArea.Move 0, 0, wid, hgt
```

When the application is ready to display the preview, the DrawPreview subroutine copies the hidden picture into the ScrollArea picture box using the PaintPicture method. DrawPreview uses PaintPicture to draw the entire hidden preview image so that it fills the ScrollArea picture box. Because ScrollArea has been resized for the appropriate scale, the image will be shrunk to fit. ExpenseReporter does not provide any magnified previews with scales greater than 1.0. If it did, PaintPicture would stretch the preview image to fit the enlarged ScrollArea.

```
Sub DrawPreview()
    ' Copy the hidden picture to the scroll area.
    ScrollArea.Cls
    ScrollArea.PaintPicture HiddenPicture.Image, _
        0, 0, _
        ScrollArea.Width, _
        ScrollArea.Height, _
        0, 0, _
        HiddenPicture.Width, _
        HiddenPicture.Height, _
        vbSrcCopy
End Sub
```

An alternative strategy for displaying preview images at different scales would be to draw the image directly on the ScrollArea picture box. You could use ScrollArea's scaling properties to make the image appear at the correct size. For two reasons this method does not work well for ExpenseReporter.

First, this method takes longer. Whenever the user changed the preview scale, the program would need to redraw the picture at the new scale. The current implementation requires ExpenseReporter to draw the image only once. When the scale changes, the program can quickly copy the image using Paint-Picture. If the image is very complicated, redrawing it every time will take much longer.

Second, the computer is not able to produce every font at every scale. To display 8 point Arial with a scale factor of 0.375, the computer would need to produce Arial at 3 point. Most computers cannot produce this font. Faced with this dilemma the computer would select the font that it thought was closest to the required font. That might be 4 point Arial, 4 point Times Roman, or even 8 point Arial, depending on the fonts available. A drawing with lines and boxes scaled by a factor of 0.375 but text at 8 point instead of 3 point looks terrible.

On the other hand, if the program does not produce text, redrawing the image at each scale will produce a better result. The PaintPicture method tends to lose detail when it shrinks or stretches an image. At small scales the image can be very hard to understand. If the program redraws the image at the smaller scale, it will be able to take better advantage of the computer's full resolution.

Managing Two Scroll Bars

The last new technique used by the print preview screen involves the two scroll bars. The way the two scroll bars work and the way the program sets their Min, Max, SmallChange, and LargeChange properties is very similar to the way these tasks are handled for ExpenseReporter's main form. Because there are two scroll bars instead of one, however, there is a difference in the way the program decides when the scroll bars are necessary.

Suppose the vertical scroll bar is needed because the preview image is too tall to fit on the form. In that case, the vertical scroll bar takes up some space on the right edge of the form; that, in turn, makes the area available for the preview image narrower. The preview area may not be as wide as the form, but it may be wider than the narrowed area now available. In that case, the horizontal scroll bar is also needed. That, in turn, reduces the amount of vertical space available. The following code fragment shows how the ArrangeControls subroutine determines which scroll bars are needed.

```
' See if we need the horizontal scroll bar.
need_hscroll = (need_wid > got_wid)
If (need_hscroll) Then _
    got_hgt = got_hgt - HScroll.Height

' See if we need the vertical scroll bar.
need_vscroll = (need_hgt > got_hgt)
If (need_vscroll) Then
    got_wid = got_wid - VScroll.Width
    ' If we do not already need it, see if we
    ' need the horizontal scroll bar now that
    ' the available area is narrower.
    If Not need_hscroll Then
        need_hscroll = (need_wid > got_wid)
        If (need_hscroll) Then _
            got_hgt = got_hgt - HScroll.Height
    End If
End If
```

Printing with a Dialog

When an ExpenseReporter user selects the Print command from the File menu or presses Ctrl-P, the program prints a single page on the currently selected printer. In some applications it is appropriate to give the user more printing options. For example, an application could allow the user to select the range of pages to print or indicate the number of copies to print. Figure 2.5 shows a print dialog that allows the user to make these choices.

In Visual Basic, an application can use a common dialog control to allow the user to make these choices. The program should first set the dialog's Flags property to indicate any special features the dialog should have. For instance, if the Flags are set to cdlPDHidePrintToFile, the dialog will not display the Print to file check box.

Next, the program should present the dialog to the user by invoking the dialog's ShowPrinter method. When the dialog is finished, its properties indicate the choices the user made. Some of these properties are straightforward; others interact strangely with the Printer object.

For example, if the printer and its device driver support hardware printing of multiple copies, the dialog will set Printer.Copies to indicate the number of copies the user entered. It will then set the dialog's Copies property to one. This allows the printer to generate the copies rather than making your application send the printout to the printer multiple times. Printing copies in hardware is generally much faster than printing them in software.

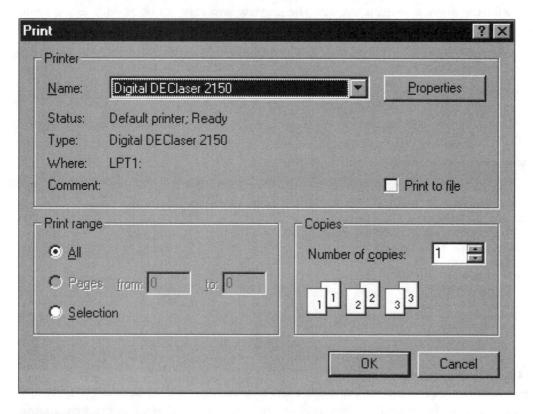

FIGURE 2.5 A print dialog.

If the printer does not support multiple copies, the dialog's Copies property will indicate the number entered by the user. The application must then generate the printout several times.

When the dialog is finished, some of the Printer object's properties may have been modified. For example, if the printer produced multiple copies in hardware, Printer.Copies will no longer be one. If the application does not reset this value before the next time it produces a printout, the program will again generate multiple copies.

The ExpenseReporter application prints only a single page, and it does not provide a print dialog. A Print Dialog command is included in the File menu, but its Visible property is set to false so it is hidden. It can be enabled by checking its Visible property using the Visual Basic Menu Editor.

ExpenseReporter's Print Dialog command uses the following code to display the print dialog. Notice how the routine is prepared to produce multiple copies of the expense report in case the printer cannot produce multiple copies itself. It does this by creating several document pages all in the same print document rather than by creating separate documents.

```
Private Sub mnuFilePrintDialog_Click()
Dim num_copies As Integer
Dim i As Integer

    ' Prepare the common dialog.
    FileDialog.Flags = _
        cdlPDHidePrintToFile + _
        cdlPDNoPageNums + _
        cdlPDNoSelection + _
        cdlPDAllPages
    FileDialog.CancelError = True

    ' Present the dialog.
    On Error Resume Next
    FileDialog.ShowPrinter

    ' If the user canceled, we're done.
    If Err.Number = cdlCancel Then Exit Sub
    If Err.Number <> 0 Then
        Beep
        MsgBox "Error printing file." & vbCrLf & _
            Err.Description, _
            vbOKOnly + vbExclamation, _
            "Printing Error"
        Exit Sub
    End If

    ' Start waiting.
    WaitStart

    ' Print to the printer.
    num_copies = FileDialog.Copies
    For i = 1 To num_copies
        PrintDocument Printer
```

```
        ' End this page.
        Printer.NewPage
    Next i

    ' Close the document.
    Printer.EndDoc

    ' Reset the printer's copy count.
    Printer.Copies = 1

    ' End waiting.
    WaitEnd
End Sub
```

Providing Printer Setup

Any application that uses the printer should allow the user to modify the printer setup. A standard printer dialog allows the user to select the printer, paper size, and orientation. It also provides a command button that presents another dialog that gives access to other printer properties. These properties are different for different kinds of printers and include such things as halftoning options, negative or mirror-image printing, scaling, and PostScript optimization. Figure 2.6 shows ExpenseReporter's print setup dialog.

Presenting the printer setup dialog is simple using the common dialog control. First, the program should set the dialog's Flags property to cdlPDPrintSetup. This tells Visual Basic that the dialog should

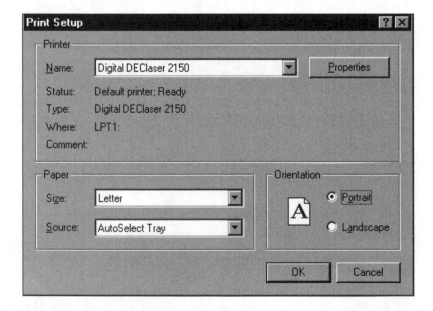

FIGURE 2.6 The print setup dialog.

be a printer setup dialog rather than a file-printing dialog similar to the one described in the previous section. Next, the program should invoke the dialog's ShowPrinter method. The following code shows how ExpenseReporter presents the print setup dialog"

```
Private Sub mnuFilePrintSetup_Click()
    ' Prepare the common dialog.
    FileDialog.Flags = cdlPDPrintSetup
    FileDialog.CancelError = False

    ' Present the dialog.
    FileDialog.ShowPrinter
End Sub
```

After the user has finished with the print setup dialog, any new settings are incorporated into the Printer object. (Note: This may not work with networked printers.) For example, if the user selects normal 8.5" by 11" paper printed in landscape (sideways) orientation, the system will redimension the Printer object so its width is 11" and its height is 8.5". The application can immediately take advantage of the new settings when it sends output to the printer or when it presents a print preview.

ExpenseReporter uses the Printer object's Width and Height properties when it displays a print preview. If a user selects landscape orientation using the Print Setup command and then invokes the Print Preview command from the File menu, ExpenseReporter uses the Printer object's dimensions. If the user selects the preview's small scale, it will be apparent that the preview shows the paper turned sideways. The expense report will still be drawn with its top at the top of the display, but the paper will be wider than it is tall. If the user then selects the Print command from the File menu, the expense report will be printed sideways.

If the user uses the print setup dialog to change the default printer, printouts will automatically be sent to the new printer. If the user selects a special device as the printer, such as a fax modem, printed output will automatically be sent to that device.

By using a common dialog, an application gets all of these features with almost no extra programming. The only way in which the application needs to be aware of the printer's setup is through the Printer object's properties. For example, ExpenseReporter sets the width of the notes field in the printout based on the Printer object's Width property. It makes the width of this field equal to Printer.Width minus space for the margins and the reconciliation fields at the right edge of the page. This very simple use of the Printer object's properties barely hints at the things an application can do to take advantage of the full printing area.

Providing Help

Like life insurance, a help system is something everyone hopes is never needed. If an application is well designed and the user interface is intuitive, users should be able to use it without accessing the help system. Unfortunately, help systems are also like life insurance in another way: By the time the user realizes it is needed, it is much too late.

Writing a high-quality help system is a huge chore. In some cases, writing a good help system is more difficult than writing the application itself. There is no room in this chapter to explain every facet of building the perfect help system, but there is room to cover the basics.

Before you read this section, however, be aware that you will need a copy of the help compiler to create help files. The help compiler is included with the Visual Basic Professional Edition. If you do not have access to the help compiler, you will not be able to build new help files (you may still find the information presented here interesting). Chapter 3 explains how you can create a Web-based help system that does not require the help compiler.

Types of Help Systems

An application can provide several different kinds of help. Some are very obvious to the user and are quite intrusive. Covering the application with a help screen can be quite distracting. On the other hand, a large help screen can give the user a lot of information very quickly. This sort of help system can also provide advanced features like an index, hypertext jumps to other topics, and keyword searching.

For occasions when the user needs a quick hint but not a full explanation, the application can provide context-sensitive help. By pressing a button or selecting a menu command, the user enters a context-sensitive help mode and the mouse pointer turns into a question mark. When the user clicks on a control, the application presents help for that control and help mode ends. Because context-sensitive help is intended to provide only a quick hint to the user, it should be brief. The user can obtain more detailed information using the screen-oriented help system.

The sections that follow describe these types of help in greater detail and explain how Visual Basic applications can support them.

Building a Help File

Building a standard help file is a complicated process. The Visual Basic 5 Enterprise Edition includes a Help Workshop that makes creating help a bit easier. By default, this program is not installed when you install Visual Basic. You can install it using the Setup.EXE program in the Tools\Hwc directory on the Visual Basic 5 compact disk.

The help compiler provided with the Visual Basic 4 Enterprise Edition is a bit more primitive. The following sections describe the steps needed to create help using this older help compiler. The steps are similar for using the Help Workshop—Workshop just packages them more nicely.

Creating a help file can be described in four steps:

1. Design the help system.
2. Create the help topic file.
3. Create the help project file.
4. Compile the help project to create the final help file.

Designing the Help System Before starting to build the help system, the help designer should invest some time in basic design. The design should include a list of major topics to be presented. It should indicate where one help topic will have hypertext links to other topics. It should also specify where the user should be able to click on a word or phrase to see a popup dialog giving more detail. Each topic should have a short name. These names or *context strings* will tie the topics together in the help files.

The description of each topic should also include a list of keywords and phrases that identify the topic for keyword searches. The help system should use many keywords. Because keywords are used only for searching, they do not clutter help topic screens; therefore, the help system should include lots of them.

The help system should not use multiple keywords that are very similar for the same topic. For example, suppose a topic describing database operations has key strings "DATABASE" and "DATABASE OPERATIONS." When the user searches for DATABASE, the help system will present both key strings because they both begin with the initial string DATABASE. Both keys lead to the same topic, however, so there is no point including them both. The help system could include only the longer key DATABASE OPERATIONS without changing the user's ability to find the topic.

A convenient way to keep all this information straight is to place each topic on a separate index card or sheet of paper. The card should include the topic's title, a brief description, its name or context string, keywords, and the names of other topics that will probably be linked to the topic in the final system.

While designing the topics, it is important to remember that people do not read help the way they read a book. They jump freely from topic to topic. Occasionally a user will follow a sequence of topics. More often the user will jump to a topic in the middle of the help file, read part of a single help screen, and then return to the main application.

To make this style of reading easier, each help topic must be as self-contained as possible. Each should be short enough to fit on a single screen. A topic must never assume that the user has just read the previous topic and is familiar with specialized terms. Whenever possible, a help topic should not force the user to visit another topic in order to understand the current one.

If a topic must use an advanced term, it should contain a hypertext link or a popup dialog describing that term so the user does not need to perform a separate keyword search.

Creating the Topic File With a design complete, the help programmer can turn to the actual help content. The content must be stored in a file using the Rich Text Format. The help compiler uses an arcane set of footnotes and text formats to provide help functionality; an editor that can provide these features is required.

Different topics must be separated by hard page breaks. In Microsoft Word page breaks are inserted by selecting the Break command from the Insert menu, clicking the Page Break button, and pressing OK.

Footnotes are used to give the help compiler special information about the help topics. Footnotes are inserted in Microsoft Word by placing the cursor at the beginning of the topic and selecting the Footnote command from the Insert menu. The text of the footnote contains the information being set for the help compiler. The footnote mark tells the compiler what kind of information it is receiving. For example, a footnote marked with a number sign (#) tells the compiler that the footnote text is the topic's name or context string. Table 2.1 lists some of the more important kinds of footnotes that can be included in a help topic file. The following sections describe some of the other important concepts used by help context files.

Hypertext Links　*Hypertext links* or *jumps* are displayed as green and underlined when presented to the user. If the user clicks on a hypertext link, the help system presents the corresponding help topic.

Hypertext links are indicated in the help topic file using the ~~strikethrough~~ or <u>double underline</u> format. The context string for the topic that the jump will activate should be placed immediately after the link text. That text should have the hidden format. In Microsoft Word hidden text is visible only when invisible characters such as paragraph marks and spaces are visible. When it is visible in Word, hidden text is displayed with a <u>dotted underline</u>.

For example, clicking on the <u>double underlined</u> <u>DOUBLE_UNDERLINE</u> text in this sentence would make the help system open up the topic with context string DOUBLE_UNDERLINE.

A common mistake in creating hypertext links is to put a space or paragraph mark between the link text and the context string. In Microsoft Word using copy and paste to copy the context string into position results in a space being inserted before the pasted text. If the context string does not immediately follow the link text, the link will not work.

Popups　In addition to hypertext links, the help system can display help popups. The user sees popup references as green text with a dotted underline. When the user clicks on this text, the help system displays a small popup window that contains a line or two of text giving further details about the text. The next time the user clicks the mouse, the popup text disappears.

Creating a popup is similar to creating a hypertext link. The popup trigger string should have the <u>single underlined</u> style. The popup topic's context string should immediately follow. That text should have the hidden style, just as the context strings for hypertext links do.

TABLE 2.1 Important Topic File Footnotes

Footnote Mark	Footnote text	Use
#	Context string	The context string is used in other topics to jump to this topic.
$	Topic title	Topic titles are displayed in the list box when the user performs a key word search.
K	Keywords	Keywords are used for keyword searches. Multiple keywords may be separated by semi-colons.
+	Browse sequence	The browse sequence is used to define browse sequence groups.

Browse Sequences A browse sequence defines a series of help topics that the user may want to view in order. For example, the topics in a browse sequence might define the steps needed to perform some complicated procedure.

The user can press the help system's >> and << buttons to move forward and backward through a browse sequence. The format of a browse sequence's identifier is group:number, as in "menus:20." Topics within a browse sequence group are presented in numerical order. The topic with sequence number menus:20 comes before menus:21 and after menus:19.

Sequence numbers need not be consecutive. In fact, it is generally best to skip numbers between each topic so that other topics can be added to the sequence later if necessary. For example, the topics in a browse sequence might initially be numbered menus:10, menus:20, menus:30, and so forth.

Nonscrolling Regions Some help topics are quite long. In those cases, it may make sense to place some text in a nonscrolling region at the top of the help screen. Nonscrolling regions can appear only at the top of help screens. Many help files place a title for each topic in a large font within a nonscrolling region.

In the help context file, text to be placed in nonscrolling regions is marked with the "keep with next" attribute. In Microsoft Word, text is given this attribute by selecting the text, invoking the Paragraph command in the Format menu, selecting the Text Flow tab, and checking the Keep with Next box.

Creating the Help Project File The help project file gives the help compiler more information about how to build the help system. The project file is a plain ASCII file. If the project file is accidentally saved in Microsoft Word format or Rich Text Format, the help compiler will be unable to read the file. By custom, help project files are usually given a .HPJ extension.

The project file contains several sections, each beginning with the section title in square brackets. Table 2.2 lists the most important sections.

To make building and reading project files easier, one file can be included within another using the #include directive, as in the following code:

```
#include <file_name>
```

TABLE 2.2 Important Help Project Sections

Title	Purpose
[OPTIONS]	Specifies compiler options. This section should be first so the options apply for the rest of the file.
[FILES]	Lists the help topic files. This section is required.
[MAP]	Associates context strings with context numbers that can be used in Visual Basic applications.

The number sign must be the first character on the line, and the angle brackets are required.

The [OPTIONS] Section Some of the more useful commands that can be specified in the [OPTIONS] section are listed in Table 2.3.

The [FILES] Section The FILES section lists the help project's topic files. This section is required and should contain at least one file. Otherwise, the help file will be empty.

The [MAP] Section If a Visual Basic application will invoke a particular help topic from the help system, the topic must be given a numeric context value. The MAP section assigns numeric values to help topics. This section contains a list of context strings followed by their numeric values. For example, the following code assigned the value 100 to the topic with context string CONTENTS.

```
[MAP]
CONTENTS        100
```

The same context numbers can also be defined in a .BAS module. Then a Visual Basic application can include the module and use meaningful values to refer to topic numbers in the help file.

```
Public Const HLP_CONTENTS 100
```

The example below shows the complete ExpenseReporter help project file Expense.HPJ.

```
[OPTIONS]
COPYRIGHT = Copyright 1997, John Wiley & Sons, Inc. All rights reserved.
TITLE = ExpenseReporter

[FILES]
EXPENSE.RTF
```

TABLE 2.3 [OPTIONS] Section Commands

Command	Purpose
CONTENTS = string	Sets the context string for the help file's table of contents topic. If this topic is not specified, it defaults to the first topic in the help topic file.
COPYRIGHT = string	Adds a copyright string seen when the user selects the Help menu's Version command from within the help system. The string can be from 35 to 75 characters long.
ERRORLOG = file	Specifies the file where the help compiler should write error messages.
ROOT = path	Specifies directories where the help compiler should look for files listed in the [FILES] section. Multiple paths should be separated with commas.
TITLE = title	Specifies the title displayed in the help system's title bar.

```
[MAP]
CONTENTS        1
OVERVIEW        2
PRINT_PREVIEW   3
CTX_NAME        101
CTX_ID          102
CTX_DEPT        103
CTX_PROJ        104
CTX_FROM_DATE   105
CTX_TO_DATE     106
CTX_DATE        107
CTX_LOCATION    108
CTX_CATEGORY    109
CTX_DESCR       110
CTX_AMOUNT      111
CTX_NOTES       112
CTX_TOTAL       113
CTX_PREPAID     114
CTX_ADVANCE     115
CTX_DUE_EMP     116
CTX_DUE_COMP    117
```

Compiling the Help Project Once the help topic and help project files are complete, compiling them is relatively simple.

Visual Basic 5's Help Workshop is a Windows program that includes a help compiler. By default, it is not installed when you install Visual Basic. To install Help Workshop, run the Setup.EXE program in the Tools\Hwc directory on the Visual Basic 5 compact disk. Once the program is installed, it can load and compile help projects.

The help compiler provided with Visual Basic 4 is located in Visual Basic's Hc subdirectory and is called Hc.EXE. This compiler has a command-line interface so it should be run from an MS-DOS window. For example, the following command shows how to compile the help project Expense.HPJ located in the current directory.

```
C:\Projects> C:\Vb4\Hc\HC Expense.HPJ
```

If all goes well, the compiler will create a compiled help file with the same name as the project file and a .HLP extension. The file can be opened and tested by double-clicking on it in Windows Explorer or by using the Open command in the File menu of any help application.

Help compilation often does not go smoothly. If all of the context strings used by hypertext links in the topic file are not properly defined by the appropriate footnotes, the compiler will produce error messages. Ensuring that all hypertext links are consistently defined can be quite confusing and debugging a large help project can be very difficult. The process is easier if the help files are built incrementally. Starting with small files, gradually adding to them and testing frequently can prevent a tangle of hypertext links from becoming too complicated to debug.

Eventually, even this process becomes cumbersome. When the number of help topics becomes extremely large, compiling the entire project may take hours. In that case, incrementally adding to the project will take a very long time.

The process can be improved by placing the help topics in several files and including them all in the help project file's [FILES] section. Then, after a particular file has been thoroughly tested, it can be commented out by placing a semi-colon in front of its INCLUDE statement. The help compiler will not load any commented files, so the build will be faster. Of course, if hypertext links in the remaining files lead to topics in a file that has been commented out, the compiler will generate warning messages.

Using a Help File in Visual Basic

Once the help file is compiled, presenting help in Visual Basic is fairly simple using a common dialog control. The application starts by setting the control's HelpFile property to the name of the compiled help file. If the application does not specify a complete path, the system will look for the file in the application's default directory.

When the program is ready to present help, it should set the dialog's HelpCommand property to indicate the operation the help system should perform. Table 2.4 lists some of this property's more important values.

Note that newer versions of the help compiler do not support cdlHelpContents and cdlHelpIndex. An application should use the "help finder" constant. Unfortunately, this constant is not defined by Visual Basic 5.0. An application can define an appropriate constant using the following code:

TABLE 2.4 Important HelpCommand Property Values

Value	Meaning
cdlHelpContents	Presents the help file's table of contents.
cdlHelpContext	Displays help for the context number specified in the dialog's HelpContext property.
cdlHelpContextPopup	Displays help for the context number specified in the dialog's HelpContext property in a popup dialog.
cdlHelpHelpOnHelp	Displays standard help on how to use help.
cdlHelpIndex	Presents the help file's index of keywords.
cdlHelpKey	Displays help for the keyword specified in the dialog's HelpKey property. This can be confusing if more than one topic uses that keyword.
cdlHelpQuit	Tells the help application that the help file is no longer needed by the program. All applications should execute this command before exiting.

```
Public Const HelpFinder = 11
```

Finally, after the application has set the dialog's HelpCommand property, it should use the dialog's ShowHelp method to present the help to the user. For example, when the user selects the Contents command from the Help menu in ExpenseReporter, the application uses the following code to present the help file's contents page.

```
Private Sub mnuHelpContents_Click()
    FileDialog.HelpCommand = cdlHelpContents
    FileDialog.ShowHelp
End Sub
```

ExpenseReporter uses the following code when the user selects the About This Screen command. The help context value 2 is defined in the MAP section of the help file's .HPJ file.

```
Private Sub mnuHelpScreen_Click()
    ExpenseForm.FileDialog.HelpCommand = cdlHelpContext
    ExpenseForm.FileDialog.HelpContext = 2
    FileDialog.ShowHelp
End Sub
```

Providing Context-Sensitive Help

Visual Basic provides support for context-sensitive help in two styles: Windows 3.x style and Windows 95 style. A Visual Basic application indicates which style to use by setting a form's WhatsThisHelp property. If this property is true, the program uses the Windows 95 "what's this" style help. If WhatsThisHelp is false, the program uses Windows 3.x style help.

Before using either style of help, the application must be associated with a help file. In the Visual Basic 4 development environment, this is done using the Options command in the Tools menu. On the Project tab, the Help File field should be filled in to indicate the location of the help file.

In the Visual Basic 5 development environment, the corresponding dialog is accessed with the Properties command at the bottom of the Project menu. This dialog's General tab contains a Help File Name field that should contain the name of the help file.

Windows 3.x Style Help

Windows 3.x style help presents help for a control when that control has the focus and the user presses F1. When this happens, Visual Basic automatically presents the help using the context number specified by the control's HelpContextID property.

For example, in the Visual Basic design environment, the HelpContextID property for ExpenseReporter's NameText was set to 101. The [MAP] section of the program's help project file associates this context number with the context string CTX_NAME.

```
[MAP]
    :
CTX_NAME         101
```

If the user clicks on the name field to give it focus and then presses F1, Visual Basic presents the help topic with the context string CTX_NAME.

When Visual Basic presents Windows 3.x style help, a separate help window appears displaying the selected topic. The help window runs as a separate application with a life of its own. The user can click on the main application to resume working there, and the help screen will keep running. If the user later invokes help for another field or uses a Help menu command, the system uses that same window to display the new help. Figure 2.7 shows ExpenseReporter with Windows 3.x style context-sensitive help.

Windows 95 Style Help

Windows 95 style presents help for a control when the mouse is over that control and the user presses F1. Note that the field does not need to have the input focus. The mouse merely needs to be above the field. This allows the user to obtain help for objects such as label controls that cannot accept the input focus. The user simply points the mouse at the control and presses F1.

As is the case with Windows 3.x style help, Visual Basic automatically presents the help using the context number specified by the control's WhatsThisHelpID property.

When the system presents Windows 95 style help, the help topic appears in a popup. When the user clicks on the popup or on any other part of the screen, the popup disappears. Figure 2.8 shows ExpenseReporter displaying Windows 95 style context-sensitive help.

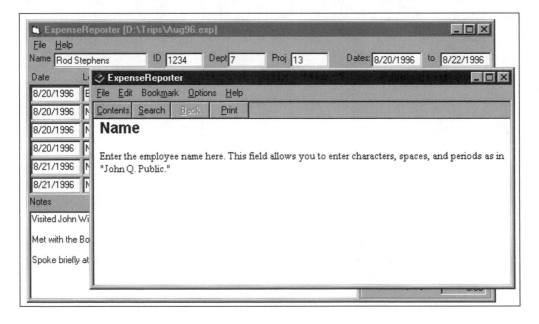

FIGURE 2.7 Windows 3.x style context-sensitive help.

Because the popup disappears when the user clicks on it, the help topic presented should not contain hypertext jumps or other help popups. If the user tries to click on a hypertext link, the help popup will disappear rather than display the new topic. For this reason, context-sensitive help topics should be dead ends in the help topic file. They should provide no links to other topics, and they should not be part of browse sequences.

Because the help is presented in a popup, the information it displays should be brief. It should not include a large title that will waste a lot of screen space. The user does not have the option of using links or other popups to define confusing terms, so the topic should be as self-contained as possible.

Because context-sensitive help topics are so restricted, they generally are not useful as part of the normal screen-oriented help system. In that case, they should not have search keys either because there is little point in letting the user find these topics using the help program's search features. Instead, the help file should provide more complete screen-oriented entries that duplicate the context-sensitive entries. These topics can include hypertext links, popups, and search keys as usual.

None of this needs to be true for Windows 3.x style help. Because this style of help presents topics in a full help application, links and help popups will work normally. These topics can include title text and keys, and they can be part of browse sequences.

If a form's WhatsThisButton property is true and if its MinButton and MaxButton properties are false, Visual Basic adds a special question mark button to the window's title bar. In Figure 2.8, ExpenseReporter displays this button. When the user clicks on the What's This button, the mouse

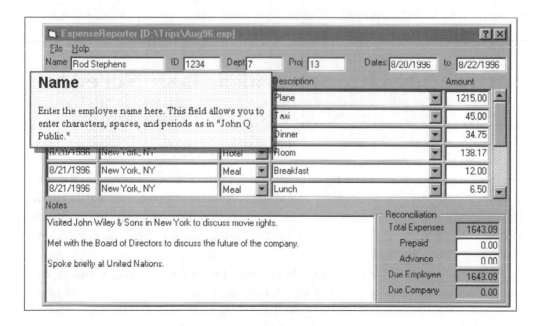

FIGURE 2.8 Windows 95 style context-sensitive help.

pointer turns into a question mark. If the user then clicks on a control, Visual Basic presents the context-sensitive help for that control.

Unfortunately, to display the What's This button, the form's MinButton and MaxButton properties must be false. That means the user cannot easily minimize and maximize the form. Fortunately, there is another way an application can display the Minimize and Maximize buttons and present context-sensitive help without using the What's This button.

A control's ShowWhatsThis method presents the context-sensitive help for that control. To present the help for a text box named IDText, an application could use the following statement:

```
IDText.ShowWhatsThis
```

An application can use ShowWhatsThis to display the context-sensitive help for fields in a program-specific manner. For example, the program could set a form's KeyPreview property to true and examine key presses. When the user pressed **F1**, the program could identify the control that currently held the input focus and invoke that control's ShowWhatsThis method.

A form's WhatsThisMode method provides an even better solution. This method puts the form in What's This mode just as if the user had pressed the What's This button. The mouse cursor changes to a question mark, and the system presents help when the user clicks on a control.

An application can use this method to effectively replace the What's This button. The program should include a command button on the form or a command in a menu to start What's This mode. The button or command's Click event handler invokes WhatsThisMode as in the following code:

```
Private Sub mnuHelpWhatsThis_Click()
    WhatsThisMode
End Sub
```

Displaying About Dialogs and Splash Screens

The one standard Help menu entry that is different from the rest is the About command. This command presents a dialog box that gives the name and version of the application. It often contains brief copyright information and sometimes identifies the registered owner of the application. The dialog contains an OK button that allows the user to close it at any time.

A splash screen is a form that appears when the user first starts the application. It contains the same information as an about dialog. The only difference is that the splash screen remains visible for a certain amount of time, generally two or three seconds, and then disappears on its own when the application is ready to begin work. The user does not need to press an OK button, and the splash screen does not provide one.

An application can use the same dialog both as an about dialog and as a splash screen. The application should include a form with a timer control and an OK button, as shown in Figure 2.9. The form's BorderStyle property should be set to 3 (Fixed Dialog) so that the user cannot resize the form. Its ControlBox, MinButton, and MaxButton properties should all be false because these options are not necessary on an about dialog or splash screen. The form should contain the application's name and version number, copyright information, and colorful, eye-catching graphics. The splash screen is the first thing the user will see when the application starts—it should make a good impression.

Next, the form should provide a Boolean AboutDialog property let function. The main application will invoke this function to tell the form whether it is being used as an about dialog or as a splash screen. The AboutDialog code presented later prepares the form appropriately.

If the main application sets AboutDialog to true, the form will be used as an about dialog. In that case, AboutDialog disables the splash screen timer. It makes the OK button visible and sets the height of the form to be large enough to display the button. Finally, it sets the form's Caption property. This is important because it makes the form display a title bar. The user can grab the title bar with the mouse and drag it to other parts of the screen.

If the main application sets AboutDialog to false, the form will be used as a splash screen. In that case, AboutDialog enables the splash screen timer. In design mode, the timer's Interval property should be set to indicate the minimum length of time the splash screen will be displayed. This value should not be greater than two or three seconds (2000 or 3000 milliseconds), or the user may be annoyed.

AboutDialog next makes the OK button invisible and sets the height of the form to a reasonable value given that the OK button is hidden. Finally, it blanks the form's Caption property so that the form

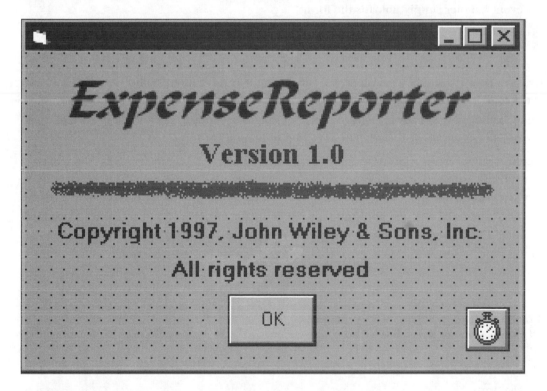

FIGURE 2.9 A form used for a splash screen and an about dialog.

has no title bar. The user does not need to be able to move the splash screen because it will be displayed for only a short time.

```
Property Let AboutDialog(value As Boolean)
Const MARGIN = 240

    If value Then
        SplashTimer.Enabled = False
        CmdOk.Visible = True
        Height = CmdOk.Top + _
            CmdOk.Height + MARGIN
        Caption = "About ExpenseReporter"
    Else
        SplashTimer.Enabled = True
        CmdOk.Visible = False
        Height = RightsLabel.Top + _
            RightsLabel.Height + MARGIN
        Caption = ""
    End If
End Property
```

When the form is displayed as an about dialog, it handles the OK button in a simple way. The OK button's Click event handler simply unloads the form.

```
Private Sub CmdOk_Click()
    Unload Me
End Sub
```

When the form is displayed as a splash screen, unloading it is a bit more complicated. The splash screen should unload itself whenever the minimum amount of time has expired or when the application has finished loading and is ready for work, whichever comes second. To keep track of both of these events, the form defines two Boolean variables in its declarations section.

```
Dim timer_expired As Boolean
Dim ready_to_unload As Boolean
```

The splash screen's Load event procedure sets both of these variables to false, indicating that the timer has not yet expired and that the application is not yet ready for the splash screen to unload. The Load event handler also centers the form on the user's computer and ensures that no other screen can be moved on top of it. It performs this last feat using the SetWindowPos API function.

```
Private Sub Form_Load()
Dim status As Long

    ' Initially the form has just been presented
    ' and is not ready for unloading.
    timer_expired = False
    ready_to_unload = False

    ' Center the form.
    Left = (Screen.Width - Width) / 2
    Top = (Screen.Height - Height) / 2
```

```
' Make this window stay on top of others.
status = SetWindowPos(hWnd, HWND_TOPMOST, _
    0, 0, 0, 0, SWP_NOMOVE + SWP_NOSIZE)
End Sub
```

The form provides a property let procedure, ReadyToUnload. The main program calls this procedure when it has finished initialization and it is ready to begin work. ReadyToUnload sets the value of the form's ready_to_unload variable to true. If the timer_expired variable also has the value true at that time, the procedure unloads the splash screen. ReadyToUnload also enables the application's main form and sends the input focus to that form.

```
Property Let ReadyToUnload(value As Boolean)
    ready_to_unload = value

    If timer_expired Then
        Unload Me
        ExpenseForm.Enabled = True
        ExpenseForm.SetFocus
    End If
End Property
```

The timer's Timer event handler is similar. It sets timer_expired to true and unloads the form if ready_to_unload is also true.

```
Private Sub SplashTimer_Timer()
    timer_expired = True
    SplashTimer.Enabled = False

    If ready_to_unload Then
        Unload Me
        ExpenseForm.Enabled = True
        ExpenseForm.SetFocus
    End If
End Sub
```

Now the main application can use the form as both a splash screen and an about dialog. The main application's Load event handler presents it as a splash screen as shown in the following code. Notice that the program disables the application's main form before presenting the splash screen. This prevents the user from interacting with the main application while the splash screen is visible. The splash screen's ReadyToUnload and SplashTimer_Timer routines reenable the main form before unloading the splash screen.

```
Private Sub Form_Load()
    ' Disable the form. The splash screen will
    ' enable the form when it unloads.
    Enabled = False

    ' Display the splash screen.
    Splash.AboutDialog = False
    Splash.Show vbModeless
```

```
' Force the splash screen to display itself.
Splash.Refresh

' Load data, arrange controls, and perform other initialization.
:

' Tell the splash screen we have finished initialization.
Splash.ReadyToUnload = True
End Sub
```

It is even easier to use the form as an about dialog. The form is displayed modally so the user must close the dialog before returning to the main application. The following code shows how the About command in ExpenseReporter's Help menu displays the about dialog.

```
Private Sub mnuHelpAbout_Click()
    Splash.AboutDialog = True
    Splash.Show vbModal
End Sub
```

Summary

Chapters 1 and 2 explain a collection of application programming techniques that give an application a polished look. Most users have seen advanced features such as scrolling areas, recent file lists, and print preview in commercial applications. Adding these familiar features to an application makes users comfortable and makes the application appear sophisticated.

Chapter 3

AppointmentBook

The AppointmentBook application tracks meetings and appointments. The user enters information about an appointment, and AppointmentBook presents a reminder message when the time for the appointment draws near.

The first section in this chapter, "Using AppointmentBook," describes the program's key features from the user's point-of-view. It explains how the user enters, modifies, and deletes appointment information. It also describes the application's HTML help system. This help system provides an alternative to the compiled help used by the ExpenseReporter application.

Note that the help system is implemented using the WebBrowser control provided with Visual Basic 5.0. Since it uses the WebBrowser control, the program will not work with earlier versions of Visual Basic. If you are using an earlier version, you may still want to read about the techniques described in this chapter, but you will be unable to run AppointmentBook as it is written.

The next section, "Key Techniques," briefly lists the most important Visual Basic programming methods used to implement AppointmentBook. The rest of the chapter describes these techniques in detail.

Using AppointmentBook

Before reading about how AppointmentBook was designed and coded, take a few minutes to run the program and test some of its features. The section "Using the Compact Disk" in the Introduction explains how you can load the program's source files from the compact disk. AppointmentBook is contained in the ApptBook.VBP project in the Ch3 directory.

AppointmentBook reads and writes appointment data to the file Appts.DAT. Because there is no way to know when you will run the program, Appts.DAT is not included in the Ch3 directory. The first time you run the program, AppointmentBook will tell you it cannot find Appts.DAT, and it will ask if it should create a new data file. Press the Yes button, and the program will be ready to run.

Figure 3.1 shows the AppointmentBook application in action. The following sections describe AppointmentBook's features from the user's point-of-view.

Selecting Dates

AppointmentBook has two main display areas: the month area on the left and the daily appointment area on the right.

The month area highlights dates that hold appointments by giving them a slightly darker background color. The months are labeled vertically to save space on the screen. Adjacent months have different background colors so it is easy to see where one month ends and the next begins.

When the user clicks on the month area to select a date, the program displays the selected date with white text on a black background. In Figure 3.1 April 1 is the selected date.

The month area's scroll bar allows the user to move the calendar forward and backward through time. By clicking on the scroll bar's up and down arrows, the user can move the selected date by one week. Clicking between the scroll bar's slider and one of its arrows moves the selected date by four weeks.

By dragging the slider, the user can move the selected date by many weeks at a time. The month area is relatively slow to draw, so it is not redrawn until the user finishes dragging the slider. The date label above the daily appointment area shows the date the user is selecting as the slider is dragged.

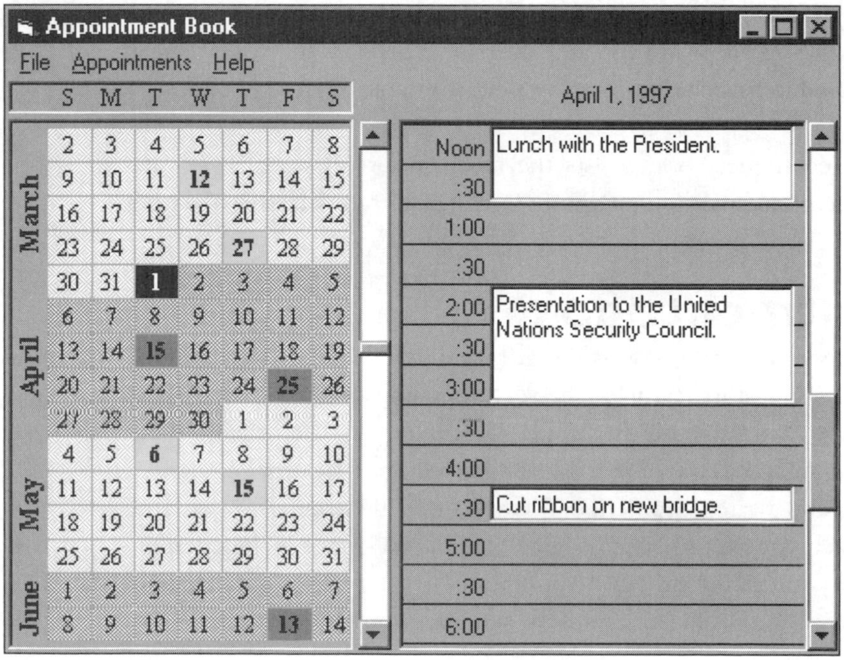

FIGURE 3.1 The AppointmentBook application.

AppointmentBook also allows the user to change the selected date using the arrow keys. When the user presses an arrow key, the program selects the corresponding adjacent date. For instance, if the user presses the up arrow, the program moves the selected date to one week earlier.

If the user holds down the shift key and presses the up or down arrow, the program moves the selected date by four weeks. If the user holds down the shift key and presses the left or right arrow, the program moves the selected date to the previous Sunday or next Saturday.

The Select Today command in the Appointments menu allows the user to select the current date easily. At first this function may seem unnecessary because the user can select the current date using the month area's scroll bar. However, the month area contains a lot of dates. It displays the current year and the previous and next years, for a total of almost 1100 days. Finding today's date using the scroll bar can be difficult. Because a user will often want to create appointments near the current date, it makes sense to create a special function to select that date.

Viewing Appointments

The daily appointment area shows the appointments for the date selected in the month area. The label above the appointment area shows the selected date textually. This label is important because it displays the selected date's year; the month area does not.

The daily appointment area shows text describing the appointments on the selected date. Morning appointments are shown with lighter background colors than appointments in the afternoon.

The text describing an appointment is displayed in a multiline text box, which allows the user to highlight the text and use Ctrl-C to copy it to the clipboard. The user can then use Ctrl-V to paste the text into other applications.

The appointment area's scroll bar allows the user to examine all of the appointments on the selected date. When the user selects a new date, the appointment area scrolls to show the date's first appointment.

Creating Appointments

To create a new appointment entry, the user should first select the appointment's date. When the user selects the New Appointment command from the Appointment's menu, the dialog shown in Figure 3.2 appears. The user should enter the appointment's Start and Stop Times, the Warning time, and a brief message describing the appointment. When the user clicks the OK button, AppointmentBook creates the appointment entry.

The warning time indicates when AppointmentBook should remind the user of the appointment. For example, if the appointment is scheduled for 9:00 AM and the warning time is 30 minutes, the program will remind the user of the appointment at 8:30 AM. Figure 3.3 shows a typical reminder message.

Modifying or Deleting Appointments

To modify or delete an appointment, the user should select the appointment's date and double-click on the appointment's text in the daily appointment area. The program will display a dialog similar to the one shown in Figure 3.2, used to create a new appointment. To modify the appointment, the user should

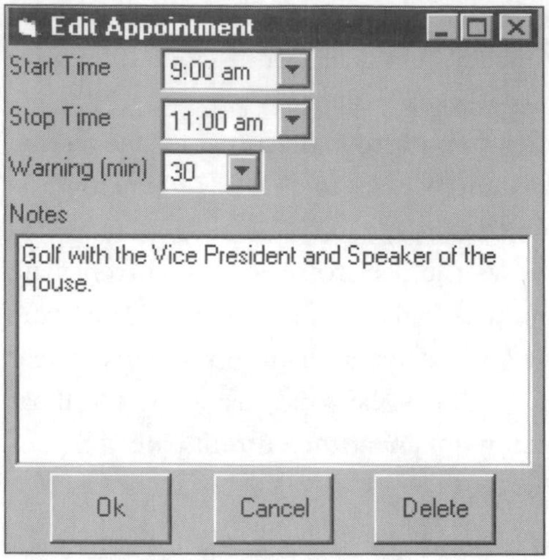

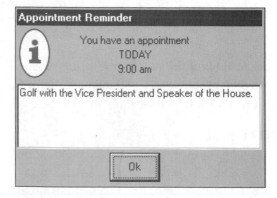

FIGURE 3.2 The appointment editing dialog.

make the required changes and click the OK button. To delete the appointment, the user should click the Delete button.

Loading and Saving Data

AppointmentBook loads the data contained in the file Appts.DAT when it starts. Later, whenever appointment data changes, the program saves the updated data in Appts.DAT. Saving the data is very quick so this does not inconvenience the user. It also ensures that the data is safe at all times. This means the user can exit AppointmentBook without explicitly saving the data. The data is safe if the program crashes or if the user stops the program with the Task Manager or some other external method. The data is even safe if the computer halts unexpectedly due to a power failure or the user pressing the computer's Reset button.

FIGURE 3.3 The appointment reminder dialog.

This feature is particularly important for a program such as AppointmentBook that may be running all the time. The system can start AppointmentBook when it boots. The user can shut down the computer without worrying about whether the AppointmentBook data is saved. This allows Appointment-Book to run continuously so it can display reminder messages whenever they are needed.

Purging Old Data

AppointmentBook displays past appointments so the user can review them. The user can flush the old data from the system by selecting the Purge command from the Appointments menu. Because removed data cannot be restored, the program asks the user to confirm the operation before it deletes the old data.

Displaying Help

AppointmentBook does not use a standard help system as does the ExpenseReporter application described in Chapters 1 and 2. Rather than using a compiled help file, AppointmentBook displays help using a collection of HTML (Hypertext Markup Language) documents similar to those displayed on the World Wide Web.

The constant HELP_DIR defined in the URLHelpForm's declares section indicates the location of the help documents. In AppointmentBook this value is set to http://Beauty/HelpHTML/. You need to change this value to reflect the location of the documents on your system before you can test the help. The help files are in the Ch3\HelpHTML directory on the compact disk.

If the user selects the Contents command from the Help menu, the program displays the contents page shown in Figure 3.4. By clicking on the HTML links on this page, the user can navigate to other help topics.

If the user selects the Index command from AppointmentBook's Help menu, the program displays the index page shown in Figure 3.5. The letters across the top of the page provide links to sections within the page. For example, if the user clicks the letter M, the browser will scroll down to display index entries that start with M.

By clicking on an index topic, the user can navigate to a help page that explains that topic. Figure 3.6 shows the help page describing the month area. Help pages such as this one can use any features supported by HTML including links to other topics and graphics.

AppointmentBook displays help documents in a customized browser form. The browser's Navigate menu provides commands to display the help contents or the help index, return to the previously displayed help page, and refresh the current display. It also contains a list of the last 10 help pages it has displayed. If the user selects one of these pages, the browser quickly redisplays it.

Displaying Context-Sensitive Help

The user can obtain context-sensitive help by clicking on part of AppointmentBook and pressing F1. The month area, daily appointment area, and the appointment description text have their own help topics.

Context-sensitive help for the scroll bars leads to the corresponding area's help topic. For instance, if the user clicks on the month area's scroll bar and presses F1, the help system displays help about the month area.

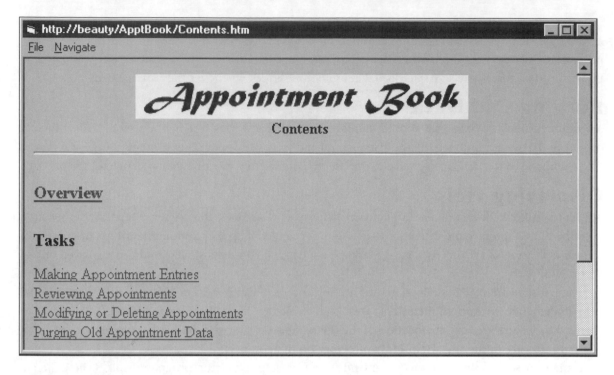

FIGURE 3.4 The help contents page.

If no control with context-sensitive help is selected when the user presses F1, the help system presents AppointmentBook's help contents page.

Viewing the About Dialog

Like ExpenseReporter, AppointmentBook displays a splash screen when it starts. If the user selects the About AppointmentBook command from the Help menu, the program uses the same screen to provide an about dialog giving version and copyright information. Figure 3.7 shows AppointmentBook's about dialog. Its unusual shape makes it more eye-catching than the dialogs provided by ExpenseReporter and adds interest to an otherwise routine feature.

Keeping Pieces Synchronized

Different parts of AppointmentBook are tied closely to the data and to each other. A single function or change to the data may cause several changes to the visible display.

For example, suppose the user scrolls the month far into the future. If the user invokes the Select Today command from the Appointments menu, the program updates its display in five ways:

1. The month area scrolls to show the current date and the dates immediately after it. It highlights the current date.

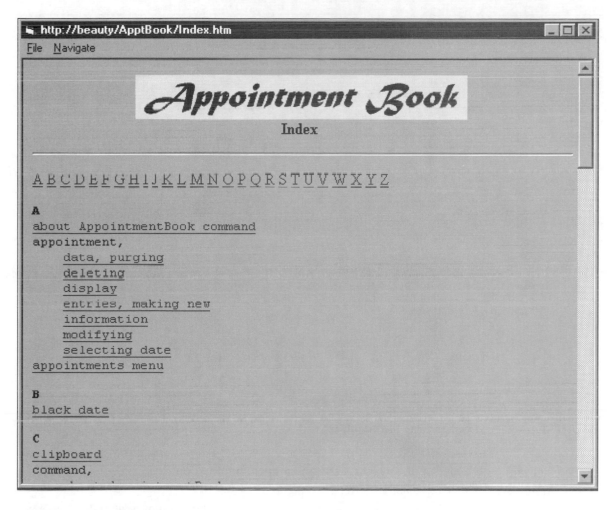

FIGURE 3.5 The help index page.

2. The month area's scroll bar adjusts to indicate the position of the current date within the larger calendar.
3. The daily appointment area displays the appointments for the current date.
4. The daily appointment area's scroll bar adjusts to indicate the position of the displayed appointments within the daily schedule.
5. The date label above the appointment area displays the current date.

Other simple actions also have complicated consequences. If the user creates a new appointment for a past date that did not have an appointment before, the program updates its display in three ways:

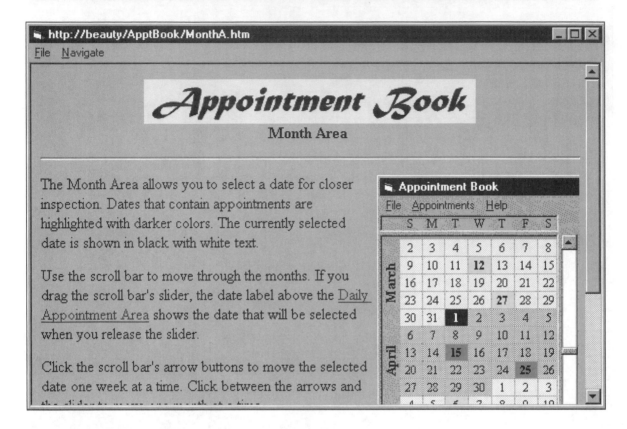

FIGURE 3.6 A help page describing the month area.

1. The daily appointment area displays the new appointment information.
2. The month area changes to display the date highlighted.
3. The program presents a message indicating that the user missed the appointment because it is in the past.

Keeping the different parts of the program synchronized is one of AppointmentBook's most important and complex features.

Key Techniques

Despite the apparent simplicity of its mission, AppointmentBook is a rather complex application. The interactions among the data and different parts of the user interface are particularly complicated. Taken individually, however, AppointmentBook's features are easy to understand. Even the elaborate user interface interactions can be broken into pieces that are simple enough to implement reliably.

The key Visual Basic techniques used to break AppointmentBook into manageable pieces are outlined in the following list. The rest of this chapter describes them in detail.

FIGURE 3.7 AppointmentBook's about dialog.

- **Using Bit Masks**. AppointmentBook uses bit masks to represent changes in the data. This section explains how a program can use bit masks to describe several Boolean or on/off features in a single integer or long integer.
- **Using the MVC Paradigm**. The model/view/controller (MVC) paradigm uses a set of simple class objects to represent a complex assortment of interactions. This section explains MVC and how it is used by AppointmentBook.
- **Creating Fonts**. To save screen space, AppointmentBook displays the names of the months in the month area using a rotated font. This section describes the CreateFont API function used to create rotated text.
- **Scrolling Large Amounts of Data**. AppointmentBook's month area displays data for the previous, current, and next years. This section explains techniques for managing very large amounts of data so AppointmentBook can scroll through almost 1100 days' worth of data.
- **Setting Alarms**. Visual Basic's timer control is useful for managing periodic events that occur fairly frequently (more than once a minute or so). This section tells how an application can wait for isolated events that may occur far in the future.
- **Creating Nonrectangular Forms**. AppointmentBook's splash screen and about dialog use a distinctive, nonrectangular form. This section explains how an application can use irregularly shaped forms to add extra interest to an otherwise routine function.
- **Presenting Help**. AppointmentBook provides help using HTML documents. This section describes the program's help documents and its customized help browsing system.

Using Bit Masks

Computers store any data item as a series of bits, each of which can have the value zero or one. For example, in Visual Basic an integer is represented by a series of 16 bits; a long integer is represented by 32 bits.

A program can use the bits in one of these data types to record Boolean or on/off features. A feature is present, true, or on if the corresponding bit in the integer is a one. It is absent, false, or off if the bit is a zero. The series of bits 00...011 would indicate that only the last two features were present. A program can use an integer if it will need no more than 16 features and a long integer if it needs up to 32 features.

A *bit mask* is a value that represents a specific collection of values. Often a mask represents a single feature. For instance, the value 00...001 represents a value with only the last feature present.

The following sections explain how to use bit masks and how they are used in AppointmentBook. If you are already familiar with bit masks, you may want to skip to the section titled "Bit Masks in AppointmentBook."

Defining Bit Masks

The following code defines bit mask values that describe specific vehicle features:

```
Public Const VEH_4WD = &H1              ' Four-wheel drive.
Public Const VEH_ABS = &H2              ' Anti-lock brakes.
Public Const VEH_Airbag1 = &H4          ' Driver-side airbag.
Public Const VEH_Airbag2 = &H8          ' Passenger airbag.
Public Const VEH_Automatic = &H10       ' Automatic transmission.
Public Const VEH_PowerSteering = &H20   ' Power steering.
Public Const VEH_PowerBrakes = &H40     ' Power brakes.
Public Const VEH_PowerWindows = &H80    ' Power windows.
Public Const VEH_RemoteKeyless = &H100  ' Remote keyless entry.
    :
```

This code illustrates several important points. First, each mask's name begins with "VEH_." This makes it easy to remember that the values represent vehicle features. Defining the masks using names such as "ABS"" and "4WD" without the "VEH_" prefix would make other parts of the code that use the masks harder to understand.

The definition of each mask includes a comment that indicates exactly what the mask means. The mask name itself should be as meaningful as possible, but it is still a good idea to place comments near the definitions. Later, if it is unclear what VEH_DOHC means, a quick search for the string "VEH_DOHC =" will locate the comment. In this example, it would also be best to change the name to something less cryptic, such as "VEH_DualOverheadCam."

Finally, the values are defined using hexadecimal. This makes it easy to keep track of the next integer value that has only a single bit set. In base 10, the numbers with a single bit set are 1, 2, 4, 8, 16, 32, 64, ... In hexadecimal, the same numbers are 1, 2, 4, 8, 10, 20, 40, ... The sequence consists of the digits 1, 2, 4, and 8 followed by different numbers of zeros. This simple pattern makes it easy to generate as many hexadecimal values as necessary.

Alternatively, mask values can be specified in terms of the preceding values. A mask value with a single bit set multiplied by two gives the next value with a single bit set. The following code defines the first few vehicle codes using this method:

```
Public Const VEH_4WD = 1                    ' Four-wheel drive.
Public Const VEH_ABS = VEH_4WD * 2          ' Anti-lock brakes.
Public Const VEH_Airbag1 = VEH_ABS * 2      ' Driver-side airbag.
Public Const VEH_Airbag2 = VEH_Airbag2 * 2  ' Passenger airbag.
     :
```

This method has the advantage that it requires few changes to move items around in the list. The following code shows the same list with the new value VEH_Automatic inserted in the middle. Only the new line and the following line required changes.

```
Public Const VEH_4WD = 1                       ' Four-wheel drive.
Public Const VEH_ABS = VEH_4WD * 2             ' Anti-lock brakes.
Public Const VEH_Automatic = VEH_ABS * 2       ' Automatic transmission.
Public Const VEH_Airbag1 = VEH_Automatic * 2   ' Driver-side airbag.
Public Const VEH_Airbag2 = VEH_Airbag2 * 2     ' Passenger airbag.
     :
```

Many programs use two special masks: a mask with no bits set and a mask with every bit set. A mask with no bits set represents an object with none of the defined features. This mask can be defined by giving it the value 0.

A mask that has every bit set represents an object with every defined feature. Because Visual Basic's bitwise Not operator switches the values of every bit in an integer value, this value is the bitwise negation of the value with no bits set.

```
Public Const VEH_NoFeatures = 0                   ' No features.
Public Const VEH_AllFeatures = Not VEH_NoFeatures ' Every feature.
```

Combining Bit Masks

A program can manipulate bit masks using the bitwise operators And, Or, Not, and Xor. The bitwise And of two integer values A and B contains a one in any position where the corresponding bits of A and B are both one.

```
    00...01101
And 00...01010
    00...01000
```

The bitwise Or of two integer values A and B contains a one in any position where the corresponding bit of either A or B is one.

```
   00...01001
Or 00...01010
   00...01011
```

The bitwise Not or *bitwise negation* of an integer value A contains a one in every position where A has a zero. It has a zero in each position where A has a one.

```
Not 00...01010
    11...10101
```

Finally, the bitwise Xor or *exclusive or* of two values A and B contains a one in any position where the corresponding bit of either A or B but not both is a one.

```
    00...01011
Xor 00...00010
    00...01001
```

To define a value that represents more than one bit mask feature, a program can combine the separate bit masks using the bitwise Or operator. The following code creates a value representing a vehicle with four-wheel drive, anti-lock brakes, and dual airbags. The vehicle does not have any other features such as power steering or automatic transmission.

```
Dim car_features As Integer

    car_features = _
        VEH_4WD Or _
        VEH_ABS Or _
        VEH_Airbag1 Or _
        VEH_Airbag2
```

Once a program has defined bit mask values for a set of objects, it must be able to determine what the values mean. It can do this using the bitwise And operator. If the program uses And to combine a value with a mask representing a single feature, the result will be zero unless the value has the same bit set as the mask. Continuing the previous example, car_features And VEH_4WD = VEH_4WD while car_features And VEH_Automatic = 0.

In Visual Basic, nonzero integer values are treated as true in logical comparisons and zero values are treated as false. That means the program can use bit masks to easily identify objects that meet certain conditions. For example, suppose a program has an array Features that contains bit masks describing a group of vehicles. The program could use the following code to locate all of the vehicles that have four-wheel drive.

```
Dim i As Integer

    For i = LBound(Features) To UBound(Features)
        If Features(i) And VEH_4WD Then
            MsgBox "Vehicle" & Str$(i) & " has four-wheel drive."
        End If
    Next i
```

A program can combine masks using the Or operator to identify objects that have one or more of a set of features. The following code identifies vehicles that have four-wheel drive or anti-lock brakes:

```
Dim i As Integer

    For i = LBound(Features) To UBound(Features)
        If Features(i) And (VEH_4WD Or VEH_ABS) Then
            MsgBox "Vehicle" & Str$(i) & _
                " has four-wheel drive OR anti-lock brakes."
        End If
    Next i
```

In complicated tests like this one, a program must use parentheses to force Visual Basic to evaluate the expression in the correct order. Without the parentheses, Visual Basic treats the following two statements equivalently:

```
Features(i) And VEH_4WD Or VEH_ABS
(Features(i) And VEH_4WD) Or VEH_ABS
```

Because the result of the first half of the second equation is combined with VEH_ABS using the bitwise Or operator, the result will have at least the same bit set as in the mask VEH_ABS. This means the result will always be nonzero so it will be treated as logically true no matter what value Features(i) has.

A program must take special care when using both the logical and bitwise meanings of an operator. For instance, the following code seems to identify vehicles that have both four-wheel drive and anti-lock brakes:

```
If (Features(i) And VEH_4WD) And _
   (Features(i) And VEH_ABS) Then...
```

Actually, Visual Basic treats all of the And operators in this example as bitwise operators. That means this expression will return true only if Features(i), VEH_4WD, and VEH_ABS all have at least one bit set to one in the same position. Because VEH_4WD and VEH_ABS are single feature bit masks, they have no set bits in common so this will never happen.

This code must be modified so the middle And operator is logical rather than bitwise. The following code uses the CBool conversion function to convert the first and last parts of the expression from bit values into Boolean values. Then the middle And operator correctly identifies vehicles that have both four-wheel drive and anti-lock brakes.

```
Dim i As Integer

    For i = LBound(Features) To UBound(Features)
        If CBool(Features(i) And VEH_4WD) And _
           CBool(Features(i) And VEH_ABS) _
        Then
            MsgBox "Vehicle" & Str$(i) & _
                " has four-wheel drive AND anti-lock brakes."
        End If
    Next i
```

Using the Not operator a program can find objects that do not have a specific feature. Again the program must take care to avoid confusing logical and bitwise operators. The bitwise negation of a number almost always has at least one bit set so it will be regarded as logically true. What is needed in this case is the logical negation of the value. The following code finds vehicles that do not have automatic transmissions:

```
Dim i As Integer

    For i = LBound(Features) To UBound(Features)
        If Not CBool(Features(i) And VEH_Automatic) Then
```

```
            MsgBox "Vehicle" & Str$(i) & _
                " does NOT have an automatic transmission."
        End If
    Next i
```

Using other combinations of operators a program can identify objects with any combination of features. It could locate vehicles with anti-lock brakes and a driver-side airbag that do not have automatic transmissions, power windows, or remote keyless entry. In elaborate cases such as this, the program should include lots of parentheses to force Visual Basic to apply the operators in the correct order. It should also use the CBool function where necessary to convert the results of bitwise operators into logical values.

Bit Masks in AppointmentBook

AppointmentBook uses bit masks to track events using the model/view/controller (MVC) paradigm. MVC is described in detail in the following section, "Using the MVC Paradigm," but its use of bit masks is described here.

AppointmentBook uses bit masks to define certain events. For example, when the user clicks on a new date in the month area, the application selects that date. The program associates this event with an event mask defined by the following code:

```
Public Const CAL_SelectedDateChanged = &H2
```

AppointmentBook keeps a list of *views* that may be interested in certain events. Each view is an object that provides a value giving the bitwise Or of the event codes that interest it. For instance, the object that manages the daily appointment area needs to redraw the appointments whenever the user selects a new date. It also needs to redraw the appointments if the user changes an appointment's start or stop time. This object uses the following value as its mask of interesting events:

```
CAL_SelectedDateChanged Or CAL_AppointmentChanged
```

Values describing the events that are interesting to each view object are stored in the program's Events collection. References to the objects themselves are stored in the corresponding entries in the Views collection.

The NotifyViews subroutine takes as a parameter an event mask that represents the event or events that have just occurred. It uses the bit mask techniques described in the previous section to identify the views that are interested in the events. For each interested view, it invokes the view's Notify subroutine, passing it the event mask so the routine can tell what event just took place.

```
Private Sub NotifyViews(event_mask As Long)
Dim i As Integer

    For i = 1 To Views.Count
        ' Notify this view if necessary.
        If event_mask And Events.Item(i) Then _
            Views.Item(i).Notify event_mask
    Next i
End Sub
```

Using the MVC Paradigm

The interactions among AppointmentBook's various user interface elements are quite complex. For example, when the user clicks the up arrow on the month area's scroll bar, the following actions take place:

1. The month area redraws the currently selected date so it no longer has a black background. It then selects the date one week before the currently selected date.
2. If the newly selected date is above the visible part of the month area, the area redraws to make the new date visible. The scroll bar also adjusts to show the newly selected date's position within the larger calendar.
3. The date label above the daily appointment area displays the new date.
4. The daily appointment area displays the appointments for the newly selected date with the earliest appointment shown at the top.
5. The daily appointment area's scroll bar adjusts to show where the daily appointment display is within the day's schedule.

This is one of AppointmentBook's more convoluted interactions, but many of the others are complicated enough to be quite confusing. These sorts of interactions can make program maintenance a nightmare. Suppose, for example, the program needed to display daily schedules using a new display method. Adding the new code would require removing all of the code that managed the display using the old method. Changes would be required wherever the program used the old code to update the appointment display. This occurs whenever the user performs one of the following actions:

- Selects a new date by clicking in the month area, using the month area's scroll bar, or by invoking the Select Today command in the Appointments menu
- Creates a new appointment
- Changes the start or stop time of an existing appointment
- Deletes an appointment
- Scrolls the appointments using the daily appointment area's scroll bar

Removing the older appointment display code would require changes in many different parts of the program.

The model/view/controller (MVC) paradigm uses three different kinds of objects to make managing these sorts of interactions easier. As its name implies, the three kinds of objects MVC uses are called *models*, *views*, and *controllers*.

Briefly, a *model* is an object that represents some sort of data, device, or some other thing around which the interactions are centered. A *view* is an object that provides some sort of display of a model. A *controller* is an object that manipulates a model. The following sections discuss the basic duties of these objects. They also briefly describe the specific duties of the model, view, and controller objects used by AppointmentBook. Some of these objects are described in greater detail a bit later.

The duties of models, views, and controllers are tied tightly together so you may find it difficult to understand how each object works separately. You may need to know how a view works before you can understand models, but you also need to understand models before you can fully understand views. To understand all the details, you may need to read the following sections two or three times.

Models

A model has two duties: managing application data and notifying views when the data is modified. The first duty simplifies the ways in which other parts of the program modify the data. The second makes even the most complicated object interactions manageable.

Managing Application Data It is the model's duty to manage all aspects of the actual data. The model is the only object that is allowed to do anything to the data directly. Only the model can load, save, modify, or even view the data. Other objects that need to interact with the data must do so using the model's public subroutines, functions, and property procedures.

For example, in AppointmentBook one of the many pieces of information stored in the model is the currently selected date. The model class CalendarModel provides a property let procedure SelectedDate that allows other parts of the program to select a new date. Code outside the CalendarModel class simply sets the property procedure's value to the desired date, and the model makes the actual changes to the data.

The following code shows how the Select Today command in the Appointments menu makes the current day the selected date. Visual Basic's Date function returns the current date. Because all of the data modification details are hidden within the model's SelectedDate procedure, this code is extremely simple.

```
Private Sub mnuApptToday_Click()
    TheCalendarModel.SelectedDate = Date
End Sub
```

Notifying Views The second duty of a model is to notify interested views when an event occurs. In addition to storing a representation of the data, the model must contain a list of view objects that are interested in various events that may occur. When one of the model's public routines or functions changes the data, the model must inform interested views of the change.

To make view management possible, the model should provide a RegisterView subroutine. This routine takes as parameters a reference to a view object and a bit mask indicating the events that interest the object. The model stores this information for later use.

AppointmentBook stores the objects and their event masks in the Views and Events collections. Adding a new view to the list with RegisterView is simple.

```
Private Views As New Collection
Private Events As New Collection
    :
Public Sub RegisterView(view As Object, event_mask As Long)
    Views.Add view
```

```
        Events.Add event_mask
End Sub
```

When an event occurs, the model must notify the interested views. The NotifyViews subroutine described in the earlier section, "Bit Masks in AppointmentBook," does this. It takes as a parameter a mask indicating which event or events just took place. For each view interested in the events, Notify-Views invokes the object's Notify subroutine.

```
Private Sub NotifyViews(event_mask As Long)
Dim i As Integer

    For i = 1 To Views.Count
        ' Notify this view if necessary.
        If event_mask And Events.Item(i) Then _
            Views.Item(i).Notify event_mask
    Next i
End Sub
```

Finally, if views may eventually be destroyed by a program, the model should provide an Unregister-View subroutine. When a view no longer needs to be informed of the model's events, the program should use UnregisterView to remove it from the model's list of views. This is important for preventing the model from trying later to invoke the Notify subroutine of an object that no longer exists.

```
Public Sub UnregisterView(view As Object)
Dim i As Integer

    For i = 1 To Views.Count
        If view Is Views.Item(i) Then
            ' Remove this view and its event mask.
            Views.Remove i
            Events.Remove i
            Exit Sub
        End If
    Next i
End Sub
```

At first one might think a view object's Class_Terminate event handler would be an ideal place to call UnregisterView. Then when the program destroyed an object, the call would happen automatically.

Unfortunately, this does not work. Visual Basic does not invoke an object's Class_Terminate event handler until the object is actually destroyed. Visual Basic will destroy an object only when the program contains no more references to the object. Because a view object is included in the model's list of views, the program contains a reference to the object so the Visual Basic will not destroy it. Therefore, the Class_Terminate event will not occur, so the call to UnregisterView will not happen.

To destroy a view object correctly, the program must first call UnregisterView and then destroy the object. The following code shows how a program could destroy a view of the MyView class"

```
Dim my_view As MyView
    :
    ' Initialise my_view, register it, etc.
```

```
Set my_view = New MyView
    :
' Destroy my_view.
TheModel.UnregisterView my_view
Set my_view = Nothing
```

Model Summary In summary, the model class must understand the application data. It must provide subroutines, functions, and property procedures that allow other parts of the program to view and modify the data. Finally, it must notify views when the data changes.

The model does not need to know why another part of the program needs to view or modify the data. It also does not need to understand why views are interested in different events. For example, when it changes the selected date, the model notifies the views that are interested in that event. It does not understand the complex series of changes this may cause.

Views

A view object has only one responsibility: to provide some sort of display of a model. A view uses the model's public routines and property procedures to obtain information about the data so it can present an appropriate display. Usually this display is visible through a user interface, though in theory the display could provide information to another program rather than the user.

The view should be registered with the model so it receives notification whenever a change to the data would affect the view's display. When the view receives notification, it should update its display as necessary.

Before a view object can receive event notifications, the program must register the view with the model, specifying the events that it finds interesting. A reasonable place to do this is in a view class subroutine named Initialize. This routine can take as parameters the model and any other information the view needs for initialization.

The DateLabelV class in AppointmentBook is a very simple view that manages the date display label above the daily appointment area. This label displays the currently selected date textually. When the user drags the month area's scroll bar slider, this label displays the date that would be selected if the user were to release the slider.

AppointmentBook's main form CalendarForm uses code similar to the following to declare and initialize the variable TheDateLabelV. This is the date label view object used by the program to manage the date label.

```
' Declare the view.
Private TheDateLabelV As New DateLabelV
    :
    ' Initialize the view.
    TheDateLabelV.Initialize TheCalendarModel, DateLabel
```

The Initialize subroutine for the DateLabelV class takes as parameters the model and the label control that will later display the selected date. The routine saves references to these for later use. It then registers itself with the model indicating that it should be notified when the selected date changes and when the "temporary date" changes. The temporary date is the date selected while the user is dragging the month area's scroll bar slider.

```
Public Sub Initialize(model As Object, ctl As Label)
    ' Save the label control for later use.
    Set TheLabel = ctl

    ' Save the model for later use.
    Set TheModel = model

    ' Register with the calendar model.
    model.RegisterView Me, _
        CAL_SelectedDateChanged Or _
        CAL_TemporaryDateChanged
End Sub
```

Controllers

A controller manipulates the data in a model. The controller must manipulate the data indirectly using the public routines provided by the model. Those routines modify the data as needed and then notify any views that are interested in the change. If a controller were to modify the data directly, the model would not have the opportunity to notify the views.

Sometimes a controller may need to make several changes to the data before the model notifies the views. When performed individually, the changes might cause notification to be sent several times to the same views. That, in turn, might force a view to redraw itself several times unnecessarily.

In cases like this, it is tempting to provide routines in the model that do not perform view notification. The controller would use those routines until the last modification, when it would use the normal data modification routine. This is not a wise practice. If the last call to the normal modification routine is omitted or later removed, the views will never be updated.

A better solution is to create a new model subroutine that performs all of the data modifications in a single subroutine call and then notifies the views when it is finished.

View/Controllers

In many programs the distinction between views and controllers blurs. In AppointmentBook the month area acts as a view when it displays a calendar showing which dates contain appointments. It acts as a controller when the user clicks on it to select a new date. The month area acts as both a view and a controller.

View/controllers often arise from the direct-manipulation nature of Windows programs. The month area allows a user to view and manipulate the data so it is both a view and a controller. Many other Visual Basic controls work similarly. Text boxes, option buttons, check boxes, combo boxes, scroll bars, lists, and others can all be used both to display and manipulate information. When a class is tied closely to one of these controls, chances are good the class will be both a view and a controller.

When working with a view/controller class, a program should keep the view and controller functions as separate as possible. Programs that use one routine to play the roles of both view and controller can be very confusing.

In particular, whenever possible the program should not make controller routines update the view's display. Instead, the model should tell the view/controller, acting as a view, to update itself. For example, when the user clicks on AppointmentBook's month area, the area must select a new date and update its display to show the new date. Rather than performing both of these actions in the single subroutine, the CalVC class uses the model's subroutines only to set the new date. The model then notifies the view of the change so it can update its display.

This technique does not work with Visual Basic controls that automatically update their own appearances. For instance, suppose a program has a view/controller object that manages a text box. Then suppose program code changes the value of the text. This generates a Changed event for the text box. Acting as a controller, the object detects the change and updates the model. The model then notifies the object that a change to the text has occurred. Now acting as a view, the object updates the text box. This generates another Changed event, which causes the object to act as a controller again and notify the model of the change. This causes another event notification, which causes a text update, which causes yet another event notification, and so forth.

In cases such as this one, the program needs a way to break out of the infinite cascade of changes and event notifications. AppointmentBook's view/controller objects do this with a Boolean variable IgnoreChanges. Just before the object (acting as a view) modifies the display, it sets IgnoreChanges to true. When the object detects a change, it checks the value of IgnoreChanges. If the value is true, it ignores the change. Otherwise, it reports the change (acting as a controller) to the model. After the object (acting as a view) finishes modifying the display, it sets IgnoreChanges back to false so changes made by the user are reported to the model in the future.

The following code fragment shows how AppointmentBook prevents event cascades for the month area's scroll bar:

```
Private IgnoreChanges As Boolean
    :
' The model is notifying us that the selected date has changed.
Public Sub Notify(event_mask As Long)
    :
    ' Verify that the selected date has changed.
    If event_mask And CAL_SelectedDateChanged Then
        IgnoreChanges = True     ' Prevent an event cascade.

        ' Change the scroll bar value to reflect the new date.
        TheScrollBar.Value = _
            DateDiff("ww", TheModel.FirstDate, _
                TheModel.SelectedDate)

        IgnoreChanges = False    ' Report future events to the model.
    End If
End Sub


' Someone (the user or the program) has changed the scroll bar value.
Public Sub ValueChanged(Value As Integer)
```

```
  ' If IgnoreChanges is true, the program made the change.
  ' Do not start an event cascade.
  If IgnoreChanges Then Exit Sub

  ' The user made the change. Tell the model about it.
  TheModel.SelectedWeek = Value
End Sub
```

MVC in AppointmentBook

This section lists the data events used by AppointmentBook. It then explains the duties of the application's model, views, and controllers. This section focuses mainly on how the objects interact using the MVC paradigm. It does not describe class details such as how the CalVC object draws the month area. Although these implementation details require quite a bit of Visual Basic code, they are relatively straightforward and are not important for the discussion of the more advanced topic of MVC. You can see all of the code on the compact disk.

To make it a bit easier to remember the purposes of the classes, the names of view classes end with the letter V, the names of controller classes end with a C, and view/controller classes have names ending with VC.

Events AppointmentBook defines the following data events in the module CalStuff.BAS:

- **CAL_AllEvents**. This bit mask has every bit set. It is used mainly when the data file is first loaded. By passing this event to the NotifyViews subroutine, the model ensures that every registered view updates its display.
- **CAL_TopDateChanged**. The topmost visible date in the month area has changed. This may have happened because the user adjusted the month area's scroll bar, pressed an arrow key, or invoked the Select Today command in the Appointments menu.
- **CAL_SelectedDateChanged**. The selected date changed. This will happen when the user clicks on a date in the month area. It is also generated in the same ways as CAL_TopDateChanged: scrolling the month area, pressing an arrow key, or invoking Select Today.
- **CAL_TemporaryDateChanged**. The temporary date changed. While the user is dragging the month area's scroll bar slider, this date is the date that would be selected if the user released the slider. Dragging the slider is the only way to generate this event.
- **CAL_YearsChanged**. The years represented by the data have changed. This happens only when the data file is first loaded.
- **CAL_Resized**. The month area has changed size. This occurs when the user resizes the form.
- **CAL_AppointmentChanged**. One of the selected date's appointments has been modified.
- **CAL_DailyApptDeleted**. The user deleted the last appointment for some date other than the selected date. This occurs when the user invokes the Purge command in the Appointments menu.
- **CAL_UserWasWarned**. The program presented a message warning the user that it was almost time for an appointment.

CalendarModel   The CalendarModel class defined in module CalModel.CLS is AppointmentBook's model class. It is responsible for loading, saving, and providing access to the data, in addition to the standard model duties of registering views and providing event notification.

CalVC   The CalVC view/controller class defined in CalVC.CLS manages the month area. As a view, the class redraws the month area whenever it receives notification of a CAL_TopDateChanged, CAL_Resized, CAL_AppointmentChanged, or CAL_DailyApptDeleted event.

The class also responds to the CAL_SelectedDateChanged event that indicates that a new date has been selected. If the event is combined with one of the previous events, the other event causes the calendar to be completely redrawn so no further action is needed. Otherwise, the Notify subroutine highlights the newly selected date.

As a controller, CalVC interacts with the model in three ways. When the program resizes the month area, the Resize event for the area's picture box invokes the CalVC's Resized subroutine. This routine, in turn, calls the model's Resized subroutine. That routine notifies interested views that the area has resized. Because CalVC is an interested view, it will be notified so it can redraw itself.

CalVC's second controller function handles key presses. When AppointmentBook receives a KeyUp event, it invokes CalVC's KeyUp subroutine. That routine decides whether the key was an arrow key and how it should change the selected date. It then uses the model's SelectedDate property procedure to select the new date. Note that CalVC decides which date should be selected and then tells the model. This keeps the model simple.

Finally, CalVC responds to mouse events. The MonthPict picture box contains the month area. When MonthPict receives a MouseUp event, it invokes CalVC's MouseUp subroutine. This routine uses the coordinates where the user clicked to determine which date should be selected. It then uses the model's SelectedDate property procedure to select the new date. Once again, CalVC decides which date should be selected and then tells the model. It is the model's job to make changes and notify the appropriate views, not to decide what changes to make.

ScrollVC   The ScrollVC view/controller class defined in ScrollVC.CLS manages the month area's scroll bar. As a view, the class resets the scroll bar's Min, Max, LargeChange, and Value properties whenever it is notified of a CAL_YearsChanged or CAL_Resized event. When it receives a CAL_SelectedDateChanged event, it resets only the scroll bar's value.

As a controller ScrollVC has two purposes. When the scroll bar's value changes, ScrollVC's Scroll subroutine invokes the model's SelectedWeek subroutine indicating the week that should contain the selected date. SelectedWeek determines the correct date and selects it. In this case the model does a bit more work than it does when the CalVC tells it exactly what date to select. This is convenient because the model needs to check the new date to ensure that it lies within the bounds of the available data. The model can adjust the selected date if necessary to keep it in bounds.

In its second controller function, ScrollVC uses the model's TemporaryWeek property procedure. When the user drags the month area's slider, ScrollVC sets TemporaryWeek to indicate the week that would be selected if the user releases the slider. TemporaryWeek is very similar to SelectedWeek except it sets the model's temporary date instead of its selected date. This allows the DateLabelV view described in the next section to display the temporarily selected date above the daily appointment area.

DateLabelV The DateLabelV view class defined in LabelV.CLS manages the date label above the daily appointment area. This view is quite simple. When it is notified of a CAL_SelectedDateChanged event, it displays the selected date in text form. When it is notified of a CAL_TemporaryDateChanged event, it displays the temporary date.

DailyV The DailyV view class defined in DailyV.CLS is also fairly simple. It manages the daily appointment display. When it is notified of a CAL_SelectedDateChanged or CAL_AppointmentChanged event, it redisplays the appointments for the selected date.

Even the way in which DailyV displays the appointments is simple. First, it uses the model's Get-DailyAppt subroutine to get a reference to the DailyAppt object that represents the appointments for the selected date. It then invokes the DailyAppt object's ShowAppts subroutine to make the object display itself. The DailyAppt object's ShowAppts subroutine does the hard part.

Scrolling Daily Appointments AppointmentBook draws the selected date's complete schedule in the daily appointment area. A scroll bar allows the user to scroll through the schedule. This operation is so simple that it really does not need a special class as does scrolling the month area. The scroll bar's Change event adjusts the top of the scrolling area much as the scroll bar does in ExpenseReporter.

```
Private Sub DailyVScroll_Change()
    DailyPict.Top = -DailyVScroll.Value
End Sub
```

AlarmV The AlarmV view class defined in AlarmV.CLS is slightly different from the other views in AppointmentBook. The other views react to changes in the data and present updated displays of the data. When the selected date changes, for example, the month area highlights the newly selected date.

The AlarmV view, on the other hand, does not immediately display any data. When it is notified of a change in the appointment data, this view schedules an action to occur later.

AlarmV is notified when an appointment is modified, when an appointment is deleted, and when the user is warned about an appointment. When AlarmV receives notification, it examines all of the appointments to find the one the user will need to be notified about next. It then sets an alarm to wait until the time at which it needs to notify the user. The method AppointmentBook uses to set alarms is described in the later section, "Setting Alarms."

Creating Fonts

The Windows API function CreateFont creates a new font that a program can use in a form or picture box. CreateFont is declared with the following code:

```
Declare Function CreateFont Lib "gdi32" Alias "CreateFontA" ( _
    ByVal Height As Long, ByVal Width As Long, _
```

```
ByVal Escapement As Long, ByVal Orientation As Long, _
ByVal Weight As Long, ByVal Italic As Long, _
ByVal Underline As Long, ByVal StrikeOut As Long, _
ByVal CharSet As Long, ByVal OutputPrecision As Long, _
ByVal ClipPrecision As Long, ByVal Quality As Long, _
ByVal PitchAndFamily As Long, ByVal Face As String) _
As Long
```

The CreateFont function returns a handle to a *logical font* that describes the font requested by the CreateFont function. The *font mapper* then uses this description to select a *physical font* that matches the description as closely as possible on the computer. The match may not be very close if the fonts available on the computer cannot provide the requested features. Many of the parameters passed to CreateFont determine how the font mapper acts if it cannot exactly match the description.

Generally, a program will specify the Face parameter to indicate the font name that should be used and the Height parameter to indicate the font's size. Many of the other parameters take on default values if they are set to the value zero.

CreateFont's parameters are described briefly in the following list. For more information, search for CreateFont in the online help file WIN31WH.HLP.

- **Height**. Gives the height for the font in logical units.
- **Width**. Gives the average width of characters. If zero, the font mapper selects a Width that matches the Height.
- **Escapement**. The angle of the text's slope in tenths of degrees, measured counterclockwise from horizontal. To create vertical text, AppointmentBook uses an escapement of 900 (90 degrees in tenths of degrees).
- **Orientation**. Gives the orientation of the characters in tenths of degrees. Windows assumes this is the same as Escapement so it ignores Orientation.
- **Weight**. Gives the font's weight. For a default font weight, the program should specify 0. For other weights it should specify a multiple of 100 up to 900, 100 indicating a thin weight and 900 indicating a very heavy weight. The most commonly used values are 400 for a normal font and 700 for bold.
- **Italic**. If not zero, indicates an *italic* font.
- **Underline**. If not zero, indicates an <u>underlined</u> font.
- **StrikeOut**. If not zero, indicates a font with ~~strikeout~~.
- **CharSet**. Specifies the font's character set. Usually a program should set this parameter to 0 to indicate an ANSI character set.
- **OutputPrecision**. Specifies how closely the font must match the height, width, escapement, character orientation, and pitch parameters. The program should specify 0 for the font's default precision. It can also specify a value between 1 and 8 where smaller values generally indicate less precision.

- **ClipPrecision**. Indicates how characters that are partially visible should be clipped. If the program is using a font with nonzero escapement, it should add the value CLIP_LH_ANGLES (16) to the precision. The default precision is 0.
- **Quality**. Indicates how closely the physical font must match the logical font. This parameter can have one of three values:

    0. Default. The font's quality is not too important.

    1. Draft. The font mapper will scale a raster font if necessary to get the size requested. This may produce jagged results if the closest available size is not too close to the size specified.

    2. Proof. The font's quality is very important. The font mapper will not scale raster fonts. Instead, it will select a font that matches the size specified even if it does not exactly match the other parameters.

- **PitchAndFamily**. Specifies the pitch and family of the font, combined using the **Or** operator. This determines what kind of font is used if the font mapper cannot find a very good match.

    Pitch. Tells whether the font's characters all have the same cell size. The value 0 indicates the default pitch for the font. The value 1 indicates a fixed pitch font like this one. The value 2 indicates a variable pitch font like this one.

    Family. Tells generally what sort of appearance the font should have. Table 3.1 lists values the program can use.

- **Face**. The font face name such as "Times New Roman" or "Courier New."

Windows 3.1 comes with the Arial, `Courier New`, and Times New Roman fonts. Each of these comes in **bold**, *italic*, and ***bold italic*** varieties. Even though there is no guarantee that these fonts will be available on all computers, they are more likely to be available than many other fonts. If a program uses them, it increases the chances that it will run correctly on a wide variety of computers.

TABLE 3.1 Font Family Values

Value	Meaning	Examples
0	Default.	(Depends on the font.)
16	Roman. Variable width strokes with serifs.	Times New Roman
32	Swiss. Variable width strokes, no serifs.	FrankfurtGothic
48	Modern. Constant width strokes, with or without serifs.	`Courier New`
64	Script. Designed to look like handwriting.	*Script*
80	Novelty fonts.	**Arabia**

Using CreateFont

After the program obtains a logical font handle using CreateFont, it can use the SelectObject API function to make a form or picture box use the font. SelectObject returns the handle of the previously selected font. When the program is done using the new font, it should reselect the original font with SelectObject and then delete the new font with the DeleteObject function. This frees system resources that are held by the font.

The VerticalText subroutine in AppointmentBook's module CalVC.CLS creates a font rotated by 90 degrees. It takes as parameters the text to be displayed, the X coordinate that should mark the left edge of the text, and two Y coordinate values between which the text should be centered. It also takes parameters indicating the font's height and weight, plus values the subroutine should pass to CreateFont indicating whether the font should have *italic*, underlined, or strike-out style. The final parameter gives the font's face name.

In AppointmentBook only the text string and the location of the text change each time VerticalText is called. The other parameters could be coded directly into the VerticalText subroutine. Making these values parameters makes the routine much more flexible, however, so it may be useful in other programs.

```
Sub VerticalText(txt As String, X As Single, ymin As Single, _
    ymax As Single, hgt As Long, wgt As Long, use_italic As Long, _
    use_underline As Long, use_strikeout As Long, font_name As String)
Dim newfont As Long
Dim oldfont As Long
Dim Y As Single

    ' Create the sideways font.
    newfont = CreateFont(hgt, 0, 900, 0, wgt, _
        use_italic, use_underline, use_strikeout, _
        DEFAULT_CHARSET, OUT_TT_ONLY_PRECIS, _
        CLIP_LH_ANGLES Or CLIP_DEFAULT_PRECIS, _
        PROOF_QUALITY, TRUETYPE_FONTTYPE, _
        font_name)

    ' Select the new font.
    oldfont = SelectObject(ThePictureBox.hDC, newfont)

    ' Display the text.
    ThePictureBox.CurrentX = X
    Y = (ymin + ymax - ThePictureBox.TextWidth(txt)) / 2

    ' Print only if the text will fit.
    If Y >= ymin Then
        ThePictureBox.CurrentY = _
            (ymin + ymax + ThePictureBox.TextWidth(txt)) / 2
        ThePictureBox.Print txt
    End If

    ' Restore the original font.
    newfont = SelectObject(ThePictureBox.hDC, oldfont)
```

```
    ' Delete the new font to free resources.
    If DeleteObject(newfont) = 0 Then
        Beep
        MsgBox "Error deleting font object.", vbExclamation
    End If
End Sub
```

Scrolling Large Amounts of Data

AppointmentBook's daily appointment area displays a list of the selected date's appointments. The amount of data this scrolling area must display is relatively limited. When the application is maximized, this area can show about 8 of the 24 possible hours' appointments.

Because it is fairly easy to draw the complete schedule, and because a large portion of the schedule is visible, the program can use a relatively simple method for scrolling the appointment area. The program draws the entire schedule and then uses picture boxes to adjust the portion of the schedule that is visible. This is similar to the method used by the ExpenseReporter application described in Chapters 1 and 2.

In contrast, AppointmentBook's month area takes longer to draw and shows a much smaller portion of its total data. Using the same strategy for scrolling this area would be quite slow. As the user dragged the scroll bar's slider, the frequent slow updates would be particularly annoying. In cases like this, where the program must display a large amount of data and updating the display takes a long time, the program can use a different scrolling strategy to improve performance.

The program should not draw all of the data into a picture box at once and then adjust the picture box's Top property. Instead, it should draw only the data it needs to display as it is required. The scroll bar, rather than indicating how to adjust the Top property of a picture box, indicates the parts of the data that need to be displayed.

Updating the display will still be slow, however, if the program redraws the data whenever the scroll bar receives a Scroll event. As the user drags the scroll bar's slider, Visual Basic generates many Scroll events. In order to respond to each event, the program would need to redraw the data constantly. If redrawing the data takes a long time, as it does in AppointmentBook, this will be slow and will make the display seem to jump awkwardly.

To prevent this problem, the program should not update its data display during Scroll events. When the user finishes scrolling and releases the scroll bar's slider, the scroll bar will receive a final Change event and the program can update the display then.

While the program should not redraw during the Scroll event, it is important to provide the user with some type of feedback. When it receives a Scroll event, AppointmentBook calculates the date that would be selected if the user were to finish scrolling at that point. It then displays the new date in the date label above the daily appointment area. This makes it much easier for the user to select a particular date using the scroll bar.

This strategy is similar to one used by Microsoft Word. In a long document, if the user grabs the scroll bar slider and drags it, Word does not immediately change the display. Instead the status bar shows the number of the page that would be selected if the slider were released at that point. Only when the user releases the slider does Word take the time to display the new page.

Setting Alarms

Visual Basic's timer control executes periodic commands. The control's Interval property determines the number of milliseconds that pass between calls to the control's Timer event. For instance, if the Interval property is 1000, the control receives a Timer event approximately every 1000 milliseconds or every 1 second.

Timer controls work well for scheduling periodic events that occur fairly frequently, but the Interval property can have values up to only 65,535. That means the longest interval a program can schedule to elapse between Timer events is roughly 65 seconds.

AppointmentBook needs to arrange notification for events far in the future. For example, suppose it is currently 10:00 AM, the program's next scheduled appointment starts at 3:30 PM, and Appointment-Book needs to give a 30-minute warning before the appointment. In that case, the program needs to warn the user of the appointment at 3:00 PM—five hours in the future. Unfortunately, the program cannot set a timer control's Interval property to five hours.

The solution to this problem is fairly simple. First, the program stores the time at which it needs to take action. In this example, the program needs to warn the user of the next appointment at 3:00 PM. Next, the program sets a timer control's Interval property to a relatively large value, for example, 60,000. This will make the Timer event handler trigger once every minute. When it triggers, the event handler checks to see if the desired time has arrived. If so, it disables the timer and takes whatever action is necessary. Otherwise, it does nothing. The Timer event will continue to occur every minute until it is time for action.

The following source code shows how AppointmentBook implements a simple, self-contained alarm system. ScheduleWakeup is a public subroutine defined in the main form CalendarForm. This form contains the timer control AlarmTimer used by the alarm system.

ScheduleWakeup takes as parameters the time the alarm should occur and an object to receive the alarm. The subroutine stores these values for later use and then enables a timer control. The control's Timer event checks to see if the alarm's time has arrived. If it has, it disables the timer control and invokes the object's WakeUp subroutine. The WakeUp subroutine performs whatever actions are necessary at the alarm's scheduled time.

```
    :
' Object that notifies the user of an appointment.
Private WakeupObject As Object

' The time at which we should notify the user.
Private WakeupTime As Date
    :
Public Sub ScheduleWakeup(wakeup_time As Date, wakeup_obj As Object)
    ' Save the wakeup time and object for later use.
    WakeupTime = wakeup_time
    Set WakeupObject = wakeup_obj
```

```
     ' Activate the timer.
     AlarmTimer.Interval = 60000
     AlarmTimer.Enabled = True

     ' Trigger the Timer event now in case the
     ' wakeup time has already passed.
     AlarmTimer_Timer
End Sub

Private Sub AlarmTimer_Timer()
     ' If not time yet, wait for the next Timer event.
     If Date + Time < WakeupTime Then Exit Sub

     ' Disable the timer.
     AlarmTimer.Enabled = False

     ' Activate the alarm object.
     WakeupObject.WakeUp
     Set WakeupObject = Nothing
End Sub
```

AppointmentBook's AlarmV view class uses this system to set alarms. The AlarmV object is notified whenever appointment data changes and when an appointment is created or deleted. It is also notified when the user is warned about an appointment so the AlarmV object can prepare to notify the user of the next appointment. AlarmV uses the following code to schedule an alarm to notify the user of the next appointment.

The model's GetNextAppointment function locates the earliest appointment that has not yet been reported to the user. The code is reasonably straightforward so it is not presented here. You can see it on the compact disk.

```
Private Sub ResetAlarm()
     ' Get the next appointment.
     TheModel.GetNextAppointment _
         next_appt, next_time, next_warn

     ' If there is no next appointment, do nothing.
     If next_appt Is Nothing Then Exit Sub

     ' Schedule the wakeup call.
     CalendarForm.ScheduleWakeup next_warn, Me
End Sub
```

Creating Nonrectangular Forms

Irregularly shaped screens can be eye-catching, but they also have a few disadvantages. Appointment-Book's splash screen, for example, has no title bar or borders. This means the user cannot move it or resize it. The user does not need to move or resize a splash screen, so this is not a problem in this case. This could cause trouble for other forms, however, so a program must use irregularly shaped forms with caution.

The main step in creating an irregularly shaped form is to set the form's window region. This region determines which parts of the form are visible. The Windows API provides several functions for creating round, elliptical, rectangular, and polygonal regions. AppointmentBook uses the CreatePolygonRgn function to create a polygonal region. Once the program has created a region, it uses the SetWindowRgn API function to restrict the form's visible portion to that region.

When AppointmentBook's splash screen loads, it invokes the ShapeForm subroutine. This routine initializes an array of the user-defined data type POINTAPI. Each POINTAPI variable has two fields, X and Y, that define the coordinates of a point. The array of POINTAPI variables defines the polygonal boundary for the form. After initializing the POINTAPI values, ShapeForm uses the CreatePolygonRgn API function to create the polygonal region.

Next, subroutine ShapeForm uses the SetWindowRgn API function to set the form's background area to the region created by the Polygon function. To make the edges of the form easy to see, it also uses the Polygon function to draw a black border along the region's edges. It uses a special pen with a width of two to ensure that the lines are not too thin.

```
Sub ShapeForm()
Const NUM_PTS = 24

Dim status As Long
Dim pts(1 To NUM_PTS) As POINTAPI
Dim rgn As Long
Dim old_rgn As Long
Dim pen As Long
Dim old_pen As Long

    pts(1).X = 132
    pts(1).Y = 155
        :
    ' More points omitted.
        :
    pts(24).X = 82
    pts(24).Y = 191

    ' Set the form region.
    rgn = CreatePolygonRgn(pts(1), NUM_PTS, WINDING)
    old_rgn = SetWindowRgn(hWnd, rgn, True)

    ' Create a pen to draw the region's edge.
    pen = CreatePen(PS_SOLID, 2, vbBlack)
    old_pen = SelectObject(hDC, pen)

    status = Polygon(hDC, pts(1), NUM_PTS)

    pen = SelectObject(hDC, old_pen)
    status = DeleteObject(pen)
End Sub
```

To make the splash screen easy to use, the form provides two public methods, ShowSplash and ShowAbout, that display the form. ShowSplash presents the form as a splash screen. It enables the form's timer so it can keep the screen visible for a certain minimum amount of time. This is accomplished just as it is by the splash screen used in ExpenseReporter. ShowSplash then hides the form's OK button because it is not needed when the form is presented as splash screen.

Next, ShowSplash presents the form and uses the Refresh method to force itself to display immediately. The form is presented modelessly so the application can continue loading the application's main form and initializing itself. The call to the Refresh method is necessary to guarantee that the splash screen is completely drawn before the main program continues initializing.

```
Public Sub ShowSplash()
    SplashTimer.Enabled = True
    CmdOk.Visible = False
    Me.Show vbModeless
    Me.Refresh
End Sub
```

When AppointmentBook's main form loads, it invokes ShowSplash and then continues preparing the main form. When it has finished, it calls the splash screen's ReadyToUnload subroutine. The splash screen unloads itself when ReadyToUnload is called or when a certain minimum amount of time has passed, whichever happens second.

```
Private Sub Form_Load()
    ' Disable the main form so the user cannot
    ' interact with it. The splash screen will
    ' enable the form when it unloads.
    Enabled = False

    ' Display the splash screen.
    Splash.ShowSplash

    ' Arrange controls, initialize data, etc.
        :
    ' Make the form visible.
    Me.Show

    ' Load the appointment data.
    ' This will draw the month area and notify the other views.
    TheCalendarModel.LoadData

    ' Indicate we have finished initialization.
    Splash.ReadyToUnload = True
End Sub
```

Subroutine ShowAbout presents the splash screen as an about dialog. It disables the timer because it is not needed when the form is presented as an about dialog. ShowAbout makes the OK button visible so the user can close the dialog. It then presents the form modally. Since the dialog is presented modally, other parts of the application will not interact with the user until the OK button is clicked. This guarantees that the dialog will be completely displayed so the program does not need to use the Refresh command explicitly.

```
Public Sub ShowAbout()
    SplashTimer.Enabled = False
    CmdOk.Visible = True
    Me.Show vbModal
End Sub
```

Presenting Help

The ExpenseReporter application described in Chapters 1 and 2 uses a standard help system. Chapter 2 explained how to use the help compiler that comes with the Visual Basic Professional Edition to create a help file.

Compiled help has several drawbacks. It is difficult to program, requiring an arcane system of footnotes to indicate index topics, keywords, and browse sequences. Compiling large help systems can be slow so making incremental changes is time-consuming.

Rather than using a compiled help file, AppointmentBook displays help using a collection of HTML (Hypertext Markup Language) documents similar to those displayed on the World Wide Web. HTML documents have several advantages over compiled help files. They are plain-text files with text control tags so they are easy to edit. They do not require any compilation because they are interpreted when they are displayed. That means a single document in the help system can be modified without requiring recompilation of the entire help system. This makes incremental changes quick and easy.

HTML documents are also designed to be distributed across a network. That makes it simple to place the help system at a single network location where many application users can share it. This capability is particularly attractive when all of the users are on a common network. Keeping the help files centralized saves space on the users' computers and allows easy updating of the centralized help documents. For instance, this would allow a company to give its customers access to a constantly updated help system available on the World Wide Web.

At the same time, HTML help does have several disadvantages that do not affect compiled help systems. Displaying a compiled help file is usually faster than displaying HTML documents. This is particularly true if the help documents are served remotely across a heavily used network. Duplicating an HTML help system requires copying many files. This makes installing the help system on a customer's computer a bit awkward. Instead of installing a single compiled help file in a format that the user already understands, a potentially large set of files must be installed.

An HTML help system is also restricted to using commands that are part of the hypertext markup language. This language is still evolving, but it currently does not provide a wide variety of layout and design features. Different document viewers and Web browsers may display HTML commands differently or not at all. The Table statement, for example, is interpreted differently by different browsers. This problem is reduced slightly if an application builds its own help browser, but it is even greater if the help system is to be placed on the World Wide Web.

Finally, while the help compiler may not provide strong support for debugging a help project, it docs detect certain kinds of errors. If the help topic file references a topic that does not exist, the compiler will issue a warning. References to remote documents in an HTML file are plain text. The system cannot know that the reference is invalid until someone actually tries to use that link to visit the document. That means HTML help systems must be carefully debugged with every link tested by hand.

Even with all of these disadvantages, an HTML help system is ideal for certain applications. An application used within a large company is a perfect candidate. The help system can reside on the company's private network. If the application provides its own help browser, or if the company has standardized on a particular commercial Web browser, compatibility issues are not a problem. While a heavily loaded network may still give reduced performance, this is balanced by the space savings allowed by having the users share the help files.

The next section describes the help browser provided by AppointmentBook and describes some of the HTML documents used by AppointmentBook. This chapter is too short to describe the entire hypertext markup language, but it does explain the most important HTML tags used by AppointmentBook's help system.

Building a Help Browser

An application could use a commercial Web browser to display HTML help pages. Commercial browsers, however, do not all display HTML documents in the same way. They also include many features of limited use in a help system, and they do not provide easy methods for connecting to an application. For example, if a browser was already displaying help on one topic, it would be difficult for the application to make the browser display help for a different topic. It would be annoying if the application displayed a new browser every time the user clicked on a field and pressed F1.

AppointmentBook avoids these problems by using the WebBrowser control to build its own help system. This control's help file is Tools\Unsupprt\Webbrwsr\Webbrows.HLP on the Visual Basic 5 compact disk.

Presenting Basic Help The WebBrowser control is fairly primitive. It allows a program to load and display an HTML document, but it is missing many of the features provided by more powerful Web browsers. For example, it does not give a program access to the HTML content it displays. Some of these missing functions are provided by the Internet transfer control, also included with Visual Basic 5. This control is described further in Chapters 18 and 19.

AppointmentBook's URLHelpForm contains a WebBrowser control. The form's public PresentTopic and PresentURL subroutines give the main application command over the WebBrowser. The PresentURL subroutine takes as a parameter the URL (Uniform Resource Locator) of an HTML document. The URL gives the location of a document on the network. PresentURL uses the WebBrowser's Navigate command to open and display the indicated document. It then invokes the URLHelpForm's Show method in case the form is not yet visible, and it uses the form's ZOrder method to move the form to the top of the stacking order.

```
Public Sub PresentURL(the_url As String)
    ' Display the URL.
    On Error Resume Next
    Browser.Navigate the_url
    On Error GoTo 0

    ' Show the form if it's not already visible.
    Me.Show

    ' Move the form to the top.
    Me.ZOrder
End Sub
```

Subroutine PresentURL takes as a parameter a topic name. It adds the directory path defined by the HELP_DIR constant to the front of the name, and the string ".htm" to the end to make a complete URL. It then uses PresentURL to display the file referenced by the URL.

AppointmentBook defines the constant HELP_DIR to be http://Beauty/HelpHTML/. Before you can run the program, you will need to change this value so it indicates the location of the help files on your computer. This can be a network address such as http://Beauty/HelpHTML/, or it can be a file name like D:\Ch3\HelpHTML\.

```
' The location of the help files.
Private Const HELP_DIR = "http://Beauty/HelpHTML/"

Public Sub PresentTopic(topic As String)
    PresentURL HELP_DIR & topic & ".htm"
End Sub
```

AppointmentBook's main form uses a URLHelpForm to provide both topical and context-sensitive help. The Contents command in the Help menu uses the URLHelpForm's PresentTopic subroutine to display the file Contents.HTM. Similarly, the Help menu's Index command displays the HTML file Index.HTM.

```
Private Sub mnuHelpContents_Click()
    HelpBrowser.PresentTopic "Contents"
End Sub

Private Sub mnuHelpIndex_Click()
    HelpBrowser.PresentTopic "Index"
End Sub
```

To provide context-sensitive help, AppointmentBook's main form examines KeyDown events looking for the F1 key. When the user presses F1, the program checks the Tag property of the control that currently has the input focus. If that property is nonblank, it contains the name of the help topic that should be presented. For example, the Tag property of the month area's picture box is "MonthA." If the user clicks on the month area and then presses F1, the program presents the help file MonthA.HTM. If no control on the form currently has the input focus, or if the control's Tag property is blank, the program presents the help contents screen Contents.HTM.

```
Private Sub Form_KeyDown(KeyCode As Integer, Shift As Integer)
Dim topic As String
```

```
If KeyCode = vbKeyF1 Then
    ' If there's no topic, use Contents.
    topic = "Contents"

    If Not ActiveControl Is Nothing Then
        If ActiveControl.Tag <> "" Then
            topic = ActiveControl.Tag
        End If
    End If

    ' Present the help.
    HelpBrowser.PresentTopic topic
End If
End Sub
```

Providing Navigation Features AppointmentBook's URLHelpForm uses its WebBrowser control to provide several navigation commands. The Navigate menu's Contents and Index commands use the PresentURL subroutine to display the files Contents.HTM and Index.HTM, respectively.

```
Private Sub mnuNavContents_Click()
    PresentTopic "Contents"
End Sub

Private Sub mnuNavIndex_Click()
    PresentTopic "Index"
End Sub
```

The Navigate menu's Back command invokes the browser's GoBack method to retrieve the previously displayed HTML file. It is important that this routine use the On Error Resume Next statement to protect itself from errors generated by the browser. If the user invokes the Back command too many times, the browser will try to move beyond the first document it loaded. In that case, the control will fail and will generate an error.

```
Private Sub mnuNavBack_Click()
    On Error Resume Next
    Browser.GoBack
End Sub
```

The Navigate menu's Refresh command uses the browser's Refresh method to reload the document it is currently displaying. This is useful if the document was changed after it was last loaded into the browser. This is particularly helpful in building and testing the help system.

```
Private Sub mnuNavRefresh_Click()
    On Error Resume Next
    Browser.Refresh
End Sub
```

The URLHelpForm's Navigate menu also provides a list of the 10 documents most recently visited by the browser. If the user selects one of the entries, the help system reloads the corresponding document.

The 10 menu entries that hold the list are all named mnuNavigate, and they have Index property values 1 through 10. Initially their Caption properties are all blank, and their Visible properties are set to false.

After the browser loads a new document, it receives a NavigateComplete event. In the Navigate-Complete event handler, AppointmentBook updates the navigation history menu entries. First it sets the URLHelpForm's Caption to the name of the newly loaded document. Next the program inserts the document's name at the top of the history list, moving the other entries down one position to make room. When it has finished, the program sets the Visible property of the menu entries with nonblank captions to true so the user can select them.

```
Private Sub Browser_NavigateComplete(ByVal URL As String)
Dim i As Integer
Dim j As Integer

    ' Set the window's caption.
    Caption = Browser.LocationName

    ' See if this URL is in the History menu.
    For i = 1 To 10
        If mnuNavigate(i).Caption = URL Then Exit For
    Next i
    If i > 10 Then i = 10

    ' i now points to the current location of
    ' this URL or 10 if it is not in the list.
    ' Move entries above this one down one spot
    ' to make room for this URL at the top.
    For j = i To 2 Step -1
        mnuNavigate(j).Caption = mnuNavigate(j - 1).Caption
    Next j

    ' Insert this URL at the top.
    mnuNavigate(1).Caption = URL

    ' Make the nonblank menu entries visible.
    For i = 1 To 10
        If mnuNavigate(i).Caption <> "" Then _
            mnuNavigate(i).Visible = True
    Next i
End Sub
```

When the user invokes one of the menu history commands, the program presents the help file associated with the menu entry.

```
Private Sub mnuNavigate_Click(Index As Integer)
    On Error Resume Next
    PresentURL mnuNavigate(Index).Caption
End Sub
```

URLHelpForm's last interesting menu command is the File menu's Close command. Rather than destroying the help form, this command hides it. When the main program later presents help again, it can quickly reuse the existing form instead of creating a new one. This allows the form to retain the history list presented in its Navigate menu.

Making the Close command in the File menu hide the form does not prevent the user from destroying the form by selecting the Close command from the form's system menu. To prevent this from occurring, the form's QueryUnload event handler checks the method by which the user is attempting to unload the form. If the user selected the Close command from the System menu, the routine cancels the unload event and hides the form instead of unloading it.

```
Private Sub mnuFileClose_Click()
    On Error Resume Next
    Me.Hide
End Sub

Private Sub Form_QueryUnload(Cancel As Integer, UnloadMode As Integer)
    If UnloadMode = vbFormControlMenu Then
        Cancel = 1
        Me.Hide
    End If
End Sub
```

Building Help Documents

Although there is no room here to describe the entire hypertext markup language, this section explains the most important elements used to build AppointmentBook's help documents. Some more advanced HTML commands are described in Chapters 14 through 19.

The following section describes the HTML commands used by AppointmentBook's help documents. Almost all of these are demonstrated by the file Contents.HTM, so the next section lists that file. It also shows a picture of the help system displaying Contents.HTM so you can see how some of the commands are displayed.

The last section in this chapter briefly describes the file Index.HTM. This file uses only a few commands not already demonstrated by Contents.HTM, but it has a rather interesting design.

The other documents used by AppointmentBook's help system are fairly similar to Contents.HTM. If you want to examine them in detail, you will find them in the Ch3\HelpHTML directory on the compact disk.

HTML Tags HTML formatting instructions are defined by *tags*. Most tags come in pairs with one tag starting a formatting mode and a corresponding tag ending it. For example, the tag "<B>" marks the beginning of bold text, and the tag "</B>" ends the bold text. The HTML code "<B>text</B>" would display the word "text" in bold characters.

The following list describes the tags used in AppointmentBook's HTML help files.

- **<HTML>...</HTML>**. Surrounds the entire HTML document.
- **<HEAD>...</HEAD>**. Contains the document's heading information.

- **<BODY>...</BODY>**. Contains the body of the document. This includes everything after the heading information.
- **<TITLE>...</TITLE>**. The document's title. Web browsers display the title in their banners.
- **<CENTER>...</CENTER>**. Centers the contents horizontally in the browser.
- **<IMG SRC="ApptBook.GIF" ALT="[ApptBook]" ALIGN="Right">**. Inserts the image in the file ApptBook.GIF. The value specified after ALT indicates the text that a browser should display if it cannot display the image. Setting the ALIGN parameter to "Right" tells the browser to allow text to fill to the left of the picture. ALIGN can also be "Left" or "Center."
- **
**. Causes a line break. The following text starts on a new line in the browser.
- **<B>...</B>**. The enclosed text is bold.
- **<HR SIZE=3>**. Creates a horizontal rule (line) three pixels thick. SIZE can be 1 through 10.
- **<A HREF="Overview.htm">...</A>**. Defines an anchor for a hypertext jump or link. The text between the tags is highlighted by the browser. If the user clicks on it, the browser displays the document specified by the HREF parameter.
- **<A NAME="Here">...</A>**. Defines the location of the included text within the file as position "Here." This location can be used by the anchor tag described next.
- **<A HREF="#Here">...</A>**. Defines an anchor for a hypertext link to the location "Here" within the current document. If the user clicks on the highlighted text, the browser scrolls to the indicated location. The HREF parameter can specify both a new document and a location, as in "Overview.htm#Here."
- **<H3>...</H3>**. The enclosed text is displayed in the browser's heading level three style. Smaller heading numbers correspond to larger, more important text. For example, <H1>...</H1> produces a very large heading.
- **<P>**. Begins a new paragraph. The browser decides how it will separate paragraphs.
- **<PRE>...</PRE>**. Preformatted text. The browser displays the text with the exact spacing given in the HTML document including spaces and carriage returns. Text is displayed in the fixed width font so the code can use spaces to make text line up exactly. For example, this code:

```
<PRE><B>Column 1    Column 2    Column 3</B>
Value 1     Value 2     Value 3
Value 4     Value 5     Value 6</PRE>
```

produces this result:

```
Column 1    Column 2    Column 3
Value 1     Value 2     Value 3
Value 4     Value 5     Value 6
```

- **<!-- ... -->**. Comment. The text between the "<!--" and the "-->" delimiters is ignored by the browser.

Contents.HTM The output produced by the file Contents.HTM is shown in Figure 3.8. This page displays a list of important subjects the user might want to examine in detail. Hypertext links are shown as underlined by the browser. If the user clicks on one of these, the browser displays the corresponding document.

The following HTML source code shows Contents.HTM:

```
<HTML>

<HEAD>
<TITLE>AppointmentBook: Contents</TITLE>
</HEAD>

<BODY>

<CENTER>
<IMG SRC="ApptBook.GIF" ALT="[ApptBook]">
<BR><B>Contents</B>
</CENTER>
<HR SIZE=3>

<A HREF="Overview.htm"><H3>Overview</H3></A><BR>

<H3>Tasks</H3>
<A HREF="Make.htm">Making Appointment Entries</A><BR>
<A HREF="Review.htm">Reviewing Appointments</A><BR>
```

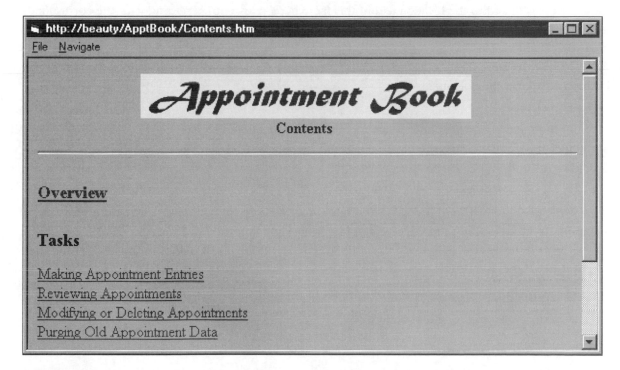

FIGURE 3.8 The help contents page.

```
<A HREF="Modify.htm">Modifying or Deleting Appointments</A><BR>
<A HREF="Purge.htm">Purging Old Appointment Data</A><BR>

<H3>Parts of AppointmentBook</H3>
<A HREF="MonthA.htm">Month Area</A><BR>
<A HREF="DailyA.htm">Daily Appointment Area</A><BR>
<A HREF="Menus.htm">Menus</A><BR>

</BODY>
</HTML>
```

Index.HTM The output produced by the file Index.HTM is shown in Figure 3.9. This page lists keywords found in AppointmentBook's help system documents. The words are linked to the pages in which they appear.

AppointmentBook's help pages are fairly short so the words are linked only to the documents. If the pages were very long, the words could be linked to specific locations within the documents using anchors such as the following:

```
<A HREF="Document.HTM#word_location">key word</A>
```

This would let the user jump directly to the words' exact locations.

Because Index.HTM is a fairly long document, it begins with a list of the letters A through Z. Each of these letters is linked to the location within this file where index entries starting with the corresponding letter begin. For example, if the user clicks on the letter N, the browser scrolls so the entries beginning with N are visible.

The body of Index.HTM begins by defining these links. The following code defines the link to the location N later in the document:

```
<A HREF="#N">N</A>
```

Next the file creates the index entries themselves. Each lettered section begins with the definition of the location's name within the file. For instance, the following code defines the location N. The text is bold so it stands out from the index entries.

```
<A NAME="N"><B>N</B></A>
```

The file uses preformatted text for every index entry. This makes it easier to align entries that share a common prefix word or phrase. For example, consider the following code:

```
date,
    <A HREF="MonthA.htm">containing an appointment</A>
    <A HREF="MonthA.htm">selected</A>
    <A HREF="MonthA.htm">selecting</A>
```

This code produces the following output:

```
date,
    containing an appointment
    selected
    selecting
```

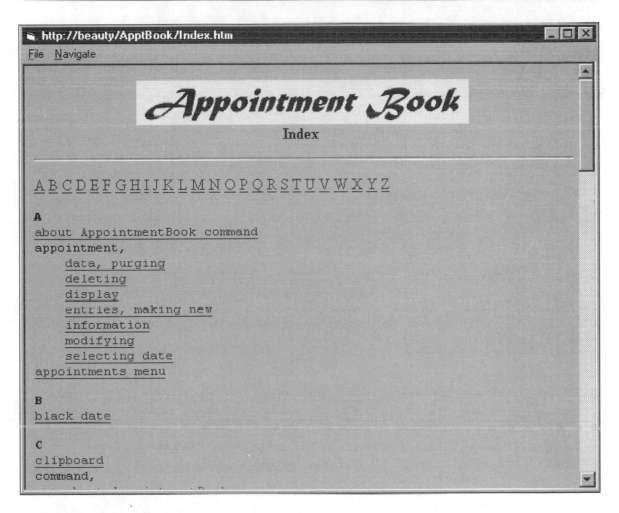

FIGURE 3.9 The help index page.

Some letters such as Q have no index entries. Omitting those letters from the list at the top of the file could be confusing. It would also make it more difficult to add entries to those categories later.

To allow the user to select these unused letters, locations are defined for them within the document. Location Q is defined just before location R. To properly define a location, its anchor tags must include some text. Because no visible text is needed here, the tags include a single space character. If the user clicks on the Q link at the top of the page, the browser scrolls down to display this space character. Because that character is immediately before the entries beginning with the letter R, those entries will be displayed. The following code shows how the Q and R locations are defined in Index.HTM:

```
<A NAME="Q"><B> </B></A>              <!-- Entries starting with Q -->
<A NAME="R"><B>R</B></A>              <!-- Entries starting with R -->
<A HREF="Overview.htm">reminder</A>
```

The code below shows pieces of Index.HTM. The file repeats several steps 26 times—once for each letter in the alphabet. To save space, most of the duplicated steps have been removed. You can find the complete HTML code in the Ch3\HelpHTML directory on the compact disk.

```
<HTML>
    :
    <!-- HEAD, BODY, etc. omitted -->
    :
    <!-- Jumps to lettered sections -->
<A HREF="#A">A</A>
<A HREF="#B">B</A>
    :
<A HREF="#Z">Z</A>


<!-- The index entries -->
<PRE><A NAME="A"><B>A</B></A>          <!-- Entries starting with A -->
<A HREF="Menus.htm">about AppointmentBook command</A>
appointment,
    <A HREF="Purge.htm">data, purging</A>
    <A HREF="Modify.htm">deleting</A>
    <A HREF="CtxAppt.htm">display</A>
    <A HREF="Make.htm">entries, making new</A>
    <A HREF="CtxAppt.htm">information</A>
    <A HREF="Modify.htm">modifying</A>
    <A HREF="MonthA.htm">selecting date</A>
<A HREF="Menus.htm">appointments menu</A>


<A NAME="B"><B>B</B></A>              <!-- Entries starting with B -->
<A HREF="MonthA.htm">black date</A>
    :
    <-- Other entries omitted -->
    :
<A NAME="P"><B>P</B></A>              <!-- Entries starting with P -->
<A HREF="Overview.htm">parts of AppointmentBook</A>
<A HREF="Menus.htm">purge command</A>
<A HREF="Purge.htm">purging old appointment data</A>
<A NAME="Q"><B> </B></A>              <!-- Entries starting with Q -->
<A NAME="R"><B>R</B></A>              <!-- Entries starting with R -->
<A HREF="Overview.htm">reminder</A>
<A HREF="Review.htm">reviewing appointments</A>
<A HREF="Purge.htm">removing old appointment data</A>
    :
    <-- More entries omitted -->
    :
</PRE>
</BODY>
</HTML>
```

Summary

This chapter on AppointmentBook demonstrates several useful programming techniques. It shows how to use the model/view/controller paradigm to manage complex interactions, and how an application can display large amounts of data. It also demonstrates API functions thata program can use to create rotated fonts and to present nonrectangular screens. These features are easy to implement and they make an application stand out from the crowd. Similar techniques are used by programs throughout the rest of the book.

Add-Ins

An add-in is a special kind of application that a developer can incorporate directly into the Visual Basic development environment. The Add-In Manager installs add-ins in the environment's Add-Ins menu. The developer can then call on the add-ins to make routine programming chores easier.

Chapter 4 describes the PropertySetter add-in. PropertySetter allows an application developer to examine and modify the properties of several controls at the same time. This is particularly useful for changing properties, such as the Name property, that the Visual Basic development environment will not change in a group.

Chapter 5 explains the Aligner add-in. Aligner lets a developer easily arrange the controls on a form in rows, columns, or grids. Using similar techniques an add-in could arrange controls in other ways such as in circles, cascading over each other, or tiled to fill the form without overlapping.

The ExpenseReporter application described in Chapters 1 and 2 uses scrolling regions to manage more information than will fit on the screen at one time. Chapter 6 describes the Scroller add-in that allows a developer to quickly create similar scrolling regions in other applications.

Creating an add-in is a simple but detailed task. Add-ins are designed to automate such tasks. Chapter 7 describes AddIn-Maker, an add-in that automates the creation of other add-ins. Using AddInMaker a developer can create other add-ins quickly and easily.

Chapter 4

PropertySetter

PropertySetter allows an application developer to examine and modify the properties of many controls all at once. This is particularly helpful for changing properties that the Visual Basic development environment will not change in a group.

For instance, Visual Basic will change the Name property of more than one control at one time. Suppose an application includes a control array named Address that contains 50 controls. Changing the array's name to StreetAddress is a lot of work. The developer must select each of the 50 controls individually and change their names one by one. PropertySetter allows the developer to select all of the controls and change their names in a single step.

A developer must install an add-in before it can be used. The following section, "Installing PropertySetter," explains how to place an add-in in the Add-Ins menu using the Add-Ins Manager.

The next section, "Using PropertySetter," describes this add-in's main features from the user's point-of-view. It explains how a developer can use PropertySetter to examine and modify property values in the design environment.

The "Key Techniques" section briefly lists the most important Visual Basic programming methods used to implement PropertySetter. The rest of the chapter describes these methods in detail.

Unfortunately, many of the details of creating an add-in are different in Visual Basic 4 and Visual Basic 5. The following sections explain the differences as they describe the different steps required to build an add-in.

Installing PropertySetter

Before an add-in can be used, it must be installed in the development environment's Add-Ins menu. This section describes the installation process from the developer's point-of-view. It does not explain the steps necessary to prepare the add-in for installation. Those steps are described in later sections.

To install the PropertySetter add-in, the developer first selects the Add-In Manager command from Visual Basic's Add-Ins menu. Figure 4.1 shows the Add-In Manager. After selecting the PropertySetter add-in, the developer clicks the OK button and the Add-In Manager installs the add-in.

Removing an add-in is just as simple. The developer opens the Add-In Manager, removes the check in the box next to the add-in's name, and presses the OK button.

Using PropertySetter

The ExpenseReporter and AppointmentBook applications described in Chapters 1, 2, and 3 are designed for use by typical business users. Add-ins, on the other hand, are designed to assist application developers. The end users of these programs are Visual Basic programmers.

This section explains how an application developer can use the PropertySetter add-in, assuming the add-in is correctly built and installed. Later sections explain how to build an add-in.

Before using PropertySetter, the developer should select a group of controls on a form in the Visual Basic development environment. The Set Properties command in the Add-Ins menu will then activate PropertySetter, displaying a dialog similar to the one shown in Figure 4.2. In this example, the developer selected four controls called NameLabel, CmdOk, AddressLabel, and CmdCancel.

The developer can then enter the name of a property in the Property text box. Pressing the Get Values button makes PropertySetter display the selected controls' property values. In Figure 4.2, PropertySetter displays the values of the controls' Caption properties.

To change a property value, the developer should enter the property name as before and place the new value in the New Value text box. When the developer clicks the Set Values button, PropertySetter updates the property for each of the selected controls.

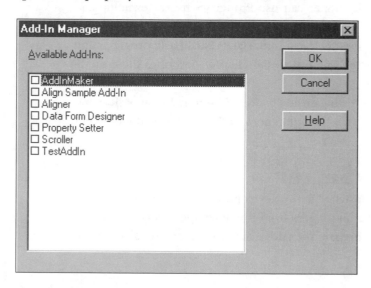

FIGURE 4.1 The Add-In Manager.

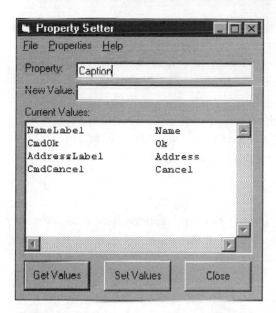

FIGURE 4.2 The PropertySetter add-in.

Both the Get Values and Set Values commands work only for controls that actually have the indicated property. For example, Figure 4.2 shows PropertySetter with two labels and two command buttons selected. Suppose the developer enters Default into the Property text box and clicks Get Values. Because command buttons have a Default property but text boxes do not, PropertySetter will return values only for the command buttons.

PropertySetter provides four menu commands. The File menu's Close command closes Property-Setter. The Get Values and Set Values commands on the Properties menu duplicate the functions of the command buttons. They are provided as menu commands for convenience, and they support the short-cut keys Ctrl-G and Ctrl-S.

The Help menu's About PropertySetter command presents an about dialog. Like other about dialogs, this one gives version and copyright information. It also gives a brief explanation of how to use PropertySetter. This gives PropertySetter some simple help with a minimum of effort.

Key Techniques

This chapter's main purpose is to explain how to create and install a basic add-in. While PropertySetter itself is a simple program, it demonstrates useful techniques for accessing the controls selected in the development environment. It also shows how an add-in can read and modify the properties of those controls. The key techniques described in this chapter are listed briefly below. They are described in detail in the following sections.

- **Understanding OLE**. Add-ins are OLE servers used by the Visual Basic programming environment. This section explains how add-ins can provide OLE services to client applications.
- **Creating Add-Ins**. Creating an add-in is a complicated process. This section describes the steps needed to create and install an add-in using Visual Basic 4 and Visual Basic 5. This section ends with a summary of the steps required.
- **Testing Add-Ins**. Because add-ins are invoked by the Visual Basic development environment, testing them is different from testing other applications. This section explains how the add-in designer can use two instances of the Visual Basic development environment to test an add-in.

Understanding OLE

Object Linking and Embedding, or *OLE*, is a standard that defines how applications should use objects to interact with each other. Starting with the release of Visual Basic 5, Microsoft has changed the name OLE to *ActiveX*. For most purposes, the two names are interchangeable. In order to understand OLE, one must first understand classes and objects.

Version 4.0 of Visual Basic introduced classes to the language. In many ways, a class is similar to a form that has no user interface. Like a form, a class can have variables, subroutines, functions, and property procedures. Variables, subroutines, and functions can be private to the class module or public so other parts of an application can interact with them.

After a class is defined, an application can create instances of the class, much as it would create new instances of a form. If the class MyClass is defined, the program can create new instances using either of the following two methods:

```
Dim instance_1 As New MyClass    ' Declare and initialize instance_1.
Dim instance_2 As MyClass        ' Declare instance_2.

    Set instance_2 = New MyClass ' Initialize instance_2.
```

Once a program has created an instance of a class, it can access the public variables, subroutines, functions, and property procedures of the instance much as it would access similar objects for a form. If the object my_obj belongs to a class that has defined a public subroutine FactorAll, the program could invoke the object's FactorAll subroutine, as in my_obj.FactorAll.

This is all so similar to the way forms work that classes would only deserve a brief mention in this chapter except for one new twist: A program can make class objects available to other applications. One application can create and manipulate objects that are defined in another. It takes a little thought to understand the power of this seemingly trivial ability.

Classes are more than just abstract data types like those defined using the Type statement. They can include subroutines and functions that perform complex actions. In fact, the subroutines and functions could perform all of the actions of a complete application. Suppose a class performed all the tasks needed by a full-featured word processor. Then any other application could create objects of that class and incorporate all of the word processor's features. For example, it would be easy to add spell checking, dictionary, and thesaurus functions to an electronic mail application. This allows developers to reuse the code in the word processing application easily, without rewriting the word processing code.

OLE defines how applications use this sort of class interaction. When an application defines a class for use by other programs, that application is called an *OLE server*. Other programs that use the server to create objects are called *OLE clients*.

An application can use classes in OLE servers to reuse the code implemented by the servers. Some commercial applications expose objects that other applications can use. Some commercial applications can even use server classes defined by a Visual Basic application. The Visual Basic programming environment is one such application. It can use specially constructed server classes as add-ins to make common programming chores easier.

Creating Add-Ins

There are four steps to creating an application that can act as an add-in OLE server. The steps are listed below and described in the following sections:

- Setting Project Options
- Creating the Add-In Class
- Creating Sub Main
- Creating the Server DLL

Creating and installing an add-in is a complicated process. After the following four sections describe the process, a summary presents a detailed list of the steps required.

Setting Project Options

To make a project behave as a proper add-in, several of its properties must be set. These properties are slightly different in Visual Basic 4 and Visual Basic 5.

Project Properties in Visual Basic 4 In Visual Basic 4 these properties are set by selecting the Options command on the Tools menu. The Project tab of the Options dialog is shown in Figure 4.3.

Three options must be set on the project Options dialog to create an add-in: Startup Form, Project Name, and StartMode.

OLE servers, including add-ins, do not need to display startup forms. Instead, Visual Basic 4 begins execution with a subroutine named Main. To indicate that the project will start by running this subroutine, the Sub Main option should be selected from the Startup Form list.

The Project Name option determines the name by which the server will be known to the system registry. Other applications will use this name to access the server. For example, if a project's name is set to MyProject in the options dialog, and the project defines a server class named MyClass, then

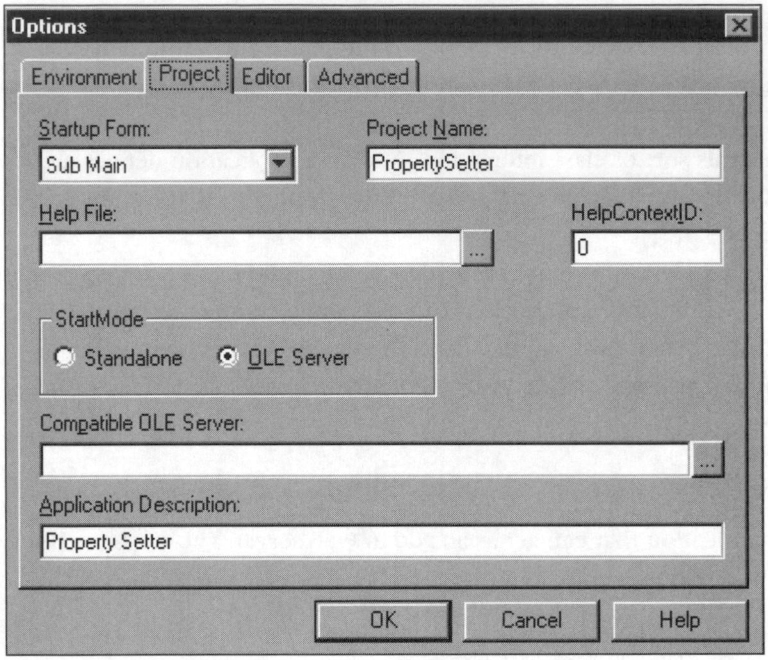

FIGURE 4.3 The project Options dialog.

another application could refer to the server class as MyProject.MyClass. Because other applications will need to use the project name, it should be relatively short and easy to remember.

Normally an OLE server runs only when it is serving a client application. If an OLE server program is started from within the Visual Basic programming environment, no client will be ready for the server so the program will immediately end. For testing purposes, however, it is convenient to keep a server running even if it has no clients. Then a client application can invoke the server and connect to the running application.

Checking the OLE Server option button in the project Options dialog tells the Visual Basic development environment to keep the program running even if it has no clients. This option affects the application only when it is running in the Visual Basic development environment. This option does not change the program's behavior when it is running as a normal OLE server.

Project Properties in Visual Basic 5 In Visual Basic 5, the Properties command in the Project menu presents the project Options dialog. The General tab of the Project Properties dialog is shown in Figure 4.4.

In Visual Basic 5, only two options must be set on the Project Properties dialog: Project Type and Project Name.

Setting the project type to ActiveX DLL or ActiveX EXE indicates that the application is an ActiveX or OLE server. This tells Visual Basic to keep the application running in the development environment even

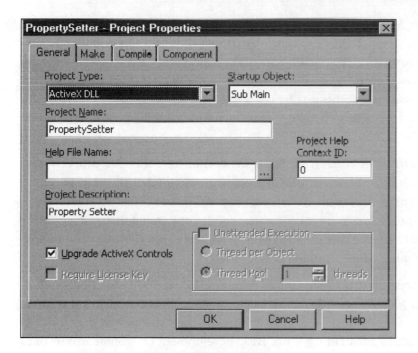

FIGURE 4.4 The Project Properties dialog.

if it does not have a client, much as selecting the OLE Server option does in Visual Basic 4. It also makes the Startup Object irrelevant. In Visual Basic 5, this object can be set to either Sub Main or "(None)." In either case, when Visual Basic 5 runs an OLE server in the development environment, it does not execute Sub Main. This has consequences that are described in the later section, "Creating Sub Main."

The Project Name should be set as it is for Visual Basic 4.

Creating the Add-In Class

If a class is to be used as an add-in, it must have certain standard property values, and it must provide certain standard subroutines. Some of these are slightly different in Visual Basic 4 and Visual Basic 5. The following two sections, "Class Properties in Visual Basic 4" and "Class Properties in Visual Basic 5," describe the properties that should be set for an add-in. The next three sections describe the standard Connect-AddIn, DisconnectAddIn, and AfterClick subroutines that should be provided by the add-in class.

Class Properties in Visual Basic 4 In Visual Basic 4, the Public property of the add-in class should be set to true. This can be done using the class module's Properties window. Setting Public to true allows client applications to create instances of the class. Because the Visual Basic development environment is not part of the application, it needs permission to create objects of this class.

The class module's Instancing variable should be set to Creatable SingleUse (1) or Creatable MultiUse (2). This indicates how the server should provide objects from the class. If Instancing is set to Creatable SingleUse, the system will create a separate server for each client requesting an instance of the class.

If Instancing is set to Creatable MultiUse, the system will allow one server to serve more than one client at a time. The clients will be assigned different class objects, but they will run in the same execution space. If the server application uses global variables, all of the clients will have access to the same global variables through their server objects. Because the system will not need to start several servers to satisfy multiple client requests, satisfying clients may be faster if Instancing is Creatable MultiUse. On the other hand, the server must be careful that multiple clients do not interfere with each other while accessing global variables.

Class Properties in Visual Basic 5 In Visual Basic 5, add-ins do not have a Public property. The Instancing variable determines both how the server provides objects and whether the objects can be created by external applications. For an add-in, the Instancing property should be set to MultiUse (5). This indicates both that external applications can create instances of the object and that a single server will provide multiple server objects. As is the case in Visual Basic 4, the server must ensure that multiple clients do not interfere with each other while accessing global variables.

ConnectAddIn Visual Basic expects add-ins to implement two standard subroutines: ConnectAddIn and DisconnectAddIn. The Add-In Manager uses these routines to connect and disconnect the add-in server from the Add-Ins menu.

When the Add-In Manager installs an add-in in the Visual Basic development environment, it invokes the add-in's ConnectAddIn subroutine. This routine should take whatever action is necessary to incorporate the server into the Visual Basic environment. Generally, this means placing new submenus and menu items in the Add-Ins menu.

Figure 4.5 shows the Visual Basic 4 Add-Ins menu after the PropertySetter server has installed itself. PropertySetter adds a single menu command, Set Properties, to the Add-In menu.

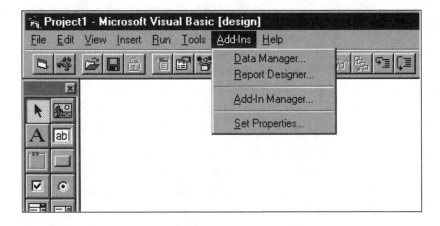

FIGURE 4.5 The Add-Ins menu with PropertySetter installed.

Visual Basic provides a number of objects that the add-in can use to manipulate the programming environment. These objects are defined in a development environment module that the add-in project must reference.

In Visual Basic 4, this is done using the References command in the Tools menu. In the References dialog, the Microsoft Visual Basic 4.0 Development Environment entry should be selected.

In Visual Basic 5, the corresponding dialog is presented by the References command in the Project menu. In this dialog, the Microsoft Visual Basic 5.0 Extensibility reference should be selected.

The ConnectAddIn subroutine is passed a single parameter of type VBIDE.Application. This object is a reference to the running Visual Basic development environment. The ConnectAddIn subroutine can access other objects such as the menus, forms, and controls in the current environment using this object.

PropertySetter's ConnectAddIn subroutine begins by saving a reference to the VBIDE.Application object for later use. Next the subroutine creates a new menu item in the Add-Ins menu. The VBIDE.Application's AddInMenu property is a reference to the Add-Ins menu object. That object's Menu-Items property is a collection containing objects that describe the items in the menu. ConnectAddIn uses this collection's Add function to create the new menu command.

The Add function returns an object of type VBIDE.MenuLine. This object represents the new command line in the menu. VBIDE.MenuLine objects provide a function ConnectEvents that associates the menu item with an event handler object that should be activated when the item is selected. When the developer selects the item from the Add-Ins menu, Visual Basic invokes the event handler object's AfterClick subroutine.

To respond to the menu item, the add-in should contain an event handler class that has an AfterClick subroutine. The ConnectAddIn subroutine should create an instance of this class and pass it to the menu item's ConnectEvents function. Because the add-in server creates this object, not the client, the event handler class does not need to have its Instancing property set to allow outside applications to create event handler objects directly.

In the PropertySetter application, the PropSet class provides the AfterClick event handler routine as well as the ConnectAddIn and DisconnectAddIn subroutines. Because PropertySetter provides only a single menu item, these three subroutines can all be contained by one class without causing confusion.

A program, however, could implement an add-in that provided more than one command in the Add-Ins menu. In that case, it could create a different event handler class for each of the menu commands. The Scroller add-in described in Chapter 7 demonstrates how to build an add-in that provides more than one Add-Ins menu item.

After the ConnectEvents function attaches the event handler object to the menu item, it returns a connection ID. The program should save this ID for later use. Subroutine DisconnectAddIn needs this ID to remove the add-in properly from the Add-Ins menu.

The following code shows the ConnectAddIn subroutine used by the PropertySetter add-in. The global variables VBInstance, SetPropLine, and SetPropID are set by ConnectAddIn and are used later by DisconnectAddIn.

```
' The environment instance.
Dim VBInstance As VBIDE.Application

' The menu command line.
Dim SetPropLine As VBIDE.MenuLine

' The event connection ID. This represents the
' event handler to menu line connection.
Dim SetPropID As Long

Sub ConnectAddIn(vb_instance As VBIDE.Application)
    ' Save the Visual Basic instance for later.
    Set VBInstance = vb_instance

    ' Add the command.
    Set SetPropLine = _
        VBInstance.AddInMenu.MenuItems.Add("&Set Properties...")

    ' Connect the event handler object to the menu line.
    SetPropID = SetPropLine.ConnectEvents(Me)
End Sub
```

DisconnectAddIn When the developer uses the Add-In Manager to remove an add-in from the Add-Ins menu, the Add-In Manager invokes the add-in's DisconnectAddIn subroutine. This routine should remove any menu items and commands created by the ConnectAddIn subroutine.

PropertySetter's PropSet class needs to perform only two tasks in DisconnectAddIn. First, it uses the event connection ID saved in subroutine ConnectAddIn to disconnect the event handler from the add-in's menu item. Second, it removes the menu item from the Add-Ins menu.

```
Sub DisconnectAddIn(mode As Integer)
    ' Disconnect the event handler.
    SetPropLine.DisconnectEvents SetPropID

    ' Remove the command.
    VBInstance.AddInMenu.MenuItems.Remove SetPropLine
End Sub
```

AfterClick The AfterClick subroutine provides the add-in's functionality. It can perform such tasks as creating new controls, moving controls around on a form, and adding new forms to the project. The PropertySetter add-in displays and sets property values for the selected controls. Its AfterClick subroutine is relatively simple.

First, AfterClick sets the prop_set variable in the SetterDialog form to indicate the currently running PropSet class instance. The SetterDialog will use this instance later to obtain information about the controls that the developer has selected.

Subroutine AfterClick then presents the SetterDialog. All of the rest of the work is performed by the SetterDialog.

```
Public Sub AfterClick()
    ' Present the dialog.
    Set SetterDialog.prop_setter = Me
    SetterDialog.Show vbModal
    Unload SetterDialog
End Sub
```

SetterDialog is also fairly simple. It uses functions provided by the PropSet class to perform all of the interesting work. For example, when the dialog is first loaded, it executes the following code to create the initial list of selected controls. Code to manipulate the selected controls is kept within the PropSet class, and SetterDialog deals exclusively with user interface issues.

```
Private Sub Form_Load()
Dim values As String

    values = prop_setter.GetValues("")
    ValuesText.Text = values
End Sub
```

The value of the rather lengthy variable VBInstance.ActiveProject.ActiveForm.SelectedControlTemplates contains a collection of the *control templates* for the currently selected controls, on the active form, in the active project, in the current instance of the Visual Basic development environment. Note that this collection does not hold the actual controls: It holds ControlTemplate objects that describe the controls.

ControlTemplate objects have a property named Properties. This is a collection of Property objects. The Property objects represent the actual properties of the controls themselves. The add-in can access a control's property by using the property's name as an index into the Properties collection just as it might index into any other collection. For example, to set the Name property of a control with template object control_template to "BigBox," an add-in could use either of the following two statements:

```
control_template.Properties.Item("Name") = "BigBox"
control_template.Properties("Name") = "BigBox"
```

Using this collection of selected control templates, the add-in can perform operations on all of the selected controls. The following code aligns the selected controls on the left by setting all of their Left properties to 1440:

```
Dim ctl As VBIDE.ControlTemplate

    For Each ctl In _
        VBInstance.ActiveProject.ActiveForm.SelectedControlTemplates
            ctl.Properties("Left") = 1440
    Next ctl
```

The GetValues function in PropertySetter's PropSet class uses a similar technique to obtain property values for the selected controls. It uses the On Error Resume Next statement to protect itself in cases where a control does not support the specified property. For example, this allows it to safely attempt to read the value of the Text property for a collection of controls even though some of the selected controls may not support the Text property.

The SetValues function is very similar. It first sets the value of the indicated property for all of the selected controls. Then it uses the GetValues function to return a revised list of the property values.

```
Public Function GetValues(prop_name As String) As String
Dim ctl As Object
Dim controls As VBIDE.SelectedControlTemplates
Dim txt As String
Dim value As String
Dim field_name As String
Dim idx As String

    GetValues = ""
    If NoControls() Then Exit Function

    Set controls = VBInstance.ActiveProject. _
        ActiveForm.SelectedControlTemplates

    txt = ""
    For Each ctl In controls
        field_name = ctl.Properties("Name")
        ' Deal with indexes if the control
        ' is part of a control array.
        idx = ctl.Properties("Index")
        If idx <> "-1" Then _
            field_name = field_name & _
            "(" & idx & ")"
        txt = txt & field_name & _
            Space$(20 - Len(field_name))

        On Error Resume Next
        value = ctl.Properties(prop_name)
        If Err.Number = 438 Then
            ' Property not supported.
            value = ""
        ElseIf Err.Number <> 0 Then
            ' Some other error.
            Beep
            MsgBox "Error reading property." & _
                Error.Description, _
                vbOKOnly + vbInformation, _
                "Property Error"
            Exit Function
        End If
        On Error GoTo 0

        txt = txt & value & vbCrLf
    Next ctl
    GetValues = txt
End Function

Public Function SetValues(prop_name As String, _
    prop_value As String) As String
```

```
Dim ctl As Object
Dim controls As VBIDE.SelectedControlTemplates
Dim txt As String
Dim field_name As String
Dim idx As String

    SetValues - ""
    If NoControls() Then Exit Function

    Set controls = VBInstance.ActiveProject. _
        ActiveForm.SelectedControlTemplates

    For Each ctl In controls
        On Error Resume Next
        ctl.Properties(prop_name) = prop_value
        If Err.Number <> 0 And Err.Number <> 438 Then
            ' Some error other than an unsupported property.
            Beep
            MsgBox "Error setting property." & _
                Error.Description, _
                vbOKOnly | vbInformation, _
                "Property Error"
            Exit Function
        End If
        On Error GoTo 0
    Next ctl
    SetValues = GetValues(prop_name)
End Function
```

These routines must be careful when accessing SelectedControlTemplates. This collection is deeply buried within objects contained in other objects contained in other objects. If any of the objects in the chain are not initialized, the program could run into trouble. For example, if no form is currently active, then VBInstance.ActiveProject.ActiveForm will have the value Nothing. In that case, the program cannot access the SelectedControlTemplates collection.

To avoid accessing the properties of an object that is not initialized, both GetValues and SetValues use function NoControls to decide if it is safe to access the SelectedControlTemplates collection. NoControls returns true if there are no controls selected and false otherwise.

```
Function NoControls() As Boolean
    ' Assume there will be trouble.
    NoControls = True

    ' Sneak up on the collection of selected
    ' controls so we don't try to access an
    ' object that is Nothing.
    If VBInstance.ActiveProject Is Nothing Then _
        Exit Function
    If VBInstance.ActiveProject.ActiveForm _
        Is Nothing Then _
        Exit Function
```

```
If VBInstance.ActiveProject.ActiveForm. _
    SelectedControlTemplates.Count < 1 Then _
    Exit Function

NoControls = False
End Function
```

Creating Sub Main

At this point, the add-in has a server class that can add items to the Add-In menu with the ConnectAddIn subroutine. It can remove those items with the DisconnectAddIn subroutine. The project also has one or more event handler classes with AfterClick subroutines. If the add-in supports a single command, as is the case with the PropertySetter add-in, the same class can handle all three functions.

The developer still cannot use the add-in because the Add-In Manager and the operating system do not know that the add-in exists.

The Add-In Manager learns about add-ins by examining an entry in an initialization file. In Visual Basic 4, this file is VB.INI. In Visual Basic 5, it is VBADDIN.INI. In Windows 95, these files are located in the computer's Windows directory. In Windows NT, the files are in the WinNT directory.

If the server is a 16-bit application, an entry should be made in the "Add-Ins16" section of the initialization file. If the server is a 32-bit application, the entry belongs in the "Add-Ins32" section.

Entries in the initialization file give the Add-In Manager the names of the add-in applications and the classes that contain the ConnectAddIn and DisconnectAddIn subroutines. For example, suppose a project named MyProject contains an add-in class named Connector that provides the ConnectAddIn and DisconnectAddIn subroutines. Then the initialization file should contain an entry for a value named MyProject.Connector.

The initialization file entry should specify a value of either zero or one. The value one means new instances of the Visual Basic programming environment should automatically load the server into the Add-Ins menu when they start. Initially an add-in should set this value to zero. Visual Basic will change the value to one when the developer loads the add-in using the Add-In Manager. This will make the add-in automatically load the next time the developer starts the programming environment.

The following lines show how the 32-bit version of the PropertySetter add-in is declared in the 32-bit section of the initialization file:

```
[Add-Ins32]
PropertySetter.PropSet=0
```

This entry could be created by editing the initialization file using a text editor. This would be rather cumbersome. Traditionally, an add-in provides a subroutine that creates the appropriate entries in the initialization file.

In Visual Basic 4, an add-in project begins execution with the Main subroutine. The add-in can create its initialization file entry in the Main subroutine. Then the developer can make the add-in create its entry by running the application in the development environment. The following code uses the Get-

PrivateProfileString and WritePrivateProfileString API functions to create an entry for the PropertySetter add-in for the Visual Basic 4 development environment:

```
#If Win16 Then
    Declare Function GetPrivateProfileString Lib "Kernel" _
        (ByVal lpApplicationName As String, _
        ByVal lpKeyName As Any, ByVal lpDefault As String, _
        ByVal lpReturnedString As String, _
        ByVal nSize As Integer, ByVal lpFileName As String) _
            As Integer
    Declare Function WritePrivateProfileString Lib "Kernel" _
        (ByVal lpApplicationName As String, _
        ByVal lpKeyName As Any, ByVal lpString As Any, _
        ByVal lplFileName As String) As Integer
#Else
    Declare Function GetPrivateProfileString Lib "Kernel32" _
        Alias "GetPrivateProfileStringA" _
        (ByVal lpApplicationName As String, _
        ByVal lpKeyName As Any, ByVal lpDefault As String, _
        ByVal lpReturnedString As String, ByVal nSize As Long, _
        ByVal lpFileName As String) As Long
    Declare Function WritePrivateProfileString Lib "Kernel32" _
        Alias "WritePrivateProfileStringA" _
        (ByVal lpApplicationName As String, _
        ByVal lpKeyName As Any, ByVal lpString As Any, _
        ByVal lpFileName As String) As Long
#End If

Sub Main()
Dim section As String
Dim val As String * 256
Dim length As Long

    ' Check the correct section of VB.INI.
    #If Win16 Then
        section = "Add-Ins16"
    #Else
        section = "Add-Ins32"
    #End If

    ' See if PropertySetter.PropSet is already in VB.INI.
    length = GetPrivateProfileString(section, _
        "PropertySetter.PropSet", "", val, _
        256, "VB.INI")

    ' If not, add it.
    If length = 0 Then _
        WritePrivateProfileString section, _
            "PropertySetter.PropSet ", "0", _
            "VB.INI"
End Sub
```

When an add-in application is run in the Visual Basic 5 development environment, the Main subroutine is not executed. The application, however, can still provide a subroutine to install the add-in. In this case, the developer will need to explicitly invoke the subroutine to create the necessary entry. The developer can do this by executing the subroutine in Visual Basic's Immediate window.

Creating the Server DLL

Once the appropriate entry has been added to the correct initialization file, the Add-In Manager knows what class objects it should use to connect and disconnect the server from the Add-Ins menu. Before an application can create an instance of a class defined by the server, the system registry needs to contain entries that describe the server in more detail.

The registry entries also give the name that the Add-In Manager displays when the developer selects add-ins. This name may be different from the project name. The project name is used by the Add-In Manager to invoke the server's ConnectAddIn and DisconnectAddIn subroutines. If the project's name is MyProject and the class containing the ConnectAddIn subroutine is named Connector, then the Add-In Manager will invoke the subroutine MyProject.Connector.ConnectAddIn.

The name placed in the registry tells the Add-In Manager what to display in its list of add-ins. Figure 4.6 shows the Add-In Manager. Here the PropertySetter add-in has the name Property Setter.

Dealing directly with the system registry entries needed to set the add-in's name is quite complicated. Fortunately, Visual Basic handles this detail automatically.

In Visual Basic 4, when the add-in designer invokes the Make OLE DLL File command from the File menu, Visual Basic creates the appropriate registry entries. Similarly, in Visual Basic 5, when the designer selects the Make PropSet.dll or Make PropSet.exe commands from the File menu, Visual Basic creates these entries. These commands are described further in a few paragraphs.

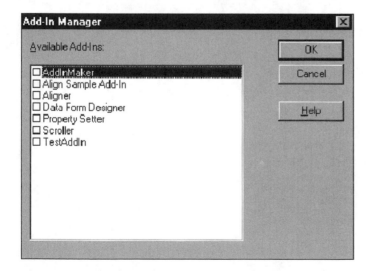

FIGURE 4.6 The Add-In Manager.

When Visual Basic makes these entries, it specifies the server's registry name using a value supplied by the Visual Basic programming environment. The add-in designer can set this value by entering the name the Add-In Manager should display in the Description box in the Member Options dialog shown in Figure 4.7.

The way the Member Options dialog is accessed is different in Visual Basic 4 and Visual Basic 5. In either case, the add-in designer begins by opening the Object Browser by pressing F2 or by selecting the Object Browser command from the View menu. The designer then selects the class that contains the ConnectAddIn and DisconnectAddIn subroutines.

Figure 4.8 shows the Visual Basic 4 Object Browser at this point. When the designer clicks the Object Browser's Options button, the Member Options dialog appears.

When using the Visual Basic 5 Object Browser, the designer should locate the class that provides the ConnectAddIn and DisconnectAddIn subroutines and click the right mouse button over that class. This makes a context menu appear, as shown in Figure 4.9. If the designer selects the Properties command from this menu, the Member Options dialog appears.

Once the add-in's name is specified, the designer can create the OLE server. In Visual Basic 4, this is done by selecting the Make OLE DLL File command from the File menu.

In Visual Basic 5, the designer should select the Make PropSet.dll or Make PropSet.exe command from the File menu. After the designer enters the name of the file that should contain the results and clicks the OK button, Visual Basic creates the file. It also creates the system registry entries that identify the server and tell the Add-In Manager the server's name.

If the initialization file entry is correctly created but the server DLL is not, the Add-In Manager will be unable to install the add-in. When a developer opens the Add-In Manager, it will present an error message similar to the following:

Visual Basic cannot load PropertySetter.PropSet because it is not in the system registry.

Please ensure that all Add-Ins have been installed correctly.

FIGURE 4.7 Setting the server's name in the Member Options dialog.

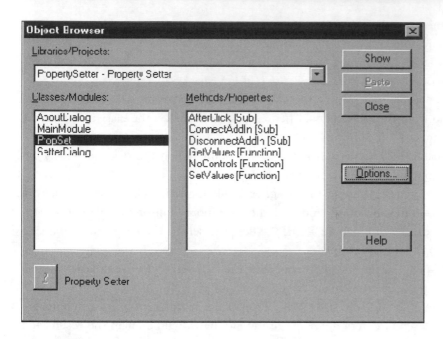

FIGURE 4.8 Locating the server class in the Visual Basic 4 Object Browser.

This warning usually means there is a mismatch between the project's registered name and the project name specified in the initialization file. For example, suppose an add-in designer creates a DLL for a project with the name "PropSetter." At that point, Visual Basic would create system registry entries that describe the PropSetter server. Now suppose the application's Main subroutine creates the following initialization entry:

```
[Add-Ins32]
PropertySetter.PropSet=0
```

When the Add-In Manager starts, it learns from the initialization file that there is an add-in with ConnectAddIn subroutine contained in the class PropertySetter.PropSet. It then checks the system registry to obtain a server for that class. Because the project name was PropSetter when the DLL was created, the Add-In Manager will be unable to find an entry for PropertySetter.PropSet.

Summarizing Add-In Creation

Creating an add-in server is a complicated process. Each step is simple, but there are so many steps that it is easy to miss one. The following list summarizes the steps required to create an add-in in Visual Basic 4 and Visual Basic 5:

1. Start a new project.
2. Set the project options. In Visual Basic 4, use the Options command in the Tool menu to set the Startup Form, Project Name, and StartMode. In Visual Basic 5, use the Properties command in the Project menu to set the Project Type and Project Name.

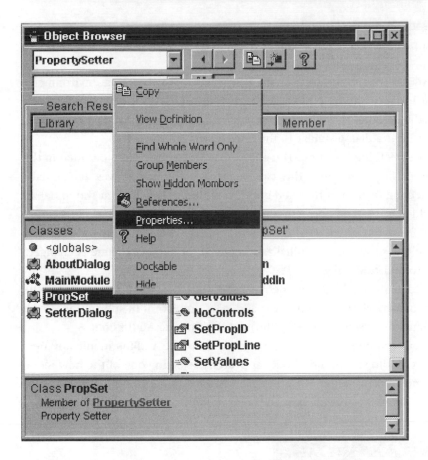

FIGURE 4.9 Locating the server class in the Visual Basic 5 Object Browser.

3. Create an add-in class that supplies the ConnectAddIn and DisconnectAddIn subroutines.
4. Create event handler classes with AfterClick subroutines. If the add-in performs a single task, the class created in step 3 can also provide the AfterClick subroutine.
5. Create Sub Main. It should register the server in the proper section of VB.INI or VBADDIN.INI.
6. Using the Object Browser, set the name that should be displayed by the Add-In Manager.
7. Create the server DLL.

To install the add-in using Visual Basic 4, run the application. To install the add-in using Visual Basic 5, run the subroutine that adds the server entries to VBADDIN.INI.

Testing Add-Ins

Because add-ins are invoked by the Visual Basic development environment, testing them is a bit unusual. The add-in designer should load the add-in project into the Visual Basic programming environment and set breakpoints in the add-in's subroutines. The project should then be executed. In Visual Basic 4, the program executes the Main subroutine, but that routine does nothing visible. In both Visual Basic 4 and Visual Basic 5, the application appears as if it is not doing anything. It is actually waiting for clients to request service.

Next the developer should start a second instance of the Visual Basic programming environment. Temporarily minimizing the first instance can help make the screen appear less cluttered and confusing. In the second environment, the designer should select the Add-In Manager command from the Add-Ins menu. The Add-In Manager displays a dialog similar to the one shown in Figure 4.10.

If the new add-in is not listed, something is wrong. The add-in may not be correctly installed in the initialization file VB.INI or VBADDIN.INI. One way this can occur is if the add-in was accidentally installed it in the "Add - Ins 32" section instead of the "Add-Ins32" section. A close look at the initialization file should verify that the add-in is installed correctly there.

The add-in also might not be installed correctly in the system registry. This will happen if the project's name is not the same as the one shown in the initialization file. If the project's name is changed, the add-in's DLL must be rebuilt to update the registry.

If the add-in is listed in the Add-In Manager, the designer can check the box next to it and click the OK button. At this point, the Add-In Manager will execute the add-in's ConnectAddIn subroutine. Using the first programming environment, the designer can step through the ConnectAddIn code.

In the second programming environment, if the designer now opens the Add-Ins menu, any new menu items created by the ConnectAddIn subroutine should appear. By selecting one of the new menu items, the designer can activate the corresponding event handler's AfterClick subroutine. The designer can use the first programming environment to step through the execution.

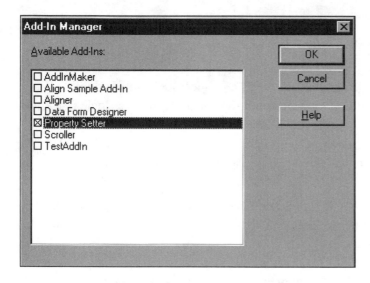

FIGURE 4.10 Selecting PropertySetter in the Add-In Manager.

When the add-in is thoroughly tested, the designer should open the Add-In Manager in the second development environment, uncheck the box next to the add-in, and click the OK button. At this point, the Add-In Manager invokes the add-in server's DisconnectAddIn subroutine. Again, the designer can step through the code using the first programming environment to verify that it works.

The designer should open the second programming environment's Add-Ins menu one last time to verify that the DisconnectAddIn subroutine successfully removed the add-in's menu entries.

Now the designer can stop the add-in server running in the first environment. The server must not stop until the client programming environment has removed the server from its Add-Ins menu. Otherwise, the server will not be running when the Add-In Manager needs to invoke the DisconnectAddIn subroutine. If the Add-In Manager cannot run DisconnectAddIn, the menu items created by the add-in will remain in the client's Add-Ins menu until the client exits from Visual Basic.

Summary

This chapter covers the essentials of add-in creation. It explains how to build the methods necessary to implement an add-in and how to install an add-in for use in the development environment. Property-Setter shows how an add-in can modify the properties of the controls contained within a project.

Using a similar technique, Chapter 5 adjusts the Left and Top properties of a group of controls to align them in rows and columns. Chapters 6 and 7 use more advanced add-in techniques to add new controls and new source code to a project.

Chapter 5

Aligner

Aligner arranges controls in rows, columns, or both in the development environment. Architecturally Aligner is similar to PropertySetter. Both add-ins use a single class to implement the ConnectAddIn, DisconnectAddIn, and AfterClick subroutines. In the Aligner add-in, that class is named AlignHandler.

The first section in this chapter, "Using Aligner," explains how this add-in works from an application developer's point-of-view. It explains how a developer can use Aligner to arrange controls on a form quickly.

The "Key Techniques" section briefly lists the most important Visual Basic programming techniques used to implement Aligner. The rest of the chapter describes these techniques in detail.

Using Aligner

Aligner allows an application developer to arrange controls in rows, columns, or both. First the developer selects two or more controls on a form. When the developer selects the Align command from the Add-Ins menu, a dialog similar to the one shown in Figure 5.1 appears. Using the dialog's tabs, the developer can specify row, column, or row and column arrangements. The controls on each tab allow the developer to specify arrangement details. For row alignment, the developer can indicate that the controls should be aligned at the top, middle, or bottom. For column alignment, the developer can specify right, left, or center alignment.

For row and column alignment, the developer can specify several parameters. These include the number of rows and columns, the spacing between rows and columns, and whether Aligner should make all rows and columns the same size.

Key Techniques

Chapter 4 explains how to create and install the PropertySetter add-in. Because Aligner's architecture is similar to PropertySetter's, its creation and installation are also similar, so those topics are not covered here.

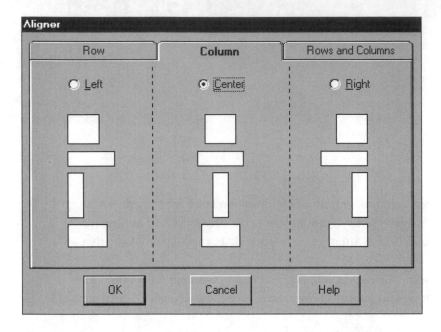

FIGURE 5.1 The Aligner add-in.

This chapter shows how an add-in can use the Left, Top, Width, and Height properties of a group of selected controls to arrange them in rows and columns. Using similar techniques, an add-in could arrange controls in other ways such as the cascade or circle shown in Figure 5.2. (Note: Although not described in this book, the Circles Add-In is included in the compact disk's Ch5\Circles directory. It was created using the AddInMaker application described in Chapter 7.)

The following list briefly describes the key techniques explained in this chapter. They are described in greater detail in the following sections.

- **Providing AfterClick**. When the developer invokes an add-in, its AfterClick subroutine is triggered. This section describes Aligner's AfterClick subroutine and shows how it calls other subroutines to arrange the controls appropriately.
- **Aligning Controls in Columns**. Aligning controls in rows is very similar to aligning them in columns. This section explains how the Aligner add-in aligns controls in columns.
- **Aligning Controls in Rows and Columns**. Aligning controls in rows and columns is a little more complicated than aligning them in columns. This section explains how Aligner arranges controls in rows and columns.

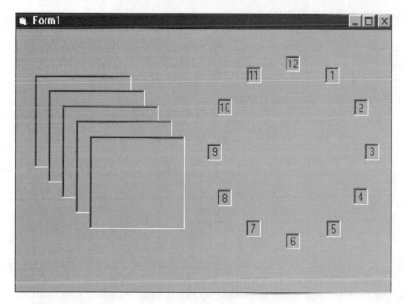

FIGURE 5.2 Controls arranged in a cascade and a circle.

Providing AfterClick

Aligner's AlignHandler class provides the add-in's ConnectAddIn, DisconnectAddIn, and AfterClick subroutines. ConnectAddIn and DisconnectAddIn are very similar to the PropertySetter add-in's corresponding routines that were described Chapter 4 (they are not described here).

The AfterClick subroutine first makes sure the developer has selected at least two controls. If not, it presents a message indicating that the developer should do so before using Aligner. If at least two controls are selected, AfterClick presents the AlignerDialog form. This dialog allows the user to select different alignment options. If the user cancels the dialog, AfterClick does nothing more. Otherwise, it invokes the AlignControls subroutine to actually arrange the controls.

```
Public Sub AfterClick()
Dim no_controls As Boolean

    ' See if fewer than two controls are selected.
    If NoControls() Then
        no_controls = True
    ElseIf VBInstance.ActiveProject.ActiveForm. _
        SelectedControlTemplates.Count < 2 Then
            no_controls = True
    Else
            no_controls = False
    End If
```

```
    ' If fewer than two controls are selected, say so.
    If no_controls Then
        Beep
        MsgBox "Please select two or more controls before you start Aligner.", _
            vbOKOnly + vbInformation, _
            "No Controls Selected"
        Exit Sub
    End If

    ' Show the dialog and get the user's choices.
    AlignerDialog.Show vbModal

    ' If the user canceled, we're done.
    If AlignerDialog.Canceled Then Exit Sub

    ' Align the controls.
    AlignControls
End Sub
```

Subroutine AlignControls checks the type of alignment specified by the user and calls the AlignRow, AlignCol, or AlignRowsAndCols subroutine to arrange the controls appropriately.

```
Sub AlignControls()
    ' See what kind of alignment the user wants.
    Select Case AlignerDialog.Tabs.Tab
        Case ALIGN_ROW            ' Align as a row.
            AlignRow
        Case ALIGN_COL            ' Align as a column.
            AlignCol
        Case ALIGN_ROW_AND_COL    ' Align as rows and columns.
            AlignRowsAndCols
    End Select
End Sub
```

Aligning Controls in Columns

The AlignCol subroutine performs most of the work of arranging the selected controls in a column. AlignRow is very similar so it is not described here. You can find its complete source code in the Ch5 directory on the compact disk.

AlignCol begins by determining the X coordinate to which the controls should be aligned. If the developer specifies left alignment, the X coordinate used is the value of the controls' smallest Left property. If the developer specifies right alignment, the X coordinate used is the largest value of the controls' Left + Width properties. Finally, if the developer specifies centered alignment, the X coordinate is set to the average of the values Left + Width / 2 over all the controls.

After determining the alignment X value, AlignCol modifies each of the selected controls' Left properties to align the controls as required.

```
Sub AlignCol()
Dim the_controls As VBIDE.SelectedControlTemplates
Dim ctl As Object
Dim x As Single
Dim wid As Single
Dim test_x As Single
Dim test_wid As Single

    Set the_controls = VBInstance.ActiveProject _
        .ActiveForm.SelectedControlTemplates

    ' Align the controls appropriately.
    If AlignerDialog.ColOption(ALIGN_LEFT).value Then
        x = the_controls.Item(0).Properties("Left")
        For Each ctl In the_controls
            test_x = ctl.Properties("Left")
            If x > test_x Then x = test_x
        Next ctl

        For Each ctl In the_controls
            ctl.Properties("Left") = x
        Next ctl
    ElseIf AlignerDialog.ColOption(ALIGN_CENTER).value Then
        x = 0
        wid = 0
        For Each ctl In the_controls
            test_x = ctl.Properties("Left")
            test_wid = ctl.Properties("Width")
            x = x + test_x
            wid = wid + test_wid
        Next ctl

        x = (x + wid / 2) / the_controls.Count
        For Each ctl In the_controls
            ctl.Properties("Left") = x - _
                ctl.Properties("Width") / 2
        Next ctl
    Else
        x = the_controls.Item(0).Properties("Left") + _
            the_controls.Item(0).Properties("Width")
        For Each ctl In the_controls
            test_x = ctl.Properties("Left") + _
                    ctl.Properties("Width")
            If x < test_x Then x = test_x
        Next ctl

        For Each ctl In the_controls
            ctl.Properties("Left") = x - _
                ctl.Properties("Width")
        Next ctl
```

```
    End If
End Sub
```

Aligning Controls in Rows and Columns

Aligner's AlignRowsAndCols subroutine is more complicated than subroutine AlignCol. Figure 5.3 shows the AlignerDialog tab that allows the developer to specify row and column arrangements. Using this dialog, the developer can indicate whether rows should be aligned at the top, middle, or bottom and whether columns should be aligned on the left, center, or right. It also allows the developer to specify the number of rows and columns, the spacing Aligner should use between rows and columns, and whether rows and columns should be given the same sizes.

AlignRowsAndCols needs to arrange the selected controls in a specific order. It must place the controls in rows and columns starting with those at the upper right and moving down toward the lower left. This will place the controls as close to their original positions as possible. Generally, controls that begin on the left will still be on the left in the new arrangement.

The SelectedControlTemplates collection does not provide an Add method, so sorting the control templates within this collection is difficult. The add-in cannot add and remove control templates to sort them within SelectedControlTemplates. To overcome this problem, AlignRowsAndCols first copies the control templates into an array that it can more easily manipulate.

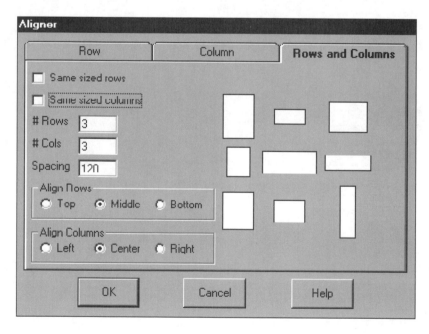

FIGURE 5.3 Specifying row and column alignment.

At the same time, the subroutine creates arrays that contain the Left and Top properties of each control. These values are used frequently in the following calculations, and storing them in arrays is much faster than repeatedly accessing them through the control templates' Properties collections.

Next AlignRowsAndCols uses subroutine SortControls to rearrange the control templates in the controls array. SortControls first sorts the templates so those with the smallest Top values come first. This will make it easy to place those controls in the upper rows of the new arrangement. SortControls then sorts the templates within each row so the controls with the smallest Left values come first.

After sorting the control templates, AlignRowsAndCols uses subroutine ArrangeRowColControls to place the controls in their new positions. This subroutine examines the controls in each row to determine how tall the row must be. Similarly, it examines the controls in each column to see how wide each column must be. If the developer checks the Same sized rows or Same sized columns boxes on the AlignerDialog, ArrangeRowColControls uses the largest row and column size for every row and column, respectively.

Once it has determined how large each row and column should be, ArrangeRowColControls moves the controls to their final locations.

```
Sub AlignRowsAndCols()
Dim the_controls As VBIDE.SelectedControlTemplates
Dim controls() As VBIDE.ControlTemplate
Dim tops() As Single
Dim lefts() As Single
Dim num_rows As Integer
Dim num_cols As Integer
Dim spacing As Single
Dim i As Integer

    On Error GoTo AlignError

    Set the_controls = VBInstance.ActiveProject _
        .ActiveForm.SelectedControlTemplates

    ' Get user input values.
    num_rows = CInt(AlignerDialog.NumRowsText.Text)
    num_cols = CInt(AlignerDialog.NumColsText.Text)
    spacing = CSng(AlignerDialog.SpaceText.Text)
    If num_rows * num_cols <> the_controls.Count Then
        Beep
        MsgBox "(# Rows) * (# Cols) does not equal the number of controls you selected.", _
            vbOKOnly + vbInformation, _
            "Error Aligning Controls"
        Exit Sub
    End If

    ' Allocate room for the control tamplates.
    ReDim controls(0 To the_controls.Count - 1)
```

```
    ReDim tops(0 To the_controls.Count - 1)
    ReDim lefts(0 To the_controls.Count - 1)

    ' Copy the selected controls' templates.
    For i = 0 To the_controls.Count - 1
        Set controls(i) = the_controls(i)
        tops(i) = controls(i).Properties.Item("Top")
        lefts(i) = controls(i).Properties.Item("Left")
    Next i

    ' Sort the controls by rows and columns.
    SortControls num_rows, num_cols, controls, tops, lefts

    ' Arrange them.
    ArrangeRowColControls num_rows, num_cols, spacing, controls, tops, lefts
    Exit Sub

AlignError:
    Beep
    MsgBox "Error aligning controls." & vbCrLf & _
        Err.Description, _
        vbOKOnly + vbInformation, _
        "Error Aligning Controls"
    Exit Sub
End Sub


Sub SortControls(num_rows As Integer, num_cols As Integer, controls() As VBIDE.ControlTemplate,
tops() As Single, lefts() As Single)
Dim tmp_ctl As VBIDE.ControlTemplate
Dim max_ctl As Integer
Dim i As Integer
Dim j As Integer
Dim r As Integer
Dim min_i As Integer
Dim max_i As Integer
Dim best_value As Single
Dim best_j As Single

    ' Sort by Top value.
    max_ctl = num_rows * num_cols - 1
    For i = 0 To max_ctl - 1
        best_value = tops(i)
        best_j = i
        For j = i + 1 To max_ctl
            If best_value > tops(j) Then
                best_value = tops(j)
                best_j = j
            End If
        Next j
        If best_j <> i Then
            Set tmp_ctl = controls(i)
```

```
                    Set controls(i) = controls(best_j)
                    Set controls(best_j) = tmp_ctl
                    tops(best_j) = tops(i)
                    tops(i) = best_value
                    best_value = lefts(best_j)
                    lefts(best_j) = lefts(i)
                    lefts(i) = best_value
            End If
        Next i

    ' Sort the controls in each row by Left.
    For r = 1 To num_rows
        min_i = (r - 1) * num_cols
        max_i = min_i + num_cols - 2
        For i = min_i To max_i
            best_value = lefts(i)
            best_j = i
            For j = i + 1 To max_i + 1
                If best_value > lefts(j) Then
                    best_value = lefts(j)
                    best_j = j
                End If
            Next j
            If best_j <> i Then
                Set tmp_ctl = controls(i)
                Set controls(i) = controls(best_j)
                Set controls(best_j) = tmp_ctl
                lefts(best_j) = lefts(i)
                lefts(i) = best_value
                best_value = tops(best_j)
                tops(best_j) = tops(i)
                tops(i) = best_value
            End If
        Next i
    Next r
End Sub

Sub ArrangeRowColControls(num_rows As Integer, num_cols As Integer, spacing As Single, controls() As
VBIDE.ControlTemplate, tops() As Single, lefts() As Single)
Dim max_row As Integer
Dim max_col As Integer
Dim max_ctl As Integer
Dim same_rows As Boolean
Dim same_cols As Boolean
Dim row_align As Integer
Dim col_align As Integer
Dim row_hgt() As Single
Dim col_wid() As Single
Dim i As Integer
Dim r As Integer
Dim c As Integer
```

```
Dim start_x As Single
Dim start_y As Single
Dim x As Single
Dim y As Single
Dim val As Single

    max_row = num_rows - 1
    max_col = num_cols - 1
    max_ctl = num_rows * num_cols - 1

    ReDim row_hgt(0 To max_row)
    ReDim col_wid(0 To max_col)

    ' Get the row and column alignment values.
    For i = 0 To 2
        If AlignerDialog.RCRowOption(i).value Then Exit For
    Next i
    row_align = i

    For i = 0 To 2
        If AlignerDialog.RCColOption(i).value Then Exit For
    Next i
    col_align = i

    ' Find the row and column sizes.
    same_rows = (AlignerDialog.SameRowCheck.value = vbChecked)
    If same_rows Then
        ' Make all rows the height of the
        ' tallest rectangle.
        y = controls(0).Properties.Item("Height")
        For i = 1 To max_ctl
            val = controls(i).Properties.Item("Height")
            If y < val Then y = val
        Next i
        For i = 0 To max_row
            row_hgt(i) = y
        Next i
    Else
        ' Find the height for each row.
        For r = 0 To max_row
            row_hgt(r) = controls(r * num_cols) _
                .Properties.Item("Height")
            For c = 1 To max_col
                val = controls(r * num_cols + c) _
                    .Properties.Item("Height")
                If row_hgt(r) < val Then _
                    row_hgt(r) = val
            Next c
        Next r
    End If
```

```
same_cols = (AlignerDialog.SameColCheck.value = vbChecked)
If same_cols Then
    ' Make all columns the width of the
    ' widest rectangle.
    x = controls(0).Properties.Item("Width")
    For i = 1 To max_ctl
        val = controls(i).Properties.Item("Width")
        If x < val Then x = val
    Next i
    For i = 0 To max_col
        col_wid(i) = x
    Next i
Else
    ' Find the width for each column.
    For c = 0 To max_col
        col_wid(c) = controls(c).Properties.Item("Width")
        For r = 1 To max_row
            val = controls(c + num_cols * r) _
                .Properties.Item("Width")
            If col_wid(c) < val Then _
                col_wid(c) = val
        Next r
    Next c
End If

' Find the upper left corner.
start_x = lefts(0)
start_y = tops(0)
For i = 1 To max_ctl
    If start_x > lefts(i) Then start_x = lefts(i)
    If start_y > tops(i) Then start_y = tops(i)
Next i

' Position the rectangles.
y = start_y

' Lay out the rows.
i = 0
For r = 0 To max_row
    x = start_x
    For c = 0 To max_col
        Select Case col_align
            Case ALIGN_LEFT
                controls(i).Properties.Item("Left") = _
                    x
            Case ALIGN_CENTER
                controls(i).Properties.Item("Left") = _
                    x + (col_wid(c) - _
                    controls(i).Properties.Item("Width")) / 2
            Case ALIGN_RIGHT
                controls(i).Properties.Item("Left") = _
```

```
                            x + col_wid(c) - _
                            controls(i).Properties.Item("Width")
            End Select
            Select Case row_align
                Case ALIGN_TOP
                    controls(i).Properties.Item("Top") = _
                        y
                Case ALIGN_MIDDLE
                    controls(i).Properties.Item("Top") = _
                        y + (row_hgt(r) - _
                        controls(i).Properties.Item("Height")) / 2
                Case ALIGN_BOTTOM
                    controls(i).Properties.Item("Top") = _
                        y + row_hgt(r) - _
                        controls(i).Properties.Item("Height")
            End Select

            x = x + col_wid(c) + spacing
            i = i + 1
        Next c
        y = y + row_hgt(r) + spacing
    Next r
End Sub
```

Summary

Aligner modifies the Left and Top properties of a group of selected controls to arrange them in rows and columns. Using similar techniques an add-in could arrange controls vertically, horizontally, in circles, tiled to fill the form without overlap, or in all sorts of other ways.

PropertySetter and Aligner modify the properties of controls created by the developer. Chapters 6 and 7 demonstrate more advanced add-in techniques to add completely new controls and new source code to a project.

Chapter 6

Scroller

The ExpenseReporter application described in Chapter 1 uses two scrolling areas. With two picture boxes and a scroll bar, it builds a region that the user can scroll to display more information than would otherwise fit on the screen. Building a scrolling area is not a difficult task, but it requires many tedious steps. The Scroller add-in automates those steps to create scrolling areas easily and quickly.

The first section in this chapter, "Using Scroller," explains how this add-in works from an application developer's point of view. It tells how a developer can use Scroller to create scrolling areas quickly.

The "Key Techniques" section that follows briefly lists the most important Visual Basic programming techniques used by Scroller. The rest of the chapter describes these techniques in detail.

Using Scroller

When it is installed, Scroller adds a Scroller submenu in the development environment's Add-Ins menu. This submenu contains two commands: Create Scrolling Area and About. Figure 6.1 shows the new Add-In menu commands.

The About command presents a standard about dialog giving Scroller version and copyright information as well as a little help.

If the developer selects one or more controls and then invokes the Create Scrolling Area menu command, Scroller creates a scrolling area to contain the controls. Scroller creates three new picture boxes and two scroll bars that work together to display the controls. Figure 6.2 shows schematically how these controls are arranged.

The controls the developer selected are placed inside a picture box with a template named scroll_area. It is important to remember that scroll_area is a template representing a picture box, not the picture box itself. By default, Visual Basic will give the control a less descriptive name like Picture1.

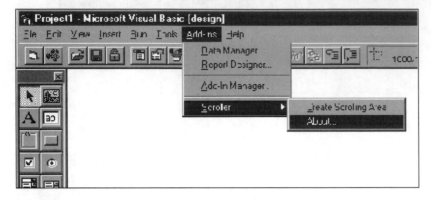

FIGURE 6.1 Scroller's Add-In submenu and commands.

Scroller makes the scroll_area object large enough to hold all the selected controls. Its border style is set to vbTransparent so it will be invisible on the form.

The scroll_area object is contained within an object with a template named viewport. This object has visible borders. As the program moves scroll_area within viewport, viewport's edges clip off the parts of scroll_area that should not be visible.

Beside viewport are the two scroll bars with templates hscroll and vscroll. They behave much as the scroll bars described in Chapter 1 do. When their values change, they move scroll_area within viewport accordingly.

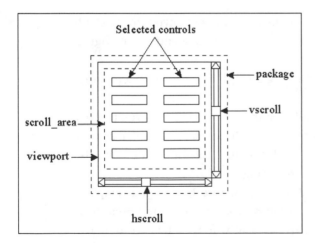

FIGURE 6.2 Control arrangement produced by Scroller.

Finally, all of these controls are contained in a picture box with a template named package. This object keeps the others together. It also provides a reference for setting properties for the scroll bars.

While the Scroller add-in can do most of the work, the application developer must perform three tasks to make the scrolling area work properly. First, the controls created by Scroller use several subroutines defined in the module Scroller.BAS. The developer must add this module to the project.

Second, when the form is first loaded, the program should call the package control's Resize event handler. This allows the scrolling to arrange itself so it will be ready for display.

Finally, the form's Resize event handler can resize the scrolling area if desired. For example, the following code shows a form's Resize event handler that makes the package control Picture3 occupy all of the form's available space.

```
Private Sub Form_Resize()
    Picture3.Move 0, 0, ScaleWidth, ScaleHeight
End Sub
```

After it creates the scrolling area, Scroller presents a message reminding the developer to perform these tasks.

Key Techniques

Scroller performs a single, well-defined task so it does not need to present a dialog box to ask the user for extra information. This makes it slightly different from the PropertySetter and Aligner add-ins described in the last two chapters. Those add-ins use a single Add-Ins menu command to present a dialog. Scroller creates two commands within a submenu in the Add-Ins menu.

The following list briefly describes the key techniques demonstrated by Scroller. The sections in the rest of this chapter describe these techniques in greater detail.

- **Creating Add-In Submenus**. Unlike the add-ins described previously, Scroller adds a submenu containing two commands to the Add-Ins menu. This section describes the ConnectAddIn and DisconnectAddIn commands that add and remove these menu items.
- **Creating the Scrolling Area**. To create the scrolling area, Scroller must create new controls, and it must properly arrange controls within each other. This section tells how Scroller accomplishes these two tasks.
- **Arranging Scrolling Area Controls**. The package control Scroller creates contains a Resize event handler that arranges the controls it contains. This section lists the subroutines used to arrange the controls and set parameters for the scroll bars.

Creating Add-In Submenus

Scroller works slightly differently than the add-ins described in previous chapters. PropertySetter and Aligner present dialogs that allow the developer to indicate what properties to set and how controls should be aligned. A command button on the dialog allows easy access to a simple help screen that explains briefly what the add-in does.

Scroller, on the other hand, does not need any additional information to perform its task. It takes the selected controls and builds a scrolling area for them without presenting a dialog to get extra information. Because there is no dialog, there is no obvious place to provide help.

To provide help, Scroller installs an About command in the Add-Ins menu. To avoid cluttering the menu too much, it creates a separate submenu to hold the Create Scrolling Area and About commands, as shown in Figure 6.3.

Scroller creates the submenu and the menu commands in its ConnectAddIn subroutine. It removes them in DisconnectAddIn. Because Scroller creates two menu commands, it uses two global MenuLine variables and two global event handler IDs.

The main class that contains the ConnectAddIn and DisconnectAddIn subroutines is named Scroller. It also contains an AfterClick event subroutine that responds to the About menu command. This AfterClick subroutine presents an about dialog giving version and copyright information. It is similar to previous about dialog code so it is not described here.

The ScrollerHandler class contains the AfterClick subroutine triggered by the Create Scrolling Area menu command. ScrollerHandler.AfterClick, which actually creates the scrolling area, is described in the next section.

```
' The environment instance.
Dim VBInstance As VBIDE.Application

' The Add-Ins submenu.
Dim ScrollerMenu As VBIDE.SubMenu

' The command lines.
```

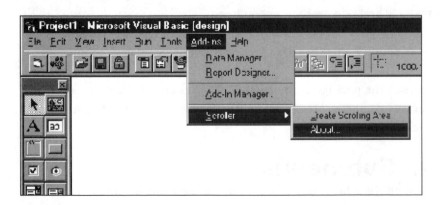

FIGURE 6.3 Scroller creates its own submenu in the Add-Ins menu.

```vb
Dim AboutLine As VBIDE.MenuLine
Dim ScrollerLine As VBIDE.MenuLine

' The event connection IDs. These represent the
' event handler to menu line connections.
Dim AboutID As Long
Dim ScrollerID As Long

Sub ConnectAddIn(vb_instance As VBIDE.Application)
' Command event handler objects.
Dim scroller_handler As New ScrollerHandler

    ' Save the Visual Basic instance for later.
    Set VBInstance = vb_instance

    ' Add the submenu to the Add-Ins menu.
    Set ScrollerMenu = _
        VBInstance.AddInMenu.MenuItems.AddMenu _
            ("&Scroller")

    ' Add the submenu's commands.
    Set ScrollerLine = _
        ScrollerMenu.MenuItems.Add("&Create Scrolling Area")
    Set AboutLine = ScrollerMenu.MenuItems.Add("About...")

    ' Connect event handler objects to the menu
    ' commands. Event handler objects have Public
    ' AfterClick subroutines.
    ScrollerID = ScrollerLine.ConnectEvents(scroller_handler)
    ' This object will handle the About AfterClick.
    AboutID = AboutLine.ConnectEvents(Me)

    ' Give the scroller event handler object
    ' the handle to the Visual Basic environment.
    Set scroller_handler.VBInstance = VBInstance
End Sub

Sub DisconnectAddIn(mode As Integer)
    ' Disconnect the event handlers.
    ScrollerLine.DisconnectEvents ScrollerID
    AboutLine.DisconnectEvents AboutID

    ' Remove the submenu commands from the submenu.
    ScrollerMenu.MenuItems.Remove ScrollerLine
    ScrollerMenu.MenuItems.Remove AboutLine

    ' Remove the submenu.
    VBInstance.AddInMenu.MenuItems.Remove ScrollerMenu
End Sub
```

Creating the Scrolling Area

When the developer selects the Create Scrolling Area command from the Add-Ins menu, the system invokes a ScrollerHandler object's AfterClick event handler. This routine must perform two tasks to create the scrolling area. First, it must create the new picture boxes and scroll bars that make up the scrolling area. Second, it must properly arrange the containments of the controls. For example, the controls selected by the developer must be contained by the inner scroll_area picture box. The following sections describe these two tasks.

Creating Controls

The first thing the ScrollerHandler object's AfterClick event handler must do is create new controls. The ControlTemplates collection provides an Add method that creates new controls and adds them to the active form. This method takes as its only parameter the name of the class of control that it should create. For example, the following code creates a new picture box control:

```
Set scroll_area = frm.ControlTemplates.Add("PictureBox")
```

Setting Control Containment

A control template's Container property indicates the template of the form or control that contains the control. Scroller moves each of the controls selected by the developer into the picture box scroll_area using code similar to the following:

```
Set ctl.Container = scroll_area
```

The AfterClick subroutine also writes event handler code for the package picture box's Resize event, and for the two scroll bars' Change and Scroll events. It begins by creating a temporary file. Next, using Print statements, it writes the event handlers into the file. It then uses the active form's InsertFile method to add the contents of the file to the form's source code. Finally, AfterClick uses the Kill command to delete the temporary file.

It is important that the new controls' event handlers be created using the controls' correct names. The variable hscroll, for example, is merely a template describing a control, not the control itself. That means the control's Scroll event handler is not called hscroll_Scroll. It is more probably named something similar to HScroll1_Scroll. The AfterClick subroutine uses each control template's Name property to determine the actual name of the control that was created. For example, the true name of the control represented by the hscroll variable is given by hscroll.Properties.Item("Name").

When it has finished creating controls and adding event handler code, AfterClick presents a message box reminding the developer to perform a few final tasks. The developer must add Scroller.BAS to the project, invoke the package control's Resize event handler when it is first created, and optionally resize the package control when the form is resized.

```
Public Sub AfterClick()
Const MARGIN = 60
Dim min_x As Single
Dim max_x As Single
```

```
Dim min_y As Single
Dim max_y As Single
Dim x As Single
Dim y As Single
Dim ctl As Object
Dim controls As VBIDE.SelectedControlTemplates
Dim frm As Object
Dim scroll_area As Object
Dim viewport As Object
Dim hscroll As Object
Dim vscroll As Object
Dim package As Object
Dim scroll_area_name As String
Dim viewport_name As String
Dim hscroll_name As String
Dim vscroll_name As String
Dim package_name As String
Dim scroll_area_wid As Single
Dim scroll_area_hgt As Single
Dim viewport_wid As Single
Dim viewport_hgt As Single
Dim package_wid As Single
Dim package_hgt As Single
Dim filename As String
Dim fp As Integer

    If NoControls() Then Exit Sub

    Set frm = VBInstance.ActiveProject.ActiveForm
    Set controls = frm.SelectedControlTemplates

    ' Find the largest and smallest coordinates.
    Set ctl = controls.Item(0)
    min_x = ctl.Properties("Left")
    max_x = min_x
    min_y = ctl.Properties("Top")
    max_y = min_y

    For Each ctl In controls
        On Error Resume Next
        x = ctl.Properties("Left")
        If Err.Number = 0 Then
            If min_x > x Then min_x = x
            If max_x < x Then max_x = x
            y = ctl.Properties("Top")
            If min_y > y Then min_y = y
            If max_y < y Then max_y = y
        End If
        x = x + ctl.Properties("Width")
        If Err.Number = 0 Then
            If min_x > x Then min_x = x
```

```
            If max_x < x Then max_x = x
            y = y + ctl.Properties("Height")
            If min_y > y Then min_y = y
            If max_y < y Then max_y = y
        End If
        On Error GoTo 0
Next ctl

' Create the scrolling area.
Set scroll_area = frm.ControlTemplates.Add("PictureBox")
With scroll_area.Properties
    .Item("Left") = 0
    .Item("Top") = 0
    scroll_area_wid = max_x - min_x + 2 * MARGIN
    scroll_area_hgt = max_y - min_y + 2 * MARGIN
    .Item("Width") = scroll_area_wid
    .Item("Height") = scroll_area_hgt
    .Item("BorderStyle") = vbTransparent
End With

' Move the items into the scrolling area.
For Each ctl In controls
    Set ctl.Container = scroll_area
    With ctl.Properties
        .Item("Left") = .Item("Left") - min_x + MARGIN
        .Item("Top") = .Item("Top") - min_y + MARGIN
    End With
Next ctl

' Create the scrolling area controls.
Set viewport = frm.ControlTemplates.Add("PictureBox")
Set hscroll = frm.ControlTemplates.Add("HScrollBar")
Set vscroll = frm.ControlTemplates.Add("VScrollBar")
Set package = frm.ControlTemplates.Add("PictureBox")

Set viewport.Container = package
Set hscroll.Container = package
Set vscroll.Container = package
Set scroll_area.Container = viewport

With viewport.Properties
    .Item("Left") = 0
    .Item("Top") = 0
    viewport_wid = .Item("Width") - _
        .Item("ScaleWidth") + scroll_area_wid
    viewport_hgt = .Item("Height") - _
        .Item("ScaleHeight") + scroll_area_hgt
    .Item("Width") = viewport_wid
    .Item("Height") = viewport_hgt
    .Item("BorderStyle") = vbBSSolid
End With
```

```
With hscroll.Properties
    .Item("Left") = 0
    .Item("Top") = viewport_hgt
    .Item("Width") = viewport_wid
End With
With vscroll.Properties
    .Item("Left") = viewport_wid
    .Item("Top") = 0
    .Item("Height") = viewport_hgt
End With
With package.Properties
    .Item("Left") = min_x
    .Item("Top") = min_y
    package_wid = viewport_wid + _
        vscroll.Properties.Item("Width")
    package_hgt = viewport_hgt + _
        hscroll.Properties.Item("Height")
    .Item("Width") = package_wid
    .Item("Height") = package_hgt
    .Item("BorderStyle") = vbTransparent
End With

' Create a file containing code for the
' scrolling area.
scroll_area_name = scroll_area.Properties.Item("Name")
viewport_name = viewport.Properties.Item("Name")
hscroll_name = hscroll.Properties.Item("Name")
vscroll_name = vscroll.Properties.Item("Name")
package_name = package.Properties.Item("Name")

fp = FreeFile
filename = App.Path & "\Scroller.TMP"
Open filename For Output As fp
Print #fp, "Private Sub " & package_name & "_Resize()"
Print #fp, "    ' Call ArrangeScrollingArea to"
Print #fp, "    ' set scroll bar parameters."
Print #fp, "    ArrangeScrollingArea _"
Print #fp, "        " & package_name & ", _"
Print #fp, "        " & viewport_name & ", _"
Print #fp, "        " & hscroll_name & ", _"
Print #fp, "        " & vscroll_name & ", _"
Print #fp, "        " & scroll_area_name
Print #fp, "End Sub"
Print #fp, "Private Sub " & hscroll_name & "_Change()"
Print #fp, "    ' Move the scrolling area."
Print #fp, "    " & scroll_area_name & _
    ".Left = -" & hscroll_name & ".Value"
Print #fp, "End Sub"
Print #fp, "Private Sub " & hscroll_name & "_Scroll()"
Print #fp, "    ' Move the scrolling area."
Print #fp, "    " & scroll_area_name & _
```

```
                ".Left = -" & hscroll_name & ".Value"
    Print #fp, "End Sub"
    Print #fp, "Private Sub " & vscroll_name & "_Change()"
    Print #fp, "    ' Move the scrolling area."
    Print #fp, "    " & scroll_area_name & _
        ".Top = -" & vscroll_name & ".Value"
    Print #fp, "End Sub"
    Print #fp, "Private Sub " & vscroll_name & "_Scroll()"
    Print #fp, "    ' Move the scrolling area."
    Print #fp, "    " & scroll_area_name & _
        ".Top = -" & vscroll_name & ".Value"
    Print #fp, "End Sub"
    Close fp

    ' Insert the file into the Form's code.
    frm.InsertFile filename

    ' Delete the file.
    Kill filename

    ' Give the user a reminder popup.
    MsgBox "Remember to:" & vbCrLf & vbCrLf & _
        "1. Add file Scroller.BAS to your project." & vbCrLf & _
        "2. Invoke " & package_name & _
        "_Resize in this form's Load event handler." & vbCrLf & _
        "3. (Optional) Add code to resize " & _
        package_name & " when the form resizes.", _
        vbOKOnly + vbInformation, "Reminder"
End Sub
```

Arranging Scrolling Area Controls

When Scroller creates the scrolling area controls, it gives the package control a Resize event handler. When this control is resized, the event handler calls the ArrangeScrollingArea subroutine, as shown in the following code.

```
Private Sub Picture3_Resize()
    ' Call ArrangeScrollingArea to
    ' set scroll bar parameters.
    ArrangeScrollingArea _
        Picture3, _
        Picture2, _
        HScroll1, _
        VScroll1, _
        Picture1
End Sub
```

The code placed in this event handler refers to the actual control names as they are created by Visual Basic. For example, if Visual Basic named the package control Picture7 instead of Picture3, this subroutine would be named Picture7_Resize and it would use Picture7 as the first parameter to the Arrange-ScrollingArea subroutine.

ArrangeScrollingArea, contained in module Scroller.BAS, places the scrolling area controls and sets the scroll bars' parameters. It determines which scroll bars are necessary and hides any that are not.

```
Sub ArrangeScrollingArea(package As PictureBox, _
    viewport As PictureBox, hscroll As HScrollBar, _
    vscroll As VScrollBar, scroll_area As PictureBox)
Dim viewport_xgap As Single
Dim viewport_ygap As Single
Dim need_wid As Single
Dim need_hgt As Single
Dim got_wid As Single
Dim got_hgt As Single
Dim need_hscroll As Boolean
Dim need_vscroll As Boolean

    ' See how big things are.
    viewport_xgap = viewport.Width - viewport.ScaleWidth
    viewport_ygap = viewport.Height - viewport.ScaleHeight
    got_wid = package.ScaleWidth - viewport_xgap
    got_hgt = package.ScaleHeight - viewport_ygap
    need_wid = scroll_area.Width
    need_hgt = scroll_area.Height

    ' See which scroll bars we need.
    If need_wid > got_wid Then
        need_hscroll = True
        got_hgt = got_hgt - hscroll.Height
    End If
    If need_hgt > got_hgt Then
        need_vscroll = True
        got_wid = got_wid - vscroll.Width
        If Not need_hscroll Then
            If need_wid > got_wid Then
                need_hscroll = True
                got_hgt = got_hgt - hscroll.Height
            End If
        End If
    End If

    ' Make sure we don't make things too small.
    got_wid = got_wid + viewport_xgap
    got_hgt = got_hgt + viewport_ygap
    If got_wid < vscroll.Width Then _
        got_wid = vscroll.Width
    If got_hgt < hscroll.Height Then _
        got_hgt = hscroll.Height

    ' Rearrange the controls.
    viewport.Move 0, 0, got_wid, got_hgt
    If need_hscroll Then _
        hscroll.Move 0, got_hgt, got_wid
    hscroll.Visible = need_hscroll
```

```
If need_vscroll Then _
    vscroll.Move got_wid, 0, vscroll.Width, got_hgt
vscroll.Visible = need_vscroll
scroll_area.Move 0, 0

' Set the scroll bar parameters.
If need_hscroll Then
    hscroll.Min = 0
    hscroll.Max = scroll_area.Width - viewport.ScaleWidth
    hscroll.SmallChange = 0.1 * viewport.ScaleWidth
    hscroll.LargeChange = 0.9 * viewport.ScaleWidth
End If
If need_vscroll Then
    vscroll.Min = 0
    vscroll.Max = scroll_area.Height - viewport.ScaleHeight
    vscroll.SmallChange = 0.1 * viewport.ScaleHeight
    vscroll.LargeChange = 0.9 * viewport.ScaleHeight
End If
End Sub
```

Summary

The PropertySetter and Aligner add-ins described in Chapters 4 and 5 modify the properties of controls that already exist in a project. Scroller adds completely new controls and new source code to a project. It uses the code and controls to automatically build scrolling regions.

Using similar techniques an add-in could add other more complex combinations of new controls and source code to a project. The AddInMaker add-in described in Chapter 7, for example, creates new source code to make implementing other add-ins easy.

Chapter 7

AddInMaker

Like many programming tasks, creating add-ins is simple taken one step at a time. There are enough interrelated steps, however, that making a mistake is easy. For instance, if the steps taken in ConnectAddIn are not correctly reversed in DisconnectAddIn, the add-in will not properly uninstall itself. This would leave useless menu items in the Add-Ins menu after the add-in server has stopped.

Add-ins were invented to automate routine programming tasks. Although building add-ins may not exactly be routine, it is certainly possible to automate the process. AddInMaker is an add-in that helps create other add-ins.

The first section in this chapter, "Using AddInMaker," describes the add-in from the developer's point-of-view. It explains how the developer can use the add-in to create other add-ins. The "Key Techniques" section briefly lists the main programming techniques used to implement AddInMaker. The rest of the chapter describes these techniques in detail.

Using AddInMaker

To begin creating an add-in, the developer selects the Create Add-In command from the Add-Ins menu. AddInMaker displays a dialog similar to the one shown in Figure 7.1

In this dialog, the developer defines menu entries for the new add-in. The Project Name field indicates the name of the server project as it will be used by the Add-In Manager. For example, if a server class object will be referenced by MyProject.MyClass, then the project name is MyClass.

The developer enters the names of the submenus and commands that should be placed in the Add-Ins menu, checking the Submenu checkbox for the submenus. For menu commands, the developer enters the name of the class that will handle that command.

For example, the entries shown in Figure 7.1 define one submenu containing two menu commands. The commands will be handled by the AfterClick subroutines in the Test-AddIn.RunTest and TestAddIn.AboutTest classes. Figure 7.2 shows the menus produced by these entries. You can find the source code for this test add-in in the Ch7\TestAdd directory on the compact disk.

Create Add-In

Project Name: TestAddIn

	Caption	Class Name
☑ Submenu	&Test Add-In	
☐ Submenu	&Run The Test	RunTest
☐ Submenu	&About...	AboutTest
☐ Submenu		

[OK]   [Cancel]   [Help]

FIGURE 7.1 The AddInMaker dialog.

When the developer clicks the OK button, AddInMaker writes a Main subroutine that registers the new add-in in VB.INI. To make installing the add-in in Visual Basic 5 easier, AddInMaker also creates an AddToINI subroutine that registers the add-in in VBADDIN.INI rather than VB.INI. To create the initialization file entries in Visual Basic 5, the developer can execute AddToINI in Visual Basic's Immediate window. In Visual Basic 4, AddToINI would be unused.

AddInMaker also creates a class called Connector that provides the ConnectAddIn and Disconnect-AddIn subroutines that install and uninstall the add-in's menu items. Finally, AddInMaker builds classes providing AfterClick events to respond to the menu commands.

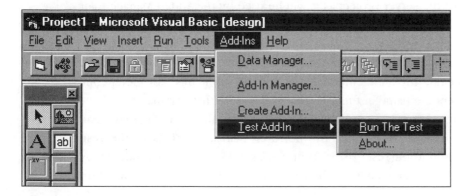

FIGURE 7.2 The Add-Ins menu commands created by the entries shown in Figure 7.1.

To finish creating the add-in, the developer must add code to the AfterClick event handlers and perform the normal add-in installation tasks. These tasks include setting the project name, setting StartMode to OLE Server, and creating the OLE DLL file. When it finishes, AddInMaker presents a dialog reminding the developer to perform these tasks.

Key Techniques

Architecturally, AddInMaker is similar to the PropertySetter and Aligner add-ins described in previous chapters. All three of these add-ins present a dialog to obtain information from the user. All three provide a Help button so all three need only a single command in the Add-Ins menu. This makes AddIn-Maker's ConnectAddIn and DisconnectAddIn subroutines similar to those used by PropertySetter and Aligner (they are not reproduced here).

In a way, AddInMaker is an in-depth review of how add-ins work. To correctly write an add-in that creates other add-ins, one must understand add-in concepts fairly well.

The following list briefly describes the key techniques used to implement AddInMaker. The rest of this chapter describes these techniques in detail.

- **Managing AddInMaker's Dialog**. AddInMaker's AfterClick subroutine presents the add-in's dialog. This section shows how AddInMaker uses the dialog to gather information from the user. The following sections describe the routines that use the information to create the new add-in.
- **Building Sub Main**. The Main and AddToINI subroutines register the new add-in with the appropriate initialization files. This section explains how AddInMaker creates these routines for the new add-in.
- **Building ConnectAddIn and DisconnectAddIn**. Subroutine ConnectAddIn creates the submenus and menu commands displayed for the new add-in in the Add-Ins menu. Subroutine DisconnectAddIn removes the entries created by ConnectAddIn. This section tells how AddInMaker creates these two important subroutines.
- **Creating Command Classes**. For each menu command specified by the developer, AddInMaker creates a class with an AfterClick event handler. This section shows how AddInMaker creates these classes.

Managing AddInMaker's Dialog

AddInMaker's AfterClick event subroutine presents the dialog. If the user clicks the OK button, AfterClick invokes the CreateAddIn subroutine. CreateAddIn calls other subroutines to create the new add-in's Main and AddToINI subroutines, the Connector class that contains the ConnectAddIn and DisconnectAddIn routines, and the menu command classes themselves.

When it is finished, CreateAddIn presents AddInMaker's AboutDialog. AboutDialog is used both to present simple help when the user clicks the dialog's Help button and as a reminder to perform extra add-in installation chores after the add-in has been built. By setting AboutDialog's About property to false, CreateAddIn tells it to format itself as a reminder dialog rather than as a help screen.

```
Sub CreateAddIn()
    ' Create Sub Main.
    CreateSubMain

    ' Create the connector class.
    CreateConnector

    ' Create the classes.
    CreateClasses

    AboutDialog.About = False
    AboutDialog.Show vbModal
End Sub
```

AddInMaker's most interesting code is contained in the three subroutines CreateSubMain, Create-Connector, and CreateClasses. These subroutines are described in the following sections.

Building Sub Main

The CreateSubMain subroutine writes the new add-in's Main and AddToINI subroutines. It creates a file named SubMain.BAS in the development environment's default directory. It then writes the code that belongs in the new add-in's main module using Print statements.

CreateSubMain begins by placing the following statement in the new file:

```
Attribute VB_Name = "SubMain"
```

This statement tells the programming environment that the new module's name is SubMain. When the developer loads this file into a project, this name appears in the Name field on the module's Property screen.

The main task of subroutines Main and AddToINI is to register the class containing the ConnectAddIn and DisconnectAddIn subroutines in the appropriate initialization file. AddInMaker gives the new add-in a class named Connector that contains these subroutines. CreateSubMain uses the project name entered in the AddInMaker dialog as the new add-in's name. For example, if the developer entered TestAddIn in this field, CreateSubMain writes code to register the application as TestAddIn.Connector in the initialization file.

Writing Visual Basic source code into a file can be a little strange. Printing double quotation marks can be particularly tricky. Inside a string the code must use two double quotation marks to indicate that the Print statement should print one double quotation mark. A quotation mark at the end of a string appears even stranger. Two double quotation marks in the string print one double quotation mark in the file. Then a third double quotation mark ends the string. For example, consider the following statement:

```
Print #fp, "Attribute VB_Name = ""SubMain"""
```

This statement produces the following output in the file:

```
Attribute VB_Name = "SubMain"
```

When CreateSubMain has finished writing the main module's source code, it closes the file Sub-Main.BAS. It then uses the active project's AddFile method to add the file to the project. This is different from the InsertFile method used by Scroller to add source code to a form. The InsertFile method copies a file into one of the project's existing modules. AddFile makes the file a new module within the project.

The following code shows CreateSubMain. The code that produces the API function declarations has been omitted. This code is similar to code used in previous programs so it is nothing new. It is quite long and formats so badly it is hard to read anyway.

```
Sub CreateSubMain()
Dim filename As String
Dim fp As Integer
Dim project_name As String

    project_name = Trim$(AddInDialog.ProjectNameText.Text)

    ' Create the file SubMain.BAS.
    fp = FreeFile
    filename = App.Path & "\SubMain.BAS"
    Open filename For Output As fp

    Print #fp, "Attribute VB_Name = ""SubMain"""
    Print #fp, "Option Explicit"
    Print #fp, ""
    Print #fp, "#If Win16 Then"
        :
        <Code to declare GetPrivateProfileString and
        WritePrivateProfileString omitted>
        :
    Print #fp, "#End If"

    ' Create the Main subroutine for VB 4.
    Print #fp, "Sub Main()"
    Print #fp, "Dim section As String"
    Print #fp, "Dim val As String * 256"
    Print #fp, "Dim length As Long"
    Print #fp, ""
    Print #fp, "    #If Win16 Then"
    Print #fp, "        section = ""Add-Ins16"""
    Print #fp, "    #Else"
    Print #fp, "        section = ""Add-Ins32"""
    Print #fp, "    #End If"
    Print #fp, ""
    Print #fp, "    ' See if the add-in is in VB.INI."
    Print #fp, "    length = GetPrivateProfileString(section, _"
    Print #fp, "        """ & project_name & ".Connector"", """", val, _"
    Print #fp, "        256, ""VB.INI"")"
    Print #fp, ""
```

```
Print #fp, "    ' If not, add it."
Print #fp, "    If length = 0 Then _"
Print #fp, "        WritePrivateProfileString section, _"
Print #fp, "            """ & project_name & ".Connector"", ""0"", _"
Print #fp, "            ""VB.INI"""
Print #fp, "End Sub"

' Create the AddToINI subroutine for VB 5.
Print #fp, "Sub AddToINI()"
Print #fp, "Dim section As String"
Print #fp, "Dim val As String * 256"
Print #fp, "Dim length As Long"
Print #fp, ""
Print #fp, "    #If Win16 Then"
Print #fp, "        section = ""Add-Ins16"""
Print #fp, "    #Else"
Print #fp, "        section = ""Add-Ins32"""
Print #fp, "    #End If"
Print #fp, ""
Print #fp, "    ' See if the add-in is in VBADDIN.INI."
Print #fp, "    length = GetPrivateProfileString(section, _"
Print #fp, "        """ & project_name & ".Connector"", """", val, _"
Print #fp, "        256, ""VBADDIN.INI"")"
Print #fp, ""
Print #fp, "    ' If not, add it."
Print #fp, "    If length = 0 Then _"
Print #fp, "        WritePrivateProfileString section, _"
Print #fp, "            """ & project_name & ".Connector"", ""0"", _"
Print #fp, "            ""VBADDIN.INI"""
Print #fp, "End Sub"
Close fp

    VBInstance.ActiveProject.AddFile filename
End Sub
```

Building ConnectAddIn and DisconnectAddIn

The new add-in's Connector class contains the ConnectAddIn and DisconnectAddIn subroutines. These routines build and remove the menu items needed by the new add-in in the Add-Ins menu.

CreateConnector creates the file Connector.CLS to hold the new class. It then writes some preliminary information into the file to identify it as a Creatable, MultiUse class named Connector. It creates global variables that the new add-in will use to manage the Add-Ins menu items and event handlers.

Finally, CreateConnector invokes subroutines CreateConnectAddIn and CreateDisconnectAddIn to create the ConnnectAddIn and DisconnectAddIn subroutines. When these subroutines have finished, CreateConnector closes the file and uses the active project's AddFile method to add the Connector class module to the project.

```
Sub CreateConnector()
Dim filename As String
Dim fp As Integer
Dim max_line As Integer

    max_line = AddInDialog.MaxLine

    fp = FreeFile
    filename = App.Path & "\Connect.CLS"
    Open filename For Output As fp

    ' Write class information.
    Print #fp, "VERSION 1.0 CLASS"
    Print #fp, "BEGIN"
    Print #fp, "  MultiUse = -1   'True"
    Print #fp, "End"
    Print #fp, "Attribute VB_Name = ""Connector"""
    Print #fp, "Attribute VB_Creatable = True"
    Print #fp, "Attribute VB_Exposed = True"
    Print #fp, "Attribute VB_Description = ""Connector"""

    ' Write module global variables.
    Print #fp, "Option Explicit"
    Print #fp, ""
    Print #fp, "' The environment instance."
    Print #fp, "Dim VBInstance As VBIDE.Application"
    Print #fp, ""
    Print #fp, "' Submenu lines."
    Print #fp, "Dim SubmenuLine(0 to" & Str$(max_line - 1) & ") As VBIDE.Submenu"
    Print #fp, ""
    Print #fp, "' Menu command lines."
    Print #fp, "Dim CommandLine(0 to" & Str$(max_line - 1) & ") As VBIDE.MenuLine"
    Print #fp, ""
    Print #fp, "' Event connection IDs."
    Print #fp, "Dim EventID(0 to" & Str$(max_line - 1) & ") As Long"

    ' Create the ConnectAddIn subroutine.
    CreateConnectAddIn fp, max_line

    ' Create the DisconnectAddIn subroutine.
    CreateDisconnectAddIn fp, max_line

    Close fp

    VBInstance.ActiveProject.AddFile filename
End Sub
```

The CreateConnectAddIn and CreateDisconnectAddIn subroutines are described in the following sections.

CreateConnectAddIn

Subroutine CreateConnectAddIn writes the ConnectAddIn subroutine for the Connector class. ConnectAddIn must create the new add-in's menu entries specified in AddInMaker's dialog. It uses the choices entered there to decide which entries should be submenus and which should be commands.

AddInMaker allows only one level of submenu. It places command items inside the previous submenu. It places commands that come before any submenu entries in the Add-Ins menu itself.

For command entries, CreateConnectAddIn also writes code to connect the command to an event handler class. It uses the class name specified in the dialog. The new add-in's ConnectAddIn code creates an object of the appropriate class and connects the object to the menu command, saving the event handler ID for later use by DisconnectAddIn.

```
Sub CreateConnectAddIn(fp As Integer, max_line As Integer)
Dim line_caption As String
Dim line_class As String
Dim prev_menu As Integer
Dim i As Integer

    Print #fp, "Sub ConnectAddIn(vb_instance As VBIDE.Application)"
    Print #fp, "Dim obj As Object"
    Print #fp, ""
    Print #fp, "    ' Save the Visual Basic instance for later."
    Print #fp, "    Set VBInstance = vb_instance"
    Print #fp, ""
    Print #fp, "    ' Create the submenus and commands."
    prev_menu = -1
    For i = 0 To max_line - 1
        line_caption = Trim$(AddInDialog.CaptionText(i).Text)
        If AddInDialog.SubmenuCheck(i).value = vbChecked Then
            ' Create a new submenu.
            Print #fp, "    Set SubmenuLine(" & _
                Str$(i) & _
                ") = VBInstance.AddInMenu.MenuItems.AddMenu(""" & _
                line_caption & """)"
            prev_menu = i
        Else
            ' Create a new command.
            line_class = Trim$(AddInDialog.ClassNameText(i).Text)
            If prev_menu < 0 Then
                ' Put it directly in the Add-Ins menu.
                Print #fp, "    Set CommandLine(" & _
                    Str$(i) & _
                    ") = VBInstance.AddInMenu.MenuItems.Add(""" & _
                    line_caption & """)"
            Else
                ' Put it under the last submenu.
                Print #fp, "    Set CommandLine(" & _
                    Str$(i) & ") = SubmenuLine(" & _
                    Format$(prev_menu) & _
```

```
                            ").MenuItems.Add(""" & _
                            line_caption & """)"
                End If

                    ' Connect the event handler.
                Print #fp, "      Set obj = New " & _
                        line_class
                Print #fp, "      Set obj.VBInstance = VBInstance"
                Print #fp, _
                        "      EventID(" & Str$(i) & ") = CommandLine(" & _
                        Str$(i) & ").ConnectEvents(obj)"
            End If
            Print #fp, ""
        Next i
        Print #fp, "End Sub"
End Sub
```

CreateDisconnectAddIn

Subroutine CreateDisconnectAddIn writes the DisconnectAddIn subroutine. DisconnectAddIn uses the event IDs saved by ConnectAddIn to remove the connection between commands in the Add-Ins menu and the event handler objects that respond to them. It then removes the new add-in's submenus and menu commands from the Add-Ins menu.

```
Sub CreateDisconnectAddIn(fp As Integer, max_line As Integer)
Dim line_caption As String
Dim line_class As String
Dim prev_menu As Integer
Dim i As Integer

    Print #fp, "Sub DisconnectAddIn(mode As Integer)"
    Print #fp, "    ' Remove the submenus and commands."

    For i = max_line - 1 To 0 Step -1
        If AddInDialog.SubmenuCheck(i).value = vbUnchecked Then
            ' It's a command line.
            ' Disconnect the event handler.
            Print #fp, "    CommandLine(" &
                Str$(i) & ").DisconnectEvents EventID(" & _
                Str$(i) & ")"

            ' Find the submenu holding the command.
            For prev_menu = i - 1 To 0 Step -1
                If AddInDialog.SubmenuCheck(prev_menu).value = _
                    vbChecked Then Exit For
            Next prev_menu

            ' Remove the command.
            If prev_menu < 0 Then
                ' The command is directly in the
                ' Add-Ins menu.
```

```
            Print #fp, _
"    VBInstance.AddInMenu.MenuItems.Remove CommandLine(" & _
                Str$(i) & ")"
        Else
            ' The command is in the submenu.
            Print #fp, "    SubmenuLine(" & Str$(prev_menu) & _
                ").MenuItems.Remove CommandLine(" & Str$(i) & ")"
        End If
        Print #fp, "    Set CommandLine(" & _
            Str$(i) & ") = Nothing"
    Else
        ' It's a submenu.
        Print #fp, _
"    VBInstance.AddInMenu.MenuItems.Remove SubmenuLine(" & _
            Str$(i) & ")"
        Print #fp, "    Set SubmenuLine(" & _
            Str$(i) & ") = Nothing"
    End If
    Print #fp, ""
Next i
Print #fp, "End Sub"
End Sub
```

Creating Command Classes

The new add-in's ConnectAddIn subroutine creates event handler objects for the menu commands specified in AddInMaker's dialog. Subroutine CreateClasses uses the CreateClass subroutine to define each of the event handler classes.

```
Sub CreateClasses()
Dim i As Integer

    For i = 0 To AddInDialog.MaxLine - 1
        If AddInDialog.SubmenuCheck(i).value = vbUnchecked Then
            CreateClass Trim$(AddInDialog.ClassNameText(i).Text)
        End If
    Next i
End Sub
```

CreateClass builds a simple class with the name given by its parameter. It begins by writing information into a new class module to identify the module as a class definition. CreateClass then gives the class a simple AfterClick subroutine. Initially AfterClick presents a message box that acts as a place holder for whatever code the developer wants to insert. When it finishes, CreateClass adds the new module to the project.

```
Sub CreateClass(class_name As String)
Dim filename As String
Dim fp As Integer

    On Error GoTo CreateClassError
    fp = FreeFile
```

```
filename = App.Path & "\" & class_name & ".CLS"
Open filename For Output As fp

    ' Class information.
Print #fp, "VERSION 1.0 CLASS"
Print #fp, "BEGIN"
Print #tp, "  MultiUse = -1  'True"
Print #fp, "End"
Print #fp, "Attribute VB_Name = """ & class_name & """"
Print #fp, "Attribute VB_Creatable = True"
Print #fp, "Attribute VB_Exposed = True"
Print #fp, "Attribute VB_Description = """ & class_name & """"

    ' Module global variables.
Print #fp, "Option Explicit"
Print #fp, ""
Print #fp, "' The environment instance."
Print #fp, "Public VBInstance As VBIDE.Application"

    ' Create the AfterClick subroutine.
Print #fp, "Public Sub AfterClick()"
Print #fp, _
    "    MsgBox ""Insert code for " & class_name & " here."""
Print #fp, "End Sub"

Close fp

VBInstance.ActiveProject.AddFile filename
Exit Sub
End Sub
```

Summary

Add-ins are designed to automate simple, detailed tasks. Building an add-in is itself a simple but detailed task, so it makes sense to create an add-in that builds other add-ins. AddInMaker does just that. Using AddInMaker a developer can easily create the framework needed to implement a new add-in.

AddInMaker can create multiple add-in submenus, each containing one or more commands. A more elaborate program could use similar techniques to create an even more complex series of cascading add-in menus.

Part Three

Databasics

Some of the programs presented in earlier chapters store data in files. For example, the AppointmentBook application described in Chapter 3 saves appointment information in the file Appts.DAT. Saving data in files is quite convenient for simple programs that do not need to share their data. It is rather cumbersome, however, if the data must be used by more than one application.

Applications that store data in a standardized database can share information much more easily. Using a database also frees the application developer from building customized routines for reading and writing data to files. Chapters 8 through 10 demonstrate database techniques that simplify data management.

The PeopleWatcher application described in Chapter 8 uses data controls and bound controls to allow the user to examine and modify data in a simple personnel database. It also shows how an application can implement privileges and password protection. It uses those privileges to customize its user interface to suit the needs of different users.

The Query application described in Chapter 9 uses data access objects to process commands written in the industry-standard *structured query language* (SQL). Query takes advantage of the flexibility of SQL to implement a powerful data management tool.

Chapter 10 describes PeopleWatcher Remote. This application extends the PeopleWatcher application described in Chapter 8 across a network. By allowing its database to run on a remote computer, PeopleWatcher Remote gives users from all over a network access to the personnel file.

Chapter 8

PeopleWatcher

PeopleWatcher is a simple company personnel application that allows users to create, view, and modify employee information. In a way, PeopleWatcher is like a glorified phone book. It allows users to look up employees and read information about them.

The next section, "Using PeopleWatcher," describes PeopleWatcher from the user's point of view. It explains how PeopleWatcher allows users to create, view, and modify personnel records.

The "Key Techniques" section briefly describes the most important programming methods used to build PeopleWatcher. The rest of the chapter describes these methods in detail.

Using PeopleWatcher

When PeopleWatcher starts, it presents a password dialog similar to the one shown in Figure 8.1. The user enters a user name and password. PeopleWatcher uses these to determine what privileges the user has so it can adjust its user interface accordingly.

Figure 8.2 shows the running PeopleWatcher application. The outline control on the left displays a list of employees grouped by their last initials. The user can click on the plus sign next to a letter to see the entries for employees with last names starting with that letter. In Figure 8.2 the list of employees with last initial S is expanded.

The middle portion of PeopleWatcher shows information about the selected employee. The Basic, Home, HR, and Salary tabs allow the user to view different types of information.

Because the Employee table contains sensitive data, not every user can be allowed to view and modify all of the data fields without violating employee privacy. For example, salary information is confidential so only certain users, such as managers, can view the Salary tab.

The right portion of PeopleWatcher shows a picture of the selected employee.

PeopleWatcher allows certain users to modify some pieces of personnel data, depending on the user's privileges. For example, a secretary can view and modify an employee's basic information and can view Home and HR information. A secretary cannot even view Salary data.

Password

User ID	sam
Password	*********

OK   Cancel

FIGURE 8.1 PeopleWatcher's password dialog.

If an employee has permission to modify a data field, the field is shown with a white background. All of the fields shown in Figure 8.2 are editable so they all have white backgrounds. If the user does not have permission to modify a field, the field's background is gray. This color coding allows a user to instantly recognize the editable fields.

If the user is not allowed to view a certain type of data, that data is not visible. Figure 8.3 shows Home data viewed by a secretary user. The fields are gray because secretaries are not allowed to modify Home data. The Salary tab is not present because secretaries are not allowed to view Salary information.

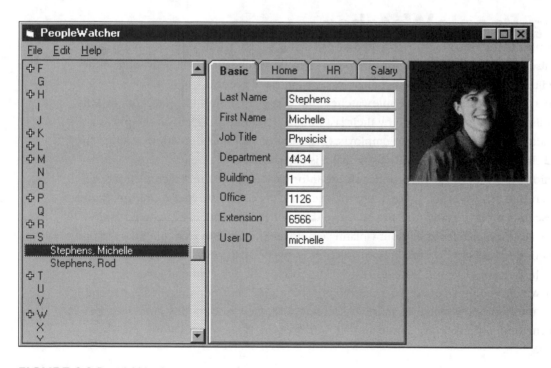

FIGURE 8.2 PeopleWatcher.

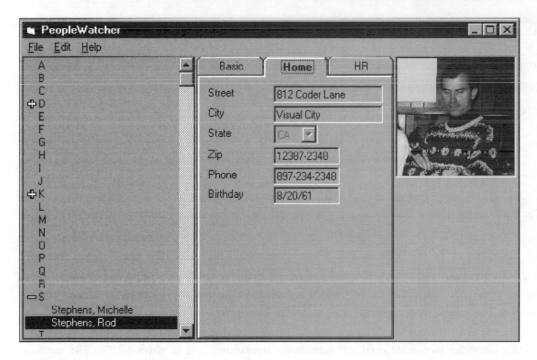

FIGURE 8.3 Home data viewed by a secretary user.

PeopleWatcher divides employee data into four categories: Basic, Home, HR (human resources), and Salary. Basic information is public and is available to everyone. It includes such items as employee name, phone number, office number, and the employee's picture.

Home information concerns the employee's personal life. It includes the employee's home address, home phone number, and birth date. This sort of information is generally private, though a secretary or manager might need it to contact an employee at home.

HR information includes the employee's ID number, Social Security number, hire date, and number of hours of unused vacation and sick leave. This data is also private.

Salary information includes the employee's job level, salary, and pay interval. It is the most sensitive information of all, so it is available to the fewest users.

Table 8.1 lists the permissions granted to each group of users.

To make testing PeopleWatcher easier, the database included on the compact disk defines one user in each group. The users defined in the database and their passwords are listed in Table 8.2.

A user with edit privileges can begin editing either by selecting the Edit command in the Edit menu or by typing directly into an editable field. Because a user cannot type directly into a picture, users who are allowed to modify pictures must do so in a different way. If the user double-clicks on the picture, PeopleWatcher presents a file selection dialog. The user should select the file containing the employee's new picture.

TABLE 8.1 User Groups and Privileges

Group	Privileges
General	View Basic information only.
Secretary	View Basic, Home, and HR information. Modify Basic information.
Manager	View all data.
HR	View and modify all data. Create and delete records.

Once the user has finished making changes, the Edit menu's Accept Changes command makes the changes permanent. The Cancel Changes command removes the changes and restores the fields to their original values.

Users with appropriate privileges can also create and delete records. For these users, People-Watcher's Edit menu includes the New, Copy, and Delete commands. The New command creates a new blank employee record. The Copy command creates a new record using the same values contained in the current record. The user can change the values before saving the changes to the data. The Delete command asks the user to confirm the deletion before it removes the record.

PeopleWatcher provides two additional commands for managing user passwords. The File menu's Logon User command presents a password dialog. This allows the user to log on to PeopleWatcher as a different user. This is particularly useful if the user initially enters an incorrect password. In that case, the program will not display any information until the user selects the Logon User command and logs on correctly.

PeopleWatcher's Change Password command in the File menu presents the dialog shown in Figure 8.4. Here the user should enter a current user name and password, which are required to prevent one user from changing another's password.

The user should then enter a new password twice. The password is entered twice to guard against typing mistakes. If the same value is entered in both new password fields, the user probably did not make any typing errors.

TABLE 8.2 Predefined PeopleWatcher Users

User Name	Password	Group
harry	humanresources	HR
mandy	manager	Manager
sam	secretary	Secretary
gus	general	General

FIGURE 8.4 PeopleWatcher's Change Password dialog.

Key Techniques

PeopleWatcher demonstrates many important Visual Basic programming techniques. The following list describes these techniques briefly. The rest of the chapter explains them in detail.

- **Understanding Databases**. This section briefly describes database engines and the compatibility issues related to the engines provided with different versions of Visual Basic. It also describes the Data Manager, an add-in that can be used to create and maintain Access databases.
- **Using the Data Control**. There are several ways to access data in Visual Basic. This section explains how a program can access data using the data control.
- **Using Data Access Objects**. Data controls work closely with data access objects. This section explains how a program can use Workspace, DBEngine, and Recordset objects to perform such actions as creating, editing, and deleting records.
- **Understanding PeopleWatcher**. This section describes the most important parts of PeopleWatcher. It explains how PeopleWatcher uses an outline control to list database records, how it customizes its user interface for users with different privileges, and how it orchestrates the editing of records.
- **Testing Database Applications**. The data control is complex and can create many strange situations. This section lists a few of the situations that an application should watch for to prevent errors.

Understanding Databases

There are many different kinds of databases. Visual Basic's "native" database format is the same as the format Microsoft Access uses. Because it is designed specifically to work with Access databases, Visual Basic provides the best performance with them.

Visual Basic can also manipulate data in many other database formats, including Btrieve, dBASE, Microsoft FoxPro, and Paradox. This chapter and those that follow deal only with Access databases. For information on how to use other kinds of databases, search the Visual Basic help for "Accessing External Databases" and consult the other database's documentation.

The following section provides a brief overview of database engines. It describes compatibility issues involving the engines that come with different versions of Visual Basic. The next section describes the Data Manager, a Visual Basic add-in that can be used to create and maintain Access databases. If you already understand Access databases thoroughly, you may want to skim these sections or skip directly to the following section, "Using the Data Control."

Database Engines

A *database engine* is the software that provides database functionality. It provides support routines with which an application can manipulate data stored in database files. Visual Basic uses the Microsoft Jet database engine; Microsoft Access uses this engine as well.

Visual Basic 4 and Visual Basic 5 come with two versions of the Jet engine and can work with databases of two major types. Version 2 databases are for use with 16-bit applications. Version 3 databases are for use with 32-bit applications. The features provided by both of these versions are similar so a developer rarely needs to worry about the difference. One place the differences are important, however, is in loading database files.

The Jet engines provide backward compatibility. That means the version 3 engine can read a data file written by a version 2 engine. The reverse is not true. A version 2 engine cannot read a version 3 database. If a version 2 engine attempts to load a version 3 database, it presents a message similar to the following: Run-time error '3049': Can't open database 'C:\People30.MDB'. It may not be a database, or the file may be corrupt.

The database files on the compact disk are all Jet version 2.5 databases so they can be opened by either 16-bit or 32-bit applications. The example programs should run on either platform.

Before an application can use data access objects to manipulate data, the application needs to give Visual Basic a reference to the object library it will use. The References command in the Tools menu makes the References dialog box appear. Checking the box next to Microsoft DAO 2.5 Object Library allows the application to use the 16-bit object library. Checking the box next to Microsoft DAO 3.0 Object Library allows the program to use the 32-bit version. The 16-bit version of Visual Basic 4 lists only the 16-bit object library because it cannot use the 32-bit version.

The Data Manager

The Visual Basic 4 Add-Ins menu comes with the Data Manager application already installed. Visual Basic 5 includes a Visual Data Manager add-in. Both of these programs can be used to create and manage databases. Their functions are similar, but their details differ so they are not described here. Both are fairly easy to use and both provide online help.

Just as there are multiple versions of the Jet database engine, there are multiple versions of the Data Manager. The Add-Ins menu in the 16-bit version of Visual Basic 4 starts the 16-bit version of the Data Manager. This version creates new databases using the Jet 2.5 engine, and it cannot open Jet version 3.0 databases. The Add-Ins menu in the 32-bit version of Visual Basic 4 starts the 32-bit version of the Data Manager. This version creates new databases using the Jet 3.0 engine. It can open both version 2.5 and version 3.0 databases.

Using the Data Control

Visual Basic provides two main methods for interacting with databases: the data control and data access objects (DAO). The data control allows a developer to build simple database applications with little or no programming. While the data control is simple, it is also fairly limited. Data access objects allow programs to manipulate the database in much more sophisticated ways, though they require more work on the developer's part.

The data control and DAO work closely together. Many programs, including PeopleWatcher, use a data control to manage basic interactions between text boxes and the database. They use data access objects to perform more complicated operations such as database navigation, record creation and deletion, and table management.

The following sections describe the data control. If you already have a sound understanding of the data control, and if you know how to select records by placing SQL statements in its RecordSource property, you may want to skim this section or skip directly to the section, "Using Data Access Objects."

The Data Control

Using a data control and other controls attached to it, an application can interact with a database using little or no Visual Basic code. Before describing the more advanced database operations performed by PeopleWatcher, this section explains how an application can use the data control to access data with a minimum of effort. The Simple.VBP project located in the Ch8\Simple directory on the compact disk demonstrates this minimalist approach.

A data control's DatabaseName property indicates the name of the file that contains the database the control should manipulate. Its RecordSource property indicates the way the control relates to the database. The RecordSource can be an SQL statement similar to the ones described later in this chapter, or it can be the name of a table.

In the Simple.VBP project, the data control PeopleData has DatabaseName property set to D:\Ch9\Simple\Simple.mdb. Before you can test the program Simple on your computer, you will need to change this value to reflect the location of the database on your system. The PeopleData control has RecordSource value People. Together these properties indicate that the control should gather data from the People table in the database file D:\Ch9\Simple\Simple.mdb.

Other controls in an application can be connected to a data control. A control's DataSource property indicates the name of the data control to which another control is connected. The control's DataField property indicates the field selected by the data control that should supply the data for the control. A control connected to a data control in this way is called a *data bound control*.

Project Simple contains two text boxes named LastNameText and FirstNameText. Both are bound to the data control PeopleData. The DataField property of LastNameText is set to LastName; this indicates that the text box should be filled with data from the LastName field in the data selected by the database control. Similarly, the DataField property of FirstNameText is set to FirstName, indicating it should be populated with values from the data control's FirstName field.

Project Simple is ready to run with no additional source code. Even though it does not include a single line of code, project Simple can perform several basic database chores. The data control's left and right arrow buttons move the control through the People table. The start-of-file and end-of-file buttons, the buttons with arrows pointing to lines, move the control to the first and last record in the table. As the data control moves through the table, the text boxes automatically display the values of the records' LastName and FirstName fields.

If the user enters text in one of the program's two text boxes, the data control automatically begins editing the corresponding database record. When the user moves to another record by clicking one of the movement buttons, the data control automatically updates the database. Figure 8.5 shows this simple program in action.

Binding Other Controls

Just as an application can bind text boxes to a data control, it can bind other types of controls. For example, an application can bind an image or picture box control to a database field that contains pictures. As is the case with text boxes, the control's DataSource property should be set to the name of the data control. Its DataField property should be set to the name of the data field that contains the appropriate images.

Different databases have different ways of storing large chunks of binary data such as pictures. These objects are often called *binary large objects* or *BLOBs*. Some databases provide a BLOB data type. Access databases do not, but their Long Binary data type can be used to store pictures. To make an image control display a picture, the application should set its DataField property to indicate a field that has the Long Binary data type. As the data control moves through the database, the image control will automatically display the pictures in the corresponding records.

A non-Access database may store pictures in a different way. For example, it might store pictures in fields of the BLOB data type. It is also possible that there is no easy way for the database to store a picture. In that case, it may be easiest to store the images in files on a hard disk and then keep only the names of the files in the database itself.

Selecting Records

In program Simple described in the previous section, the data control's DatabaseName property is set to the location of the People.MDB database file. Its RecordSource property is set to the name of the People database table. When the program runs, it uses these properties to create a list of records for the

FIGURE 8.5 A simple database program using the data control.

data control to manage. This list is called a *recordset*. In this simple example, the recordset includes all of the records in the People table, but there are other ways a program can define a data control's recordset.

One of the most flexible ways to define a recordset is by using an SQL statement. SQL stands for *Structured Query Language*, an industry-standard language for manipulating relational databases. The complete SQL language includes commands for creating and dropping tables from the database; adding, deleting, and updating records in the tables; composing complex queries; and performing many other data manipulation tasks. An SQL SELECT statement can be used to select the records that should be contained in a data control's recordset.

For example, in the Simple project the PeopleData control's RecordSource property could be set to the following SQL statement instead of the table named People.

```
SELECT * FROM People ORDER BY LastName
```

Then when the program runs, the data control's recordset includes all the records in the People table sorted by the LastName field. The records are ordered by LastName, but they are not ordered by First-Name. The names Ursula Jones, Harry Jones, and Xavier Jones appear in an undefined order—Harry does not necessarily come first. This can be easily fixed by adding the FirstName field to the SELECT statement's ORDER BY clause.

```
SELECT * FROM People ORDER BY LastName, FirstName
```

Now when the data control lists the records, Harry comes first, Ursula comes second, and Xavier comes last.

Another important clause that can be included in a SELECT statement is the WHERE clause. The WHERE clause allows a statement to specify criteria a record must meet to be included in the recordset. For example, the following SELECT statement would select only records that have the LastName field value Jones.

```
SELECT * FROM People WHERE LastName='Jones' ORDER BY LastName, FirstName
```

The following statement selects records that have LastName values that come alphabetically before Jones:

```
SELECT * FROM People WHERE LastName<'Jones' ORDER BY LastName, FirstName
```

In these statements the value Jones is surrounded by single quotation marks. An SQL statement can use either single or double quotation marks to delimit text values. Single quotes are a bit easier to handle in Visual Basic because SQL statements are usually stored in String variables. Single quotes are easier to embed in strings in Visual Basic code.

SQL statements are case insensitive. Even database table and field names can be in uppercase or lowercase. That means the previous SELECT statement is equivalent to the following:

```
Select * from people WhErE LASTname='Jones' order by lastNAME, FirstName
```

Statements are easier to read, however, if SQL keywords like SELECT are entered in all capital letters and if table and field names are capitalized as they are defined in the database.

You can search the Visual Basic help for "SELECT queries, defining" to find much more information.

Coding for the Data Control

By placing a SELECT statement in a data control's RecordSource property, an application can select a specific group of records. The application can display the list sorted in a useful order, and it can allow the user to edit records without including a single line of Visual Basic source code. With just a little code, an application can change a data control's RecordSource property and produce different recordsets at run time.

For example, an application could use a set of option buttons to allow the user to select one of several SQL statements. The first statement might order the records by last name while the second might order them by first name. The SQL statements could even be placed in each option button's Tag property so the option buttons' Click event handler would not need to know anything about the SQL statements involved. If it was necessary to change the statements, the changes would be made in the buttons' Tag properties. The following code shows how the option buttons' click event handler code could select the different SQL statements:

```
Private Sub SQLOption_Click(Index As Integer)
    PeopleData.RecordSource = SQLOption(Index).Tag
    PeopleData.Refresh
End Sub
```

With this little bit of code, an application can allow users to choose different data orderings or completely different select statements. With an additional text box and command button, an application can search for data values entered by the user. For example, if the user enters a value in the SearchText text box, the application could find the records with matching last names using the following code:

```
Private Sub CmdSearch_Click()
    PeopleData.RecordSource = _
        "SELECT * FROM People WHERE LastName='" & _
        SearchText.Text & "' ORDER BY LastName, FirstName"
    PeopleData.Refresh
End Sub
```

Using Data Access Objects

Earlier this chapter mentioned that data controls work closely with data access objects. This is made obvious by the fact that a data control's Recordset property is actually a reference to a Recordset data access object. An application can use the Recordset object to manipulate the records in a data control's recordset.

Recordset objects provide methods for moving through the recordset, examining the recordset's selected fields, and adding, updating, and deleting records. The data control attached to a recordset automatically updates any bound controls to reflect any actions taken by the Recordset object. You can search the Visual Basic online help for "recordsets" to obtain more information on Recordset objects and their methods.

The following sections describe the Recordset and other data access objects. If you already know how to create and manipulate data access objects, you may want to skim this section or skip directly to the section, "Accessing Records with the Outline Control."

Creating Recordsets

The Visual Basic Professional Edition allows applications to create Recordsets and other data access objects directly. This means an application can create Recordsets that are not attached to a data control. Unattached Recordsets are ideal for working with data that should not be displayed directly by bound controls.

For example, a program might need to perform some sort of statistical analysis on a large group of records. Displaying each of the records in rapid succession within bound text boxes would look strange to the user. Using an unattached Recordset object, the program can select the records and examine them internally before displaying only the summary results.

Before a program can create a Recordset object, it must give Visual Basic some contextual information by creating a couple of other data access objects. Data controls generate this information automatically; the program needs to follow these steps only if it is creating an unattached Recordset.

The data access object at the highest level of abstraction is DBEngine. The DBEngine object represents an instance of the Jet database engine, the software that runs the database. The main reason the program needs to use the DBEngine object is to access Workspaces.

A Workspace object defines a database session for a particular user. Different Workspaces can be attached to different databases, and they can perform different operations without interfering with each other.

Workspaces also manage user privileges and security if the database has security features enabled. Even though a Visual Basic program can manage user security using data access objects, it cannot actually create a secure database. A secure database must be created using Microsoft Access. Then a program can open it in Visual Basic.

The DBEngine contains a collection named Workspaces that contains references to Workspace objects. The entry Workspaces(0) is created by default. A program can use the DBEngine's CreateWorkspace method to create additional Workspace objects if they are needed.

A Workspace object's OpenDatabase method opens a particular database file and associates it with a Database object. The following code uses the default Workspace to open the file Employees.MDB. It saves the returned Database object instance for later use in the variable TheDB.

```
Dim TheDB As Database

    Set TheDB = DBEngine.Workspaces(0).OpenDatabase("Employees.MDB")
```

Once a program has opened a database, it can finally create a Recordset object. The following code uses the Database object's OpenRecordset method to create a Recordset that lists the names in the Employees table:

```
Dim TheRS As Recordset
Dim query As String

    query = "SELECT * FROM Employees ORDER BY LastName, FirstName"
    Set TheRS = TheDB.OpenRecordset(query, dbOpenDynaset)
```

The second parameter to the OpenRecordset method is a constant that determines the type of Recordset created. A Visual Basic application can create several different kinds of Recordset objects, as described in the next section. The sections after that explain how to use Recordset objects to manipulate data. They tell how a Recordset object can create, edit, copy, and delete records. The next section explains how a data control can validate changes made by a Recordset object. Finally, the last section before the discussion of PeopleWatcher begins describes the relationship between Recordset objects and bookmarks.

Types of Recordset Objects   The second parameter to the Database object's OpenRecordset method indicates the type of Recordset to open. This parameter can be dbOpenTable, dbDynaset, dbOpenDynamic, dbOpenSnapshot, and dbOpenForwardOnly.

The value dbOpenTable makes OpenRecordset create a table type Recordset. A table type Recordset represents a table in the database. Some operations, such as locating records using the Seek method, are allowed only on table type Recordsets.

The value dbOpenDynaset makes OpenRecordset create a dynaset type Recordset. Dynasets can select records using an SQL statement and can select fields from more than one database table. For example, the following statement selects employee names from the Employees table. It also selects each employee's salary from the Salaries table. This query uses the EmployeeID fields in the two tables to decide which salary value goes with each employee name.

```
SELECT LastName, FirstName, Salary FROM Employees, Salaries _
    WHERE Employees.EmployeeID = Salaries.EmployeeID
```

The value dbOpenDynamic creates a Recordset similar to a dynaset. Any changes made to the data by other users will be reflected in the dynamic Recordset.

The value dbOpenSnapshot makes the OpenRecordset method create a snapshot-type Recordset. Snapshots contain a copy of the data as it existed when the snapshot was created. If another database user adds, deletes, or modifies a record, the snapshot will not know about the change unless it is recreated. Snapshots can select records using an SQL statement much as a dynaset can.

The value dbOpenForwardOnly creates a Recordset similar to a snapshot, but the program can only move forward through the records, thereby providing faster performance than a snapshot.

Table Recordsets are generally the fastest. Dynasets are somewhat slower but give much more flexibility. Snapshots provide a balance between the two. They can select records using SQL statements, but they do not allow records to be updated. Because they are generally faster than dynasets, however, they are a better choice if the program will not need to update the records selected.

Manipulating Data with Recordsets   After an application creates a Recordset, the Recordset is considered to point at a "current" record. Recordset methods allow a program to manipulate the current record. For example, the Recordset's Delete method deletes the current record from the database.

Visual Basic code can use an exclamation mark (!) to access the value of a particular field within a Recordset's current record. For example, rs!LastName refers to the value of the LastName field in the rs Recordset's current record.

A program can also retrieve a field's value from a Recordset's Fields collection by specifying the field's name as the index for the collection. Using this method, the LastName field in the rs Recordset's current record is rs.Fields("LastName"). This method is particularly useful for programs that do not know which fields will be accessed until run time.

Other Recordset methods allow a program to make other records become the current record. The MoveNext and MovePrevious methods move the current record to the next or previous record, respectively. The MoveFirst and MoveLast methods move the current record to the first or last record in the Recordset.

A Recordset's BOF (beginning of file) property is true if the Recordset is positioned *before* the first record in the recordset. Similarly, the EOF (end of file) property is true if the Recordset is positioned *after* the last record. The following code uses the MoveNext method and the EOF property to build a text string listing all of the names in the Employees table:

```
Dim db As Database
Dim rs As Recordset
Dim query As String
Dim txt As String

    ' Open the database.
    Set db = DBEngine.Workspaces(0).OpenDatabase("Employees.MDB")

    ' Create the Recordset.
    query = "SELECT LastName, FirstName FROM Employees " & _
        "ORDER BY LastName, FirstName"
    Set rs = db.OpenRecordset(query, dbOpenSnapshot)

    ' Build the list of names.
    txt = ""
    Do Until TheRS.EOF
        txt = txt & rs!LastName & ", " & rs!FirstName & vbCrLf
        TheRS.MoveNext
    Loop
```

Checking the BOF and EOF properties is important whenever a program manipulates data using a Recordset. Many of the Recordset methods fail if there is no current record. For example, if EOF is true (the program is beyond the last record) and the program executes the MoveNext command, Visual Basic generates run time error 3021: No current record. The program will also receive this error if it invokes the Delete method when there is no current record.

Creating Records A program can create a new record by invoking a Recordset object's AddNew method. This method creates a memory buffer to contain the new record. If the Recordset is associated with a data control, any fields bound to the control are cleared so the user can enter data for the new record.

The program can provide Accept and Cancel buttons to allow the user to accept the data and create a new record or to cancel the operation and not create a new record. If the user clicks the Accept button, the program should invoke the Recordset's Update method to create the new record. If the user clicks the Cancel button, it should invoke the CancelUpdate method.

Editing Records If the user begins typing in a bound control, the attached data control automatically begins editing its current data record. An application can initiate editing programmatically by calling the Recordset object's Edit method.

As is the case when creating a new record, the program should allow the user to accept or cancel changes to the data. If the user clicks the Accept button, the program should invoke the Recordset's Update method to update the database. If the user clicks the Cancel button, it should invoke the CancelUpdate method to leave the database unchanged.

Copying Records The Recordset object does not directly provide a method for copying records. To give users this capability, a program should first save the data values for the record to be copied into variables. It could save the values in a collection. Next it should use the Recordset's AddNew method to allocate memory for a new record. It should then copy the saved values into the new record's fields. The easiest way to do that is to copy the saved values into bound controls. The program can then allow the user to edit the copied data before accepting or canceling the changes.

Deleting Records To delete a record, a program can use the Recordset's Delete method. The Delete method immediately removes the Recordset's current record permanently from the database.

When creating a new record or editing an existing one, the program can allow the user to accept or cancel the operation. Similarly, it should give the user a chance to cancel a delete operation. Because the Delete method takes effect immediately and is irreversible, the program should first ask the user to confirm that it should delete the record. It can do this using a message box, as shown in the following code:

```
Private Sub mnuEditDelete_Click()
    If MsgBox("Are you sure you want to delete this record?", _
        vbYesNo, "Delete Record?") = vbYes _
    Then
        ' Delete the record.
        rs.Delete
    End If
End Sub
```

Validation A data control receives a Validate event just before a new record becomes the current record. It also receives the Validate event before the Update, Delete, Close, or Unload operations. In all of these cases, changes to the data may be pending. The program's Validate event handler can take actions to verify the correctness of the data and either save or discard the changes.

The event handler's Action and Save parameters can help the program determine what sort of event is in progress. The Action parameter indicates the action that is about to occur—update, delete, and so forth. The event handler can set Action to the value vbDataActionCancel to cancel the action.

The Save parameter initially indicates whether bound data has changed. The program can set Save to false if it wants to continue the action but not save the changes.

The event handler can also validate the data entered by the user and decide whether to allow the operation that caused the event. For example, suppose the Action parameter initially has the value vbDataActionUpdate, indicating that changes to the current record are about to be saved. The program could examine the data to make sure the data values make sense. It could check that data values entered in date fields have valid date formats, that numeric values lie within certain ranges, and so forth. If the values do not pass validation, the subroutine can present an error message asking the user to fix the problems. It can then set the Action parameter to vbDataActionCancel to indicate that the update should not take place. The user can click the program's Accept button again after fixing the problems in the data.

For another example, suppose the user begins editing a record and then invokes the Close command in the application's control box. The program needs to know whether to save the changes to the data before it exits. Before the data control's form unloads, Visual Basic invokes its Validate event handler. This routine can ask the user if the pending changes should be saved before quitting. If the user wants to save the changes, the program should set the Save parameter to true. If the user wants to discard the changes, the program should set Save to false. If the user decides to cancel the operation and not unload the form, the program should set Action to vbDataActionCancel. In that case, the form's unload operation will not occur, and the user can resume modifying the record.

Bookmarks   Each record in a recordset has an associated *bookmark*. A bookmark is a set of bytes that uniquely identifies that record in that particular recordset. If a program saves a record's bookmark in a string, it can later quickly return to that record by setting the recordset's Bookmark property to the string's value. The following code fragment shows how a program could use a bookmark to return to a record quickly after performing other operations on a recordset.

```
Dim rs As Recordset
Dim bm As String            ' The bookmark.

    ' Initialize the recordset, etc.
    :
    ' Save the bookmark.
    bm = rs.Bookmark

    ' Perform other operations with the recordset.
    :
    ' Return to the original record.
    rs.Bookmark = bm
```

Bookmarks are not shared among recordsets. Even though two recordsets may contain the exact same records, bookmarks from one are not usable in the other.

Understanding PeopleWatcher

As has already been mentioned, PeopleWatcher is a personnel file application. Using a data control and bound text boxes, one could build a simple version of this program, but it would have several problems. The program would use a data control that selected data from an Employee table containing fields for the employees' last names, first names, Social Security numbers, salaries, and so forth. Data bound controls would display the record information. Without including a line of Visual Basic source code, this program could display and update personnel records. Unfortunately, this simplified personnel system has several problems.

First, locating records would be difficult. The user would need to start at the beginning of the data control's recordset and step through the records one at a time until reaching the correct record. If the database contains only a dozen or so employee records, this is not a big problem. If the personnel file contains records for hundreds or thousands of employees, however, this would be impractical. The program needs a search facility or some other mechanism to make locating specific records easier.

This program would also be usable by only a few people in the company. Because the Employee table contains sensitive information, such as employee Social Security numbers and salaries, only a few users would be able to use the system without violating employee privacy.

The following sections explain how the PeopleWatcher program solves these problems. They also describe in detail how PeopleWatcher implements standard database operations such as creating, modifying, and deleting records.

Managing the Outline Control

PeopleWatcher uses an outline control to provide a list of employee names grouped by their last initials. To locate the record for Michelle Stephens, the user scrolls through the list to find the entry for the initial S. Clicking on the plus sign next to the letter S then opens the entry to display a list of names with that initial. Unless the database is extremely large, finding a particular entry in the list is easy.

Figure 8.6 shows PeopleWatcher displaying the record for employee Michelle Stephens. The outline control is on the left of the screen with the entry for this record highlighted.

The LoadNameOutline subroutine that follows uses Recordset methods to fill the NameOutline control with a list of employee names grouped by last initial. Initially the Recordset variable TheRS is attached to the data control EmployeeData. To prevent the data control from updating bound text boxes as the routine examines each record in the Recordset, LoadNameOutline begins by setting Employee-Data.Recordset to Nothing.

After it has finished building the list of employee names, the subroutine moves the Recordset object back to its first record and sets the EmployeeData.Recordset property back to TheRS. This restores the link between the Recordset and the data control. It also makes the data control immediately update the text boxes and other bound controls to display the data for the Recordset's first record.

```
Sub LoadNameOutline()
Dim query As String
Dim i As Integer
Dim j As Integer
Dim last_name As String
Dim first_name As String
Dim letter As Integer
Dim new_letter As Integer
```

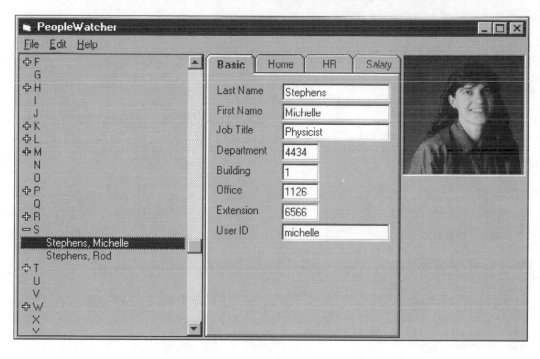

FIGURE 8.6 PeopleWatcher displaying the record for Michelle Stephens.

```
' Start with an empty list.
NameOutline.Clear

' Disconnnect the Data control.
Set EmployeeData.Recordset = Nothing

' Get the employee names.
On Error GoTo LoadNameError
query = "SELECT * FROM Employees " & _
    "ORDER BY LastName, FirstName"
Set TheRS = TheDB.OpenRecordset(query, dbOpenDynaset)

' Load the names.
letter = Asc("A") - 1
i = 0
Do Until TheRS.EOF
    last_name = TheRS!LastName
    first_name = TheRS!FirstName
    new_letter = Asc(UCase$(Left$(last_name, 1)))
    If new_letter <> letter Then
        ' Add letters.
        For j = letter + 1 To new_letter
            NameOutline.AddItem Chr$(j)
            NameOutline.Indent(i) = 1
```

```
                i = i + 1
        Next j
        letter = new_letter
    End If

      ' Add the name.
    NameOutline.AddItem last_name & ", " & first_name
    NameOutline.Indent(i) = 2
    Bookmarks.Add CStr(TheRS.Bookmark)
    NameOutline.ItemData(i) = Bookmarks.Count
    i = i + 1

    TheRS.MoveNext
Loop

  ' Add remaining letters.
For j = letter + 1 To Asc("Z")
    NameOutline.AddItem Chr$(j)
    NameOutline.Indent(i) = 1
    i = i + 1
Next j

  ' Reconnnect the Data control. This generates
  ' a Reposition event.
TheRS.MoveFirst
Set EmployeeData.Recordset = TheRS

Exit Sub

LoadNameError:
    Beep
    MsgBox "Error" & str$(Err.Number) & _
        " reading employee names." & vbCrLf & _
        vbCrLf & Err.Description, _
        vbOKOnly + vbInformation, _
        "Error Reading Names"
    Exit Sub
End Sub
```

The variable Bookmarks is a global collection. When LoadNameOutline creates an entry for an employee record in the outline control, it saves the record's bookmark as a string in the Bookmarks collection. It also stores the index of the bookmark in the collection using the corresponding ItemData property in the outline control. For example, if the 10th entry in the NameOutline control corresponds to a database record and not a last name initial, then NameOutline(10).ItemData is the index of the record's bookmark in the Bookmarks collection.

Later, when the user clicks on an entry in the outline control's list, the program uses the following code to find the item's bookmark and quickly reload the corresponding record. The code uses the outline control's Indent property to decide if the selected entry is an employee name rather than an initial. Employee names are indented two levels in the outline control's display.

```
Private Sub NameOutline_Click()
Dim i As Integer
Dim bm As Integer

    i = NameOutline.ListIndex
    If NameOutline.Indent(i) = 2 Then
        bm = NameOutline.ItemData(i)
        TheRS.Bookmark = Bookmarks.Item(bm)
    End If
End Sub
```

When the user selects a record using the outline control, the NameOutline_Click subroutine updates the data control so it displays the selected record. There are also occasions when the data control moves to a new record of its own accord. For example, if the user deletes the current record, the data control moves to a new record. In cases such as this, the program must update the outline control so that it shows the correct record as selected. It does this in the data control's Reposition event handler. If the data control has a current record, the event handler calls subroutine SelectName to highlight the corresponding name in the outline control.

```
Private Sub EmployeeData_Reposition()
    If TheRS.EOF Then
        ' Select no name.
        NameOutline.ListIndex = -1
    Else
        ' Select this name in the list.
        SelectName
    End If
End Sub
```

SelectName searches through the outline's list until it finds an item with a bookmark that matches the bookmark of the current record. It then selects that item in the list.

```
Private Sub SelectName()
Dim mark As String
Dim i As Integer
Dim bm As Integer
Dim level As Integer
Dim parent As Integer

    ' If there is no record selected, do nothing.
    If TheRS.EOF Then Exit Sub

    ' Find the outline entry.
    mark = TheRS.Bookmark
    For i = 0 To NameOutline.ListCount - 1
        level = NameOutline.Indent(i)
        If level = 1 Then
            parent = i
        Else
            bm = NameOutline.ItemData(i)
            If mark = Bookmarks.Item(bm) Then
```

```
                       ' Expand the parent.
                   NameOutline.Expand(parent) = True
                       ' Select this name.
                   NameOutline.ListIndex = i
                   Exit For
               End If
           End If
       Next i
End Sub
```

Displaying Appropriate Commands

An application should allow the user to invoke only the commands that make sense at any given time. For example, when editing a database record, the program should not allow the user to delete a different record. If the program provides too many unrelated commands, the user may become confused or forget that an edit operation is in progress.

The data control attempts to avoid these issues by automatically saving changes whenever the user moves to a new record. For example, if the user clicks the data control's next record button (right arrow), the control automatically saves any pending changes. Similarly, if the user closes the application, the data control automatically saves any changes.

This strategy is a *what-you-see-is-what-you-get* (WYSIWYG, pronounced *wizzy-wig*) interface. When the user makes a change to the data, that change is reflected in the database as far as the user is concerned.

Unfortunately, this approach causes a few problems. First, the data control does not really update the database when the user modifies the data, but only later when the user moves to a new record. This what-you-see-is-*almost*-what-you-get interface can cause some very subtle problems if several users access the database at the same time. For example, suppose one user opens a records and makes some changes. If another user opens the same record, the changes will not be visible because the first user has not yet moved to a new record and the changes have not yet been saved to the database.

The data control's default behavior also uses a poor user interface style. Ideally, an application will allow the user to undo changes made to the application's data. Failing that, the program should at least give the user the chance to confirm or cancel major changes that cannot be undone. By default, the data control saves changes with no chance to confirm or cancel, and it does not allow the changes to be undone.

PeopleWatcher requires the user to explicitly accept or cancel any changes to the database. When the user edits a record, PeopleWatcher uses the SetControlsEditing subroutine to enable only the commands appropriate for editing and to hide the others. The EndEditing subroutine does the opposite. It is so similar to SetControlsEditing that it is not presented here. By allowing only the commands that are appropriate at a given moment, PeopleWatcher helps the user stay focused on the task of editing a record.

```
Sub SetControlsEditing()
    mnuFileLogon.Enabled = False
    mnuFileChangePassword.Enabled = False
    mnuFileExit.Enabled = False
    mnuEditRefresh.Enabled = False
```

```
        mnuEditNew.Enabled = False
        mnuEditEdit.Enabled = False
        mnuEditCopy.Enabled = False
        mnuEditDelete.Enabled = False
        NameOutline.Enabled = False
        EmployeeData.Enabled = False
        mnuEditAccept.Enabled = True
        mnuEditCancel.Enabled = True
End Sub
```

Editing Records

To edit PeopleWatcher's current record, the user can begin typing in any of the data bound controls. The program detects the change and calls subroutine BeginEditing. For example, the FirstNameText control's Change event is invoked when the user changes the data in the first name field. Visual Basic sets the text control's DataChanged property to true if the value of the bound control has been modified other than by retrieving a new record. In particular, DataChanged will be true if the user has changed the data.

```
Private Sub FirstNameText_Change()
    If FirstNameText.DataChanged Then BeginEditing
End Sub
```

Subroutine BeginEditing first checks to see if the application is already editing the record. If not, it uses the Recordset's Edit method to prepare the database for changes to the data. It then uses the SetControlsEditing subroutine described in the previous section to enable the commands that are appropriate for editing. No other work is necessary until the user decides to accept or cancel the changes.

```
Sub BeginEditing()
    If Editing Then Exit Sub
    Editing = True
    EditStatus = EDIT_STATUS_UNKNOWN

    ' Start editing (if we are not adding a new
    ' record).
    If TheRS.EditMode = dbEditNone Then TheRS.Edit

    ' Set the controls for editing.
    SetControlsEditing
End Sub
```

Editing Images

Normally the user modifies a record's data using a bound control such as a text box. However, the user cannot enter data into an image control. PeopleWatcher must provide some method for changing the picture contained in each employee's record.

If the user double-clicks on PeopleWatcher's employee image control, the program begins the process of selecting a new employee picture. First it checks that the user has permission to modify employee pictures. If the user does not, the program ignores the double-click. Privileges are described in a later section.

Next the program presents a file selection dialog. The user can use the dialog to select an image file. The program loads the file into the employee image control.

Because the program, rather than the user, makes the change to the image control, the program does not automatically detect this change. The data bound image control does not have a Changed event so the program does not automatically enter editing mode. The program explicitly begins editing the record by calling the BeginEditing subroutine.

```
Private Sub EmployeeImage_DblClick()
Dim status As Boolean

    ' If the user does not have the UPDATE_BASIC
    ' privilege, do nothing.
    If Not TheUser.HasPrivilege("UPDATE_BASIC") _
        Then Exit Sub

    ' Prepare the file common dialog.
    FileDialog.Flags = cdlOFNFileMustExist + _
        cdlOFNHideReadOnly + cdlOFNExplorer + _
        cdlOFNLongNames
    FileDialog.DialogTitle = "Select Employee Picture"
    FileDialog.filename = "*.bmp"
    FileDialog.CancelError = True

    ' Present the dialog.
    On Error Resume Next
    FileDialog.ShowOpen

    ' If the user canceled, we're done.
    If Err.Number = cdlCancel Then Exit Sub

    ' If there is some other error, say so.
    If Err.Number > 0 Then
        Beep
        MsgBox "Error" & str$(Err.Number) & _
            " reading file name. " & vbCrLf & _
            Err.Description, _
            vbOKOnly + vbExclamation, "Error"
        Exit Sub
    End If

    ' Save the directory for next time.
    FileDialog.InitDir = _
        Left$(FileDialog.filename, _
            Len(FileDialog.filename) - _
            Len(FileDialog.FileTitle))

    ' Load the image file.
    EmployeeImage.Picture = _
        LoadPicture(FileDialog.filename)
    If Err.Number > 0 Then
```

```
        Beep
        MsgBox "Error" & str$(Err.Number) & _
            " loading image. " & vbCrLf & _
            Err.Description, _
            vbOKOnly | vbExclamation, "Load Error"
        Exit Sub
    End If

    ' If we succeeded, enter editing mode.
    BeginEditing
End Sub
```

Accepting and Canceling Changes

Normally the user will edit a new or existing record and then select either the Cancel Changes or Accept Changes command from the Edit menu.

The Cancel Changes command sets the global variable EditStatus to EDIT_STATUS_CANCEL. This value allows the data control's Validate event handler to know that the user wants to cancel the changes. The Cancel Changes command then calls the Recordset's CancelUpdate method to cancel the changes to the data. Finally, it calls EndEditing to enable the commands that are appropriate when the user is not editing data.

```
Private Sub mnuEditCancel_Click()
    EditStatus = EDIT_STATUS_CANCEL

    ' Cancel the changes.
    TheRS.CancelUpdate

    EndEditing
End Sub
```

The Accept Changes command begins by setting EditStatus to EDIT_STATUS_ACCEPT so that the data control's Validate event handler knows the user is accepting the changes. It then uses the Record set's Update method to save the changes to the database.

```
Private Sub mnuEditAccept_Click()
    EditStatus = EDIT_STATUS_ACCEPT

    ' Save the changes.
    TheRS.Update

    ' EndEditing is called during validation.
End Sub
```

Validating Data

The data control's Validate event occurs when the user attempts to accept or cancel changes to the data. It also occurs under certain other circumstances such as when the program's main form is about to unload. While a program can disable the Exit command in its File menu, it cannot be certain the user will finish editing before stopping the application. The user might close the program in some other way, such as using the Close command in the form's control box. The user may even shut down the operating system.

In these cases, an editing operation may be in progress. Because the user has neither accepted nor canceled the changes to the data, the program cannot know whether to save or discard the changes. The EmployeeData_Validate event handler ensures that the data is safe before it allows the program to exit.

First it checks the global variable Editing to see if the user is editing a record. If not, there are no pending changes to save so the subroutine simply exits.

Otherwise, the subroutine checks the value of EditStatus. This variable is set to EDIT_STATUS_CANCEL by the Edit menu's Cancel Changes command. If EditStatus has this value, the Validate event handler sets Save to false to tell the data control that it should discard changes to the data.

EditStatus is set to the value EDIT_STATUS_ACCEPT by the Edit menu's Accept Changes command. If EditStatus has this value, the Validate event handler sets Save to true so the data control will save the changed data values to the database.

If EditStatus has neither of these values, the edit is about to end without the user's invoking either the Cancel Changes or the Accept Changes commands. The user is probably closing the application in the middle of an edit. In this case, the program asks the user whether it should save the changes.

Finally, if the program needs to save the changes, it calls function ValidForm to validate the data. ValidForm determines whether the form's field values are valid. For example, it checks that any date fields have valid date formats. If the data values are invalid, EmployeeData_Validate sets the Action variable to vbDataActionCancel. This will make the data control cancel whatever action was about to occur. If the program was about to exit, the data control will prevent it from exiting so the user has a chance to correct the data.

```
Private Sub EmployeeData_Validate(Action As Integer, Save As Integer)
    ' If we're not editing, do nothing.
    If Not Editing Then Exit Sub

    If EditStatus = EDIT_STATUS_CANCEL Then
        ' The user pressed Cancel.
        Save = False
    ElseIf EditStatus = EDIT_STATUS_ACCEPT Then
        ' The user pressed Accept.
        Save = True
    Else
        ' Ask the user what to do.
        Save = (MsgBox("You have modified this record. Do you want to save the changes?", _
            vbYesNo, "Save Changes?") = vbYes)
    End If

    ' If the user wants to save, validate the form.
    If Save Then
        ' If the form is invalid, cancel the
        ' operation until the user fixes the data.
        If Not ValidForm() Then
            Action = vbDataActionCancel
```

```
            EditStatus = EDIT_STATUS_UNKNOWN
            Save = False
        Else
            EndEditing
        End If
    Else
        EndEditing
    End If
End Sub
```

Customizing the Interface for Users

Because the Employee table contains sensitive data, only a few people can look at all the data fields without violating employee privacy. For example, the program cannot allow every employee to read the Social Security number and salary of other employees.

An application is more widely usable if it can identify the kinds of access different groups of users require and then customize itself for each group of users. For example, depending on the company's policies, secretaries might be allowed to read personal information, such as home phone number and address, but be unable to access financial information. Managers might be allowed to view both personal and financial information.

PeopleWatcher divides employee data into four categories: Basic, Home, HR, and Salary. The first section in this chapter, "Using PeopleWatcher," describes these categories in detail.

Dividing information into categories such as these makes it easy to determine how groups of users interact with the data. Usually the data items in a particular category also share a common theme that is reflected by the name of the category. For example, information in the Home category involves the employee's home life. It includes home address, phone number, and birth date. It could also include similar information, such as the names of other members of the employee's family, the work location and phone number of the employee's spouse, and so forth.

Because these data fields share a common theme, they belong together in the user interface. The program can place the items for each data category inside some sort of container control to provide visual grouping. For example, it could place all of the home data items inside a frame control with the caption "Home." If the program should not separate the data so clearly from the other fields, the items can be placed inside a picture box control. The picture box's border can be removed if the grouping should be even less obvious to the user.

PeopleWatcher uses a separate tab in an SSTab control for each data category. This not only groups the data, but it also saves space on the screen. Figure 8.7 shows the running PeopleWatcher application. In this picture the tab containing the basic information is selected.

Placing related fields in container controls does more than create a visual separation for the data. It also allows the program to easily customize its user interface for users with different privileges. For example, if the user should not be able to see the salary data, the application can set the Visible property for the container of the salary data fields to false.

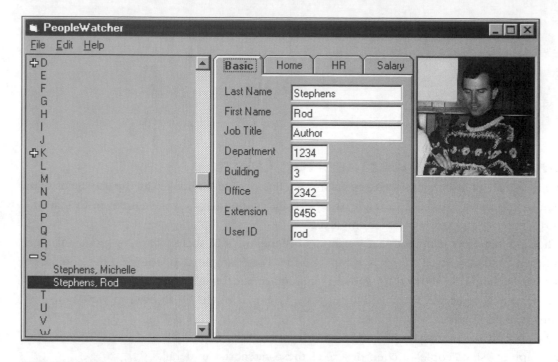

FIGURE 8.7 PeopleWatcher places data in separate tabs in an SSTab control.

Unfortunately for PeopleWatcher, a program cannot easily hide and display the tabs on an SSTab control. A tab control's Visible property applies to the entire control, not to the individual tabs it contains.

To work around this problem, PeopleWatcher does not place the data controls within the tab itself. Instead, it places them in picture boxes with no borders. It then positions these picture boxes on top of the tab control so it looks as if the picture boxes are within the tabs. When the user clicks on one of the tabs, the program sets the Visible property of the previously displayed picture box to false. It then sets Visible to true for the newly selected picture box and uses the ZOrder method to ensure that the picture box is displayed on top of any other controls. This makes it appear as if the appropriate controls are contained within the selected tab.

```
Public Sub InfoTab_Click(PreviousTab As Integer)
    TabPicture(PreviousTab).Visible = False
    TabPicture(InfoTab.Tab).Visible = True
    TabPicture(InfoTab.Tab).ZOrder
End Sub
```

Setting Field Editability Making fields visible or invisible solves half of the user configuration problem. Users can also have read-only or update privilege for each set of data fields. For instance, members of the Secretary group should be able to view Basic, Home, and HR information but update only the Basic information. The application must prevent a Secretary user from modifying Home and HR data fields.

The application can prevent a user from modifying a text box by setting the control's Locked property to true. Preventing modification of other types of controls is not as simple. Combo boxes do not have a Locked property. To prevent the user from modifying a combo box, the program should set the control's Editable property to false. This, unfortunately, makes the control appear grayed, but it does protect the field's value.

When a program makes a field noneditable, it should also change the field's background color so that it matches the background color of labels and other noneditable controls. This gives the user a visual indication that the field is not editable.

To make these operations easier, PeopleWatcher initializes two arrays of collections containing the text boxes and combo boxes used by each data group. For instance, TextBoxes(0) is a collection that lists the text boxes contained in the first picture box—those that display Basic information.

The SaveEditableControls subroutine initializes these collections for later use. It examines every control on the form and checks to see if it is contained in one of the four picture boxes. If it is, the control is saved in the appropriate collection. Subroutine SetEditable uses these collections to properly set the editability and background color of the text boxes and combo boxes for a data group.

```
Sub SaveEditableControls()
Dim ctl As Control
Dim i As Integer

    For Each ctl In Controls
        If TypeOf ctl Is TextBox Then
            For i = 0 To 3
                If ctl.Container Is TabPicture(i) Then
                    TextBoxes(i).Add ctl
                    Exit For
                End If
            Next i
        End If
        If TypeOf ctl Is ComboBox Then
            For i = 0 To 3
                If ctl.Container Is TabPicture(i) Then
                    ComboBoxes(i).Add ctl
                    Exit For
                End If
            Next i
        End If
    Next ctl
End Sub


Sub SetEditable(Index As Integer, editable As Boolean)
Dim ctl As Control
Dim color As Long
```

```
    If editable Then
        color = EmployeeData.BackColor
    Else
        color = Label1(0).BackColor
    End If

    For Each ctl In TextBoxes(Index)
        ctl.Locked = Not editable
        ctl.BackColor = color
    Next ctl
    For Each ctl In ComboBoxes(Index)
        ctl.Enabled = editable
        ctl.BackColor = color
    Next ctl
End Sub
```

Privilege Tables Using the methods described in the previous sections, an application can tailor its user interface for a user with a given set of privileges. The program still needs a way to determine the privileges that belong to each group and the groups to which each user belongs.

Most types of databases include security features that can help an application control user access to data. The Jet database engine, for example, supports security features that can allow or deny access to specific tables for each user. Some databases even allow control of user access to specific fields within a table.

Unfortunately, these features are difficult to use in Visual Basic for several reasons. First, different databases handle security differently. Without committing to a particular database engine, a program cannot take full advantage of its security features.

Second, Visual Basic cannot create a secure Access database. If a secure database is created using Microsoft Access, a Visual Basic program can access it and use its security features. The fact that Visual Basic cannot originally create the database makes securing Visual Basic's "native" database format a bit more difficult.

Finally, some user privilege issues deal more with the user interface than with data access. For example, a program might want to allow a user to view or modify data in a table but only using a certain program and not any other. A secretary might have access to a department budget program that could calculate the total of the salaries of a department's employees. At the same time, the secretary might not be allowed to use another program that listed each employee's salary individually. Databases do not provide this type of security.

PeopleWatcher uses two database tables to manage user privileges. The UserGroups table contains entries that determine the groups to which each user belongs. Each record contains a user ID and a group name. For example, the user "harry" belongs to the group "HR" so the table contains a record with UserID = harry and Group = HR.

The second table is called GroupPrivileges. This table contains pairs of group names and privilege names. For example, the HR group should be able to read Basic information so the table contains a record with Group = HR and Privilege = READ_BASIC. The HR group should also have permission to read Home, HR, and Salary information, so the table also contains entries for Group = HR with Privilege values READ_HOME, READ_HR, and READ_SALARY. In addition, the GroupPrivileges table includes records defining the corresponding update privileges, UPDATE_BASIC and so forth.

GroupPrivileges includes records with two special privileges: CREATE_RECORDS and DELETE_RECORDS. These allow users in the appropriate groups to create and delete records in the Employee table. Table 8.3 shows the privileges granted to each group in PeopleWatcher's GroupPrivileges table.

User Passwords To use the UserGroups and GroupPrivileges tables, PeopleWatcher needs to know which user is running the program. Then the program can use the UserGroups table to see to which groups the user belongs. Knowing the user's groups, it can use the GroupPrivileges table to see what privileges are granted to those groups.

Of course, the application cannot simply ask the users who they are. If the program could trust the users completely, it would not need to worry about privacy in the first place. The next best thing is to ask the user for a user name and a password.

In a fairly trusting environment, one might think user names and passwords could be stored in a database table. Unfortunately, that would mean anyone who could read the table would be able to read all the passwords. At first glance, this might not seem too horrible. After all, anyone who can read the password table can probably also read the Employee table and thus the private employee information, with or without the passwords.

Unfortunately, despite countless instructions to the contrary, many users pick the same password for several different computer systems. Someone who captured passwords from your table could try them on other corporate database systems. Chances are good that many of the user names and passwords would work on another system. Even if one application does not require the tightest security in the world, it must guard its passwords to protect the other systems in its environment.

PeopleWatcher protects its passwords using a method that is common in UNIX systems. When the user selects a password, the user's name and an encrypted version of the password are stored in the Passwords table.

TABLE 8.3 Privileges Granted in the GroupPrivileges Table

Group	Privileges
General	READ_BASIC
Secretary	READ_BASIC, READ_HOME, READ_HR, UPDATE_HOME
Manager	READ_BASIC, READ_HOME, READ_HR, READ_SALARY
HR	READ_BASIC, READ_HOME, READ_HR, READ_SALARY UPDATE_BASIC, UPDATE_HOME, UPDATE_HR, UPDATE_SALARY CREATE_RECORDS, DELETE_RECORDS

Later, when the program needs to verify a user's identify, the user reenters the user name and password. The application encrypts the newly entered password and compares it to the encrypted version stored in the database. If the two match, the user name and password are valid. Notice that the actual unencrypted password is never stored in the database or anywhere else in the system. This makes it harder for attackers to pull passwords out of the system.

The encryption system used by PeopleWatcher uses a series of hard-to-invert operations to grind the user name and password into an eight-byte output string. The process also incorporates an eight-byte randomly chosen "salt" value. The randomly chosen value means that a particular user name and password will encrypt to different values depending on the salt values chosen. For example, if the program encrypts the user name "rod" with the password "H#sg1_?6" and then it encrypts the same user name and password again with a different salt, it will get different results. This makes it very difficult for an attacker to precompute a large dictionary of encrypted user name and password pairs.

Passwords and password validation are described further in the next section.

The DBUser Class

To make working with privileges and passwords easier, PeopleWatcher uses a DBUser class. A DBUser object represents a database user with a verified user name and password.

When an application first creates a DBUser object, it should invoke the object's Initialize method to tell the object what database contains the password and privilege information. The DBUser object will search this database when it needs to validate passwords.

```
Dim TheDB As Database
Dim TheUser As DBUser
    :
    ' Open the database.
    :
    ' Tell the DBUser object about the database.
    TheUser.Initialize TheDB
```

The following sections describe the public routines provided by the DBUser class for working with privileges and passwords. Only the most important points are explained here. You can see the complete code for the DBUser class on the compact disk.

GetPrivileges and HasPrivilege The GetPrivileges subroutine examines the database to see what privileges belong to the groups to which this user belongs. The heart of the routine is the following database query:

```
query = "SELECT DISTINCT privilege " & _
        "FROM GroupPrivileges, UserGroups " & _
        "WHERE userid = '" & UserID & "' AND " & _
        "GroupPrivileges.group = UserGroups.group"
```

The subroutine adds the selected privileges to the DBUser object's Privileges collection using the following command:

```
Privileges.Add 1, Trim$(rs!Privilege)
```

This statement adds the value 1 to the Privileges collection. It uses the value of the Privilege fields returned by the query as the value's key.

The HasPrivilege property procedure searches the collection for a specific key to decide whether the user has a particular privilege.

```
Property Get HasPrivilege(priv As String) As Boolean
    On Error GoTo PrivError
    HasPrivilege = (Privileges.Item(priv) = 1)
    Exit Property

PrivError:
    HasPrivilege = False
    Exit Property
End Property
```

The PeopleWatcher application uses code similar to the following to change its user interface depending on the privileges granted to the user. You can examine the complete configuration code in the ConfigureForUser subroutine on the compact disk.

```
If TheUser.HasPrivilege("READ_BASIC") Then
    ' Do stuff for users with this privilege.
    :
End If
```

PeopleWatcher protects most fields from unauthorized users by hiding them, by setting their Editable properties to false, or by setting their Locked properties to true. These methods do not work for the EmployeeImage control. Image controls do not have Editable or Locked properties. Setting this control's Enabled property to false does not prevent the user from generating double-click events and starting the picture selection process.

To keep unauthorized users from changing an employee's picture, EmployeeImage's double-click event handler uses the following code to see if the user has the UPDATE_BASIC privilege. If not, the subroutine exits silently.

```
If Not TheUser.HasPrivilege("UPDATE_BASIC") Then Exit Sub
```

GetUserID The GetUserID subroutine prompts the user for a user name and password. It then uses the ValidPassword function to encrypt the password and decide if the combination is valid. If it is, GetUserID sets the DBUser object's public UserID variable so the application can read the newly entered user ID. If the user name and password combination is invalid, the DBUser object leaves the previous UserID value unchanged.

The ValidPassword function takes as parameters the user's ID and password. It begins by using an SQL statement to fetch the user's salt values and the correctly encrypted password from the database. The salt values are stored in the database fields salt1 through salt8. The correctly encrypted password is stored in the fields hash1 through hash8.

Next ValidPassword calls subroutine Encipher to encrypt the entered user name and password using the salt values from the database. It then compares the result to the correct encryption it got from the database.

```
Private Function ValidPassword(uid As String, pwd As String) As Boolean
Dim query As String
Dim rs As Recordset
Dim i As Integer
Dim salt(1 To 8) As Byte
Dim hash(1 To 8) As Byte

    ' Assume we will fail.
    ValidPassword = False

    On Error GoTo ValidPasswordError

    ' Get the salt and hashed values.
    query = "SELECT " & _
        "salt1, salt2, salt3, salt4, " & _
        "salt5, salt6, salt7, salt8, " & _
        "hash1, hash2, hash3, hash4, " & _
        "hash5, hash6, hash7, hash8 " & _
        "FROM Passwords WHERE userid = '" & _
        uid & "'"
    Set rs = TheDB.OpenRecordset(query, dbOpenSnapshot)

    ' If we didn't find it, it's not a valid ID.
    If rs.EOF Then GoTo ValidPasswordDone

    ' Copy the salt into the salt array.
    For i = 1 To 8
        salt(i) = rs.Fields(i - 1)
    Next i

    ' Encipher the uid using the user entered
    ' key and password, and the salt from the database.
    Encipher uid, pwd, salt, hash

    ' Verify that this is the correct hash.
    For i = 1 To 8
        If hash(i) <> rs.Fields(i + 7) Then _
            GoTo ValidPasswordDone
    Next i

    ' This user ID/password is correct.
    ValidPassword = True

ValidPasswordDone:
    ' Finish up.
    rs.Close
    Set rs = Nothing
    Exit Function

ValidPasswordError:
    <Error handling code omitted here>
```

```
    :
    Exit Function
End Function
```

The details of the Encipher subroutine are not very important so they are not described here. All that matters is that Encipher combines the user name, password, and salt values in a way that is hard to invert. In other words, given the encrypted value, the salt, and the user name, it should be difficult for an attacker to reproduce the password.

UpdatePassword The UpdatePassword subroutine allows the user to change the password corresponding to a user name. The program prompts the user to enter a user name, the current password, and a new password. The new password must be entered in two different text boxes. The dialog form that takes this information verifies that the two versions of the new password match. This helps ensure that the user did not make any errors while typing the new password.

UpdatePassword takes the user name and old password and verifies that they are a correct pair. This prevents unauthorized users from changing the password for another account.

If the application sets the DBUser object's public variable SuperUser to true, UpdatePassword skips this step and does not validate the user name and original password. This feature is useful for resetting forgotten passwords.

The SuperUser variable gives a user the ability to change any user name's password without knowing the current password. A program could manage the SuperUser variable by adding a SUPER_USER privilege to the GroupPrivileges table. It would then set SuperUser to true for users with this privilege.

Finally, UpdatePassword uses the SetPassword function to give the user name the indicated new password. If the user name did not already have an entry in the Passwords table, SetPassword creates it. Because a nonexistent user name cannot have a valid password, UpdatePassword will not create a new entry unless the DBUser object's SuperUser property is true.

The SetPassword function uses a new kind of data access object. To update a password entry, this function uses an SQL UPDATE statement. The UPDATE statement sets new values for the salt and hash fields for the given user name. The following statement shows how the program might update the entry for the user "kay."

```
UPDATE Passwords SET salt1 = 125, salt2 = 97, ...,
    hash1 = 21, hash2 = 107, ... WHERE userid = kay
```

This SQL statement modifies data in the Passwords table. Because it is not a SELECT statement, it does not create a recordset so the program cannot use the statement to define a Recordset object. Instead, the program can use a QueryDef object to execute the statement. A QueryDef object describes an SQL statement for later processing. Once it has defined a QueryDef object, the program can use the object's Execute method to execute the SQL command. The following code fragment shows how the SetPassword function updates a password entry:

```
Dim qd As QueryDef
Dim query As String
```

```
' Initialize the query string, etc.
   :
Set qd = TheDB.CreateQueryDef("", query)
qd.Execute
```

Field Validation

PeopleWatcher uses several field validations to prevent the user from entering invalid data. For example, validations on the Social Security number field prevent the user from entering strings that are not part of a valid Social Security number. These field validations are generally similar to those described in Chapter 2. However, there are a few important ways in which validations interact with database programming.

Values Not Allowed by Controls   Bound text boxes can contain almost any data loaded from the database. A text box can be bound to a typical text, integer, currency, or date/time field with no problems. Certain other types of controls combined with certain data fields can be a bit trickier.

PeopleWatcher uses two combo box controls. To ensure that the user selects only valid choices from the lists rather than typing in an invalid value, the Style property for both of these combo boxes is set to 2—Dropdown List. When the data control moves to a new record, Visual Basic uses data from the record to set the values of the combo boxes. If the value it obtains from the database is not a valid choice for a combo box, the system generates the message, "'Text' property is read only." This is its cryptic way of saying the text value it got from the database is not valid in the combo box.

To prevent this and similar problems, the values in the database must always fit into the controls designed to hold them. To prevent this specific problem in PeopleWatcher, the fields corresponding to the combo boxes have default values in the Employees table. This gives them legal values if values are not specified when a record is created.

For instance, the HomeState field contains the abbreviation for the state in which the employee lives. Using the design capabilities of the Data Manager, this field was given the default value AK. If the user, the program, or even some other program creates a new employee record and does not specify a value for HomeState, the database automatically gives the field the value AK. When the record is displayed by PeopleWatcher, HomeState contains a valid value so there is no error message. PeopleWatcher will not allow the user to select an invalid value for this field, so the value should always remain valid.

Of course, someone could change the value of the field using Data Manager or some other program. In that case, the user can enter a value that will be rejected by the combo box, so a user may later see the error message.

Values Not Allowed by Validation   When a user makes changes to an employee record and tries to accept the changes, the program's validation routines verify that the data entered is reasonable. If the program also attempts to verify data to which the user does not have access, the validation routines can cause trouble.

For example, suppose the user is a member of the Secretary group. This user has read access to Basic, Home, and HR data and update access to Basic data. The user updates an employee's Basic data and selects the Accept Changes command from the Edit menu. Now suppose the Home data's Zip Code field in the database was somehow given the value 803X1, which is not a valid Zip Code value. If the form validation routines detect this problem, they will present an error message asking the user to fix the Zip Code. Because this user does not have update access to the Zip Code field, the necessary correction is impossible. The only thing the user can do is cancel the changes and report the problem to someone else who does have update permission for the Zip Code field.

To prevent this kind of problem, form validation routines should not attempt to validate fields that the user cannot update. The validation routines used by PeopleWatcher check each control's Locked property before validating its data. If Locked is true, the user cannot edit the field so the routine skips the validation.

The following code shows the ValidateDigits function. After checking that the field is editable, the function calls ValidDigits to verify that the user has entered only digits in the field. The other data validation routines are similar.

```
Public Function ValidateDigits(ctl As TextBox, msg As String) As Boolean
Dim txt As String
    ' Skip noneditable fields.
    If ctl.Locked Then
        ValidateDigits = False
        Exit Function
    End If

    txt = ctl.Text
    If ValidDigits(txt) Then
        ValidateDigits = False
    Else
        PresentMessage ctl, msg, vbOKOnly, _
            "Invalid Digit Format"
        ValidateDigits = True
    End If
End Function


Public Function ValidDigits(txt As String) As Boolean
Dim i As Integer
Dim ch As String

    For i = 1 To Len(txt)
        ch = Mid$(txt, i, 1)
        If (ch < "0" Or ch > "9") Then
            ValidDigits = False
            Exit Function
        End If
    Next i
    ValidDigits = True
End Function
```

Testing Database Applications

Data controls are quite complicated. Whenever an application uses a data control, all of the possible actions the data control might take should be thoroughly tested. Particular attention should be given to unusual conditions such as these:

- Moving past the last record
- Moving before the first record
- Executing a query that returns no rows
- Working with a completely empty database

PeopleWatcher does not correctly handle a completely empty database. If a user deletes all of the records, the program will generate an error message when it tries to build an empty employee list. If the user then types in one of the text fields, the program generates an untrapped error and crashes when it tries to edit the nonexistent current record.

Testing for these odd cases was left out of PeopleWatcher to make it a little less complicated. Because this application is a corporate personnel file, the database should never be empty in any case. A true production application should handle all of these special cases, even if they should never occur in actual use.

Summary

PeopleWatcher demonstrates several important database programming concepts. It uses a data control and bound controls to display data and to allow the user to edit the data. It uses a Recordset object to manipulate the data behind the scenes. For example, it uses the Recordset object to build a list of employee names in an outline control without displaying all of the data in the bound controls.

PeopleWatcher also shows how an application can configure itself to meet the requirements of different groups of users. Using a relatively simple password and privilege system, PeopleWatcher customizes itself to meet the widely varying needs of the users. This not only makes the application appear sensitive to each user's demands, but it also makes the program more widely usable. Without this sort of customization, an application such as PeopleWatcher that deals with sensitive information could be used by only a few privileged people.

Chapter 9

Query

The DBUser class described in Chapter 8 uses a QueryDef object to update a user's password information in the Passwords table. It uses the object's Execute method to run an SQL UPDATE statement.

QueryDef objects can execute other SQL commands as well. The Query application described in this chapter uses this fact to implement an extremely flexible database management tool. Query allows a user to enter and execute any SQL statement.

The first section in this chapter, "Using Query," describes Query from the user's point of view. It explains how the user can enter and execute queries and save query text and results in files.

The "Key Techniques" section lists the Visual Basic programming techniques used by the Query application. The rest of the chapter describes those techniques in detail.

Using Query

Figure 9.1 shows the Query program in action. The user enters one or more SQL statements separated by semi-colons in the upper text box and clicks the Run button. The program executes the statements and presents the results in the lower text box.

The Query application interacts with three file-like items that the user may want to manipulate: the SQL statement text, the result text, and the database file itself.

After entering a series of SQL statements, the user might want to save those statements in a file so they can be easily reloaded and executed later. Query's File menu provides a standard set of New, Open, Save, and Save As commands that allow the user to manipulate SQL statement files. The File menu also provides a recent file list that shows the four SQL files most recently accessed by the program. All of these commands are similar to those used by the ExpenseReporter application described in Chapters 1 and 2.

Query is intended for use as an ad hoc database querying tool. It assumes the user will usually enter a few SQL statements, execute them, and quit. Because the user will probably not want to save the SQL statements, Query does not present a warning before exiting if the

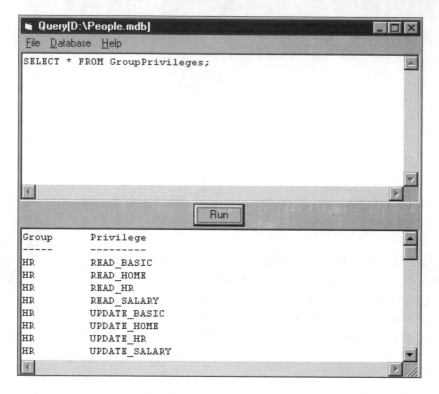

FIGURE 9.1 The Query application.

statements have not been saved to a file. It would be easy to change this behavior using the techniques described in Chapter 1.

The second file-like item in Query is the result text. This text contains success and failure messages, and the results of any SQL SELECT statements. The File menu's Save Results As command allows the user to save these results into a text file. The user can then use the results to create simple reports.

Query makes the results easier to manipulate by displaying them in a text box rather than in a label control. The user can use the mouse to copy the text in the text box and paste it into other applications. The Locked property of the text box is set to true so the user cannot accidentally modify the results within the Query program.

The final file-like item used by Query is the database file. Before the user can execute SQL statements, the program must be connected to a database. The Database menu's Connect command allows the user to open a database file. The Disconnect command closes the database so the user can open another.

The Database menu also contains a recent database list similar to the File menu's recent query file list. This list holds the names of the four most recently accessed database files. The user can select one of these to reconnect to a database quickly without searching for it using a file selection dialog.

Key Techniques

The following list describes the key concepts demonstrated by the Query application. The rest of this chapter describes these concepts in detail.

- **Creating Databases**. The Data Manager is not the only way to create a new database. This section shows how a Visual Basic application can create a new Access database.
- **Composing SQL Commands**. The structured query language provides a large assortment of commands for manipulating relational databases. This section describes some of the more important SQL commands.
- **Processing SQL Statements**. Processing SQL statements is the main goal of the Query application. This section explains how Query separates SQL statements, removes comments from them, and executes them.

Creating Databases

Subroutine ConnectToDatabase first attempts to open the specified database file using the default Workspace object's OpenDatabase method. If that method raises error number 3024, the database does not exist so the program asks the user if it should create the database.

If so, ConnectToDatabase uses the Workspace object's CreateDatabase command to create the new database. The format of the new database will depend on the version of the data access objects used by the application. If the application is a 16-bit Visual Basic program, Query uses version 2.5 of the data access objects so it creates a version 2.5 format database.

If the application is a 32-bit Visual Basic program, it can use either the 2.5 or 3.0 version of the data access objects. The References command in the Visual Basic development environment's Tools menu determines which version of the data access objects the program uses.

Whether the subroutine ConnectToDatabase opened an existing database or created a new one, it next uses the database's CreateQueryDef method to create a new QueryDef object. That object will be used later to execute SQL statements on the database.

ConnectToDatabase finishes by performing some user interface chores. It adds the database name to the program's caption and the list of recently accessed databases. It also enables commands, such as the Disconnect command, that are appropriate while a database is open.

```
Private Function ConnectToDatabase(db_name As String) As Boolean
Const DATABASE_NOT_FOUND = 3024

Dim i As Integer
Dim err_num As Long
Dim err_descr As String

    ' Start waiting.
    WaitStart
```

```
' Connect to the database.
On Error Resume Next
Set TheDB = TheWS.OpenDatabase(db_name)
err_num = Err.Number
err_descr = Err.Description
On Error GoTo DbOpenError

If err_num = DATABASE_NOT_FOUND Then
    ' The database file does not exist.
    ' See if the user wants to create it.
    Beep
    If MsgBox("This database does not exist." & _
        vbCrLf & vbCrLf & _
        "Do you want to create it?", _
        vbYesNo + vbQuestion, _
        "Create Database?") = vbNo _
    Then
        ConnectToDatabase = True
        WaitEnd
        Exit Function
    End If

    ' Create the database.
    Set TheDB = TheWS.CreateDatabase(db_name, _
        dbLangGeneral)
ElseIf err_num > 0 Then
    Err.Number = err_num
    Err.Description = err_descr
    GoTo DbOpenError
End If

' Create a QueryDef object to query with.
Set TheQD = TheDB.CreateQueryDef("")

DBName = db_name
AddRecentDB DBName
Caption = APPNAME & "[" & DBName & "]"
For i = 1 To 4
    mnuDBList(i).Enabled = False
Next i
mnuDbDisconnect.Enabled = True
mnuDbConnect.Enabled = False
CmdRun.Enabled = True
ConnectToDatabase = False
WaitEnd
Exit Function

DbOpenError:
    ' Do not leave the cursor as an hourglass.
    WaitEnd
```

```
    Beep
    MsgBox "Error" & Str$(Err.Number) & _
        " connecting to database " & db_name & _
        "." & vbCrLf & Err.Description, _
        vbOKOnly + vbExclamation, "Error"
    ConnectToDatabase = True
    Exit Function
End Function
```

Composing SQL Commands

Even though there is no room in this section to explain the entire SQL language, there is room to describe many of the most important SQL commands.

Query processes a series of standard SQL commands separated by semi-colons. It ignores carriage returns and spaces within a command.

Query can also interpret two kinds of comments. If it encounters two dashes in a row, it ignores the rest of the command text up to the end of the line. For instance, Query will execute the following SELECT statement correctly:

```
SELECT LastName, FirstName       -- Find the employees who
    FROM Employees               --    earn more than $30k.
    WHERE Salary > 30000;
```

Query also ignores comments enclosed in braces. It looks for this kind of comment before it looks for double dash comments. This can cause trouble if comments overlap. For example, consider the following statement:

```
{ Here is a comment. {Here is a nested comment.} Here is some more. }
```

In this case Query will match the first open brace with the first close brace. This produces the following code that Query will try to interpret as an SQL statement. Of course, this code is part of a comment, not an SQL statement, so Query will display an error message.

```
Here is some more. }
```

The following sections describe some of the most important SQL statements the Query application can execute. These sections describe the commands as they are most frequently used. You can search the Visual Basic help for more information about a command. For example, to learn more about the CREATE TABLE command, search for "CREATE TABLE." As you read through these sections, you may want to use the Query application to test the commands.

Sections later in this chapter explain how Query extracts the separate SQL statements from the command text, how it removes comments from the statements, and how it executes them.

CREATE

The CREATE statement builds tables, fields, and indexes. The syntax for creating a table is as follows:

```
CREATE TABLE table (field_name type [(size)] [constraint_clause], ... [, multi-field_index_name [,
...]])
```

For example, the following statement creates a table named Appointments. The table contains three fields: a 30-character text field named WhoWith, a date/time field called DateAndTime, and a currency field named Cost.

```
CREATE TABLE Appointments (
    WhoWith      TEXT (30),
    DateAndTime  DATETIME,
    Cost         CURRENCY
);
```

The Query application ignores carriage returns and spaces; an SQL statement can use these characters to improve legibility. SQL is also case insensitive so a statement can use capitalization to make itself clearer. The examples presented here set all SQL commands and keywords in uppercase, and the names of tables, fields, and indexes in mixed uppercase and lowercase.

The following SQL statement creates a table named Books to store information about books. The ID field has the counter data type. When a new record is created in this table and no value for ID is specified, the database automatically assigns the next sequential value to the ID field. The first record will receive the value 1, the next 2, and so forth.

The ID field is also the table's primary key. The key is named BooksIDKey. Primary key values must always be unique. In this case, that means that no two Books records can have the same value for the ID field. Primary keys are useful because searching for a record using the primary key is faster than searching with other fields.

The table also contains a unique multifield key named BooksAuthorTitleKey. Because this key is unique and includes the Author and Title fields, no two records in the table can have the same combination of Author and Title. Two records could have the same Author or the same Title, but not both. This key makes searching for an author, or for an author and title, faster. It does not make a search for a title alone faster.

```
CREATE TABLE Books (
    ID        COUNTER CONSTRAINT BooksIDKey PRIMARY KEY,
    Title     TEXT (30),
    Author    TEXT (30),
    Length    INTEGER,
    CONSTRAINT BooksAuthorTitleKey UNIQUE (Author, Title)
);
```

Once a table has been created, the CREATE INDEX command can build a new index for it. The syntax for the CREATE INDEX command is as follows:

```
CREATE [UNIQUE] INDEX index_name ON table_name (field [ASC|DESC], ...) [WITH { PRIMARY | DISALLOW
NULL | IGNORE NULL }]
```

The ASC and DESC keywords specify that the key values should be arranged in ascending or descending order, respectively. If neither order is specified, ascending is the default.

The PRIMARY keyword indicates that the index should be the primary index for the table. A table can have only one primary index. If the statement tries to create another primary key, the database generates an error.

If the DISALLOW NULL clause is included, the database will not accept records with null values for any of the fields specified in the key.

If the IGNORE NULL clause is included, the database will not include any records in the index if they have null values for the index fields.

The following statement creates a new Books table and then adds an index on the Title and Author fields. Because the index uses the DISALLOW NULL clause, all records must have Title and Author values.

```
CREATE TABLE Books (
     ID          COUNTER,
     Title       TEXT (30),
     Author      TEXT (30),
     Length      INTEGER
);
CREATE INDEX BooksIndex ON Books (Title, Author)
     WITH DISALLOW NULL;
```

DROP

The DROP command removes a table or index from the database. The syntax for removing a table is as follows:

```
DROP TABLE table_name
```

For example, the following statement removes the Books table from the database:

```
DROP TABLE Books
```

The syntax for removing an index from a table is just as simple.

```
DROP INDEX index_name ON table_name
```

The following statement removes the BooksIndex from the Books table:

```
DROP INDEX BooksIndex ON Books
```

DROP statements are very dangerous: They are immediate and unforgiving. Once a table has been dropped, it and all of the data it contained are gone forever.

ALTER

The ALTER TABLE command changes the definition of a table after it is created. This statement can add or drop columns and constraints. The syntax for adding a column is as follows:

```
ALTER TABLE table_name ADD COLUMN
     field_name type[(size)] [CONSTRAINT index_name]
```

For example, the following statement adds the text field Publisher to the already existing Books table:

```
ALTER TABLE Books ADD COLUMN Publisher TEXT (30)
```

The syntax for removing a field is even simpler.

```
ALTER TABLE table_name DROP COLUMN field_name
```

The following statement removes the Publisher field from the Books table:

```
ALTER TABLE Books DROP COLUMN Publisher
```

Like the DROP statement, ALTER TABLE statements can be dangerous. Any data contained in a dropped column is permanently lost.

The ALTER CONSTRAINT commands follow a similar pattern. The following two statements first add and then remove a uniqueness constraint on the Title and Author fields in the Books table.

```
ALTER TABLE Books ADD CONSTRAINT BooksTitleIndex

    UNIQUE (Title, Author);
ALTER TABLE Books DROP CONSTRAINT BooksTitleIndex;
```

SELECT

The SELECT statement is one of the most important and complex SQL commands. A complete discussion of all the possible combinations of clauses and parameters would be quite long and would waste a lot of your time on subtleties that you might never encounter. This section describes only the most commonly used varieties of the SELECT statement.

The basic syntax for the SELECT command is as follows:

```
SELECT [predicate] select_list from_clause [where_clause] [group_by_clause] [having_clause]
[order_by_clause]
```

The pieces of the SELECT statement are described in the following sections.

Predicate The predicate specifies which records should be selected. The predicate can take one of the following values:

- **ALL**. This value selects all records that meet the criteria specified by the other clauses. This is the default predicate.
- **DISTINCT**. This value omits duplicates of the values selected.
- **DISTINCTROW**. This value omits records that duplicate all fields in another record rather than just the fields selected. This is useful only under certain circumstances when the statement selects fields from more than one table.
- **TOP**. This value returns an indicated number of rows. For example, "TOP 10" indicates that the first 10 rows returned by the query should be presented. Usually a statement using TOP also specifies an ORDER BY clause (described later) to order the results so the returned rows do not seem randomly selected.

This example selects information about the 25 shortest books listed in the Books table:

```
SELECT TOP 25 * FROM Books ORDER BY Length
```

The following statement produces an alphabetized list of the authors who have written books with more than 300 pages:

```
SELECT DISTINCT Author FROM Books WHERE Length > 300 ORDER BY Author
```

Select List The select list indicates which fields are to be selected. Several of the previous examples include select lists. The select list usually includes field names or the asterisk to indicate all the fields in a table. The following statement displays all of the data in the Books table:

```
SELECT * FROM Books
```

If the statement selects fields from more than one table, and if the tables contain a field with the same name, the statement must specify the table name for those fields in the SELECT statement. For example, suppose the Books and Films tables both have a field named Title. The following statement would produce a list of books with titles that are also the titles of films. The words "Books.Title" indicate the Title field in the Books table.

```
SELECT DISTINCT Books.Title FROM Books, Films
    WHERE Books.Title = Films.Title
    ORDER BY Books.Title
```

A statement can use an AS clause to change the displayed name of a field when the statement returns results. If the new name contains space characters, the entire name should be enclosed in square brackets. The following command lists the titles and author names in the Books table, but the information from the Title field is renamed "Work." Below the SQL statement are the first few output lines produced by this command in the Query application.

```
SELECT Author, Title AS Work FROM Books;
```

```
Author     Work
------     ----
Stephens   Visual Basic Algorithms
Stephens   Visual Basic Graphic Programming
   :
```

In addition to field names and the asterisk character, the select list can include literal values and aggregate functions. Literal values can include numbers and text strings. Aggregate functions include the following:

- **Avg**. The average of the selected field's values.
- **Count**. The number of records returned by the query. Note that COUNT (*) is much faster than statements such as COUNT (*column_name*).
- **Min, Max.** The minimum or maximum value of the selected field.
- **StDev, StDevP**. An estimate of the standard deviation for a population (StDevP) or a population sample (StDev).
- **Sum**. The sum of the values in the selected column.
- **Var, VarP**. Estimates of the variance for a population (VarP) or a population sample (Var).

For example, the following statement returns the average number of pages for the books in the Books table:

```
SELECT AVG(Length) AS [Average Length] FROM Books
```

From Clause The FROM clause lists the table or tables from which the records are selected. An SQL statement can *join* together the data in multiple tables using the FROM clause in several ways. The simplest is to just list the tables. A WHERE clause can specify a link between the tables. For example, the following SQL statement displays information on books and films that share the same title. The clause "WHERE Books.Title = Films.Title" allows the database to match information from the two tables. Because both tables contain a field named Title, the statement must qualify the field as "Books.Title" or "Films.Title" so the database knows which value to select.

```
SELECT Books.Title, Author, Producer FROM Books, Films
    WHERE Books.Title = Films.Title
```

Suppose the Books table contains the records shown in Table 9.1, and the Films table contains the records shown in Table 9.2.

Then the previous SELECT statement would return these results:

```
Title                       Author          Producer
-----                       ------          --------
Visual Basic Algorithms     Stephens        Elliott
Curve Ahead                 Sierpinski      Jackson
Selected 2 records.
```

This query returns rows only if there are records in both tables with matching titles. This type of join is called an *inner join* or *equi-join*. The previous query can be rewritten to make the fact that it is an inner join more obvious, like this:

```
SELECT Books.Title, Author, Producer FROM Books
    INNER JOIN Films ON Books.Title = Films.Title
```

Sometimes it may be necessary to return all of the rows in one table plus any matching rows from the other table. This kind of join is called an *outer join*. There are two kinds of outer joins. A *left join* selects all of the rows from the first table plus any matching rows in the second. A *right join* selects all of the rows from the second table plus any matching rows in the first. The following code shows a left join statement and the results it produces.

```
SELECT Books.Title, Author, Producer FROM Books
    LEFT JOIN Films ON Books.Title = Films.Title;
```

TABLE 9.1 Records in the Books Table

Title	Author
Visual Basic Algorithms	Stephens
The Trial and Death of Socrates	Plato
Curve Ahead	Sierpinski
This Thing Called Calculus	Newton

TABLE 9.2 Records in the Films Table

Title	Producer
Visual Basic Algorithms	Elliott
Curve Ahead	Jackson
Keys to Success	Brahms
The Killer Tortoises of Maui	Kipster

```
Title                            Author         Producer
-----                            ------         --------
Visual Basic Algorithms          Stephens       Elliott
The Trial and Death of Socrates  Plato          Null
Curve Ahead                      Sierpinski     Jackson
This Thing Called Calculus       Newton         Null
Selected 4 records.
```

The next example shows a right outer join and the results it produces. Notice that the statement selects Films.Title rather than Books.Title. Because this is a right join, Books.Title will have a null value for records from the Films table that do not have a corresponding record in the Books table.

```
SELECT Films.Title, Author, Producer FROM Books
    RIGHT JOIN Films ON Books.Title = Films.Title
```

```
Title                         Author         Producer
-----                         ------         --------
Visual Basic Algorithms       Stephens       Elliott
Curve Ahead                   Sierpinski     Jackson
Keys to Success               Null           Brahms
The Killer Tortoises of Maui  Null           Kipster
Selected 4 records.
```

Where Clause The previous sections have shown several examples of WHERE clauses. A WHERE clause indicates which records should be chosen by a SELECT statement.

```
SELECT * FROM Books WHERE Length > 300
```

The WHERE clause can contain the operators =, <>, >, <, >=, and <= to select records. These operators work on fields of most data types. When comparing two date fields, for example, "date1 >= date2" means the first date falls on or after the second.

A WHERE clause can join two or more tables together, as in the following statement:

```
SELECT Books.Title, Author, Producer FROM Books, Films
    WHERE Books.Title = Films.Title
```

WHERE clauses can contain the logical operators AND, OR, and NOT to form more complex clauses.

```
SELECT Books.Title, Author, Producer FROM Books, Films
    WHERE Books.Title = Films.Title AND Length > 300
        AND Producer <> "Jackson"
```

Group By Clause The GROUP BY clause combines records with the same values in the specified fields into one record. An SQL statement can use a GROUP BY clause together with aggregate functions to produce summary values. The following statement lists the authors in the Books table and the total length of all books written by each:

```
SELECT Author, SUM(Length) As [Total Length]
    FROM Books GROUP BY Author
```

For example, if the author Newton had written 18 books with a combined length of 4763 pages, this query would return a row listing Newton and the total length 4763.

Having Clause After a query has grouped records using a GROUP BY clause, the HAVING clause specifies which output records should be displayed. This is similar to a WHERE clause that selects from among the records produced by the GROUP BY clause.

For example, the following statement produces a list of authors and the total length of their books as before, but it displays results only for authors who have written at least 1000 pages.

```
SELECT Author, SUM(Length) As [Total Length]
    FROM Books GROUP BY Author HAVING SUM(Length) >= 1000
```

Order By Clause The previous sections have shown several examples of the ORDER BY clause. This clause determines the order of the results returned by SELECT statements. The optional keyword DESC indicates that the values should be arranged in descending order. The following example produces a list of authors and the total length of their books, for authors who have written at least 1000 pages, arranged with those authors having the largest page count totals first.

```
SELECT Author, SUM(Length) As [Total Length]
    FROM Books GROUP BY Author HAVING SUM(Length) >= 1000
    ORDER BY SUM(Length) DESC
```

INSERT

An INSERT statement creates new records in a table. There are two formats for INSERT statements. The first inserts a single record into a table. Its syntax is as follows:

```
INSERT INTO table_name [(field_name, ...)] VALUES (value1, ...)
```

For example, the following statement inserts a single record into the Books table. It specifies only the Title and Author fields so any other fields in the record are given null values.

```
INSERT INTO Books (Title, Author)
    VALUES ("The Longest Day", "Bishop")
```

If an INSERT statement does not explicitly list the fields initialized, the VALUES clause must specify a value for every field in the table in the proper order. The following statement creates a record similar to the one created by the previous example. Because it omits the field list, this statement must specify a value for the Length field as well as the Title and Author fields. This statement sets the Length field to 375. Rather than giving a specific value for this field, the statement could have specified the value null to leave the field's value undefined.

```
INSERT INTO Books
    VALUES ("The Longest Day", "Bishop", 375)
```

The second kind of INSERT statement uses a subquery to select rows from one or more tables and insert them into another table. The syntax for this kind of statement is as follows:

```
INSERT INTO table_name [(field_name, ...)] subquery
```

Once again, if the statement omits the field name list it must provide values for all the fields in the table.

The following statement selects the Title and Author fields from the Books table and uses the results to create entries in the Films table.

```
INSERT INTO Films (Title, Producer)
    SELECT Title, Author FROM Books
```

UPDATE

An UPDATE statement modifies the field values in existing records. The syntax for an UPDATE statement is as follows:

```
UPDATE table_name SET field_name = value, ... where_clause
```

For example, the following statement changes the Author field to "Leibniz" for any records in the Books table that currently have Author value "Newton."

```
UPDATE Books SET Author = "Leibniz" WHERE Author = "Newton"
```

The following statement adds 100 to the Length field for every record in the Books table:

```
UPDATE Books SET Length = Length + 100
```

Using an UPDATE statement to make changes to many records is generally much faster than making a program loop through the records to update them one at a time.

Like many other SQL statements, UPDATE statements can be dangerous. A program can irreversibly damage a lot of data with a single UPDATE statement if it is not careful. In particular, if the program omits the WHERE clause, the UPDATE statement will affect every record in the table rather than just a few.

DELETE

The DELETE statement removes records from a table. The syntax for this statement is as follows:

```
DELETE FROM table_name where_clause
```

The following example deletes all the records in the Books table where the value of the Author field is Plato:

```
DELETE FROM Books WHERE Author = "Plato"
```

Using a DELETE statement to remove many records is generally much faster than making a program loop through the records to delete them one at a time.

Like the UPDATE statement, the DELETE statement can be dangerous if used carelessly. Once records have been deleted, they are gone forever. Also like the UPDATE statement, DELETE is particularly dangerous without a WHERE clause. If a program accidentally omits the WHERE clause, it will delete every record in the table instead of just a few.

One strategy for protecting data is to use the multirecord INSERT statement described previously to copy the records into a temporary table before deleting them. This reduces the size of the main data table but allows the program to recover the records later if it needs them. When it is certain the saved values are no longer necessary, the program can use the DROP command to remove the temporary table.

Another strategy for safe deletion is to first test the DELETE statement's WHERE clause in a SELECT statement. The program can present a list of the records to be deleted to the user and ask for confirmation. If the user approves the deletion, the program can run the DELETE statement using the tested WHERE clause.

If the WHERE clause selects a large number of rows, the program can use a SELECT statement with the COUNT function to determine how many rows would be deleted. The program can tell the user the number of rows that will be removed and ask for confirmation. For example, the WHERE clause in the following statement should select only a few rows. If the COUNT function returns a value larger than a dozen or so, the user should take a closer look at the data and the WHERE clause before deleting the records.

```
SELECT COUNT (*) FROM Books WHERE Author="Xeno"
```

Processing SQL Statements

The Query application processes a series of SQL statements separated by semi-colons. Executing the commands is actually easier than breaking the individual statements apart. The following sections explain the routines Query uses to separate and execute SQL commands.

ProcessAllCommands

The process of separating and executing the commands begins with the ProcessAllCommands subroutine. ProcessAllCommands uses the StripCommands subroutine to remove comments, carriage returns, and excess spaces from the commands. It then repeatedly uses the GetToken subroutine to find the separate commands delimited by semi-colons. The GetToken routine is similar to the version used by ExpenseReporter and described in Chapter 2.

ProcessAllCommands places the separated commands in a collection. When it has finished breaking apart all of the commands, it loops through the collection calling the ProcessCommand subroutine to execute each command individually.

```
Private Sub ProcessAllCommands()
Dim cmd_string As String
Dim cmd As String
Dim cmds As New Collection
Dim got_cmd As Boolean
Dim i As Integer
Dim result As String

    WaitStart

    ' Remove comments, new lines, and tabs.
    cmd_string = Trim$(InputText.Text)
    StripCommands cmd_string
```

```
    ' Seperate the commands.
got_cmd = GetToken(cmd_string, ";", cmd)
Do While got_cmd
    cmds.Add Trim$(cmd)
    got_cmd = GetToken("", ";", cmd)
Loop

    ' Process the commands.
result = ""
For i = 1 To cmds.Count
        ' Process this command.
    ProcessCommand cmds.Item(1), result
Next i

    ' Display the output.
OutputText.Text = result

    WaitEnd
End Sub
```

StripCommands

The StripCommands subroutine uses GetToken to locate different comment delimiters in the command text. First, it looks for the open braces that mark the start of a multiline comment. For each open brace it finds, the routine locates the next closing brace and discards the text between them.

After it has removed comments enclosed in braces, StripCommands uses a similar procedure to remove comments that begin with a double dash and end with a carriage return. Finally, the routine replaces new line and tab characters with spaces. This will make it easier for the ProcessCommand subroutine to determine whether a command is completely blank.

```
Private Sub StripCommands(cmd As String)
Dim new_cmd As String
Dim token As String
Dim got_token As Boolean

    ' Remove { } style comments.
    new_cmd = ""
    ' Get the command up to the first "{".
    got_token = GetToken(cmd, "{", token)
    Do While got_token
        ' Add this piece to the new command.
        new_cmd = new_cmd & token & " "

        ' Get (and ignore) the comment.
        got_token = GetToken("", "}", token)
        If Not got_token Then Exit Do

        ' Get the command up to the next "{".
        got_token = GetToken("", "{", token)
    Loop
```

```
    ' Remove -- style comments.
    cmd = ""
    ' Get the command up to the first "--".
    got_token = GetToken(new_cmd, "--", token)
    Do While got_token
        ' Add this piece to the new command.
        cmd = cmd & token & " "

        ' Get (and ignore) the comment.
        got_token = GetToken("", vbCrLf, token)
        If Not got_token Then Exit Do

        ' Get the command up to the next "--".
        got_token = GetToken("", "--", token)
    Loop


    ' Remove new lines.
    new_cmd = ""
    ' Get the first line.
    got_token = GetToken(cmd, vbCrLf, token)
    Do While got_token
        ' Add this piece to the new command.
        new_cmd = new_cmd & token & " "

        ' Get the next line.
        got_token = GetToken("", vbCrLf, token)
    Loop


    ' Remove tabs.
    cmd = ""
    ' Get the first line.
    got_token = GetToken(new_cmd, vbTab, token)
    Do While got_token
        ' Add this piece to the new command.
        cmd = cmd & token & " "

        ' Get the next line.
        got_token = GetToken("", vbTab, token)
    Loop


    ' Trim leading and trailing blanks.
    cmd = Trim$(cmd)
End Sub
```

ProcessCommand

ProcessCommand executes a single SQL statement and adds the results to the end of a result string. After checking that the statement is not empty, the routine sets the SQL property of a QueryDef object equal to the statement.

SELECT statements must be handled a bit differently from other SQL statements. SELECT statements return rows of data; other SQL statements perform actions. ProcessCommand examines the first word in the command to see if it is "SELECT."

If the command is a SELECT statement, ProcessCommand invokes the ProcessSelect subroutine to execute it. Otherwise, ProcessCommand uses the QueryDef object's Execute method to execute the command. It then performs some final calculations to present an informative message indicating that the command succeeded.

```
Private Sub ProcessCommand(cmd As String, result As String)
Dim rows As Integer
Dim verb As String
Dim reply As String

    ' If it is blank, do nothing.
    If cmd = "" Then Exit Sub

    ' "Compile" the QueryDef.
    On Error GoTo QueryDefError
    TheQD.SQL = cmd

    ' See what the command verb is.
    If Not GetToken(cmd, " ", verb) Then Exit Sub
    verb = UCase$(Trim$(verb))

    ' Execute the command.
    If verb = "SELECT" Then
        ' It's a SELECT statement.
        ProcessSelect result
    Else
        ' It's an action query. Execute it.
        TheQD.Execute

        If verb = "DELETE" Or verb = "INSERT" Or _
            verb = "UPDATE" _
        Then
            ' These affect rows.
            rows = TheQD.RecordsAffected
            If rows = 1 Then
                reply = "1 record."
            Else
                reply = Format$(rows) & " records."
            End If
            Select Case verb
                Case "DELETE"
                    verb = "Deleted "
                Case "INSERT"
                    verb = "Inserted "
                Case "UPDATE"
```

```
                      verb = "Updated "
            End Select
            result = result & verb & reply & _
                 vbCrLf & vbCrLf
        Else
             ' These affect tables, indexes, etc.
            result = result & verb & " OK." & _
                 vbCrLf & vbCrLf
        End If
    End If  ' End if SELECT ... Else ...

    On Error GoTo 0
    Exit Sub

QueryDefError:
    result = result & "Error" & _
        Str$(Err.Number) & _
        " executing command." & vbCrLf & _
        vbCrLf & Err.Description & vbCrLf & vbCrLf
    Exit Sub
End Sub
```

ProcessSelect

Because a SELECT statement returns an unknown number of rows of data, it must be handled differently than other statements. Subroutine ProcessSelect uses the QueryDef object initialized in ProcessCommand to create a Recordset object. It then examines the data types of the Recordset's fields to determine how wide each column in the result will be. For example, a short integer can be up to six characters long, as in -32767.

ProcessSelect then examines each field's name to make sure each column is wide enough to display the name. It also makes sure each column is at least four characters wide so there is room to display the value "null."

The subroutine then adds column headers to the result string. Finally, it loops through the records in the Recordset, adding each of the fields' values to the result string.

```
Private Sub ProcessSelect(result As String)
Dim rs As Recordset
Dim col_type() As Integer
Dim col_wid() As Integer
Dim max_col As Integer
Dim i As Integer
Dim j As Integer
Dim col_value As String
Dim max_rec As Integer

    ' Open the Recordset.
    Set rs = TheQD.OpenRecordset(dbOpenSnapshot, _
        dbReadOnly)
```

```vb
' See how wide each column should be.
max_col = rs.Fields.Count - 1
ReDim col_wid(0 To max_col)
ReDim col_type(0 To max_col)
For i = 0 To max_col
    col_type(i) = rs.Fields(i).Type
    Select Case col_type(i)
        Case dbDate          ' Date/Time
            col_wid(i) = 8
        Case dbText          ' <= 255 characters
            col_wid(i) = rs.Fields(i).Size
        Case dbMemo          ' <= 1.2 GB
            col_wid(i) = 0      ' Hide this.
        Case dbBoolean       ' Boolean
            col_wid(i) = 5
        Case dbInteger       ' Integer
            col_wid(i) = 6
        Case dbLong          ' Long
            col_wid(i) = 11
        Case dbCurrency      ' Currency
            col_wid(i) = 16
        Case dbSingle        ' Single
            col_wid(i) = 12
        Case dbDouble        ' Double
            col_wid(i) = 21
        Case dbByte          ' Byte
            col_wid(i) = 3
        Case dbLongBinary    ' Long Binary (OLE Object)
            col_wid(i) = 0      ' Hide this.
    End Select

    ' Allow room for the field's name.
    col_value = rs.Fields(i).Name
    If col_wid(i) < Len(col_value) Then _
        col_wid(i) = Len(col_value)

    ' Allow at least 4 spaces for "Null".
    If col_wid(i) < 4 Then col_wid(i) = 4

    ' Add an extra space between fields.
    col_wid(i) = col_wid(i) + 1
Next i  ' End setting column widths.

' Display column headers.
For i = 0 To max_col
    ' Add the name for field i.
    col_value = rs.Fields(i).Name
    result = result & col_value & _
        Space$(col_wid(i) - Len(col_value))
Next i
result = result & vbCrLf
```

```
For i = 0 To max_col
    ' Add underscores beneath field i's name.
    col_value = ""
    For j = 1 To Len(rs.Fields(i).Name)
        col_value = col_value & "-"
    Next j
    result = result & col_value & _
        Space$(col_wid(i) - Len(col_value))
Next i
result = result & vbCrLf

' Display the data.
Do Until rs.EOF
    For i = 0 To max_col
        ' Add the value for field i.
        If IsNull(rs.Fields(i)) Then
            col_value = "Null"
        ElseIf col_type(i) = dbMemo Or _
            col_type(i) = dbLongBinary Then
            col_value = "*"
        Else
            col_value = rs.Fields(i)
        End If
        result = result & col_value & _
            Space$(col_wid(i) - Len(col_value))
    Next i
    result = result & vbCrLf

    max_rec = rs.RecordCount
    rs.MoveNext
Loop

' Say how many records were selected.
If max_rec = 1 Then
    result = result & "Selected 1 record." & _
        vbCrLf & vbCrLf
Else
    result = result & "Selected" & _
        Str$(max_rec) & " records." & _
        vbCrLf & vbCrLf
End If

' Delete the Recordset.
Set rs = Nothing
End Sub
```

Privileges

Query is an extremely powerful application. With a few keystrokes, a user can delete every record in a table or even delete the table itself. Because this can be potentially disastrous, it is important that Query never falls into careless hands.

At the same time, Query makes a handy reporting utility. For a large database project used by many people, allowing more experienced users the convenience Query provides is reasonable. To ensure that these users do not damage the database, either intentionally or accidentally, Query can include user privileges and password protection features similar to those demonstrated by the PeopleWatcher application described in Chapter 8.

Query's ProcessCommand subroutine already checks for the command verbs SELECT, DELETE, INSERT, and UPDATE so it can take special actions for these commands. It could also verify that the user has permission to execute one of these commands. If the user does not have DELETE privilege, for example, Query can add a message to the output text saying that the operation is not allowed.

The program could also add other potentially dangerous commands to the list of privileges. Some of these are CREATE, DROP, and ALTER. These commands are potentially more dangerous than INSERT, UPDATE, and DELETE.

A program should refuse to allow a user to execute a command unless permission is explicitly granted in the Privileges tables. Then if the program overlooks a command, or if a future version of the data access objects supports a new DESTROY command, the user cannot slip past the program's safeguards and wreak havoc on the database.

Query is designed to be used by database administrators so it does not perform these checks. It assumes the user is responsible and knows SQL well enough not to damage the database accidentally.

Summary

The Query application uses the QueryDef object to execute practically any database command. If the user attempts to open a database that does not exist, the program can even create a new database. These features make Query a powerful tool for ad hoc reporting and database maintenance.

Chapter 10

PeopleWatcher Remote

Chapter 8 describes PeopleWatcher, a computerized personnel system that provides different views of employee data to different users based on the permissions they have. This and many other database applications can be moved onto a network with surprisingly little effort.

PeopleWatcher Remote is very similar to PeopleWatcher. The only difference between the two is in how they access the personnel data. The PeopleWatcher Remote's user interface is identical to the previous version, so this chapter does not describe the application from the user's point of view. To read a description of PeopleWatcher's user interface, see "Using PeopleWatcher" in Chapter 8.

The "Key Techniques" section that follows lists the Visual Basic programming techniques described in this chapter. Later sections describe those techniques in detail.

Key Techniques

An application can access a remote database in a couple of ways. The two most common methods are to directly access the remote database and to attach the remote tables to a local database. The following sections describe these two methods.

- **Accessing Remote Databases Directly**. One method for accessing remote data is to attach directly to the remote database. This section explains how a data control can make this attachment.
- **Attaching Remote Tables**. A second way to access remote data is to attach remote database tables to a local database. This section explains how a program can attach and detach remote tables.
- **Improving Network Performance**. Applications that transfer large amounts of data across a network often pay a price in reduced performance. This section describes several ways PeopleWatcher could be redesigned to improve its performance over a busy network.

The Ch10 directory on the compact disk contains several subdirectories that demonstrate these techniques. The project Direct.VBP in the Ch10\Direct directory uses a data control to access a remote database directly.

The projects Ch10\Attacher\Attacher.VBP and Ch10\Detacher\Detacher.VBP show how to attach and detach remote database tables to a local database. The project Ch10\PeopleW\PeopleW.VBP uses the local database to provide access to the remote tables.

Accessing Remote Databases Directly

To access a remote database directly, a program should specify the database's remote connection information when opening it. For instance, suppose the remote computer Beauty contains an Access database stored in the file C:\Ch10\People.MDB. If the network is configured so a program can access this file system from the local computer, the program can use the following code to open the remote database.

```
Dim db As Database

    Set db = DBEngine.Workspaces(0).OpenDatabase _
        ("//Beauty/C/Ch10/People.MDB", False, False, "")
```

Once the program has opened the remote database, it can work with it as if it were local. It can create, open, and delete tables, define QueryDefs, create Recordsets, and so forth.

Using Remote Databases with Data Controls

A program can also connect a data control to a remote database. The control's DatabaseName property should specify the remote connection information. To bind a data control to the database used in the previous example, the control's DatabaseName property should be set to //Beauty/C/Ch10/People.MDB.

The control's RecordSource property should be set just as it would be for a local database. The RecordSource can be set to the name of a table in the remote database or to an SQL statement.

Text boxes and other controls can be bound to the data control as usual by setting their DataSource properties to the name of the data control. The DataField property for these controls should be set to the name of a data field selected by the data control.

The example program Direct in the compact disk's Ch10\Direct subdirectory uses this technique to manipulate records in the database stored in //Beauty/C/Ch10/People.MDB. To modify this application to run on your network you must do two things:

1. Copy the database file People.MDB from the Ch10\Direct subdirectory to a remote machine. Place the files in a directory you can access from your computer.
2. In the Direct application, change the EmployeeData control's DatabaseName property to indicate the new location for the database file.

If your computer does not have access to another machine's file system, you cannot really test this program. You can change the data control's DatabaseName property to indicate the location of the database on your own computer, but then you will not be testing Visual Basic's network capabilities.

Attaching Remote Tables

The second method for accessing remote data is to attach the remote tables to a local database. When the remote tables are attached, a local name for them must be specified. This is the name the tables will be known by in the local database. Using this name, an application can access the tables as if they were local. Generally, accessing remote tables by attaching them to a local database is faster than accessing them directly, as described in the previous section.

Remote tables can be attached and detached either programmatically or by using the Data Manager. The following sections describe these two methods.

Attaching Programmatically

Normally to build a new table in a database using Visual Basic a program follows these steps:

1. Use the database object's CreateTableDef method to create a new TableDef object.
2. Use the TableDef object's CreateField method to create and define Field objects to represent the fields the table should hold.
3. Append the new Field objects to the TableDef object's Fields collection.
4. Append the new TableDef object to the database's TableDefs collection.

The following code fragment adds a new table called NewTable to the People.MDB database. The table contains one integer field named IntField and one date field named DateField.

```
Dim db As Database
Dim td As TableDef
Dim new_field As Field

    ' Open the database.
    Set db = Workspaces(0).OpenDatabase("People.MDB")

    ' Create a new TableDef.
    Set td = db.CreateTableDef("NewTable")

    ' Create and define the fields and add them to the table.
    Set new_field = td.CreateField("IntField", dbInteger)
    td.Fields.Append new_field
    Set new_field = td.CreateField("DateField", dbDate)
    td.Fields.Append new_field

    ' Add the table to the database.
    db.TableDefs.Append td
```

A program also uses a TableDef object to attach a remote table to a local database. Again, the program uses the database object's CreateTableDef method to create a new TableDef object. It should specify the name that the table should have locally in the call to CreateTableDef.

Next, the program should set the TableDef's Connect property to indicate the connection information for the remote database. The SourceTableName property should give the name of the table in the remote database. This need not be the same as the name given to the table locally, though making the names the same may prevent some confusion.

Finally, the program should append the TableDef to the database's TableDefs collection. The following code fragment attaches the remote table Employees on machine Beauty in the database file C:\Ch10\People.MDB. The local database is stored in Local.MDB. In this database the table will be known as LocalEmployees.

```
Dim db As Database
Dim td As TableDef

    ' Open the database.
    Set db = Workspaces(0).OpenDatabase("Local.MDB")

    ' Create a new TableDef.
    Set td = db.CreateTableDef("LocalEmployees")

    ' Set the connection information.
    td.Connect = ";DATABASE=\\Beauty\C\Ch10\People.MDB"
    td.SourceTableName = "Employees"

    ' Make the connection.
    db.TableDefs.Append td
```

This example is easy to generalize. The AttachTable subroutine, shown in the following code, takes the names of the remote database and table as parameters and attaches the table to the database TheDB. It makes the table's local name the same as its remote name.

```
Sub AttachTable(table_name As String, db_name As String)
Dim td As TableDef

    Set td = TheDB.CreateTableDef(table_name)
    td.Connect = ";DATABASE=" & db_name
    td.SourceTableName = table_name

    TheDB.TableDefs.Append td
End Sub
```

The Attacher application in the Ch10\Attacher subdirectory of the compact disk uses this subroutine. The Main subroutine that follows attaches the remote database tables Employees, UserGroups, GroupPrivileges, and Passwords from the People.MDB database on machine Beauty.

```
Sub Main()
Const LOCAL_DB = "D:\Ch10\PeopleW\Local.MDB"
Const REMOTE_DB = "\\Beauty\C\Ch10\People.MDB"

    On Error GoTo MainError

    Set TheDB = DBEngine.Workspaces(0). _
        OpenDatabase(LOCAL_DB)
```

```
    ' Attach the tables.
    AttachTable "Employees", REMOTE_DB
    AttachTable "UserGroups", REMOTE_DB
    AttachTable "GroupPrivileges", REMOTE_DB
    AttachTable "Passwords", REMOTE_DB

    ' Present a success message.
    MsgBox "Tables attached."
    Exit Sub

MainError:
    Beep
    MsgBox "Error" & Str$(Err.Number) & _
        " attaching tables." & vbCrLf & vbCrLf & _
        Err.Description
    Exit Sub
End Sub
```

This code attaches the tables to the local database Local.MDB. This database is empty—it contains no tables itself. It is used only to attach the remote tables.

To run this program on your network, you will need to make a few changes. First, copy the database file Ch10\Direct\People.MDB onto a remote computer that you can access from your computer. Next, change the definition of REMOTE_DB in the Attacher program's Main subroutine so it indicates the file's new location. Copy the file Ch10\PeopleW\Local.MDB onto your computer and change the definition of LOCAL_DB to indicate this file's new location.

PeopleWatcher Remote Once remote tables have been attached to a local database, a program can use those tables as if they were present locally. To make the PeopleWatcher application use the tables attached by the Attacher program, the program needs a single change. Instead of opening the People.MDB database, PeopleWatcher Remote opens the local database Local.MDB. The PeopleWatcher application in subdirectory Ch10\PeopleW on the compact disk opens this database using the following code:

```
Const DB_FILE = "D:\Src\Ch10\PeopleW\Local.MDB"
    :
    Set TheDB = DBEngine.Workspaces(0).OpenDatabase(DB_FILE)
```

No other changes are needed to PeopleWatcher. To test this program on your computer, all you need to do is change the definition of DB_FILE to indicate the location of the local database Local.MBD.

The process is even simpler if the local (empty) and remote databases have exactly the same name. For example, PeopleWatcher's databases could have been named C:\PeopleW\People.MDB on both computers. Then no changes would be necessary to PeopleWatcher. The only drawback to this method is that giving the databases the same name may make the process a little more confusing.

If the local and remote databases have the same name, making a distributed database application is a simple process:

1. Write the application using a local database.
2. Copy the application to other computers.
3. Create an empty database on each of those computers.
4. Attach the necessary tables in the original database to the empty databases.

Detaching Tables Detaching a remote table from a local database is even easier than attaching it. The program simply uses the Delete method of the database's TableDefs collection to remove the local table. The program should specify the table to be deleted by name, as in the following code:

```
db.TableDefs.Delete "Employees"
```

The Detacher application in the Ch10\Detacher uses the following code to remove the references created by program Attacher:

```
Sub Main()
Const LOCAL_DB = "D:\Ch10\PeopleW\Local.MDB"
Const REMOTE_DB = "\\Beauty\C\Ch10\People.MDB"

    On Error GoTo MainError

    Set TheDB = DBEngine.Workspaces(0). _
        OpenDatabase(LOCAL_DB)

    ' Detach the tables.
    DetachTable "Employees"
    DetachTable "UserGroups"
    DetachTable "GroupPrivileges"
    DetachTable "Passwords"

    ' Present a success message.
    MsgBox "Tables detached."
    Exit Sub

MainError:
    Beep
    MsgBox "Error" & Str$(Err.Number) & _
        " detaching tables." & vbCrLf & vbCrLf & _
        Err.Description
    Exit Sub
End Sub

Sub DetachTable(table_name As String)
    TheDB.TableDefs.Delete table_name
End Sub
```

Using Data Managers

Attaching and detaching remote tables in Visual Basic is fairly easy. It is also easy to attach and detach tables using Visual Basic 4's Data Manager or Visual Basic 5's Visual Data Manager.

Attaching with Data Manager The Data Manager command in the Visual Basic development environment's Add-Ins menu opens the Data Manager. Before attaching tables, the Data Manager must open a local database or create a new one.

The Data Manager's Attached Tables button opens a list of the database's remotely attached tables. On the Attached Tables dialog, the New button opens the New Attached Table dialog. After the dialog's data fields are filled in, clicking the Attach button will make the Data Designer attach to the remote table. Figure 10.1 shows the New Attached Table dialog. In this figure, the remote table Employees in the database \\Beauty\C\People.MDB will be attached to the local table LocalEmployees.

Attaching with Visual Data Manager Visual Basic 5's Visual Data Manager is similar to the Data Manager provided by Visual Basic 4. The Visual Data Manager command in the development environment's Add-Ins menu opens the Visual Data Manager. The Visual Data Manager must open a local database or create a new one before it can attach to remote tables.

The Attachments command in the Utility menu displays a list of the database's remotely attached tables. The New button opens a New Attached Table dialog similar to the one presented by the Visual Basic 4 Data Manager. After the dialog's data fields are filled in, clicking the Attach button creates the new attachment, just as it does in Data Manager.

Manipulating Remote Tables Once a remote table is attached to a local database, Data Manager and Visual Data Manager can manipulate it just as if it were contained within the local database. For example, double-clicking on the attached table presents a new screen where records can be inserted, edited, and deleted from the remote table.

The local database can even modify the design of the remote table. These changes affect the actual remote table, not just the local view of that table. If other applications remotely attach to the table, changes made by the local database could stop the other applications from working.

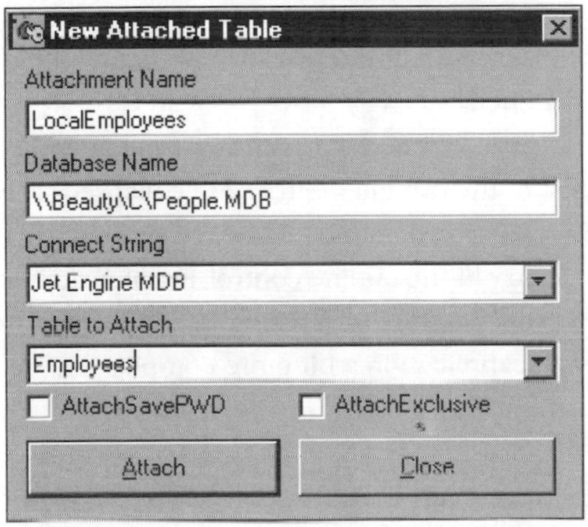

FIGURE 10.1 Attaching a remote table using Data Manager.

When the local database removes an attached table, the attachment is removed but the table itself is still present on the remote database. This can create a confusing and potentially dangerous situation. A database designer might delete a table from a database thinking the table is a remote attachment. If it is actually a table stored in the local database, all of the table's data will be permanently deleted. Designers must be extremely careful when using Data Manager to delete an attachment. Data Manager makes deleting a remote attachment and deleting a local table seem exactly the same, but the consequences are quite different.

Improving Network Performance

Although these techniques allow a program to treat remote tables as if they were present locally, it is important to keep in mind that they are not. Networks are relatively slow. If an application moves large amounts of data to and from a remote database, there may be a noticeable delay. Even when the data accessed is small, there will probably be a delay when the program first connects to the remote database.

PeopleWatcher was not designed specifically for use with remote tables. If the database contains a very large Employees table, the application's performance may suffer, particularly if the network is heavily used. There are several ways to address this situation.

First, the application can ignore the problem. PeopleWatcher's largest data transfers occur when the employee list is loaded. This happens when the application starts, when the user deletes an entry, and when the user selects the Refresh list command from the Edit menu. If the database is rarely modified, there is no need for the user to refresh the list. In that case, performance will suffer only when the application is first started. If the user starts PeopleWatcher and leaves it running all day, it will give acceptable performance most of the time. Even the largest transfers should be fairly fast unless the network is very heavily loaded or the database contains several thousand records.

A second option is to redesign the application so it does not give the user access to so much data at one time. For example, the program might require the user to specify a letter of the alphabet. The program would then present a list of only those employees having that last initial. Another strategy would be to allow the user to enter the name or part of the name of the person of interest. The program would then search the database and display only the records that matched.

A more complicated solution is to break large data transfers into a series of smaller ones. PeopleWatcher uses an outline control to list employees. Initially most of the outline's entries are collapsed. For example, the entry for names starting with "S" is not visible at first. The program could be rewritten so that it loads data only as it is needed. When the user expands the "S" entry in the outline control, PeopleWatcher would fetch the records for employees with the last initial S. This practice of fetching data only as it is needed would provide good performance, but it would make the application a bit more complicated.

Summary

An application can use remote databases either by directly accessing to the remote database, or by attaching the remote table to a local database. The latter method generally performs better. Both methods are extremely easy, so extending applications such as PeopleWatcher across a network is simple.

Part Four

Client/Server Applications

In client/server applications one application, the *server*, provides some sort of service for another application, the *client*. The Add-Ins described in Chapters 4 through 7 are servers. They provide some sort of design service for the Visual Basic development environment. The Aligner application presented in Chapter 5, for example, provides control arranging services for the development environment.

Servers usually provide access to some sort of centralized or shared resource. The resource might be a physical device such as a scanner, printer, or special-purpose processor. It could also be a logical construct such as a database or executable code. Add-Ins are this kind of server. They provide centralized access to executable code that helps a programmer work in the development environment.

In the past, client/server programming has been fairly difficult. Making two applications communicate effectively can be tricky, particularly over a network. In some applications the interprocess communication programming makes the application-specific code seem trivial by comparison.

When Visual Basic 4 introduced objects, it made client/server programming much easier. By creating a class and exposing it to the world, an application can allow other programs to create instances of the class. The class objects become servers providing whatever methods they support as services to the program that created it. Note that this kind of server can only be built using 32-bit Visual Basic, not 16-bit Visual Basic.

The following chapters describe several different methods for creating client/server applications. The TimeSync project described in Chapter 11 allows one computer to display the system date and time used by another computer. It also allows the user to synchronize the client computer's time with that of the server or to synchronize the server's time with that of the client. Even though this is a very simple application, it demonstrates the complex process of installing a remote server application.

Chapter 12 explains the QueryServer application that allows a user to select reports from remote report servers. By keeping report services centralized, QueryServer makes it easier to create and modify reporting capabilities.

The AsyncServer application described in Chapter 13 is similar to QueryServer, but it uses multiple servers to process requests for data asynchronously. The user can request several reports at the same time, and, if the reports are served by different computers, the servers can process the requests simultaneously.

Chapter 11

TimeSync

The PeopleWatcher Remote application described in Chapter 10 attaches remote database tables to a local database. This allows the program to treat the tables as if they were present on the local machine. It also allows many users on the same network to share data stored in a centralized database.

Not all programs, however, can use this database feature to provide centralized services. Many applications provide some service other than database access. To centralize these sorts of services requires true client/server programming.

The following section, "Using TimeSync," describes the TimeSync application from the user's point of view. It explains how a user can view a remote computer's date and time and synchronize the times of two computers.

The "Key Techniques" section lists the application programming techniques used by the TimeSync application. The rest of the chapter describes those techniques in detail.

Using TimeSync

As time passes, the clocks of two computers tend to drift apart. If one system has a file system remotely mounted on another, this drift can cause confusion. Sometimes a file can be created on one computer so that it looks to the other as if the file's creation time has not yet arrived. Synchronizing the two computers to within one or two seconds can prevent this sort of puzzling time travel.

The TimeSync client/server application allows a client application to access the system date and time on a server computer. The client can read the server system's time, synchronize its time to the server's time, or synchronize the server's time to its time.

Figure 11.1 shows TimeSync. When this image was taken, the TimeSync server application was running on the computer Beauty so the date and time shown in Figure 11.1 are the values for Beauty. The client program that produced the display shown in Figure 11.1 was running on the computer Beast.

FIGURE 11.1 The TimeSync application.

When the user clicks the Set Server Time button, TimeSync sets the server's time equal to the client's. In this example, the date and time on Beauty would be set equal to those on Beast.

If the user clicks the Set Client Time button, TimeSync sets the client's time equal to the server's. In this case, the values on Beast would be set equal to those on Beauty.

Key Techniques

Building and installing a remote server requires performing a complex series of tasks. Each task is relatively simple, but all must be performed correctly for the server to work.

At the same time, the application code must be debugged. Trying to debug an application served remotely on another machine while also trying to learn the server installation process can be quite confusing. Fortunately, there are ways to test and debug the server before it must be installed remotely.

Debugging an application is much easier if it is built in three distinct steps. As the steps progress, the server installation details become progressively more complicated. At the same time, the application code becomes more thoroughly tested. By the final step the server installation tasks are quite complex, but the application code has been thoroughly debugged.

The three steps and other programming techniques demonstrated by TimeSync are briefly described in the following list. The rest of Chapter 11 describes these techniques in detail.

- **Step 1: Testing within the Client**. Testing is easiest when the client and server are contained in the same application. This section describes how to test application code before adding the complexities of separate client and server programs.
- **Step 2: Testing Locally**. The next step is to test the client and server applications on the same computer. This section explains how to test the separate applications before the extra complexity of network connectivity is added.
- **Step 3: Testing Remotely**. Once the client and server are sufficiently debugged, they can be tested across a network. This section explains how to prepare a client and server for remote operation.
- **Trouble Shooting**. Solving problems with client/server applications can be quite difficult. This section lists some of the most common client/server problems and outlines their solutions.

- **Using RegClass**. The RegClass class provides functions for manipulating a client computer's system registry. This section shows how a program can use RegClass objects to learn such things as the name of a server computer.

Step 1: Testing within the Client

Debugging a single, integrated program is much easier than debugging a system with clients and servers running on different computers. Before adding the complexities of network communication to an application, it is best to start with a "client" program that contains a "server" class object. The client and server are easier to debug when they are contained in the same program.

Figure 11.2 shows schematically how the client and server relate. Here the client application directly creates an instance of the server class. It then invokes the server object's methods to obtain service. The interaction between the client application and the server object is simple and direct, making it easy to debug. At this point, there are no complex remote communication issues, so they do not interfere with debugging the application itself.

TimeSync Step 1

In the integrated step 1 TimeSync program, the TimeSetter class is the server class. This simple class provides two public functions and two public subroutines. The GetDate and GetTime functions return the current system date and time, respectively. The SetDate and SetTime subroutines set the server system's date and time.

```
Public Function GetDate() As Date
    GetDate = Date
End Function

Public Function GetTime() As Date
    GetTime = Time
End Function
```

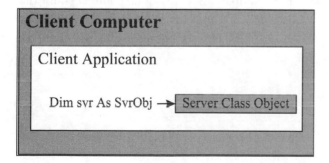

FIGURE 11.2 The server object running within the client application.

```
Public Sub SetDate(client_date As Date)
    Date = client_date
End Sub

Public Sub SetTime(client_time As Date)
    Time = client_time
End Sub
```

In addition to the server class, this program has a form that will become the client application when the client and server are separated. The form contains two text boxes. A timer control periodically updates these text boxes so they display the date and time returned by a TimeSetter object. The form also contains two buttons, one that sets the server's time equal to the client's time, and one that sets the client's time equal to the server's time. This form is shown in design mode in Figure 11.3.

The following code shows the timer and command button event handlers used by this application. You can find the complete application in the Ch11\Step1 subdirectory on the compact disk.

```
Option Explicit

Dim time_setter As New TimeSetter

Private Sub CmdSetClientTime_Click()
    Time = time_setter.GetTime
    Date = time_setter.GetDate
End Sub

Private Sub CmdSetServerTime_Click()
    time_setter.SetTime Time
    time_setter.SetDate Date
End Sub

Private Sub TimeTimer_Timer()
    TimeLabel.Caption = Format$(time_setter.GetTime)
    DateLabel.Caption = Format$(time_setter.GetDate)
End Sub
```

The time and date synchronization subroutines are quite simple. They do not take into account the delay caused by accessing the server application, and they do not compensate for additional time that may be lost due to a heavy network load. These functions are sufficient for synchronizing the clocks of the client and server computers to within a second or so.

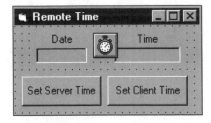

FIGURE 11.3 The Step 1 TimeSync form.

In this case, the two synchronization buttons do not do much. Because the server object runs within the client application, the client and server computers are the same machine. That means both of these buttons synchronize the computer with itself. Some server functions such as these cannot be completely tested until the client and server are running on separate machines. At this point, however, it is still worth stepping through the code in the debugger to test the server as much as possible.

Step 2: Testing Locally

Once the application code has been thoroughly debugged within a single application, it should be broken into separate client and server applications. These two pieces should then be tested within two instances of the Visual Basic development environment running on the same computer.

Figure 11.4 shows how the client and server applications interact schematically. When the client references the svr object, it is created in the server application and runs within the server application. The fact that the client and server both run on the same computer simplifies server installation and testing. The sections that follow explain how to build the client and server applications and how to test them on the same computer. The code for the step 2 TimeSync client and server programs is contained in the Client and Server subdirectories of the Ch11\Step2 directory on the compact disk.

Building the Server

A server for a client/server application is an OLE (ActiveX) server. As is the case for the Add-Ins described in Chapters 4 through 7, these OLE servers must provide some additional information so they can be correctly identified by the system. The necessary project properties are described in detail in Chapter 4, so they are listed briefly here.

Project Properties in Visual Basic 4 In Visual Basic 4, these properties are set by selecting the Options command on the Tools menu. The Project tab of the Options dialog is shown in Figure 11.5.

Three options must be set on the Project Options dialog to create an add-in: Startup Form, Project Name, and StartMode.

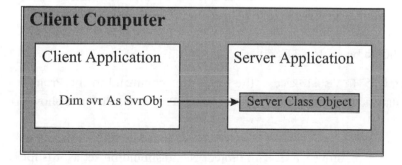

FIGURE 11.4 The client and server programs running on the same computer.

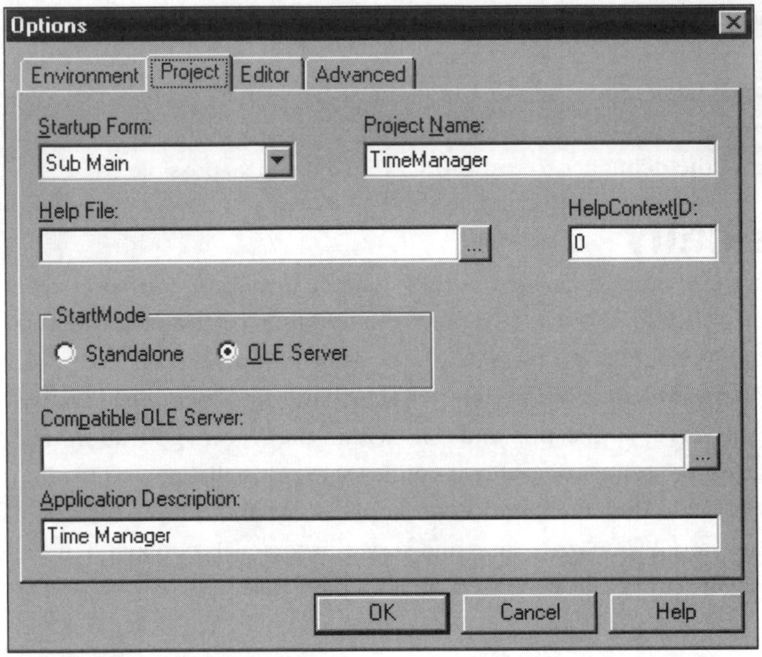

FIGURE 11.5 The Visual Basic 4 Project Options dialog.

For Visual Basic 4, the application's Startup Form should be set to Sub Main. The Main subroutine need not do anything unless the server must perform some sort of initialization at startup, but it must be present. The following code shows the Main subroutine for step 2 of the TimeSync project.

```
Sub Main()

End Sub
```

The Project Name option determines the name by which the server will be known to the system registry. Other applications will use this name to access the server. For example, in this case the project's name is TimeManager, and the timer server class is called TimeSetter. The client application will refer to this class as TimerManager.TimeSetter.

Finally, the program's StartMode should be set to OLE Server.

Project Properties in Visual Basic 5 In Visual Basic 5, the Properties command in the Project menu presents the Project Options dialog. The General tab of the Project Properties dialog is shown in Figure 11.6.

In Visual Basic 5, only two options must be set on the Project Properties dialog: Project Type and Project Name. Project Type should be set to ActiveX EXE. The Project Name should be set as it is for Visual Basic 4.

The Startup Object can be set either to Sub Main or "(None)." If it is set to Sub Main, the program must include a subroutine named Main.

The Server Class Because the step 1 program used a separate server class to provide server functions, building the server program is easy. The server class from step 1 is simply added to the server program project. All the Visual Basic code should remain the same. Only a few changes to the properties of the class are required.

In Visual Basic 4, the Public property of the class should be set to true. Its Instancing variable should be set to Creatable SingleUse (1) or Creatable MultiUse (2).

In Visual Basic 5, the Instancing variable of the server class should be set to MultiUse (5).

Running the Server At this point, the server is ready to run. When the server program is executed in the Visual Basic design environment, the program should start and then appear to do nothing. In Visual Basic 4, if the program immediately exits, the project's StartMode is probably not set to OLE Server. In Visual Basic 5, the Project Type option is probably not set to ActiveX EXE.

When the client application later executes, it will invoke the running server application. Break points in the client and server allow the execution to be studied and debugged.

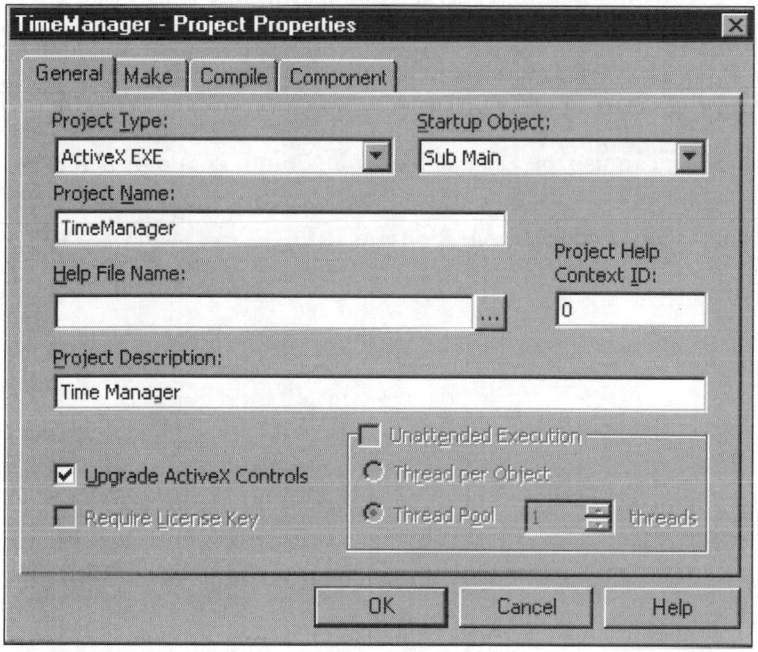

FIGURE 11.6 The Visual Basic 5 Project Properties dialog.

Building the Client

The client application should run in a separate instance of the Visual Basic programming environment. The new client program will be very similar to the step 1 version. The main difference is that the new version does not include the server class. Instead, it creates an instance of the server class using the running server application.

Before a program can use a class provided by another application, the program must contain a reference to the other application. In Visual Basic 4, the References command in the Tools menu presents a list of the project's references. In Visual Basic 5, the References command in the Project menu displays a similar list.

The running instance of the server application should be selected within the References list. This instance will have the name given to the server application—in this case, Time Manager.

When the server is highlighted, the References dialog will display the server's location. For a server running in a Visual Basic development environment, the server's location will end in ".vbp"—for example, C:\Ch11\Step2\Server\TimeSvr.vbp. Sometimes more than one server will be available. For example, the References dialog might list a Time Manager server with location C:\Ch11\Step2\Server\ TimeSvr.exe. This is an executable program, not a server running in the Visual Basic development environment.

Occasionally a client's References dialog will list a server as missing. This happens when a previously selected server executable is rebuilt. It also happens when a server running in the Visual Basic environment is started, selected in the client's References dialog, stopped, and then restarted. The old version of the server is no longer running so the class references are out of date. In these cases, the client's References dialog should be reopened and the new server selected.

Using CreateObject The client application can use the CreateObject function to create instances of an object supplied by a server. The following code shows how the TimeSync client creates an object of the TimeSetter class provided by the TimeManager server application.

```
Dim time_setter As Object

Private Sub Form_Load()
    Set time_setter = CreateObject("TimeManager.TimeSetter")
End Sub
```

Testing

At this point the client is ready for testing. When the client uses the methods of the server class object, the appropriate server code executes. Break points within the client and server code should be used to test the two programs thoroughly. Once the client and server are running on separate computers, debugging them becomes much more difficult.

Step 2 Summary

The following list shows the main steps for creating and testing the local client and server applications:

1. Build the server.
   a. Move the server class into a new Sub Main application. The Main subroutine does not need to do anything, but it must exist in Visual Basic 4.
   b. Set project options. In Visual Basic 4, set Startup Form to Sub Main, StartMode to OLE Server, and set the project name. In Visual Basic 5, set the Project Type to ActiveX EXE and set the project name.
   c. Set the server class properties. In Visual Basic 4, set Public to true and Instancing to 1 - Creatable SingleUse or 2 - Creatable MultiUse. In Visual Basic 5 set Instancing to MultiUse (5)
   d. Run the server to add the server to the client's references list.
2. Build the client.
   a. Remove the server class from the client application.
   b. Invoke the References command and select the server.
   c. Run the client.
3. Test the client and server thoroughly.

Step 3: Testing Remotely

After the client and server applications have been thoroughly tested on the same computer, it is time to test them across the network. Figure 11.7 shows the relationship between the client and server schematically. When the client references the svr object, the object is created in the server application on the remote computer. At this point, tracing the interactions between the client and server processes is more difficult than it is when the programs run on the same computer.

By now, most of the bugs should have been worked out of the client and server applications. Installing the server correctly is a complicated enough process without the extra bother of chasing application errors.

The following list shows the basic steps for installing and testing the remote server. The sections that follow explain each of these steps in detail.

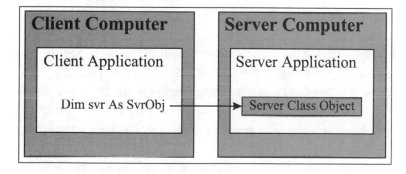

FIGURE 11.7 The client and server programs running on different computers.

1. Compile the server.
2. On the server computer do the following:
   a. Install the server program.
   b. Register the server.
   c. Grant access to the server.
   d. Start the automation manager.
3. On the client computer do the following:
   a. Register the server.
   b. Run the client.

Compile the Server

Compiling the server is easy. In Visual Basic 4, the Make EXE File command in the development environment's File menu creates the server executable. In Visual Basic 5, the Make TimeSvr.exe command builds the executable.

If the server executable already exists, Visual Basic asks if it should replace the existing file. When it does attempt to replace the file, the system may generate a Permission Denied error. This can happen if an instance of the client is loaded in the Visual Basic development environment. Even though the client is not running, Visual Basic locks the server executable so it cannot be deleted and replaced. Unloading the client application by creating a new one or exiting Visual Basic will unlock the executable so it can be replaced.

Install the Server

Installing the server is as simple as copying the executable file onto the server computer. Several Visual Basic and OLE support files must also be copied onto the server computer if it does not have Visual Basic installed.

The easiest way to install these files is to use the Application Setup Wizard. The Wizard should create a distribution kit just as if the server were being shipped to a customer.

In Visual Basic 4, the Setup Wizard provides an OLE service provider check box, as shown in Figure 11.8. Checking this box makes the Setup Wizard include OLE automation support files that the server computer needs.

The Setup Wizard may have a hard time finding all the components it needs to install the server. For example, if it cannot locate the Data Access Object library DAO3032.DLL, the location of this file must be entered into the Wizard manually. These files should be in the subdirectories of the Windows directories (\Windows in Windows 95, \WINNTxx in Windows NT). In Windows 95, these files may be in the subdirectories of \Program Files. If all else fails, the Windows Explorer's Find utility can search the entire hard disk for the missing files.

Visual Basic 5's Setup Wizard performs a similar function by asking if the component will be accessed through remote automation, as shown in Figure 11.9. Answering yes to this question makes the Wizard include the necessary automation files.

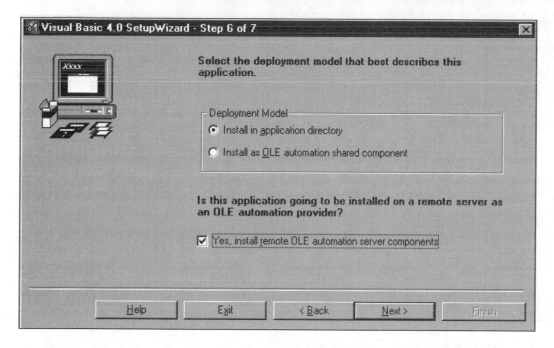

FIGURE 11.8 Selecting OLE components in the Visual Basic 4 Setup Wizard.

Register the Server

When a client needs to use the server application, it sends a request to the server computer. Entries in the system registry tell the server computer how to resolve the request.

Creating the proper registry entries is quite complicated. Fortunately, the entries need not be created by hand. If the server is installed using a setup kit created by the Application Setup Wizard, the registry entries are created automatically when the server is installed.

Otherwise, executing the server on the server computer creates the registry entries. The program will start and then stop almost immediately. Before it stops, the program will create the necessary registry entries.

Whenever an updated version of the server is copied onto the server computer, the registry entries must be updated. This can be done by executing the new version of the server.

Grant Server Access

The server computer will not allow external applications to create servers unless they have been given permission. The Remote Automation Connection Manager on the server computer manages server access permissions. This program is called RACMGR32.EXE and is located in the Clisvr subdirectory of the Visual Basic installation directory.

If the server is installed using a setup kit created by the Setup Wizard, and the appropriate OLE options are selected, the installation places RACMGR32.EXE on the server computer. It will be in one of the subdirectories of the Windows directory (\Windows in Windows 95 or \WINNTxx in Windows NT).

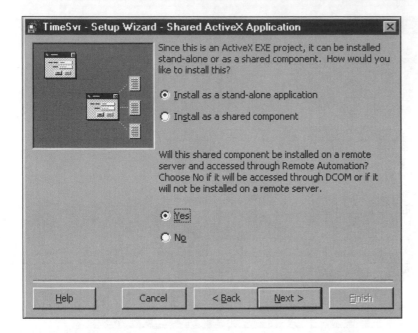

FIGURE 11.9 Selecting OLE components in the Visual Basic 5 Setup Wizard.

When the Remote Automation Connection Manager runs on the server computer, it presents a list of server applications similar to the one shown in Figure 11.10. An entry for the server class should be listed if it was correctly registered, as described in the previous section.

Clicking on the Client Access tab and selecting the Allow All Remote Creates option will let all applications on other computers create instances of server class.

Start the Automation Manager

On the server computer, the Automation Manager AUTMGR32.EXE must be running when the client attempts to use the server. This program is located in the same directory as the Remote Automation Connection Manager.

When it begins, the Automation Manager starts the protocols available on the server computer and then minimizes itself. The Automation Manager should remain running as long as the client may need to access the server.

Register the Server

The Remote Automation Connection Manager on the client computer tells the client computer where to find the server application. Clicking on the server's entry displays information about the server's location. In Figure 11.10, for example, the server class TimeManager.TimeSetter is served by the remote computer Beauty using the TCP/IP network protocol. After the appropriate network address and protocol have been entered, the Apply button makes the changes take effect.

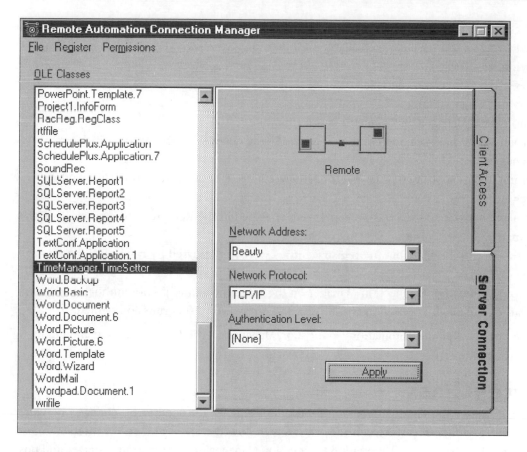

FIGURE 11.10 The Remote Automation Connection Manager.

This gives the client computer the information it needs to locate the remote server, but it does not actually select the server. The Remote command in the Remote Automation Connection Manager's Register menu selects remote service. The Local command indicates that the computer should use a local server rather than a remote one.

Run the Client

Now the client application can finally be started and tested with the remote server.

Trouble Shooting

Building a remote automation server offers many opportunities to make mistakes. During the later steps in the process, it can be difficult to find and correct problems. The following list describes some of the most likely problems and suggests ways to correct them:

• If the server is marked as missing in a client's references list, remove it from the list, close the list, reopen the list, and select the server again.

- The most common OLE automation error is Error -2147023143 OLE Automation error. This error usually means the server is unavailable for one of many reasons. Possible reasons include the following:
  - The server machine is not running.
  - The network is not running.
  - The Automation Manager on the server is not running.
  - The wrong server network address was specified in the client's Remote Automation Connection Manager.
  - The wrong network protocol was specified in the client's Remote Automation Connection Manager.
  - After a new network address and protocol were specified in the Remote Automation Connection Manager, the Apply button was not clicked.
  - A new server was installed, but the registry entries were not updated by running the new server.
- If the Remote Automation Connection Manager on the server machine has not authorized remote object creation, the client application will receive the error "Error 70 Permission denied."

  In this case, run the Remote Automation Connection Manager on the server machine and grant access to the server.

Using RegClass

The Visual Basic code for the client and server applications should not need to be changed between steps 2 and 3. The only difference between these steps is in how the client and server interact. These changes are made using the Remote Automation Connection Manager, the Automation Manager, and possibly the client's references list in the Visual Basic programming environment.

The Client and Server subdirectories of the Ch11\Step3 directory on the compact disk contain the client and server applications. The server application is identical to the server used in step 2. The client application has been modified slightly to demonstrate one more feature of remote server programming.

The RegClass class provides methods that a program can use to manipulate the system registry on a client computer. Before it can use this class, the client must include a reference to it. The RacReg entry should be selected in the project's References dialog.

RegClass objects provide two public methods. The GetAutoServerSettings function returns information about a server's registration on the client computer. This function takes as a parameter the program ID of the server class—for example, TimeManager.TimeSetter. It returns a variant containing an array of four values holding the registration information. Table 11.1 describes the values contained in these four entries.

The client application in the Ch11\Step3\Client directory calls the SetCaption subroutine. This routine uses GetAutoServerSettings to decide if the server is local or remote. If it is local, SetCaption sets the caption of the program's main form to "Local." Otherwise, it sets the caption to the name of the remote server machine contained in the second value returned by GetAutoServerSettings.

TABLE 11.1 GetAutoServerSettings Return Values

Entry Number	Description
1	True if the server is registered remotely
2	The remote machine name
3	RPC network protocol name
4	RPC authentication level

```
Sub SetCaption()
Dim reg As New RegClass
Dim result As Variant

    result = reg.GetAutoServerSettings("TimeManager.TimeSetter")
    If Not (IsEmpty(result)) Then
        If result(1) Then
            Caption - result(2)
        Else
            Caption = "Local"
        End If
    End If
End Sub
```

RegClass also provides a public SetAutoServerSettings function. A program can use this function to specify local or remote service, the server computer, and the protocol that should be used for a particular server application. The SetLocalServer subroutine that follows prepares the system to use the local server for TimeManager.TimeSetter. The SetRemoteServer subroutine makes the system use a remote server on the indicated computer.

```
Private Sub SetLocalServer()
Dim reg As New RegClass

    if reg.SetAutoServerSettings(False, _
        "TimeManager.TimeSetter") <> 0 _
    Then
        MsgBox "Error making server local."
    End If
End Sub

Private Sub PrepareRemoteServer(machine_name As String, _
    server_name As String, protocol_name As String)
Dim reg As New RegClass

    if reg.SetAutoServerSettings( _
        True, server_name, , _
        machine_name, protocol_name) <> 0 _
    Then
        MsgBox "Error making server remote."
```

```
    End If
End Sub
```

For instance, a program could use the PrepareRemoteServer subroutine like this:

```
PrepareRemoteServer "Beauty", "TimeManager.TimeSetter", "ncacn_nb_nb"
```

This statement indicates that the TimeManager.TimeSetter server should be served remotely by the computer Beauty using the protocol NetBIOS over NetBEUI.

Summary

Creating and installing a client/server application is a complicated process, however implementing the application in three stages can make the process much simpler. First, test the server within the client application. Next, test the client and server in separate instances of Visual Basic running on the same computer. Finally, after the application code is thoroughly tested, install and test the server remotely.

QueryServer

The PeopleWatcher Remote application described in Chapter 10 attaches remote database tables to a local database, allowing the program to treat the tables as if they were present on the local computer. Attaching tables gives an application quick and easy access to remote data, but it has some disadvantages.

First, processing a large number of records may be slow. Suppose a program computes a complicated function involving values contained in the records in a 1 million record database. If the program attaches to the remote table and then examines each record individually, the data for all 1 million records is transmitted across the network from the remote database. The program then examines the records to compute the complicated function. Figure 12.1 shows how the data flows from the remote database to the program.

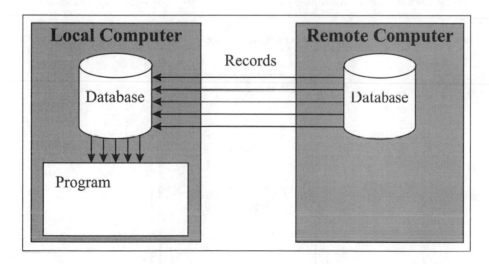

FIGURE 12.1 Attaching to a remote table requires records to be transmitted across the network.

A much more efficient solution is to use techniques similar to those used by the TimeSync application to create a server on the remote computer. The server examines the 1 million records on the remote computer and then sends only the result over the network. Sending data across a network is relatively slow. By reducing the amount of data sent over the network, the server can greatly improve the performance of the application. It also reduces the overall traffic on the network, making other network applications faster. This solution is shown in Figure 12.2.

A second problem with attaching to remote tables is that there is no centralized control over the operations being performed. That makes changing the operations difficult. Suppose an application produces a list of employee names by querying a remotely attached table. A separate copy of the application runs on each of 100 different computers so every user can see a copy of the list. Now suppose management decides that the list should also include each employee's telephone number. The application would need to be rewritten and reinstalled on all 100 of the users' computers. Figure 12.3 shows this situation. Black boxes with white text show computers where the new version would need to be installed.

Once again, a server application on the database computer provides a better solution. The server generates the employee list and sends it to the user computers. If the way in which the list is generated must be changed, only the single server application must be updated. If the user computers display the list in the same way as before, the 100 user programs can be left unchanged. Figure 12.4 shows this new arrangement. The single black box with white text represents the only computer that must be updated.

The QueryServer application uses remote servers to avoid these potential problems while providing a set of predefined reports. It uses servers to minimize network traffic and to provide a centralized location for report definition.

The following section, "Using QueryServer," explains the application from the user's point of view.

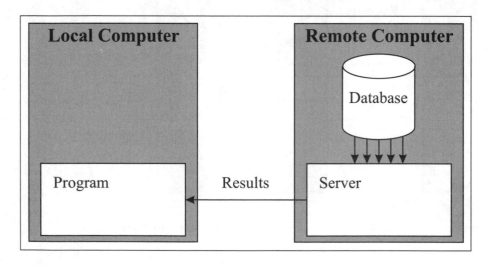

FIGURE 12.2 A remote server processes database records and transmits only results across the network.

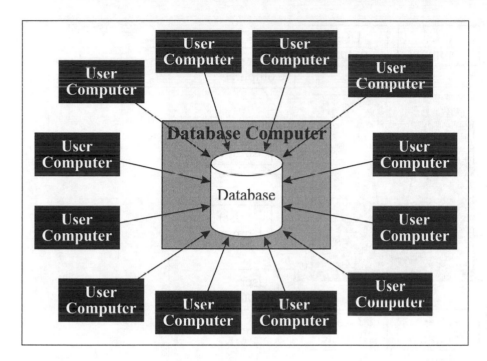

FIGURE 12.3 Updating 100 copies of an application that attaches to a remote database.

The "Key Techniques" section lists the main programming concepts demonstrated by QueryServer. The rest of the chapter describes those concepts in detail.

Using QueryServer

The complete QueryServer system consists of a family of client and server programs working together to provide reporting services. The ReportList client program presents a list of available reports. When the user selects a report, ReportList fetches it from a server and displays it. Figure 12.5 shows ReportList displaying a list of reports.

The Librarian server generates the list of available reports for ReportList to display. Librarian obtains the list by using a simple SQL query on the Reports table in the database Reports.MDB. To change the list of reports available, the only change necessary is to modify the records in this table.

The SQLServer program contains several classes, each of which implements a single report service. When the ReportList client is ready to generate a report, it creates an instance of the appropriate report class. That object uses parameters specified by the user to generate the report.

In the sample application, all of the reports are provided by a single server application, and they all come from the same database Purchase.MDB. They could just as easily be provided by different applications on different computers scattered throughout the network, each using a different database. They could even use other data sources such as text files.

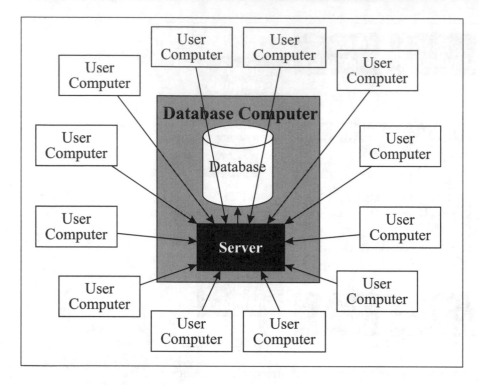

FIGURE 12.4 Updating 100 copies of an application that attaches to a remote server.

Figure 12.6 shows one alternative arrangement of the ReportList, Librarian, and SQLServer applications. In this picture, the report servers lie on two different computers and access three different databases.

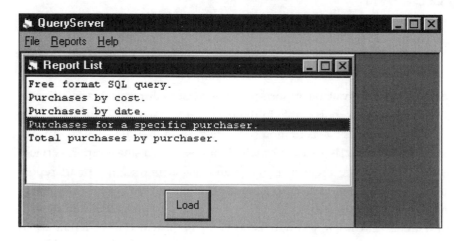

FIGURE 12.5 ReportList displaying the available reports.

Key Techniques

The QueryServer system uses the same client/server techniques described in Chapter 11. The new programming methods it uses are demonstrated by its three programs: ReportList, Librarian, and SQLServer. The following list describes these programs in brief. The rest of this chapter describes them in greater detail.

- **Building ReportList**. The ReportList client displays a list of available reports. This section explains how ReportList lists the reports, allows the user to pick one, and then generates and displays the report.
- **Building Librarian**. The Librarian server creates a list of reports for ReportList to display. This section shows how Librarian creates the list using a database query.
- **Building SQLServer**. The SQLServer program provides reporting services. This section describes SQLServer and tells how it generates different reports requested by the user.

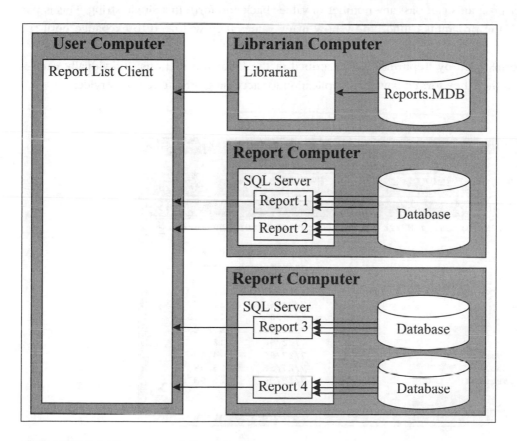

FIGURE 12.6 The pieces of QueryServer.

Building ReportList

The ReportList client program is the main user interface for the QueryServer system. It provides a list of reports, as shown in Figure 12.5. When the user selects a report, it uses an object from the SQLServer program to create the corresponding report. Figure 12.7 shows ReportList displaying a report.

The source code for the ReportList program is in the Ch12\RptList subdirectory on the compact disk. This program contains five forms and two .BAS modules. Splash.FRM contains a standard splash screen. SetPos.BAS declares the SetWindowPos API routine used by the splash screen.

Token.BAS contains the GetToken function described in earlier chapters. GetToken plays an important role in many of the system's client/server interactions. Arguments and return values for many server routines are packaged in delimited strings. For example, three values could be packed into a semi-colon-delimited string, like this:

```
value1;value2;value3;
```

The routine that receives this string uses GetToken to separate the values. Using similar techniques, client and server programs can pass any number of values back and forth in a single string. This is particularly useful if the programs cannot know how many values they will need to exchange until run time.

The other forms used by ReportList are described in the following sections. Individually, each is quite simple. Together, they form a powerful application for accessing remote report services.

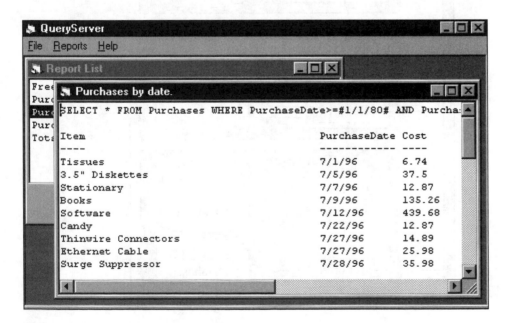

FIGURE 12.7 ReportList displaying report results.

QueryServerForm

QueryServerForm is the MDI form that contains all of the other forms in the ReportList program. This form contains almost no code. Even though it provides the menu bar for all of the other forms, it does very little to handle the menu commands. With the exceptions of the Exit and About QueryServer commands, it simply passes requests to other objects for further processing.

For example, the Refresh List command in the Reports menu invokes the LoadReportNames subroutine provided by a ReportListForm object. The ReportListForm performs the work of fetching the list of available reports.

```
Private Sub mnuRptRefresh_Click()
    ReportListForm.LoadReportNames
End Sub
```

Similarly the Save Report As command in the File menu invokes the SaveReportAs subroutine provided by the report display form. The following code uses the MDI form's ActiveForm property to make the currently active form save itself into a file.

```
Private Sub mnuFileSaveReportAs_Click()
    ActiveForm.SaveReportAs
End Sub
```

ReportListForm

The ReportListForm contains a list control and a command button. When the form is first created, its Form_Load event handler calls the LoadReportNames subroutine to fill in the list of available reports. The QueryServerForm also uses this subroutine to refresh the report list when the user invokes the Refresh List command in the Reports menu.

LoadReportNames creates a new object of the ReportLister class in the Librarian server program. It then invokes this object's GetReportNames function. For the time being, the methods used by the ReportLister object to build the list of reports is unimportant. To subroutine LoadReportNames, all that is important is that this server builds a semi-colon-delimited list of report descriptions and their servers and that it returns the number of reports available.

For example, suppose there are two reports with descriptions "Report 1" and "Report number two," and suppose they are served by the server programs Server1.Report1 and Server2.Report2. Then Librarian.ReportLister.GetReportNames would build the following text string:

```
Report 1;Server1.Report1;Report number two;Server2.Report2;
```

LoadReportNames uses the GetToken function to break this string into pieces. It places the report names in the form's list control and saves the server names in the array ServerName for later use.

```
Public Sub LoadReportNames()
Dim lister As Object
Dim txt As String
Dim i As Integer
Dim token As String
Dim not done As Boolean
```

```
    ReportList.Clear

    Set lister = CreateObject("Librarian.ReportLister")

    MaxChoice = lister.GetReportNames(txt) - 1
    If MaxChoice < 0 Then
        Beep
        MsgBox "No reports are currently available.", _
            vbInformation, "No Reports"
        End
    End If

    ReDim ServerName(0 To MaxChoice)
    not_done = GetToken(txt, ";", token)
    For i = 0 To MaxChoice
        ReportList.AddItem token
        not_done = GetToken("", ";", token)
        ServerName(i) = token
        not_done = GetToken("", ";", token)
    Next i

    ' Pop this form to the top.
    Me.ZOrder
End Sub
```

If the user double-clicks on an item in the list, the program triggers the Load command button. This button invokes the FetchReport subroutine to begin generating the selected report. When the report is finished, the subroutine determines whether the result is nonblank. If so, it creates a new ReportForm to display the results. The result will be blank if there is an error creating the report or if the user cancels the report instead of entering any required parameters.

```
Private Sub ReportList_DblClick()
    CmdLoad_Click
End Sub

Private Sub CmdLoad_Click()
Dim results As String
Dim frm As Report.Form
Dim choice As Integer

    MousePointer = vbHourglass
    DoEvents

    choice = ReportList.ListIndex
    FetchReport choice, results

    If results <> "" Then
        Set frm = New ReportForm
        frm.Caption = ReportList.List(choice)
        frm.ReportText.Text = results
```

```
        frm.Show
    End If

    MousePointer = vbDefault
End Sub
```

The FetchReport subroutine uses the server names stored in the ServerName array by the Load-ReportNames subroutine to create a server object. Visual Basic's CreateObject function takes as a parameter the name of the server object to create, and it returns an object of the appropriate type. For example, CreateObject("Server1.Report1") would return an object of the Report1 class in the Server1 program.

Once FetchReport has created the ReportList object, it uses the object's ListParameters function to obtain a string giving the parameters required by the report object. This string lists a prompt and a default value for each parameter, separated by semi-colons. For example, if the report needs the user to enter a reporting date with the default value of 12/12/99, the string might look like the following.

```
Report Date;12/12/99;
```

If the parameter string is nonblank, FetchReport creates a ParameterForm to allow the user to enter the necessary parameter values. It then takes the results and passes them to the report object's Load-Report function. This function uses the parameter values to generate and return the final report.

```
Public Sub FetchReport(i As Integer, results As String)
Dim obj As Object
Dim params As String
Dim frm As ParameterForm

    On Error GoTo FetchReportError
    Set obj = CreateObject(ServerName(i))

    params = obj.ListParameters()
    If params <> "" Then
        Set frm = New ParameterForm
        frm.SetParameters params
        frm.Show vbModal
        If frm.Canceled Then
            Unload frm
            Set frm = Nothing
            Set obj = Nothing
            Exit Sub
        End If
        params = frm.GetParameters
        Unload frm
        Set frm = Nothing
        results = ""
    End If

    results = obj.LoadReport(params)
    Set obj = Nothing
    Exit Sub
```

```
FetchReportError:
    Beep
    MsgBox "Error" & Str$(Err.Number) & _
        " creating ReportList." & vbCrLf & _
        vbCrLf & Err.Description, vbInformation, _
        "Error Creating Report"
    results = ""
End Sub
```

The FetchReport subroutine does not really understand what kind of report object it is creating. It simply uses the string obtained earlier from the Librarian as a parameter to the CreateObject function. This is crucial to making changes centralized. The ReportList program will reside on every user's computer. If this program knows anything about the reports it displays, it would need to be changed whenever the available reports change. If there were 100 user computers, the upgrade would be needed on all 100. Because FetchReport does not depend on knowledge of the reports, this is not an issue. Any necessary changes can be made either in the Librarian or in the report servers.

ParameterForm

The ParameterForm contains a label, a text box, and two command buttons. The label and text box have Index property set to 0. This form is shown in design mode in Figure 12.8.

The ReportListForm passes this form's SetParameters subroutine a semi-colon-delimited list of field names and default values. SetParameters uses Visual Basic's Load statement to create one label and one text box for each field. Figure 12.9 shows ParameterForm's layout for the following parameter list:

```
Start Date;1/1/80;End Date;12/2/96;Minimum Cost;0.00;Maximum Cost;;
```

As SetParameters creates the new text controls, it sets their Text properties to the required default values. After it has created all of the controls, it arranges them on the form.

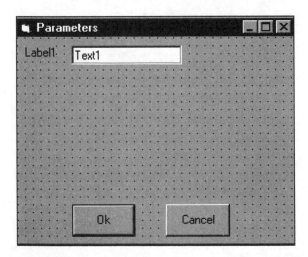

FIGURE 12.8 ParameterForm in Visual Basic design mode.

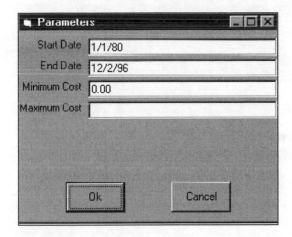

FIGURE 12.9 ParameterForm ready for user input.

```
Public Sub SetParameters(params As String)
Const gap = 60
Dim not_done As Boolean
Dim prompt As String
Dim default_value As String
Dim i As Integer
Dim y As Single
Dim dy As Single
Dim label_right As Single

    i = 0
    label_right = 0
    not_done = GetToken(params, ":", prompt)
    Do While not_done
        not_done = GetToken("", ";", default_value)

        i = i + 1
        Load PLabel(i)
        PLabel(i).Caption = prompt
        If label_right < PLabel(i).Width Then _
            label_right = PLabel(i).Width
        Load PText(i)
        PText(i).Text = default_value

        not_done = GetToken("", ":", prompt)
    Loop
    NumFields = i

    TextLeft = label_right + 2 * gap
    y = PLabel(0).Top
    dy = PText(0).Height + gap
    For i = 1 To NumFields
```

```
        PLabel(i).Move _
            label_right - PLabel(i).Width, y
        PText(i).Move TextLeft, y
        PLabel(i).Visible = True
        PText(i).Visible = True
        y = y + dy
    Next i
End Sub
```

The user should enter values in ParameterForm and then press the Ok button. The ReportListForm can then use ParameterForm's GetParameters function to obtain a semi-colon-delimited list of the values entered by the user. It passes this list directly to the ReportList object to generate the final report.

```
Public Function GetParameters() As String
Dim txt As String
Dim i As Integer

    txt = PText(1).Text
    For i = 2 To NumFields
        txt = txt & ";" & PText(i).Text
    Next i
    GetParameters = txt
End Function
```

This version of ParameterForm is quite simple. A more robust application would provide field and form validation features. This can be particularly important in database applications because the errors returned by database calls tend to be nondescriptive. For example, if the user enters "X" in the Minimum Cost field on the ParameterForm shown in Figure 12.9, the report server returns the following error message:

```
Error 3061 processing select statement.

SELECT * FROM Purchases WHERE Cost>=X ORDER BY PurchaseDate

Too few parameters. Expected 1.
```

The message "Too few parameters. Expected 1." is not very helpful to the user. Only a user experienced in SQL and familiar with the database design will be able to read the SQL statement and discover the problem.

ReportForm

ReportForm is extremely simple. All it does is display a report in a text box that has scroll bars.

One of the few nontrivial things ReportForm does is it allows the user to save the report into a file. It uses a common dialog control to allow the user to specify the file. The file dialog's initial directory is set to the value specified in the ReportDir variable. This variable is declared globally in module SetPos.BAS so all ReportForms have access to the same value.

After it has saved the report, ReportForm stores the file dialog's current directory in ReportDir. If the user saves another report using this or a different ReportForm, the file dialog will initially begin in this same directory. This is convenient for a user who keeps many reports in the same directory.

One simple enhancement that could be made to this program would be to store ReportDir in the system registry. Then it could be reloaded when the program starts. This would make the file dialog begin in the same directory each time the user ran the program.

The only other nontrivial task ReportForm performs is to manage the main MDI form's Save Report As menu item. This item should be enabled only when a ReportForm has the input focus. It would not make sense for the user to select this command when no reports were visible.

To make this command available when a ReportForm is active, the form's Activate event handler enables the command. To make the command unavailable when no ReportForm is active, the form's Deactivate and Unload event handlers disable the command.

For example, suppose ReportForm1 is active and the user clicks on ReportForm2 to bring it to the top of the other MDI child windows. First ReportForm1 receives a Deactivate event so it disables the Save Report As command. Next, ReportForm2 receives an Activate event so it reenables the command. This happens quickly so the user is never aware that the command was disabled and reenabled.

```
Private Sub Form_Activate()
    QueryServerForm.mnuFileSaveReportAs.Enabled = True
End Sub

Private Sub Form_Deactivate()
    QueryServerForm.mnuFileSaveReportAs.Enabled = False
End Sub

Private Sub Form_Unload(Cancel As Integer)
    QueryServerForm.mnuFileSaveReportAs.Enabled = False
End Sub
```

Building Librarian

The Librarian's job is to return a list of the reports that are available and the servers that support them. The Librarian project contains a single class, ReportLister, to perform this service. ReportLister performs its duty by querying the Reports table in Reports.MDB. This table contains two data fields. The Descr field contains a description of an available report. The Server field contains the name of the class that serves the report.

ReportLister's GetReportNames function selects all of the records in the Reports table and builds a semi-colon-delimited string listing the report descriptions and server names. This string is returned to the ReportList client program. ReportList separates the descriptions and server names to present the user with a list of the available reports.

```
Public Function GetReportNames(txt As String) As Integer
Dim query As String
Dim rs As Recordset

    On Error GoTo GetReportNamesError
```

```
query = "SELECT Descr, Server FROM Reports ORDER BY Descr"
Set rs = TheDB.OpenRecordset(query, dbOpenSnapshot)

' Load the names.
txt = ""
Do Until rs.EOF
    txt = txt & rs!descr & ";" & rs!Server & ";"
    rs.MoveNext
Loop
GetReportNames = rs.RecordCount
Exit Function

GetReportNamesError:
    GetReportNames = 0
End Function
```

ReportLister's **Instancing** property is set to 2 - Creatable MultiUse. When a new client requests a ReportLister object, it will be provided by an existing Librarian program if one is already running. In this program, the database connection is stored in global variable TheDB, declared in the main program's module LibrMain.BAS. If more than one ReportLister object is running within the same program, they can both access this database object. The program's Main subroutine opens the database when the server program starts running.

```
Sub Main()
Const REPORT_LIST_DB = "D:\Ch12\Libr\Reports.MDB"

    Set TheDB = DBEngine.Workspaces(0).OpenDatabase(REPORT_LIST_DB)
End Sub
```

In this application, Librarian is implemented as an OLE server. The list of reports could be built by simply querying a local database. A remote table could even be attached to the local database so the actual data could still be stored centrally. This would make generating the report list a little faster.

ReportList is simple enough, however, that it gives adequate performance implemented as an OLE server. It also provides a bit more flexibility than a direct query would.

For example, one of the next logical enhancements to the Query Server system would be user access control. With user groups and group privileges similar to those used by the PeopleWatcher application described in Chapter 8, the program could decide which users should be given access to particular reports.

This type of security is important if some of the reports contain confidential information such as employee salaries. It is also important for powerful reports such as the free-format SQL query capability provided by the SQLServer program. This "report" allows the user to execute any SQL SELECT statement so a knowledgeable user who executes this report can view any data in the database.

With only a small change to the free-format query server, the program could allow a user to execute any SQL statement. The Query application described in Chapter 9 does this. In that case, the program would need to be even more careful in granting access to the report server. Only the most trusted and skilled users should be allowed to execute powerful SQL statements such as DELETE, ALTER TABLE, or DROP TABLE.

To prevent potential damage, the program can implement user privilege checks centrally in ReportLister and allow the user access to only the appropriate report servers.

Building SQLServer

The SQLServer program in this example contains five classes, each of which serves one of the available reports. The main program does nothing, though the main module does provide two support routines used by the server classes. The ProcessSelect function executes an SQL query, much as the ProcessSelect function used by the Query application described in Chapter 9 does.

The WhereClause function takes as parameters an array of field names with operators (=, >=, <>, ...), a string containing a semi-colon-delimited list of field values, and an array of delimiters. Using these values, it constructs an appropriate SQL WHERE clause.

For example, suppose the WhereClause function is passed the following values:

```
Field names and operators:
     Quantity>=
     DateSold<
     Name=
Value string:
     12;4/1/97;Michaelson;
Delimiters:
          (empty)
     #    (number sign)
     '    (single quote)
```

Then the corresponding WHERE clause would be as follows:

```
WHERE Quantity>=12 AND DateSold<#4/1/97# AND Name='Michaelson'
```

The WhereClause function skips any fields with empty values. For instance, the value string "72;;12" contains no value for the second field so that field would be omitted from the WHERE clause.

```
Public Function WhereClause(names() As String, values As String, delimiters() As String) As String
Dim where_clause As String
Dim need_where As Boolean
Dim not_done As Boolean
Dim token As String
Dim i As Integer

    ' Compose the clause.
    need_where = True
    where_clause = ""
    not_done = GetToken(values, ";", token)
    For i = LBound(names) To UBound(names)
        If Trim$(token) <> "" Then
            If need_where Then
                where_clause = where_clause & " WHERE "
```

```
                need_where = False
            Else
                where_clause = where_clause & " AND "
            End If
            where_clause = where_clause & names(i) & _
                delimiters(i) & token & _
                delimiters(i)
        End If

        not_done = GetToken("", ";", token)
    Next i

    WhereClause = where_clause
End Function
```

A Typical SQLServer

The server classes in SQLServer are very similar. Each provides two functions: ListParameters and Load-Report. ListParameters returns to the ReportList client program a semi-colon-delimited list of prompts and default values. As described in an earlier section, ReportList separates the prompts and default values and, using a ParameterForm, allows the user to enter values for the fields.

The following code shows the ListParameters function for the Report1 class. This report takes as parameters minimum and maximum date and cost values. ListParameters uses the Visual Basic Now function to make the maximum report date be the current date.

```
Public Function ListParameters() As String
Dim date_now As String

    date_now = Format$(Now, "Short Date")
    ListParameters = "Start Date;1/1/80;" & _
        "End Date;" & date_now & ";" & _
        "Minimum Cost;0.00;" & _
        "Maximum Cost;;"
End Function
```

After ReportList uses the parameter string to obtain values from the user, it passes the results to the server object's LoadReport function. LoadReport builds an array listing the field names and operators, plus an array listing delimiters appropriate for each field's data type. Date values, for example, must be surrounded by number signs (#) in SQL queries. LoadReport passes these arrays and the values returned by ReportList into the ProcessSelect function to produce the final report. The report results are returned to ReportList for display.

```
Public Function LoadReport(params As String) As String
Dim query As String
Dim field_names(1 To 4) As String
Dim delimiters(1 To 4) As String

    ' Fill field_names with the database field
    ' names and appropriate operators (=, >, etc.)
```

```
field_names(1) = "PurchaseDate>="
field_names(2) = "PurchaseDate<="
field_names(3) = "Cost>="
field_names(4) = "Cost<="

    ' Fill in delimiters for different data types.
delimiters(1) = "#"      ' Surround dates with #.
delimiters(2) = "#"
delimiters(3) = ""       ' Numeric fields do not need delimiters.
delimiters(4) = ""

    ' Compose the query.
query = "SELECT * FROM Purchases" & _
    WhereClause(field_names, params, delimiters) & _
    " ORDER BY PurchaseDate"

    ' Execute the query.
LoadReport = query & vbCrLf & vbCrLf & _
    ProcessSelect(DB_NAME, query)
End Function
```

Free-Format SQL

Because it provides greater flexibility, the free-format SQL query may seem more complicated than other reports. Actually it is simpler. Because the user enters the SQL statement directly, the server does not need to construct a WHERE clause. It simply takes the statement provided by the user and passes it to the ProcessSelect function. ProcessSelect executes the indicated SQL query much as the ProcessSelect function used by the Query application described in Chapter 9 does.

The free-format query server code that follows is in the Report5 OLE server class.

```
Public Function ListParameters() As String
    ListParameters = "SQL Query;SELECT * FROM Purchases;"
End Function

Public Function LoadReport(params As String) As String
Dim query As String
Dim not_done As Boolean

    ' Get the query.
    not_done = GetToken(params, ";", query)

    ' Execute the query.
    LoadReport = query & vbCrLf & vbCrLf & ProcessSelect(DB_NAME, query)
End Function
```

Summary

The QueryServer application uses a client application and a collection of server programs to provide centralized report services. Keeping the report services centralized reduces network traffic and makes maintenance easier. It also provides opportunities for advanced features such as customization based on user privileges.

Maintenance becomes even simpler by the fact that the ReportList client need know only little about reports, because ReportList allows the user to specify report parameters. Using the ListParameters and LoadReport routines provided by the report server objects, ReportList can access the full power of the report servers.

Chapter 13

AsyncServer

The QueryServer application described in Chapter 12 allows a user to display reports generated on one or more different computers, but it does not take full advantage of the capabilities of all the computers available. Even though the reports may be produced by different machines, only one process can be running at one time.

Control of the client and server processes in QueryServer is strictly synchronized. Each step follows the previous one in a steady, predictable way. The client requests data from the server and waits for a reply. When the server is finished, the client displays the results and awaits the user's next command. Figure 13.1 shows a timeline of the events that occur during a synchronous call to the server. Notice that the client sits idle while the server processes the request.

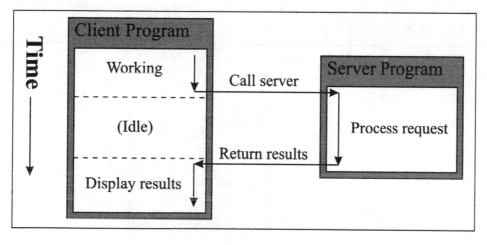

FIGURE 13.1 The timeline of events during a synchronous call to a server.

In a more efficient system, the client would call the server and then turn to other tasks. When the server finished processing the request, the client would display the results. Figure 13.2 shows the timeline for this kind of asynchronous system.

While an asynchronous server is processing a request, the client can perform other tasks. For example, it can request services from a different server. If all of the servers run on different computers, all of them can work on their separate tasks at the same time. The tasks will be finished sooner so the client program will be able to display the results sooner.

For example, suppose the client needs to display 10 reports that take 10 minutes each to generate. Using synchronous servers, the program would take 100 minutes to produce and display all the reports. If the 10 reports are requested asynchronously on 10 different computers, all of the results will be ready approximately 10 minutes later.

AsyncServer uses these techniques to generate reports. (These techniques work in Visual Basic 4.0 but not in 5.0.) The following section, "Using AsyncServer," describes the program from the user's point of view. It explains how the user can request reports and how AsyncServer displays the results.

The "Key Techniques" section after that lists the main programming concepts demonstrated by AsyncServer. The rest of this chapter explains those concepts in detail.

Using AsyncServer

In appearance, AsyncServer is very similar to the QueryServer program described in Chapter 12. It, too, queries a report librarian to present the user with a list of reports. When the user selects a report, AsyncServer uses a report server to generate the report.

Unlike QueryServer, however, AsyncServer generates the reports asynchronously. After asking a report server for a report, AsyncServer is ready to process other user requests so the user can ask for another report before the first has finished.

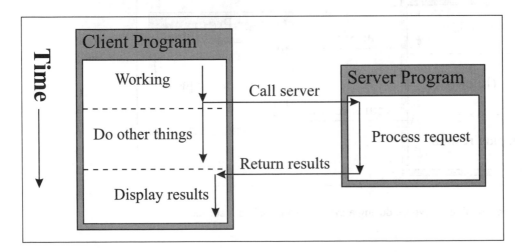

FIGURE 13.2 The timeline of events during an asynchronous call to a server.

To make its behavior a bit more clear, AsyncServer presents status messages describing operations that are pending. Figure 13.3 shows the AsyncServer application after it has requested a report listing total purchases grouped by purchaser. When the report returns, the program will update the status message to indicate that the report has arrived.

Key Techniques

The following list describes the Visual Basic programming techniques QueryServer uses to process asynchronous requests. The rest of the chapter describes these techniques in detail.

- **Building Asynchronous Servers in Visual Basic**. Visual Basic does not provide an easy way to create asynchronous applications. This section explains how a program can use timer controls to mimic asynchronicity.
- **Requesting Reports**. When the user requests a report, the ReportList client begins the process of requesting a report. This section tells how ReportList gets report parameters from the user and how it actually requests the report. It also explains how the program can display forms that imitate modality.
- **Generating Reports**. After the client requests a report, the server processes the request. This section shows how the report servers generate reports asynchronously.
- **Displaying Results**. After the server has finished generating the report, it invokes a callback object to send the results to the client. This section explains how AsyncServer displays the report server's results.

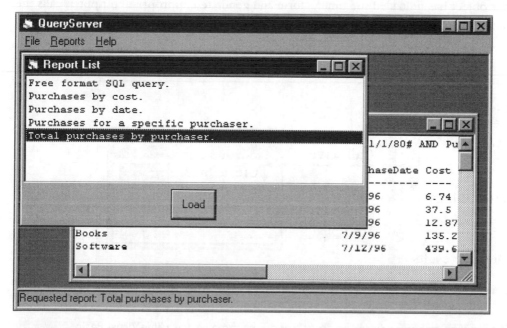

FIGURE 13.3 AsyncServer after requesting a report.

Building Asynchronous Servers in Visual Basic

Visual Basic does not provide a simple method for calling servers asynchronously. With a little work a program can create a similar effect.

When the client first calls the server, it should pass the server an object. When the server is finished processing, it will invoke one of the functions defined by this object. Because this allows the server to "call back" to the client, this object is known as a *callback* object.

It does not matter what functions the callback provides as long as the client and server agree. For example, the callback object class might define a public DisplayText subroutine that takes as a parameter some text to display. When the server invokes DisplayText, the callback object could display the text in a message box on the client machine.

The client calls the server passing it a callback object. To create the asynchronous effect, the server creates a form containing a timer control. It activates the timer and exits. This returns control to the client so it can continue performing other tasks asynchronously.

When the timer activates, it begins by disabling itself so it cannot activate again. It then creates a new server object to perform the actual server processing. For a report server, this is the object that generates the report results.

This object must also unload the form that contains the timer control. This step is extremely important. A Visual Basic program will not stop if it contains a loaded form. If the timer's form is not unloaded, the server program will continue to run even after it has finished serving the client. If clients invoke the server a dozen times, the server program will end up with a dozen forms loaded and wasting resources.

After the server object has unloaded the timer's form and generated appropriate output, it calls the designated subroutine defined by the callback object to send the results back to the client.

Figure 13.4 shows the timeline of events during this process.

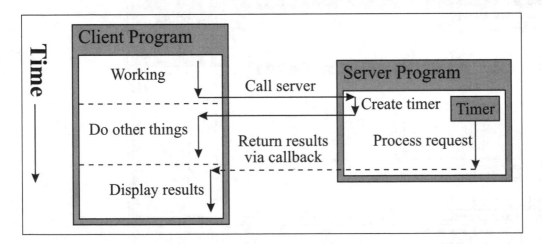

FIGURE 13.4 The timeline of events during an asynchronous call to a server using Visual Basic.

Requesting Reports

Much of the structure of AsyncServer is similar to that of the QueryServer application described in Chapter 12. Both applications use the same Librarian.ReportLister class to obtain a list of the available reports. The applications differ mainly in the ways they invoke the report servers and in how the servers work.

Both applications begin by requesting report parameters from the user. AsyncServer cannot present the parameter form modally, however, so the process is more complicated in the asynchronous version.

Getting Report Parameters

In QueryServer the FetchReport subroutine defined in the ReportListForm interacts with a report server object. FetchReport creates this object and uses its ListParameters function to obtain a list of the parameters needed by the server. It then allows the user to enter parameter values on a ParameterForm. Once it has obtained these values, FetchReport uses the server object's LoadReport command to generate the report.

The new version of FetchReport creates a server object as before. As before, it uses the object's List-Parameters function to obtain a list of the parameters needed by the report. At this point, the two versions of FetchReport start to diverge.

The previous version uses a ParameterForm to allow the user to enter parameter values. It presents this form modally so the user cannot interact with other parts of the application until the form is closed. Unfortunately, presenting forms modally can cause problems for an asynchronous program.

Suppose the program sends out an asynchronous request for a report and then the user asks for another report. The program presents a ParameterForm modally. When the earlier report finishes, it activates its callback object. In AsyncServer the callback object presents a new form to display report results. Unfortunately, Visual Basic does not allow a program to display a new form while a modal form is visible. If AsyncServer is to display report results asynchronously, it must not display ParameterForm modally.

For this reason, the program displays the ParameterForm modelessly. If the ParameterForm is displayed modelessly, the FetchReport code will continue immediately after presenting the form without waiting for the user to enter parameter values. This means the rest of FetchReport must change because the values required by the old version are not yet available. Rather than processing those values and starting the report server directly, FetchReport allows the ParameterForm to start the report-generation process after the user has entered the values.

The single exception to this rule occurs if the report server has no parameters. Then FetchReport calls the RequestReport subroutine to begin the report generation. RequestReport is also called by the ParameterForm when it finishes.

```
Public Sub FetchReport(i As Integer)
Dim obj As Object
Dim params As String
Dim frm As ParameterForm

    On Error GoTo FetchReportError
    Set obj = CreateObject(ServerName(i))
```

```
' Get parameters.
params = obj.ListParameters()
If params <> "" Then
        ' Create a ParameterForm to get the user's
        ' input and request the report.
        Set frm = New ParameterForm
        Set frm.ReportObject = obj
        frm.SetParameters params
        frm.TheCaption = ReportList.List(i)

        ' This must be modeless in case a report
        ' returns while it is running.
        frm.Show vbModeless
Else
        ' If we do not need parameters, request
        ' the report now.
        RequestReport obj, "", ReportList.List(i)
    End If

    Exit Sub

FetchReportError:
    Beep
    MsgBox "Error" & Str$(Err.Number) & _
        " creating report server." & vbCrLf & _
        vbCrLf & Err.Description, vbInformation, _
        "Error Creating Report"
End Sub
```

Imitating Modality

Although the program cannot use ParameterForm modally, it can at least ensure that the form remains on top of other application windows. With the SetWindowPos API function used to keep splash screens on top of other windows, the ParameterForm's Load event handler makes the form a topmost window.

The application's other windows are contained within an MDI form. Disabling the MDI form prevents the user from interacting with the other windows in the application until the ParameterForm is closed. If the user clicks on a form other than the ParameterForm, the application beeps just as if it had presented the ParameterForm modally.

```
Private Sub Form_Load()
Dim status As Long

    ' Make this window stay on top.
    status = SetWindowPos(hWnd, HWND_TOPMOST, _
        0, 0, 0, 0, SWP_NOMOVE + SWP_NOSIZE)

    ' Disable the main MDI form.
    QueryServerForm.Enabled = False
End Sub
```

```
Private Sub Form_Unload(Cancel As Integer)
    ' Reenable the main MDI form.
    QueryServerForm.Enabled = True
    QueryServerForm.SetFocus
End Sub
```

If the user clicks ParameterForm's Cancel button, the form simply unloads itself. If the user clicks the Ok button, the form starts the report-generation process. It does this by calling the RequestReport subroutine.

```
Private Sub CmdCancel_Click()
    Unload Me
End Sub

Private Sub CmdOk_Click()
Dim params As String

    Me.Hide
    DoEvents

    ' Create the delimited parameter list.
    params = GetParameters()

    ' Request the report.
    RequestReport ReportObject, params, TheCaption

    ' This form is done.
    Unload Me
End Sub
```

Requesting Reports

The RequestReport subroutine finally begins the actual report-generation process. It calls the report server object's LoadReport subroutine, passing it the parameters entered by the user. It also passes the server an object of class Callback.

Because asynchronous processing can be quite confusing, RequestReport displays a status message indicating that the report has been requested. The message appears in a label control inside a picture box attached to the bottom of the main MDI form. The SetStatus subroutine makes setting this message a little easier. Another message is presented when the report is returned.

```
Public Sub RequestReport(obj As Object, params As String, cap As String)
Dim cb As New Callback

    SetStatus "Requested report: " & cap
    cb.TheCaption = cap    ' Save the caption for use by the callback.
    obj.LoadReport params, cb
End Sub

Public Sub SetStatus(txt As String)
    QueryServerForm.StatusLabel = txt
```

```
        DoEvents
End Sub
```

Generating Reports

When the ReportList client invokes the report server's LoadReport subroutine, control passes to the server. The server activates a timer control to trigger the actual report generation later, and it quickly returns control to the client. This allows the client to continue operating asynchronously.

Scheduling the Report

At this point, control passes to the server object's LoadReport subroutine. In the Query Server application, LoadReport creates the report and returns the results. The new version saves the parameters and callback object for later use, and it creates a WakeUpForm object. This form contains a single timer control named Waker. LoadReport enables Waker and then exits, returning control to the client application.

```
Public Sub LoadReport(params As String, cb As Object)
    ' Save the callback object.
    Set TheCallback = cb

    ' Save the parameter string.
    TheParams = params

    ' Create a new WakeUpForm.
    Set TheWakeUpForm = New WakeUpForm

    ' Tell it what report to wake up.
    Set TheWakeUpForm.ReportObject = Me

    ' Activate the timer.
    TheWakeUpForm.Waker.Enabled = True
End Sub
```

Now the client application has finished requesting the report. Because it has no code running, the client becomes idle. The user could request a new report and begin entering parameter values on a ParameterForm. The user could also invoke a menu command or close a previously generated report.

Something rather odd occurs if the user exits the application at this point. When the report server finishes creating the report, it invokes a callback object to display the results. If the client application has exited, the callback will still create a new form to display the report. Building that form will force the application to reopen the main MDI form so the report results can lie inside it. The MDI form's Load event then causes the ReportListForm to present a list of available reports.

This behavior is decidedly strange. In other applications things might be even worse. For example, if the MDI form's Load event required the user to enter a user name and password, the program could enter a very strange state. The report results might still appear, even though the application would not necessarily be logged in as the same user.

One way to prevent this sort of behavior would be to disable the Exit command as long as a server request was still running. When no such requests were outstanding, the Exit command would behave normally.

Starting the Report Object

WakeUpForm contains a single timer control named Waker. It also declares a form-level variable, ReportObject. The LoadReport subroutine described in the previous section saves a reference to a report object in this variable. When its Timer event occurs, Waker invokes this object's MakeReport subroutine to produce the actual report.

```
Public ReportObject As Object

Private Sub Waker_Timer()
    ' Disable the timer so we don't trigger again.
    Waker.Enabled = False

    ' Wake up the report object.
    ReportObject.MakeReport
End Sub
```

Building the Report

The first thing the Report object's MakeReport subroutine does is unload the WakeUpForm. As mentioned earlier, this is extremely important. A Visual Basic program will not stop as long as it has any form running. If this form is not unloaded, the server process will keep running even after the client has finished with it.

The task manager application on the server computer can determine whether a rogue server is running invisibly. In Windows 95, pressing Ctrl-Alt-Del presents a list of running tasks. If a server appears in the list, it may need to be stopped manually. Figure 13.5 shows the Windows 95 task manager.

It is important not to confuse a runaway server process with an instance of the Visual Basic development environment that is working with the server. The server project loaded into the development environment will be named "AsyncServer - Microsoft Visual Basic [design]" in the task list. If the program is running in the development environment, the last part of this name will be "[run]" instead of "[design]." If a running server has been interrupted in the development environment, this last part will be "[break]." In Figure 13.5 the highlighted task is an AsyncServer running normally as an independent executable program. The top line shows the AsyncServer program running in the Visual Basic development environment.

In Windows NT, double-clicking on the server computer's screen background will bring up a task manager similar to the one shown in Figure 13.6. This task manager can also stop a runaway server.

After unloading the WakeUpForm, MakeReport must produce the actual report. The report parameters were stored in class variable TheParams by the LoadReport subroutine that created the WakeUpForm object.

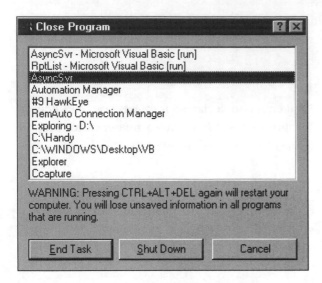

FIGURE 13.5 The Windows 95 task manager.

Once the report is finished, MakeReport invokes the callback object's DisplayReport subroutine to transfer the results back to the ReportList client application.

The following code shows the MakeReport subroutine for the Report5 class. This class processes free-format SQL queries. It is the simplest of the report server classes because it does not need to interpret the parameters specified by the user. The MakeReport subroutines of all of the example report servers waste between 5 and 10 seconds to simulate long queries. This makes the reports slow enough that the user can select a second report before the first finishes to test the application's asynchronous features.

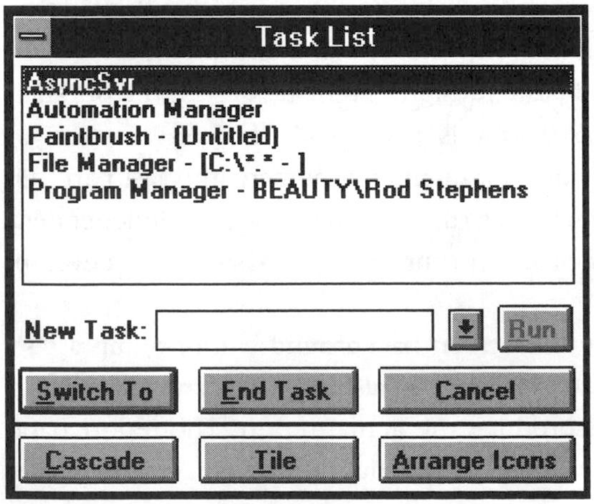

FIGURE 13.6 The Windows NT task manager.

```
Public Sub MakeReport()
Dim query As String
Dim not_done As Boolean
Dim results As String

    ' Unload the WakeUpForm.
    Unload TheWakeUpForm

    ' Get the query.
    not_done = GetToken(TheParams, ";", query)

    ' Execute the query.
    results = query & vbCrLf & vbCrLf & _
        ProcessSelect(DB_NAME, query)

    ' Waste some time to simulate a long query.
    Pause Rnd * 5000 + 5000

    ' Send the results to the callback object.
    TheCallback.DisplayReport results

    ' We don't need this any more.
    Set TheCallback = Nothing
End Sub
```

Displaying Results

When the callback object's DisplayReport subroutine is invoked, control returns to the ReportList client application. The client displays the report results and waits for the next user action or for another asynchronously generated report to return.

Displaying the ReportForm

The callback class used by ReportList is fairly simple. It contains one variable, TheCaption, which indicates the caption the report should display. This variable is set in the RequestReport subroutine that originally creates the callback object.

The callback object provides one subroutine, DisplayReport, that is called by the report server object. DisplayReport creates a new ReportForm, sets the form's Caption, and inserts the report into the form's single text control for display.

```
Public Sub DisplayReport(txt As String)
Dim frm As New ReportForm

    frm.Caption = TheCaption
    frm.ReportText.Text = txt
    frm.Show

    ' Set the MDI form's status message.
    SetStatus "Returned report: " & TheCaption
End Sub
```

Displaying the Report

ReportForm displays the report results much as the ReportForm does in the Query Server application. Its only interesting component is the SaveReportAs subroutine that allows the user to save the displayed report into a file. See the description of ReportForm in Chapter 12 for more details.

Displaying Messages

Just as a modal ParameterForm can cause problems for AsyncServer, so too can the MsgBox statement. Because MsgBox presents a modal dialog, the application can run into trouble if a callback object tries to display a report while a call to MsgBox is running.

To prevent this problem, Report List displays error messages through a form of its own rather than using MsgBox. MsgForm's ShowMsg subroutine takes as parameters a message to display and a caption to give the message dialog. It then presents the message, as shown in Figure 13.7.

MsgForm is fairly simple and does not provide many of the features available with the MsgBox statement. It does not rearrange its controls to take into account the size of the message. It also does not provide an assortment of images and buttons the way MsgBox does. It simply presents a message modelessly.

MsgForm's Form_Load event handler centers the form and uses the SetWindowPos API function to keep the window on top of the other windows in the application. Like ParameterForm, it disables the application's main MDI form. The Form_Unload event handler reenables the MDI form.

```
Public Sub ShowMsg(txt As String, cap As String)
    MsgLabel.Caption = txt
    Caption = cap
    Me.Show
End Sub

Private Sub CmdOk_Click()
    Unload Me
End Sub

Private Sub Form_Load()
Dim status As Long
```

FIGURE 13.7 MsgForm displaying an error message.

```
    ' Center the form.
    Left = (Screen.Width - Width) / 2
    Top - (Screen.Height - Height) / 2

    ' Make this window stay on top.
    status = SetWindowPos(hWnd, HWND_TOPMOST, _
        0, 0, 0, 0, SWP_NOMOVE + SWP_NOSIZE)

    ' Disable the main MDI form.
    QueryServerForm.Enabled = False
    DoEvents
End Sub

Private Sub Form_Unload(Cancel As Integer)
    ' Reenable the main MDI form.
    QueryServerForm.Enabled = True
    QueryServerForm.ActiveForm.SetFocus
End Sub
```

Summary

While Visual Basic itself does not support asynchronous processing, it provides all the tools you need to implement it yourself. After receiving a request from a client, a server can use a timer object to schedule an asynchronous action for later. It can then return control to the client so the client can perform other tasks. When the timer awakens the server, it can perform its necessary tasks and then notify the client by using a callback object when it has finished. Using these techniques, a Visual Basic program can access the full power of a network of computers that might otherwise remain underused.

Part Five

ActiveX

The Visual Basic 5 Professional and Enterprise editions introduced ActiveX to Visual Basic programming. ActiveX means different things to different people, but, in general, ActiveX is a specification detailing how objects should interact with each other.

One way the ActiveX specification can be used is to define controls made up of other controls. This kind of *ActiveX control* can be compiled into an .OCX file and distributed like any other custom control. An ActiveX control can even be loaded and used by earlier versions of Visual Basic.

Chapter 14 describes an alarm control that makes it easy for a program to wait for a specified time. The AppointmentBook application described in Chapter 3, for example, uses a standard timer control to wait for isolated events far in the future. The alarm control makes this sort of waiting easier.

The bar gauge control described in Chapter 15 allows the user to view and select values graphically. This chapter explains techniques required by any control that has a visible user interface.

Chapter 16 uses an array of bar gauge controls to build a histogram control. This control provides its own scroll bars when needed so the user can view a large amount of data graphically.

The Visual Basic 5 distribution CD contains several documents that describe ActiveX. The Tools\Docs\Ctg subdirectory of the CD contains more than two dozen files that make up the Component Tools Guide. The file CTCMP09.DOC contains the document "Building ActiveX Controls." You may want to read these documents, either before or after you read the following chapters, to learn more about building ActiveX controls.

Chapter 14

The Alarm Control

This chapter explains how to use ActiveX to build an alarm control. In some ways the alarm control is similar to the timer control provided by Visual Basic. Neither interacts directly with the end user, both are invisible at run time, and both provide a time-dependent event.

The timer control is designed to schedule periodic tasks that happen fairly often. Such events include displaying the next frame in an animation series and reversing a label's foreground and background colors to make it blink.

In contrast, the alarm control is designed for scheduling isolated events that occur infrequently. For example, the AppointmentBook application described in Chapter 3 schedules events far in advance. AppointmentBook uses a timer to schedule appointment notification, but the timer event is not designed for this task. The alarm control is much better suited for this kind of event scheduling.

The following section, "Using the Alarm Control," explains how a program can use the alarm control to schedule events. It also explains the test program AlarmTst.

The "Key Techniques" section lists and briefly describes the main concepts demonstrated by the alarm control. The rest of this chapter describes these concepts in detail.

Using the Alarm Control

As far as a client application is concerned, an ActiveX control is just like any other control supplied with Visual Basic or purchased from a third party. It has properties, methods, and events similar to those provided by any other control.

ActiveX controls come with several standard properties that require little or no effort on the control designer's part. The alarm control's Name, Enabled, Index, Left, Tag, and Top properties require no extra programming to implement.

In addition to these standard properties, the alarm control adds a single new property: AlarmDate. An application should set AlarmDate to the date and time at which the control should generate an Alarm event. If the program specifies a time but not a date, the alarm control assumes the current date. The client application should place whatever code it wants to execute in the alarm control's Alarm event handler.

The example program AlarmTst, which tests the alarm control, is shown in Figure 14.1.

When the user presses one of the buttons, the program sets the alarm control's AlarmDate property to an appropriate value. The button labeled "Now + 5 seconds" uses the following statement to set AlarmDate for five seconds after the current date and time:

```
Alarm1.AlarmDate = DateAdd("s", 5, Now)
```

The two "Time +" buttons add appropriate amounts to the current time but do not specify a date. For example, the "Time + 65 seconds" button sets AlarmDate with the following code:

```
Alarm1.AlarmDate = DateAdd("s", 65, Time)
```

After setting the alarm control's AlarmDate property, the program displays the current time and the time at which the alarm is scheduled. It then sets the alarm's Enabled property to true to activate the control. When the program's Alarm event handler triggers, it presents a message box telling how much time elapsed.

Key Techniques

The alarm control is relatively simple. It does not interact directly with the end user, has no public methods, provides only one event, and has only one nonstandard property. Even such a simple control, however, must handle several important tasks. These tasks are outlined in the following list and described more thoroughly in the rest of the chapter:

- **Working with Control Projects**. Creating an ActiveX control project is slightly different from creating other projects. This section describes the control's test application and how it interacts with the control.

- **Managing Control Display**. Controls such as the alarm control do not need to display a visible component at run time. This section explains how the control makes itself invisible at run time and how it prevents the developer from resizing the control at design time.

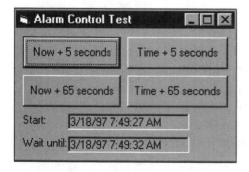

FIGURE 14.1 The AlarmTst application.

- **Implementing Property Procedures**. Property procedures allow the client application to read and set property values, both at design time and at run time. This section describes the single property procedure provided by the alarm control.
- **Setting Default Property Values**. When a control is first created, its properties should have some default values. This section tells how the alarm control sets default property values.
- **Reading and Writing Property Values**. Controls are created and destroyed many times during design and run time. This section explains how the alarm control saves and restores its property values when it is destroyed and recreated.
- **Delegating Standard Properties**. The UserControl object defines many standard properties. This section shows how the alarm control uses the UserControl object to simplify management of these properties.
- **Raising Events**. When the alarm control's AlarmDate arrives, the control generates an Alarm event. This section tells how the control declares and raises this event.

Working with Control Projects

Creating and testing an ActiveX control is a little different from creating other kinds of Visual Basic projects. This section describes some of the development environment features needed to build controls in Visual Basic. It gives a brief tour of the design environment for the alarm project group. Details on what the pieces of the projects do are presented in later sections.

The AlarmTst.VBG project in the Ch13 directory on the compact disk contains the alarm control project group. This group contains two projects: AlarmControl and AlarmTest. The AlarmControl project defines the ActiveX alarm control, and AlarmTest is its test application. The two projects are contained in the same group so they can be easily run together. Keeping them together makes it easy to change the alarm control and then run the test application.

The Project Explorer window shows a hierarchical list of the objects that make up each project. Clicking on a plus symbol in the Project Explorer expands the project hierarchies. The Project Explorer for AlarmTst.VBG is shown in Figure 14.2.

The AlarmControl project contains one object: Alarm. This is the object that defines the alarm control. The AlarmTst project contains the object AlarmTstForm. This is the main form for the test application.

The Test Application

Double-clicking on the AlarmTstForm entry presents the test program's main form. This form is shown in design mode in Figure 14.3. The form contains several command buttons and labels, plus a small control that looks like an alarm clock; that control is an alarm control. It behaves much as other controls do. The developer can grab it and drag it around, use the Properties window to examine and modify its properties, and double-click on it to see the source code associated with its event handlers.

Figure 14.4 shows the development environment's toolbox. At the bottom is the alarm control symbol; this tool allows the developer to create new alarm controls. Double clicking on the tool creates

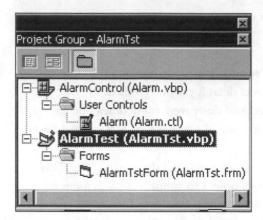

FIGURE 14.2 The Project Explorer.

an alarm control in a default position. Alternatively, the developer can click on the tool, then click and drag on the form to position the new alarm control.

The ActiveX Control

Double-clicking on the Alarm entry in the Project Explorer displays the control's *object window*. This window is very similar to a form window. It represents the UserControl object that contains the ActiveX control's components. The alarm control's UserControl object window is shown in Figure 14.5.

While this window is selected, the Properties window displays the UserControl object's properties. In this case, the UserControl's Picture property is set to an image of a small alarm clock. This makes the control display the picture when it is placed on a form.

Two other interesting properties for this control are InvisibleAtRuntime and ToolboxBitmap. InvisibleAtRuntime is set to true, indicating the alarm control should not be visible to the end user. The ToolboxBitmap property determines the appearance of the control's tool in the toolbox.

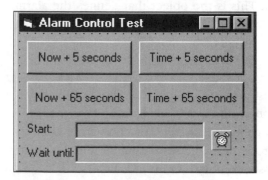

FIGURE 14.3 The alarm control test form in design mode.

FIGURE 14.4 The development environment's toolbox with the alarm control tool.

The control's object window, shown in Figure 14.5, contains a Visual Basic timer control. The alarm control uses the timer to wait until its specified alarm time. Using the toolbox, a control developer can add other controls to the object window. As usual, double-clicking on one of the controls displays its related source code.

While its object window is visible, the alarm control's tool in the toolbox is disabled. On the test application the alarm control is hatched over with lines. This indicates that the environment cannot use any of the ActiveX control's customized code that may be required at design time. This code is unavailable whenever the control's object window is open. Figure 14.6 shows the toolbox, test application, and control's object window.

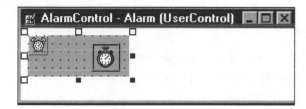

FIGURE 14.5 The alarm control's UserControl object window.

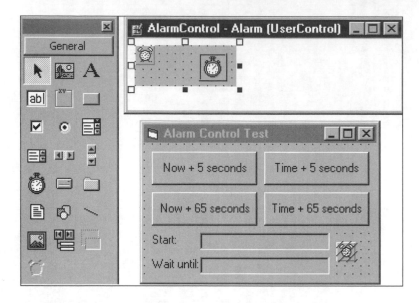

FIGURE 14.6 The toolbox and test application while the control's object window is visible.

The control can still be dragged to a new position in the test application because that is a standard operation defined for all controls. The control's standard properties, Name, Index, Left, Tag, and Top, can also be viewed and modified. The two other properties, AlarmDate and Enabled, require specialized control code that cannot execute while the object window is open, so those properties are not displayed in the Properties window.

When the control's object window is closed, the alarm tool is enabled in the toolbox, and the hatching is removed from the alarm control in the test application's main form. The AlarmDate and Enabled properties also reappear in the Properties window.

Running the Test Application
Pressing F5 or selecting the Start command from the Run menu starts the test application. If the ActiveX control's object window is open, the environment automatically closes it so that it can use the control's code.

Managing Control Display
Controls such as the timer and alarm controls do not need to display a visible component at run time. Whether an ActiveX control is visible at run time is controlled by the UserControl's InvisibleAtRuntime property. If this property is true, it will not be visible to the user at run time.

Because these controls are invisible to the user, there is no reason for the application designer to change their sizes. The alarm control's UserControl_Resize event handler triggers whenever the designer changes the control's size. The following code uses the UserControl's Size method to set the UserControl's width and height back to their proper values. Note that the width and height parameters passed to Size should be specified in twips. The Size routine uses twips no matter what ScaleMode is used by the UserControl object or the object containing the control in the client application.

```
Private Sub UserControl_Resize()
    Size 320, 320
End Sub
```

Implementing Property Procedures

An ActiveX control provides access to its properties through public property procedures. The values represented by the properties are generally stored either in variables local to the control or in the properties of controls contained within the ActiveX control.

To allow a developer or the client application to read a property, the control should provide a property get procedure. To allow a developer or application to modify a property, the control should provide a property let or property set procedure. Sometimes a control will not provide both. For example, a control can provide a read-only property by providing a property get procedure with no corresponding property let procedure.

The alarm control stores the time at which it should generate an alarm in the private variable alarm_date. The property get and let procedures named AlarmDate give developers and client applications indirect access to this value.

The AlarmDate property get procedure shown in the following code simply returns the value of alarm_date.

```
Property Get AlarmDate() As Date
    AlarmDate = alarm_date
End Property
```

The AlarmDate property let procedure that follows is a bit more complicated. First, the procedure examines the value it has been passed by the client application to see if the value includes a date (2/7/97 1:00 PM) or if it is just a time (1:00 PM). If the value is only a time, the procedure adds the current date.

Next, the procedure checks to see if the alarm date is more than 10 years from the current date. This prevents overflow problems later when the code calculates the number of seconds between the current time and the alarm date.

AlarmDate then stores the new value of alarm_date and calls the PropertyChanged subroutine. This notifies the Visual Basic environment that the value of the AlarmDate property has been changed and that the corresponding value in the Properties window must be updated. It also lets the environment know that the new value will need to be saved later in the test application's form file. This process is described in more detail in "Reading and Writing Property Values."

Finally, if the control's Enabled property currently has the value true, the AlarmDate property procedure invokes the AlarmTimer_Timer event handler. This subroutine starts the timer that controls the alarm.

```
Property Let AlarmDate(ByVal d As Date)
    ' If this is only a time and not a date,
    ' add today's date.
    ' When converted into a single, a Date's
    ' date part is to the left of the decimal
    ' and the time part is to the right. Thus
    ' a time with no date < 1.0.
    If CSng(d) < 1# Then d = d + Date

    ' Make sure the alarm is less than 10 years
    ' from now.
    If Abs(DateDiff("yyyy", Now, d)) > 10 Then Exit Property

    ' Set the alarm date.
    alarm_date = d

    PropertyChanged "AlarmDate" ' Tell VB.

    ' If we are enabled, start the timer.
    If Enabled Then AlarmTimer_Timer
End Property
```

Setting Default Property Values

When an ActiveX control is initially added to a form at design time, its properties are given default values. The control sets these values in the UserControl object's InitProperties event handler.

```
Private Const dflt_Enabled = False
    :
Private Sub UserControl_InitProperties()
    ' Do not run while loading.
    loading = True

    AlarmDate = Now
    Enabled = dflt_Enabled

    ' Run now if appropriate.
    loading = False
    AlarmTimer_Timer
End Sub
```

In this case AlarmDate is set to a calculated value: the value returned by Visual Basic's Now function. This value is unlikely to be useful to the application designer, but it makes more sense than some arbitrary constant value such as Jan 1, 1970, 1:00 PM. At least its date may be correct.

The Enabled property is initially set to the constant value false. The application designer will probably want the alarm control disabled until the program later enables it.

Using Ambient Properties

Another good method for selecting initialization values is to use the *ambient properties* of the container that holds the ActiveX control. The control can access ambient properties through the UserControl object's Ambient property. The following code shows how a control could initialize its BackColor property to the ambient BackColor value.

```
BackColor = Ambient.BackColor
```

Ambient properties give the control clues about how it can best display itself. They do not necessarily match the properties of the container that holds the control. For example, the ambient BackColor property matches the BackColor property of the form. If the form's background is blue when the new control is created, the control will have a blue background even if it is placed within a picture box that has a yellow background. If all ActiveX controls use ambient properties, the application should have a consistent appearance.

A control should generally initialize its properties to ambient values if possible. In particular, the control should use ambient values to initialize properties that affect the control's appearance, such as Fore-Color, BackColor, Font, and TextAlign.

Deferring Execution during Initialization

As a control's InitProperties event handler sets property values, it may temporarily cause the control to activate. For the alarm control InitProperties first sets the value of AlarmDate. If the Enabled property happened to be initialized by Visual Basic with the value true, the AlarmDate property let procedure will activate the alarm control. That routine will see that the alarm date has already arrived so that it will immediately trigger an Alarm event even though the application is probably not ready.

To prevent this from happening, the InitProperties routine sets the variable loading to true. The AlarmTimer_Timer subroutine checks this value to see if the control is in the middle of loading itself. If so, the routine does nothing. When InitProperties is finished loading the control, it sets loading to false and invokes AlarmTimer_Timer directly so it can take action if necessary.

Deferring action is even more important for other kinds of ActiveX controls. The bar gauge controls described in Chapter 15 have many property procedures that force the control to redraw itself. Using the loading variable to defer redrawing until every property is initialized saves many unnecessary redraws.

Reading and Writing Property Values

When a control is first added to a form in design mode, it is created. The UserControl object's Init-Properties event handler runs to set default values for the control's properties.

If the designer closes a form, the controls on the form are destroyed. At that point, the property values for the controls must be saved so they can be recovered later. ActiveX controls provide a WriteProperties event handler to perform this task.

WriteProperties takes as a parameter a PropertyBag object. Using this object's WriteProperty subroutine, the control can save its property values into the form's .FRM file.

WriteProperty takes three parameters. The first is the name of the property. The second is the value the property currently has. The last parameter is a default value. If the property's current value matches the default value, it is not saved to the file. Later, when the ReadProperties event handler loads values from the file, it sets properties with missing values to their defaults. This arrangement saves space in the form file when many properties have their default values.

The following code shows the alarm control's WriteProperties event handler. The Enabled property's default value is false, the value more likely to be specified at design time. The default value for Alarm-Date is the rather arbitrary Jan 1, 2000, 12:00 PM. Even though it is extremely unlikely that this value will ever be used by the application designer, the WriteProperty subroutine requires some default value. All that matters is that the default used when writing the property is the same as the value used when reading it (described in the next paragraphs). Then, in the unlikely event that the designer does select this value, the same value will be assigned to AlarmDate when the file is reloaded.

```
Private Const dflt_AlarmDate = #1/1/2000 12:00:00 PM#
Private Const dflt_Enabled = False
    :
Private Sub UserControl_WriteProperties(PropBag As PropertyBag)
    PropBag.WriteProperty "Enabled", Enabled, dflt_Enabled
    PropBag.WriteProperty "AlarmDate", AlarmDate, dflt_AlarmDate
End Sub
```

When the form is reloaded, the properties of the controls contained in the form must be reloaded from the form file. Like WriteProperties, the UserControl's ReadProperties event handler also uses a property bag object to manage control properties. The object's ReadProperties function takes two parameters. The first is the name of the property to be loaded. The second is the default value that should be assigned to the property if no value was stored in the form file by the WriteProperties event handler.

The following code shows how the alarm control reads its properties from the form file. Read-Properties uses the same Boolean variable loading used by the InitProperties event handler to defer action until all of the properties are loaded. This prevents the control from taking action before all the properties have been reloaded.

```
Private Sub UserControl_ReadProperties(PropBag As PropertyBag)
    ' Do not run while loading.
    loading = True

    AlarmDate = PropBag.ReadProperty("AlarmDate", dflt_AlarmDate)
    Enabled = PropBag.ReadProperty("Enabled", dflt_Enabled)

    ' Run now if appropriate.
    loading = False
    AlarmTimer_Timer
End Sub
```

Delegating Standard Properties

The UserControl object defines certain standard properties, such as BackColor, FillStyle, and Font. Rather than building these properties from scratch, an ActiveX control can *delegate* the duties needed to manage them. It does this by invoking the properties of the UserControl object.

For example, the BackColor property get procedure shown in the following code simply returns the value given by the UserControl object's BackColor property.

This routine returns a value of type OLE_COLOR. The Visual Basic design environment uses property procedure types to determine how it should present values in the Properties window. Using the OLE_COLOR data type for the BackColor property tells the environment to use standard color selection for BackColor in the Properties window.

```
Property Get BackColor() As OLE_COLOR
    BackColor = UserControl.BackColor
End Property
```

Similarly the following property let procedure sets the UserControl's BackColor property to a new value. It also uses the PropertyChanged subroutine to notify the environment that the value has been modified.

```
Property Let BackColor(new_color As OLE_COLOR)
    UserControl.BackColor = new_color
    PropertyChanged "BackColor"
End Property
```

To support standard properties such as BackColor, the event handlers for the UserControl's Init-Properties, ReadProperties, and WriteProperties events must also be modified. The InitProperties event handler should set a default value for BackColor. The ReadProperties and WriteProperties event handlers should read and write the value of BackColor to the form file just as they do for other property values.

This is all the code the control needs to support the BackColor property. Because the UserControl object provides support for BackColor, it changes the control's background color whenever necessary.

Property IDs

Each property and event defined by an ActiveX control has an identification number called a *procedure ID*. Certain key properties and events have special IDs defined by the ActiveX standard. In some situations, Visual Basic uses these properties and events by referring to their procedure IDs rather than their names. If an ActiveX control is to behave in the same way other controls do, its standard properties and events must have the correct procedure IDs.

The steps for assigning procedure IDs to standard properties and events are listed below:

1. Open the control's object window.
2. Select the Procedure Attributes command from the Tools menu.
3. Click the Advanced >> button.
4. Select a property or event in the Name box.
5. Scroll through the Procedure ID box and select the appropriate procedure ID.

Standard IDs should be assigned whenever they are defined. Standard IDs for methods are defined for click, key, mouse, and error events. Standard IDs are defined for many properties including Appearance, BackColor, BorderStyle, Enabled, FillColor, and Font.

The Enabled Property

The Enabled property behaves differently than other properties supported by the UserControl object. This property is not supported unless the control provides Enabled property procedures and Enabled has been given the standard procedure ID. If these conditions are not met, the control will not behave as other controls do.

Raising Events

Before a control can cause an event to trigger, it must declare the event. The alarm control uses the following Event statement to declare the Alarm event:

```
Public Event Alarm()
```

Later, when the control needs to trigger the event, it uses a RaiseEvent statement, like this one:

```
RaiseEvent Alarm
```

The alarm control uses a normal timer control, named AlarmTimer, to wait for the scheduled alarm time. A timer control's Interval property specifies the time between the control's Timer events in milliseconds. The Interval property can hold values up to 65,535, so the Timer events can be separated by, at most, roughly 65 seconds.

AlarmTimer's event handler begins by checking the value of the Boolean variable loading. If its value is true, the program is in the middle of initializing or reloading the control's properties; AlarmTimer_Timer takes no action.

Next AlarmTimer_Timer checks to see how far in the future the alarm time is. If the alarm time is less than one second away, the event handler disables AlarmTimer, disables the ActiveX alarm control, and raises the Alarm event.

Otherwise, if the alarm time is less than one minute away, the event handler resets AlarmTimer's Interval property so that the next Timer event will occur when the alarm is scheduled.

Finally, if the alarm time is more than one minute away, the code sets AlarmTimer's Interval property to 60,000 so that the next Timer event will occur in roughly 60 seconds. When that event occurs, the event handler will again see how far in the future the alarm is. This process continues until the alarm time arrives.

```
Private Const LONG_WAIT = 60000
    :
Private Sub AlarmTimer_Timer()
Dim remaining As Long

    '  Do not start if we're loading.
    If loading Then Exit Sub

    '  See how many seconds until alarm time.
    remaining = DateDiff("s", Now, alarm_date)

    If remaining < 1 Then
```

```
            '  Close enough. Raise the alarm.
        AlarmTimer.Enabled = False
        Enabled = False
        RaiseEvent Alarm
    ElseIf remaining < LONG_WAIT Then
            '  It's less than one minute. Set the
            '  Interval property to wait for the
            '  required number of seconds.
        AlarmTimer.Interval = remaining * 1000
        AlarmTimer.Enabled = True
    Else
            '  It's more than one minute. Set the
            '  Interval property to wait 60 seconds.
        AlarmTimer.Interval = LONG_WAIT
        AlarmTimer.Enabled = True
    End If
End Sub
```

Summary

The Alarm control is fairly simple. It has no visible interface at run time, provides just one nonstandard property, AlarmDate, and supports a single new event, Alarm. Despite its simplicity, the Alarm control performs all of the major tasks required of any ActiveX control. It initializes its property values in the InitProperties event handler, saves values in the WriteProperties event handler, and reloads them in ReadProperties. Other ActiveX controls, such as the BarGauge control described in Chapter 15, provide more complex functionality, but they all perform these same three basic tasks.

Chapter 15

Bar Gauge

The ActiveX alarm control described in Chapter 14 works behind the scenes with a client application rather than interacting directly with the end user. This control is fairly extreme in the sense that it has no user interface at run time. At the other extreme, the bar gauge control has a rich user interface. It is designed to interact directly with the end user while displaying and modifying data values.

The first section in this chapter, "Interacting with Bar Gauge," explains how the control works from the end user's point of view. It describes the control's run time user interface, and it explains the ways the user can interact with the control.

The section "Programming Bar Gauge" details the control's features from an application developer's point of view. It describes the properties and events an application can use to manage the control.

The "Key Techniques" section briefly lists the main tasks the ActiveX control must handle to support both the application developer at design time and the end user at run time. The rest of this chapter describes the bar gauge's internals and explains how the control handles these tasks.

Interacting with Bar Gauge

The bar gauge control displays a value by showing an area partially covered with a foreground color. This is similar to the way a thermometer shows the temperature by covering part of its scale with mercury or some other liquid.

When the bar gauge is enabled, the user can click and drag on it to set a new value. When the control has the input focus, it displays a dotted border and the user can modify the control's value using the arrow keys. The up and down arrow keys affect vertical gauges, and the left and right arrow keys affect horizontal gauges.

The example program group BarGauge.VBG in the Ch15\BarGauge directory demonstrates the bar gauge control. It creates four gauges, two horizontal and two vertical. When the user changes the value of a gauge, the program updates the label next to that gauge to show the new value. Figure 15.1 shows the running BarGauge program. The vertical gauge on the right displays the dotted border indicating that it has the input focus.

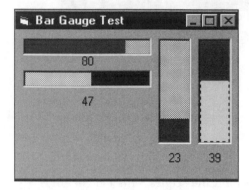

FIGURE 15.1 The BarGauge application.

Programming Bar Gauge

The bar gauge control supports several standard properties as well as a few that are customized for its own needs. The standard properties are listed in Table 15.1. They behave exactly as they do for other controls. The control's customized properties are listed in Table 15.2.

TABLE 15.1 Standard Bar Gauge Properties

Property	Type	Meaning
Appearance	AppearanceValue	This enumerated type can have the values: appears2D—Flat, two-dimensional borders appears3D—Three-dimensional borders
BackColor	OLE_COLOR	The gauge's background color
ForeColor	OLE_COLOR	The color displayed to represent the value (the mercury in a thermometer)
TabStop	Boolean	Determines whether the tab key stops at the control
Enabled	Boolean	Determines whether the user can interact with the control

TABLE 15.2 Customized Bar Gauge Properties

Property	Type	Meaning
Min	Long	The gauge's minimum value
Max	Long	The gauge's maximum value
Value	Long	The gauge's current value
KeyChangeAmount	Long	The amount Value changes when the user presses an arrow key
Style	GaugeStyle	This enumerated type can have the values: gsLeftToRight—Horizontal with Max on the right gsRightToLeft—Horizontal with Max on the left gsBottomToTop—Vertical with Max on the top gsTopToBottom—Vertical with Max on the bottom

In some ways this control is similar to the scroll bars provided by Visual Basic. The Min and Max properties determine the range of values represented by the control. The Value property determines its current value. The KeyChangeAmount property indicates the amount by which the Value is modified in response to arrow keys.

Key Techniques

The bar gauge control implements the same standard subroutines required by the alarm control described in Chapter 14 so they are not described here. These include the InitProperties, WriteProperties, and ReadProperties event handlers needed to manage an ActiveX control's properties.

The bar gauge also provides new user interaction capabilities not provided by the alarm control. The following list briefly describes those features. The rest of the chapter explains how they are implemented in detail.

- **Managing Bar Gauge Properties**. Because the bar gauge has a visible interface, many of this control's properties are handled quite differently than those used by the alarm control. This section describes the bar gauge's new properties.
- **Drawing Bar Gauge**. Most of the bar gauge's properties affect the control's appearance. This section explains how the control redraws itself when property values change.
- **Managing the Mouse**. Because the mouse is used to select a bar gauge's value, mouse events play a critical role in the bar gauge control. This section tells how the control reacts to mouse movements.

- **Handling Keyboard Events**. To make itself easier to use, the bar gauge allows the user to change the control's value using the arrow keys. This section explains how the bar gauge handles keyboard events.
- **Modifying Bar Gauge**. The bar gauge control demonstrates how an ActiveX control can handle mouse and keyboard events. This section describes slight modifications that create other gauges with very different appearances.

Managing Bar Gauge Properties

Like the alarm control's properties, the properties of the bar gauge are saved and read from a project's form file by the WriteProperties and ReadProperties event handlers. These routines are very similar to those used by the alarm control, so they are not shown here. You can find them in the Ch15 directory on the compact disk.

The bar gauge's Enabled property works just as it does for the alarm control, so it is not described here. Several other properties are more interesting; they are explained in the following sections.

Min, Max, KeyChangeAmount, and Value

The bar gauge's Min, Max, KeyChangeAmount, and Value properties are all long integers, and they are all handled similarly. Each is stored in a variable that is private to the control. For instance, the variable that stores the value for Min is declared as follows:

```
Private the_min As Long
```

The property procedures for these values are also quite similar. The property get procedures simply return the value of the private variable. The property let procedures store the new value in the control's private variable and use the PropertyChanged subroutine to notify Visual Basic that the property value has been modified. They also invoke the control's Paint subroutine. This makes the control redraw itself so that it is displayed using the new property values. The Paint subroutine is described in the section, "Drawing Bar Gauge," in this chapter.

The following code shows the property procedures for the Min property. The procedures for Max, KeyChangeAmount, and Value are very similar.

```
Public Property Get Min() As Long
    Min = the_min
End Property

Public Property Let Min(val As Long)
    the_min = val

    PropertyChanged "Min"    ' Tell VB.
    Paint    ' Redisplay the gauge.
End Property
```

BackColor and ForeColor

The UserControl object provides ForeColor and BackColor properties, so the bar gauge can delegate ForeColor and BackColor to the UserControl object. The following code shows how the control delegates the ForeColor property let procedure using the UserControl's ForeColor property. The Picture2D and Picture3D objects are not important right now. They are explained later in the section,"Appearance."

```
Public Property Let ForeColor(clr As OLE_COLOR)
    UserControl.ForeColor = clr
    Picture2D.ForeColor = clr
    Picture3D.ForeColor = clr

    PropertyChanged "ForeColor" ' Tell VB.
    Paint    ' Redisplay the gauge.
End Property
```

To make the bar gauge's foreground and background colors match the rest of the application, the bar gauge initializes these values using ambient values, as described in Chapter 14. The following code shows how InitProperties initializes the control's properties.

InitProperties uses the Boolean variable loading to defer redrawing the control until all the properties are loaded. Most of the bar gauge's property let procedures make the control redraw itself when they are invoked. Using the loading variable prevents the control from redrawing itself unnecessarily.

```
Private Sub UserControl_InitProperties()
    loading = True

    Appearance = dflt_Appearance
    BackColor = Ambient.BackColor
    ForeColor = Ambient.ForeColor
    Max = dflt_Max
    Min = dflt_Min
    Style - dflt_Style
    Value = dflt_Value
    KeyChangeAmount = dflt_KeyChangeAmount

    Enabled = dflt_Enabled

    ' Redraw now.
    loading = False
    Paint
End Sub
```

Because ForeColor and BackColor are colors, the control declares all the variables dealing with them to be of type OLE_COLOR. For example, the ForeColor property get procedure shown here is declared to return a value of type OLE_COLOR.

```
Public Property Get ForeColor() As OLE_COLOR
    ForeColor = UserControl.ForeColor
End Property
```

Declaring a color property to be of type OLE_COLOR allows Visual Basic to present the color properly in the Properties window at design time. The entry for ForeColor is shown with a small sample of the color selected and the color value in hexadecimal. If the application designer clicks on the drop-down arrow to the right of this value, a standard color selection palette appears.

It is common, particularly in older programs, to declare color values as long integers. If the control did this, the Properties window would not display the color sample. Instead, it would show the color's value in a practically meaningless decimal form and would not provide the standard color selection palette.

Style

Declaring property procedures using the correct data type helps the Properties window display values correctly for data types other than colors, too. Declaring the Enabled property to be of type Boolean makes the Properties window display its values as true or false.

The bar gauge's Style property is an enumerated type. It can take only one of four values, each of which has a special meaning. The values are defined in the control class using the following public enum statement. The control keeps track of its style in the private variable the_style, declared as type GaugeStyle.

```
Public Enum GaugeStyle
    gsLeftToRight
    gsRightToLeft
    gsBottomToTop
    gsTopToBottom
End Enum
Private the_style As GaugeStyle
```

The Style property procedures shown here are declared using the enumerated data type GaugeStyle.

```
Public Property Let Style(val As GaugeStyle)
    the_style = val

    PropertyChanged "Style" ' Tell VB.
    Paint    ' Redisplay the gauge.
End Property

Public Property Get Style() As GaugeStyle
    Style = the_style
End Property
```

Using an enumerated type for the property procedures allows the Properties window to list the choices that are available. The window displays the enumerated value that is currently selected. Clicking on the value's drop-down arrow makes Visual Basic present a list of the allowed choices.

Using an enumerated type also has the advantage that it allows application designers to specify values for this property using the enumerated constants. The following code would make a bar gauge use the bottom-to-top vertical style.

```
BarGauge1.Style = gsBottomToTop
```

The application designer can find a list of the allowable values for an enumerated property using the Object Browser. Figure 15.2 shows the Object Browser with the Style property selected.

The last part of the description includes text that describes the purpose of the property. In this case, the text reads, "Orientation and direction (left-to-right, etc.)." This text is set by opening the control's design window and selecting the Procedure Attributes command from the Tools menu. After selecting the property from the Name list, the text to be displayed by the Object Browser should be entered in the Description box.

Clicking on the highlighted text GaugeStyle in the Object Browser makes the Browser display the definition of the type GaugeStyle. Figure 15.3 shows the Object Browser displaying this definition.

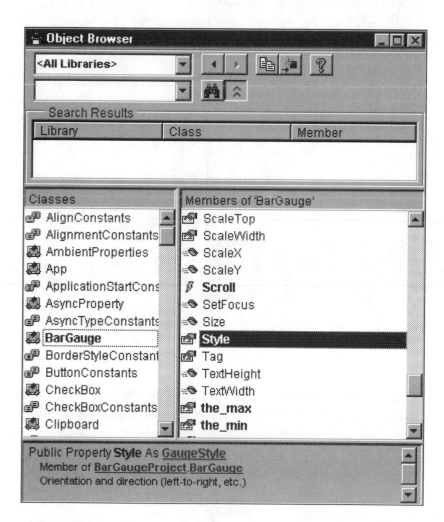

FIGURE 15.2 Examining the Style property using the Object Browser.

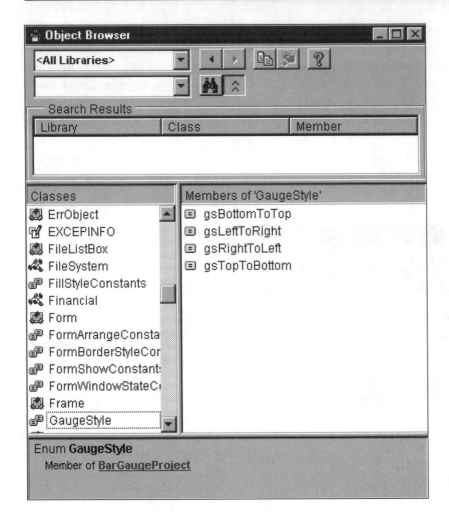

FIGURE 15.3 GaugeStyle values shown by the Object Browser.

Appearance

Some controls include properties that are available only at design time, that are available only at run time, or that are read-only at run time. Using some of these properties can present unique problems for ActiveX controls.

The Appearance property determines whether a control should appear three-dimensional or whether it should have a flat, two-dimensional appearance. Figure 15.4 shows the same bar gauges shown in Figure 15.1. The upper horizontal gauge and the vertical gauge on the left have Appearance set to 0 - appears2D.

Appearance is supported by the UserControl object, so one might think it would be easy to implement an Appearance property by delegating it. Unfortunately, the Appearance property is read-only at

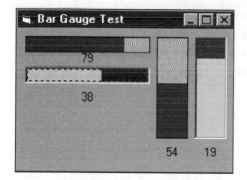

FIGURE 15.4 Two- and three-dimensional bar gauges.

run time. Whenever an ActiveX control is created, modified, or destroyed, the control's code executes. For instance, when an application designer creates a new instance of an ActiveX control, the control's InitProperties event handler is invoked. InitProperties will usually call a series of property procedures to initialize the control's properties.

While the control code executes, the control acts in run-time mode. Even though the application designer is working in design time and the application being built is in design mode, the ActiveX control is working in run time. That means it cannot set the UserControl's Appearance property because that property is read-only at run time. That means the control cannot delegate the Appearance property to the UserControl object.

There are two solutions to this problem. First, the control can manage its own Appearance property. It would store the property's value in a private variable and draw itself in a three-dimensional way when necessary. Drawing a three-dimensional Appearance property and making it match that of other controls can be difficult.

A simpler solution is to create two sets of controls within the ActiveX control, one with Appearance set to 1 - 3D and the other with Appearance 0 - Flat. The ActiveX control's Appearance property can be managed locally rather than by delegation, and the controls with the appropriate Appearance can be used to display the ActiveX control.

The bar gauge control contains two picture boxes named Picture2D and Picture3D. The first has Appearance set to 0 - Flat; the other has Appearance set to 1 - 3D. Both have BorderStyle set to 1 - Fixed Single.

The following code shows the UserControl's Resize event handler. It resizes both of the picture boxes so they fill the UserControl's drawing area.

```
Private Sub UserControl_Resize()
    Picture2D.Move 0, 0, ScaleWidth, ScaleHeight
    Picture3D.Move 0, 0, ScaleWidth, ScaleHeight
End Sub
```

The Appearance property is managed locally using the private variable the_appearance. When Appearance is modified, its property let procedure updates the value of the_apparance. It also makes the appropriate one of the two picture boxes visible and saves a reference to that picture box in the variable the_canvas. This variable is used later when drawing the bar gauge.

```
Public Enum AppearanceValue
    appears2D
    appears3D
End Enum
Private the_appearance As AppearanceValue
    :
Dim the_canvas As PictureBox
    :
Public Property Let Appearance(val As AppearanceValue)
    the_appearance = val

    ' Make the correct picture box visible.
    If the_appearance = appears2D Then
        Picture2D.Visible = True
        Picture3D.Visible = False
        Set the_canvas = Picture2D
    Else
        Picture2D.Visible = False
        Picture3D.Visible = True
        Set the_canvas = Picture3D
    End If

    PropertyChanged "Appearance"    ' Tell VB.
    Paint   ' Redisplay the gauge.
End Property
```

When the control needs to display itself, it draws on the currently visible picture box, as described in the next section.

Drawing Bar Gauge

Whenever one of the bar gauge's properties changes, the corresponding property procedure invokes the Paint subroutine to redraw the control using the new property values. Similarly, whenever either picture box Picture2D or Picture3D receives a Paint event, it invokes the Paint subroutine.

Paint starts by clearing the picture box that is currently visible. It then calculates the fraction of the picture box that should be filled to represent the control's current value. Next, it fills in the correct part of the picture box depending on the control's Style. For example, if Style is gsLeftToRight, the routine fills the left portion of the picture box.

Finally, if the control has the input focus, Paint draws a dotted box around the inside of the picture box. The line is drawn in drawing mode vbInvert. This drawing mode inverts the color values for the pixels that are drawn. By inverting, the control increases the chances that the dotted box will be visible no matter what ForeColor and BackColor properties the control has.

```
Private Sub Paint()
Dim v As Single
Dim wid As Single
Dim hgt As Single

    ' Do nothing if we're loading.
    If loading Then Exit Sub

    ' Start from scratch.
    the_canvas.Cls

    ' See how much of the gauge should be filled.
    If the_min >= the_max Then
        ' Fill in nothing.
        v = 0#
    Else
        v = (the_value - the_min) / (the_max - the_min)
    End If

    wid = the_canvas.ScaleWidth
    hgt = the_canvas.ScaleHeight

    ' Convert the value to pixels.
    If the_style = gsLeftToRight Or _
        the_style = gsRightToLeft _
    Then
        v = v * wid
    Else
        v = v * hgt
    End If

    ' Draw the gauge with the correct style.
    Select Case the_style
        Case gsLeftToRight
            the_canvas.Line (0, 0)-(v, hgt), , BF
        Case gsRightToLeft
            the_canvas.Line (wid, 0)-(wid - v, hgt), , BF
        Case gsBottomToTop
            the_canvas.Line (0, hgt)-(wid, hgt - v), , BF
        Case gsTopToBottom
            the_canvas.Line (0, 0)-(wid, v), , BF
    End Select

    ' If the gauge has the focus, outline it.
    If has_focus Then
        the_canvas.DrawStyle = vbDot
        the_canvas.DrawMode = vbInvert
        the_canvas.Line (0, 0)- _
            (wid - 1, hgt - 1), _
            , B
        the_canvas.DrawStyle = vbSolid
```

```
        the_canvas.DrawMode = vbCopyPen
    End If
End Sub
```

Managing the Mouse

When the user clicks and drags on the bar gauge, the control must adjust its value. The control handles mouse movements in MouseDown, MouseMove, and MouseUp event handlers. Because either picture box Picture2D or Picture3D might be visible at any given time, the control must handle all three mouse events for both controls. Rather than duplicating three complicated event handlers for both picture boxes, the event handlers simply invoke other routines to process the mouse events. For example, the Picture2D_MouseDown and Picture3D_MouseDown event handlers both invoke the private subroutine MouseDown.

```
Private Sub Picture3d_MouseMove(Button As Integer, _
    Shift As Integer, X As Single, Y As Single)

    MouseMove X, Y
End Sub
```

The other mouse event handlers are very similar.

MouseDown

The Boolean variable dragging allows the control to tell if the user is currently dragging the mouse to select a new value. This is important for the MouseMove event handlers because they detect mouse movement whenever the mouse crosses the picture box even if no button is pressed.

The MouseDown subroutine begins a dragging operation. First it verifies that the control's Min value is less than its Max value. Then it makes sure that the control's Enabled property is true. If either of these conditions is not met, the control cancels the operation.

Next, MouseDown sets dragging to true so that later MouseMove events know the user is changing the control's value. The routine then updates the control's Value property. This invokes the corresponding property let procedure that, in turn, calls the Paint subroutine to redisplay the control using the new value. Finally, MouseDown raises a Scroll event to indicate that the value is scrolling. The application can catch this event and perform tasks such as updating label controls to reflect the new value.

```
Private dragging As Boolean
    :
Private Sub MouseDown(X As Single, Y As Single)
    ' Do nothing if there is no range or the
    ' control is disabled.
    If (the_min >= the_max) Or (Not Enabled) Then _
        Exit Sub

    ' Start dragging.
    dragging = True
```

```
' Update the value.
Value = ComputeValue(the_canvas, X, Y)

' Generate a Scroll event.
RaiseEvent Scroll
End Sub
```

ComputeValue

The MouseDown subroutine, and the MouseMove and MouseUp routines described in the following sections, use the ComputeValue function to set the control's new value. This function begins by checking that the control's Min value is less than the Max value. If it is not, the function arbitrarily returns the Min value.

Next, ComputeValue determines at what fraction of the distance through the control the selected point lies. It uses that fraction to compute the new value. Finally, it ensures that the result remains between the Min and Max values before it returns the result.

```
Private Function ComputeValue(the_canvas As PictureBox, _
    X As Single, Y As Single) As Long
Dim fract As Single
Dim val As Long
Dim wid As Single
Dim hgt As Single

    ' No range. Pick the_min.
    If the_min >= the_max Then
        ComputeValue = the_min
        Exit Function
    End If

    ' See at what fraction of the way through
    ' the control the point lies.
    wid = the_canvas.ScaleWidth
    hgt = the_canvas.ScaleHeight

    Select Case the_style
        Case gsLeftToRight
            fract = X / wid
        Case gsRightToLeft
            fract = (wid - X) / wid
        Case gsBottomToTop
            fract = (hgt - Y) / hgt
        Case gsTopToBottom
            fract = Y / hgt
        Case Else
            ComputeValue = the_min
            Exit Function
    End Select
```

```
' Compute the result.
val = the_min + _
    (the_max - the_min) * fract

' Keep the result in range.
If val < the_min Then
    val = the_min
ElseIf val > the_max Then
    val = the_max
End If

ComputeValue = val
End Function
```

MouseMove

Subroutine MouseMove is a little simpler than MouseDown. It first checks the Boolean variable dragging to see if the user is changing the control's value. If it is, the control uses the ComputeValue function to update the control's Value property. As is the case in subroutine MouseDown, updating the value makes the control redraw using the new value. Finally, MouseMove raises a Scroll event so the application can take action if necessary.

```
Private Sub MouseMove(X As Single, Y As Single)
    ' Do nothing if the user is not selecting
    ' a value.
    If Not dragging Then Exit Sub

    ' Update the value.
    Value = ComputeValue(the_canvas, X, Y)

    ' Generate a Scroll event.
    RaiseEvent Scroll
End Sub
```

MouseUp

Subroutine MouseUp is similar to MouseMove. It, too, does nothing unless the user is changing the control's value. If the user is changing the value, the routine sets dragging to false to indicate that future mouse events are not related to this value change. It then updates the control's value with Compute-Value and raises a Change event, indicating that the user has finished the value drag operation.

```
Private Sub MouseUp(X As Single, Y As Single)
    ' Do nothing if the user is not selecting
    ' a value.
    If Not dragging Then Exit Sub
    dragging = False

    ' Update the value.
    Value = ComputeValue(the_canvas, X, Y)
```

```
    ' Generate a Change event.
    RaiseEvent Change
End Sub
```

Handling Keyboard Events

The bar gauge control handles keyboard events much as it handles mouse events. The KeyDown event handlers for Picture2D and Picture3D both invoke the KeyDown subroutine to do all the actual work.

KeyDown begins by checking the key's code and the control's Style to determine how the value should change. For example, if the control's Style is gsTopToBottom and the user has pressed the down arrow, the subroutine should increase the control's value toward Max. It will increase by the amount specified by the control's KeyChangeAmount property.

KeyDown then computes the new value and checks whether it lies between the Min and Max values. This protects the control from situations where the value could move out of bounds. This would happen, for example, if the control's value was already the same as the Max property and the arrow key would increase the value even more.

If the new value is in bounds, KeyDown updates the Value property. This invokes the Value property let procedure, which redraws the control to display the new value.

```
Private Sub KeyDown(KeyCode As Integer)
Dim dv As Long
Dim val As Long

    ' See by how much the value should change.
    Select Case KeyCode
        Case vbKeyLeft
            If the_style = gsLeftToRight Then
                dv = -value_change
            ElseIf the_style = gsRightToLeft Then
                dv = value_change
            End If

        Case vbKeyRight
            If the_style = gsLeftToRight Then
                dv = value_change
            ElseIf the_style = gsRightToLeft Then
                dv = -value_change
            End If

        Case vbKeyUp
            If the_style = gsBottomToTop Then
                dv = value_change
            ElseIf the_style = gsTopToBottom Then
                dv = -value_change
            End If

        Case vbKeyDown
            If the_style = gsBottomToTop Then
```

```
                    dv = -value_change
            ElseIf the_style = gsTopToBottom Then
                    dv = value_change
            End If

        Case Else
            dv = 0
    End Select

    ' Make the change.
    If dv <> 0 Then
        ' Make sure the new value is in bounds.
        val = the_value + dv
        If val >= the_min And val <= the_max Then
            ' Update the value.
            Value = val

            ' Generate a Change event.
            RaiseEvent Change
        End If
    End If
End Sub
```

Modifying Bar Gauge

The bar gauge control shows how an ActiveX control can handle mouse and keyboard events. By modifying the control slightly, creating other gauges with very different appearances is easy. Figure 15.5 shows several copies of four different kinds of gauge controls.

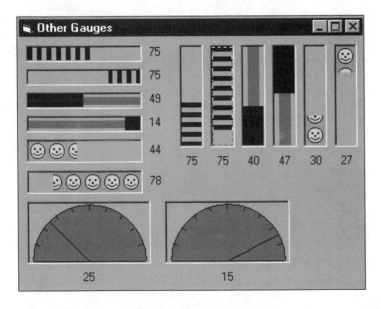

FIGURE 15.5 Modified bar gauges.

All of the controls shown in Figure 15.5 are based on the bar gauge control. They provide the same two events, Change and Scroll, and they support almost the same properties. The main difference between them is in their Paint subroutines. A few also support additional properties used to specify their particular styles. All of the controls support two- and three-dimensional appearances. All except the Dial controls shown at the bottom of Figure 15.5 also support the left-to-right, right-to-left, bottom-to-top, and top-to-bottom styles. The Dial control supports only the two horizontal styles, left-to-right and right-to-left.

The following sections briefly explain how these controls differ from the bar gauge. You can find the complete code for each of them, and for the test application shown in Figure 15.5, in the Ch15\Others directory on the compact disk.

TicGauge

The tic gauge control, shown in the upper left of Figure 15.5, displays the selected value as a series of tic marks. The tic gauge has one property that the standard bar gauge does not:TicWidth. This property determines how wide each of the tic marks is in pixels. The gap between tics is the same width as the tic marks. TicWidth is a simple numeric value with straightforward property procedures.

The only other difference between the tic gauge and the bar gauge is in the way it is drawn. The following code fragment shows the interesting parts of tic gauge's Paint subroutine.

As in the previous version, Paint starts by clearing the visible picture box and by calculating the fraction of the control that should be filled to represent the current value. It then repeatedly draws tic marks, starting at the end that is appropriate for the control's Style, and continuing until it reaches the calculated value.

Finally, if the control has the input focus, Paint draws a dotted line around the outside edge of the control.

```
Private Sub Paint()
    :
    ' Calculate how much of the gauge should be filled, etc.
    :
    ' Draw the gauge with the correct style.
    dx = TicWidth
    x1 = 0
    Do While x1 < v
        x2 = x1 + dx
        If x2 > v Then x2 = v

        Select Case the_style
            Case gsLeftToRight
                the_canvas.Line (x1, 0)-(x2, hgt), , BF
            Case gsRightToLeft
                the_canvas.Line (wid - x1, 0)-(wid - x2, hgt), , BF
            Case gsBottomToTop
                the_canvas.Line (0, hgt - x1)-(wid, hgt - x2), , BF
            Case gsTopToBottom
                the_canvas.Line (0, x1)-(wid, x2), , BF
```

```
      End Select

      x1 = x2 + dx + 2
  Loop

  ' If the gauge has the focus, outline it.
  :
End Sub
```

WidGauge

The wide gauge control uses bars of two different thicknesses and colors to display values. The controls third and fourth from the top on the left in Figure 15.5 are wide gauge control's.

The control's ForeColor property determines the color of the larger bar as it does for the bar gauge. The BackColor property determines the color shown behind the narrower bar.

The new property NarrowColor determines the color of the narrower bar. The numeric property NarrowPercent determines how thick the narrow bar is. For example, when NarrowPercent is 50, the narrow bar is 50 percent as wide as the thick bar.

The wide gauge's Paint subroutine is very similar to the one used by the original bar gauge control. After clearing the control, however, this version draws the narrower bar. It then draws the thick bar on top of the narrow one.

The following code fragment shows how the Paint subroutine draws the narrower bar. The rest of the routine is the same as the original version.

```
Private Sub Paint()
    :
    ' Draw the narrow part.
    wid = the_canvas.ScaleWidth
    hgt = the_canvas.ScaleHeight
    Select Case the_style
        Case gsLeftToRight
            v1 = (hgt * NarrowPercent) / 200#
            v2 = hgt - v1
            the_canvas.Line (0, v1)-(wid, v2), NarrowColor, BF
        Case gsRightToLeft
            v1 = (hgt * NarrowPercent) / 200#
            v2 = hgt - v1
            the_canvas.Line (0, v1)-(wid, v2), NarrowColor, BF
        Case gsBottomToTop
            v1 = (wid * NarrowPercent) / 200#
            v2 = wid - v1
            the_canvas.Line (v1, 0)-(v2, hgt), NarrowColor, BF
        Case gsTopToBottom
            v1 = (wid * NarrowPercent) / 200#
            v2 = wid - v1
            the_canvas.Line (v1, 0)-(v2, hgt), NarrowColor, BF
    End Select
```

```
    ' Draw the thick bar as before.
    :
End Sub
```

PicGauge

The picture gauge control fills a bar area with copies of a picture. The bottom two horizontal gauges in Figure 15.5 are picture gauges.

The picture gauge displays a value by tiling an area with a picture rather than by filling it with a solid color. This means it does not need a ForeColor property so this control does not support ForeColor. Instead, it has a FillPicture property that specifies the picture that should be used to tile the area.

FillPicture is declared as type StdPicture. This allows the Visual Basic Properties window to display the picture in a standard way. If the application programmer clicks on the value's drop-down arrow, Visual Basic presents a standard picture selection dialog.

Because a variable of type StdPicture is an object, an application using the FillPicture property should initialize variables using the Set statement—for example:

```
Set PicGauge1.FillPicture = LoadPicture("MY_PICT.BMP")
```

This means FillPicture must have a property set procedure rather than a property let procedure.

```
Public Property Set FillPicture(pic As StdPicture)
    Set fill_picture = pic

    PropertyChanged "FillPicture" ' Tell VB.
    Paint    ' Redisplay the gauge.
End Property
```

The picture gauge's Paint subroutine begins by calculating the amount of the gauge that should be filled as usual. Then, much like the tic gauge, it begins filling small regions in the control until it has filled the desired area. The process is somewhat more complicated here because the PaintPicture routine used to draw the picture is not as simple as the Line statement used to draw tic marks.

For example, suppose the control has the right-to-left style. The control's value will probably make the control display only part of the leftmost picture, just as the last horizontal gauge in Figure 15.5 displays roughly half of its leftmost picture. The Paint subroutine must not only calculate the fraction of the picture that must be drawn, but it must draw the rightmost portion of the picture. The PaintPicture statement is designed to draw portions of pictures from the left, so Paint must do a bit of work to place the correct piece of the picture in the proper position.

The following code shows the parts of the Paint subroutine that are unique to the picture gauge:

```
Private Sub Paint()
    :
    ' If there is no picture, do nothing.
    If FillPicture Is Nothing Then Exit Sub
    :
    ' Calculate v, the amount to fill, as usual.
    :
```

```
' See how big the picture is.
pic_wid = CInt(ScaleX(FillPicture.Width, vbHimetric, vbPixels))
pic_hgt = CInt(ScaleY(FillPicture.Height, vbHimetric, vbPixels))

' Draw the gauge with the correct style.
Select Case the_style
    Case gsLeftToRight
        x1 = 0
        y1 = 0
        Do While x1 < v
            If x1 + pic_wid > v Then pic_wid = v - x1
            If pic_wid > 0 Then
                the_canvas.PaintPicture FillPicture, _
                    x1, y1, pic_wid, pic_hgt, _
                    , , pic_wid, pic_hgt
                x1 = x1 + pic_wid
            Else
                x1 = v + 1
            End If
        Loop

    Case gsRightToLeft
        x1 = pic_wid
        y1 = 0
        Do While x1 - pic_wid < v
            If x1 <= v Then
                the_canvas.PaintPicture FillPicture, _
                    wid - x1, y1, pic_wid, pic_hgt, _
                    , , pic_wid, pic_hgt
                x1 = x1 + pic_wid
            Else
                x2 = x1 - v
                x1 = v
                pic_wid = pic_wid - x2
                If pic_wid > 0 Then
                    the_canvas.PaintPicture FillPicture, _
                        wid - x1, y1, pic_wid, pic_hgt, _
                        x2, , pic_wid, pic_hgt
                End If
                Exit Do
            End If
        Loop

    Case gsBottomToTop
        x1 = 0
        y1 = pic_hgt
        Do While y1 - pic_hgt < v
            If y1 <= v Then
                the_canvas.PaintPicture FillPicture, _
                    x1, hgt - y1, pic_wid, pic_hgt, _
                    , , pic_wid, pic_hgt
```

```
                         y1 = y1 + pic_wid
                 Else
                     y2 = y1 - v
                     y1 = v
                     pic_hgt = pic_hgt - y2
                     If pic_hgt > 0 Then
                         the_canvas.PaintPicture FillPicture, _
                             x1, hgt - y1, pic_wid, pic_hgt, _
                             , y2, pic_wid, pic_hgt
                     End If
                     Exit Do
                 End If
         Loop

     Case gsTopToBottom
         x1 = 0
         y1 = 0
         Do While y1 < v
             If y1 + pic_hgt > v Then pic_hgt = v - y1
             If pic_hgt > 0 Then
                 the_canvas.PaintPicture FillPicture, _
                     x1, y1, pic_wid, pic_hgt, _
                     , , pic_wid, pic_hgt
                 y1 = y1 + pic_wid
             Else
                 y1 = v + 1
             End If
         Loop

 End Select
     :
 ' Draw the focus outline as usual (if necessary).
     :
 End Sub
```

Dial

At first glance, the dial gauges shown at the bottom of Figure 15.5 seem to be completely unrelated to the standard bar gauge. Actually, the two types of controls are very similar. The main differences are in the way the controls draw themselves and in the way they calculate new values based on mouse events.

The dial gauge supports an extra FillColor property that determines the color that fills the face of the dial. It also provides a simple numeric property TicSpacing that determines the distance between tic marks on the dial. TicSpacing is measured in the same units as the control's Min, Max, and Value properties. For example, suppose the control's Min, Max, and TicSpacing values are 0, 100, and 10, respectively. Then the control will display a tic mark every 10 units along the face of the dial.

This control's Paint subroutine is simplified slightly by the fact that it supports only the horizontal left-to-right and right-to-left styles. After clearing the control, Paint draws the dial's semicircular face, filling it with the value specified by the FillColor property. It then draws the tic marks around the inside edge of the dial. It draws the value needle and finishes by drawing the focus rectangle if the control has the input focus.

```
Private Sub Paint()
Dim r1 As Single      ' Outer radius.
Dim r2 As Single      ' Inner (tic) radius.
Dim x0 As Single      ' The origin of the circle.
Dim y0 As Single
Dim x1 As Single
Dim y1 As Single
Dim x2 As Single
Dim y2 As Single
Dim wid As Single
Dim hgt As Single
Dim theta As Single
Dim dtheta As Single
Dim stheta As Single
Dim ctheta As Single

    ' Do not redraw while loading.
    If loading Then Exit Sub

    ' Start from scratch.
    the_canvas.Cls

    ' Don't bother if Min >= Max.
    If the_min >= the_max Then Exit Sub

    'Draw the circle.
    wid = the_canvas.ScaleWidth
    hgt = the_canvas.ScaleHeight
    r1 = hgt - 2
    r2 = wid / 2 - 1
    If r2 < r1 Then r1 = r2
    r2 = 0.9 * r1
    x0 = wid / 2
    y0 = hgt - 1
    the_canvas.FillStyle = vbSolid
    the_canvas.Circle (x0, y0), r1, , -0.0000001, -PI
    the_canvas.FillStyle = vbFSTransparent

    ' Draw the tic marks.
    If tic_spacing > 0 Then
        dtheta = PI * tic_spacing / (the_max - the_min)
        For theta = dtheta To PI Step dtheta
            If Style = gsLeftToRight Then
                ctheta = Cos(PI - theta)
            Else
                ctheta = Cos(theta)
            End If
            stheta = Sin(theta)
```

```
            x1 = x0 + r1 * ctheta
            x2 = x0 + r2 * ctheta
            y1 = y0 - r1 * stheta
            y2 = y0 - r2 * stheta

            the_canvas.Line (x1, y1)-(x2, y2)
        Next theta
    End If


    ' See where the needle belongs.
    If the_style = gsLeftToRight Then
        theta = PI * (1 - (the_value - the_min) / (the_max - the_min))
    Else
        theta = PI * (the_value - the_min) / (the_max - the_min)
    End If


    ' Draw the needle.
    the_canvas.Line (x0, y0)- _
        (x0 + r1 * Cos(theta), y0 - r1 * Sin(theta))

    ' If the gauge has the focus, outline it.
    If has_focus Then
        the_canvas.DrawStyle = vbDot
        the_canvas.DrawMode = vbInvert
        the_canvas.Line (0, 0)- _
            (wid - 1, hgt - 1), _
            , B
        the_canvas.DrawStyle = vbSolid
        the_canvas.DrawMode = vbCopyPen
    End If
End Sub
```

Apart from its appearance, the main difference between the dial gauge and the others is in how it determines the value selected by mouse events. The previously described gauges see how far across the control the mouse has moved and then calculate the appropriate value between the control's Min and Max values.

The dial gauge's ComputeValue function is only a little more complicated. First it calculates the angle between the horizontal and the line connecting the point selected to the center of the dial. This angle is shown in Figure 15.6.

ComputeValue then sees where this angle lies between the right horizontal angle 0 and the left horizontal angle P (3.14159265). It uses the result to determine the value selected.

For example, if the angle is 0.79 radians, it is roughly one-quarter of the distance from the angle 0 to the angle P. If the control has the right-to-left style, the value selected is one-quarter of the distance from the control's Min value to its Max value.

```
Private Function ComputeValue(the_canvas As PictureBox, _
    X As Single, Y As Single) As Long
Dim fract As Single
```

```
Dim val As Long
Dim wid As Single
Dim hgt As Single
Dim x0 As Single
Dim y0 As Single
Dim dx As Single
Dim dy As Single
Dim theta As Single

    ' No range. Pick the_min.
    If the_min >= the_max Then
        ComputeValue = the_min
        Exit Function
    End If

    ' See at what fraction of the way through
    ' the range the point lies.
    wid = the_canvas.ScaleWidth
    hgt = the_canvas.ScaleHeight
    x0 = wid / 2
    y0 = hgt - 1
    dx = X - x0
    dy = y0 - Y
    theta = Arctan2(dx, dy)

    ' Convert that into Dial units.
    Select Case the_style
        Case gsLeftToRight
            fract = (PI - theta) / PI

        Case gsRightToLeft
            fract = theta / PI

        Case Else
            ComputeValue = the_min
            Exit Function
    End Select

    ' Compute the result.
    val = the_min + _
        (the_max - the_min) * fract

    ' Keep the result in range.
    If val < the_min Then
        val = the_min
    ElseIf val > the_max Then
        val = the_max
    End If

    ComputeValue = val
End Function
```

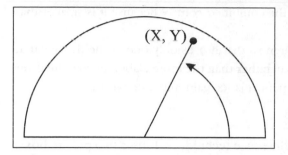

FIGURE 15.6 Calculating a selected point's angle.

A Combined Gauge

The BarGauge, TicGauge, PicGauge, WidGauge, and Dial controls have much in common. To handle similar tasks, such as setting the Min and Max properties, these controls have identical copies of the same code. This redundant code takes up a great deal of space.

The Gauge.VBG project group in the Ch15\Combined directory defines a single gauge control that is a combination of all of the others. Its Style property determines how the control draws itself and how it calculates new values selected by the user. Style is a simple enumerated value with the following definition:

```
Public Enum GaugeStyle
    styleBar
    styleDial
    stylePic
    styleTic
    styleWid
End Enum
```

The new gauge control includes all of the properties required by each of the five different gauge types. These properties are handled exactly as they were before.

By creating a new control that can behave like each of the five others, the code that is duplicated among them is removed. For example, the new control has only one copy of the Min property let procedure rather than five separate copies.

This space saving is shown by the size of the compiled controls' .OCX files. The .OCX file for the original BarGauge control is 29 KB. The .OCX for the four other separate gauges occupies 100 KB so the combined size of all five controls is almost 130 KB. The size of the new, combined .OCX is only 63 KB—less than half the size of the five separately.

Working with a single, combined control is convenient, but it is not always the best approach. In a Web-based application such as those described in Chapters 17, 18, and 19, users will need to download the .OCX file across a relatively slow network link. For some users, these links can be slow enough that a difference of a few kilobytes can have a fairly large impact. If the application truly needs all the different gauge control styles, it is better to download the combined control because it is smaller than the five separate controls.

On the other hand, if the application can be rewritten so that it uses only one of the five separate controls, it would be better to download only that control rather than the more elaborate combined version. The application would lose some variety, but the performance gain might be worth it.

Summary

The BarGauge control demonstrates several important interface techniques. It uses two picture boxes so it can provide both two- and three-dimensional appearances. These picture boxes allow it to provide design time, and even run time, access to a property that is normally unavailable to the designer and end user.

The BarGauge displays a data value. It uses mouse and keyboard events to allow the user to manipulate the value using the mouse or the arrow keys. With only minor changes to its drawing routine, it can provide a variety of different looks. These features give the BarGauge a much richer user interface than the Alarm control described in Chapter 14.

Chapter 16

Histogram

ActiveX controls can be used in almost the same ways as any other control. In particular, an ActiveX control can be used to create other ActiveX controls.

This chapter describes a histogram control built using the gauge control described in Chapter 15. The first section in the chapter, "Using Histogram," describes how the control works from the end user's point of view. It explains the control's run-time behavior and the means by which the user can interact with the control.

The next section, "Programming with Histogram," describes the control's features from an application designer's point of view. It explains the properties and events a client application can use to manage the control.

The "Key Techniques" section briefly outlines the main tasks the control performs to support both the application developer at design time and the end user at run time. The rest of the chapter describes the histogram control's internals and explains how the control handles these key tasks.

Using Histogram

The histogram control displays a series of data values using gauge controls. A scroll bar allows the user to move through the values if there are more data values than gauges. If the control's Enabled property is set to true, the user can also modify the data using the gauges.

The project group HistTest.GRP in the Ch16 directory includes the test program project HistTest.VPJ. This program displays a single form containing a histogram control. Figure 16.1 shows the HistTest program displaying test data.

Programming Histogram

The histogram control is designed primarily for use with gauge controls of the tic gauge style. For that reason, histogram supports the TicWidth property used by tic gauge controls. This property and several others are delegated to the gauge controls contained in the histogram. Table 16.1 lists properties delegated to the gauges. Table 16.2 lists the other properties supported by the histogram control.

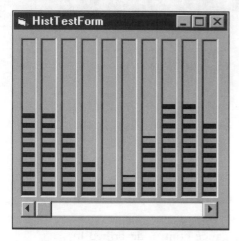

FIGURE 16.1 Test program HistTest.

The histogram control's NumBars property indicates the number of bar gauges the control should display. The control automatically calculates the width it needs to display that number of gauges with a reasonable separation between them.

TABLE 16.1 Histogram Properties Delegated to the Gauge Controls

Property	Type	Meaning
BarBackColor	OLE_COLOR	Background color for gauges
BarForeColor	OLE_COLOR	Foreground color for gauges
Enabled	Boolean	Allows the user to change gauge values
Max	Long	Maximum value displayed by gauges
Min	Long	Minimum value displayed by gauges
Style	HistStyle	The gauge style. May be one of: styleBar styleDial stylePic styleTic styleWid
TicWidth	Long	Width of gauge tic marks

TABLE 16.2 Histogram Properties That Are Not Delegated

Property	Type	Meaning
BackColor	OLE_COLOR	Background color of the histogram control
NumBars	Integer	Number of gauges
NumValues	Integer	Number of data values
Value	Long	A single data value

The NumValues property determines the number of data values the control will display. After this value is set, the application can set data values using the indexed Value property. The HistTest program uses the following code to initialize its 100 data values. The function used to calculate the values rises and falls in an interesting way.

```
Private Sub Form_Load()
Const PI = 3.14159265

Dim i As Integer

    Histogram1.NumValues = 100
    For i = 1 To 100
        Histogram1.Value(i) = 50 + 50 * _
            Sin(PI * i / 10) * _
            Sin(PI * i / 15) * _
            Cos(PI * i / 5)
    Next i
End Sub
```

If the histogram control's Enabled property has the value true, then the user can interact with the gauges to modify the data at run time. To notify the client application when this occurs, the control provides a ValueChanged event. Whenever the user modifies a value, the control invokes the program's ValueChanged event handler, passing it the index of the data value that was modified. The program can then take appropriate action, such as saving the modified value into a file.

To keep the code as simple as possible, the histogram control does not provide any other events. A reasonable addition would be a Scroll event that triggered when the user modified the control's scroll bar value. This would inform the program that the data values displayed had changed. The program could then take actions such as updating a group of labels that displayed the values shown by the gauges as text.

Key Techniques

The following list briefly describes new techniques demonstrated by the histogram control. The rest of the chapter explains these techniques in detail.

- **Managing Control Arrays.** When the histogram control's NumBars property is changed, the control must load and arrange the correct number of gauges. This section explains how the histogram control uses a control array to manage the bar gauges.
- **Scrolling Data.** Because the histogram control can contain more data values than it has gauges, it provides a scroll bar to allow the user to scroll through the data. This section tells how the control uses the scroll bar.
- **Delegating to a Control Array.** Many of the histogram control's properties are delegated to the gauges it contains. This section describes the methods the histogram uses to delegate properties to the bar gauges it contains.
- **Supporting Indexed Properties.** The histogram control represents many data values. This section explains how the histogram provides indexed properties to allow client programs to read and set the data values.
- **Raising Indexed Events.** The histogram control raises an event to notify the client application when the user changes a data value. This section shows how the control passes the event handler the index of the modified value.

Managing Control Arrays

The histogram control contains an array of gauge controls and a scroll bar. Figure 16.2 shows the control at design time. The vertical gauge control has Index property 0. When other gauges are needed, the histogram control uses Visual Basic's Load command to create gauges with indexes 1, 2, and so on.

A client application or the application designer can use the histogram's NumBars property to determine the number of bar gauges the control displays. Changing the number of gauges has several consequences. First, the control unloads any old gauge controls it no longer requires. If the user changes NumBars from 10 to 5, for example, five of the controls must be unloaded.

Next, the control loads any new gauges it needs. If the user increases NumBars from 3 to 10, the control creates seven new bar gauge controls.

After unloading and loading gauges as needed, the NumBars property let procedure saves the new number of controls loaded. It will need this number later if NumBars is changed again. Finally, the procedure invokes the ArrangeControls subroutine to arrange the gauges and the scroll bar.

```
Public Property Let NumBars(val As Integer)
Dim i As Integer

    ' There must be at least 1 gauge.
    If val < 1 Then Exit Property

    ' Unload bars no longer needed.
    For i = val + 1 To num_bars
        Unload Bar(i)
    Next i

    ' Load bars now needed.
```

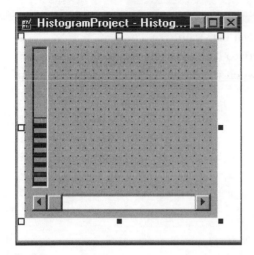

FIGURE 16.2 The histogram control at design time.

```
For i = num_bars + 1 To val
    Load Bar(i)
Next i

    ' Save the new value.
    num_bars = val

    ' Arrange the controls.
    ArrangeControls

    PropertyChanged "NumBars" ' Tell VB.
End Property
```

Subroutine ArrangeControls aligns the gauges horizontally 60 twips apart. It begins by calculating the width needed to display all of the scroll bars. It then gives the UserControl that width.

Next, the routine compares NumBars and NumValues to see if the scroll bar is needed. If not, it sets hgt to be the total height available within the UserControl. The value hgt will be used later to set the height of the gauges. If the scroll bar is needed, the subroutine makes hgt smaller to leave room for the scroll bar.

ArrangeControls then places the gauges and makes them visible. If the scroll bar is needed, the routine positions it and makes it visible as well.

The subroutine finishes by setting the scroll bar's Max and LargeChange properties. Max is set so the scroll bar can range from 0 to NumValues - NumBars. When the scroll bar has value i, the leftmost gauge displays the ith data value. When the scroll bar has value 0, the leftmost gauge displays the data value in position 1. When it has value Max, the leftmost gauge displays the value in position Max + 1. In that case, the rightmost gauge would display the value in position (Max + 1) + (NumBars - 1) =

((NumValues - NumBars) + 1) + (NumBars - 1) = NumValues. This makes sense. When the scroll bar value is as large as possible, the rightmost gauge displays the last data value.

ArrangeControls sets the scroll bar's LargeChange property to NumBars. This makes the histogram display a whole new set of values when the user clicks between the scroll bar's slider and one of its arrow buttons.

```
Private Sub ArrangeControls()
Const GAP = 60

Dim wid As Single
Dim hgt As Single
Dim tp As Single
Dim i As Integer
Dim x As Single

    If loading Then Exit Sub

    ' See how wide the control needs to be.
    wid = NumBars * (Bar(0).Width + GAP) - GAP
    Width = wid + (Width - ScaleWidth)

    ' See if we will need the scroll bar.
    If NumBars >= NumValues Then
        ' We don't need the scroll bar.
        ' Make the bars as tall as possible.
        hgt = ScaleHeight
    Else
        ' We do need the scroll bar.
        ' Place the scroll bar.
        tp = ScaleHeight - ScrollBar.Height
        ScrollBar.Move 0, tp, ScaleWidth

        ' Leave room for the scroll bar.
        hgt = ScrollBar.Top - GAP
    End If

    ' Arrange the gauges.
    wid = Bar(0).Width
    x = 0
    For i = 1 To NumBars
        Bar(i).Move x, 0, wid, hgt
        x = x + wid + GAP
    Next i

    ' Make the bars visible.
    For i = 1 To NumBars
        Bar(i).Visible = True
    Next i

    ' Make the scroll bar visible or not as appropriate.
```

```
    If NumBars >= NumValues Then
        ScrollBar.Visible = False
    Else
        ScrollBar.Visible = True

        ' Set the scroll bar's properties.
        ScrollBar.Max = NumValues - NumBars
        ScrollBar.LargeChange = NumBars
    End If
End Sub
```

Scrolling Data

When the scroll bar's value changes, its event handlers invoke the ShowValues subroutine. This routine sets the Value properties of the gauges so they display the appropriate data values.

```
Private Sub ScrollBar_Change()
    ShowValues
End Sub

Private Sub ScrollBar_Scroll()
    ShowValues
End Sub

Private Sub ShowValues()
Dim off As Integer
Dim i As Integer

    off = ScrollBar.Value
    For i = 1 To NumBars
        Bar(i).Value = Value(i + off)
    Next i
End Sub
```

Delegating to a Control Array

The histogram control delegates many of its properties to the gauge controls it contains. These properties are all handled similarly, so only the TicWidth property procedures are described here.

While the gauge control with index 0 is never visible, it is used to represent the properties of the other gauges. Whenever a gauge property value is changed, it is changed for all of the loaded gauge controls, including the one with index 0. This allows the visible controls to update their appearances. It also keeps the control with index 0 up to date so the delegated property get procedures can manage its property values.

```
Public Property Let TicWidth(val As Long)
Dim i As Integer

    For i = 0 To NumBars
        Bar(i).TicWidth = val
```

```
    Next i

    PropertyChanged "TicWidth" ' Tell VB.
End Property

Public Property Get TicWidth() As Long
    TicWidth = Bar(0).TicWidth
End Property
```

Supporting Indexed Properties

The histogram control represents many data values. To allow client programs to read and set all of these values, the histogram control's Value property is indexed.

Creating indexed property procedures is simply a matter of including an extra parameter. The first argument in the following Value property procedures is the index of the value to be returned or set.

Notice that these procedures check to make sure the index is within the range of valid values. This is extremely important. If either procedure tries to access an array value that does not exist, such as entry 0, the code will generate a "Subscript out of range" error.

```
Private the_value() As Long

Public Property Get Value(i As Integer) As Long
    If i < 1 Or i > NumValues Then
        Value = 0
    Else
        Value = the_value(i)
    End If
End Property

Public Property Let Value(i As Integer, val As Long)
    If i < 1 Or i > NumValues Then Exit Property

    the_value(i) = val

    ' Redisplay the values (we don't need to
    ' rearrange the controls).
    ShowValues

    PropertyChanged "Value" ' Tell VB.
End Property
```

This is not the only way a control can support multiple values for a single property. One alternative would be to provide property procedures that take as a parameter an array of values. The property let procedure would copy the values from the array into the control's local data structures. The property get procedure would use the control's local values to fill in the entries in the array. The procedures could also take extra arguments to allow the client application to fill in ranges of values rather than all of the possible values. Setting many values with a single procedure call will generally be faster than setting the same number of values one at a time.

Raising Indexed Events

When the user modifies a value using one of the gauges, the histogram control raises an event to notify the client application. It passes as a parameter to the event handler the index of the value modified. Then the application can take appropriate action such as saving the new value to a file.

To create an event with a parameter, the program must declare the parameter when it declares the event. The following code shows how the histogram control declares the ValueChanged event:

```
Public Event ValueChanged(Index As Integer)
```

Once the event is declared, raising it is easy. The program simply uses the parameter in the RaiseEvent statement. The following code shows how the histogram control responds to a Change event generated by one of its gauge controls:

```
Private Sub Bar_Change(Index As Integer)
Dim i As Integer

    ' Calculate the index of the changed value.
    i = ScrollBar.Value + Index

    the_value(i) = Bar(Index).Value

    ' Raise the value changed event.
    RaiseEvent ValueChanged(i)

    PropertyChanged "Value" ' Tell VB.
End Sub
```

Summary

For most purposes, ActiveX controls behave just as other controls. In particular, a program can use ActiveX controls to build other ActiveX controls. Component controls can be loaded using Visual Basic's LOAD statement. Properties can be assigned to these controls just as with simpler controls such as labels and text boxes.

Because ActiveX controls behave much like other controls, a developer can build complex controls such as the Histogram control in incremental stages. By itself, the BarGauge control is relatively simple. Using BarGauge controls to build the Histogram control is even simpler.

Part Six

ActiveX on the Web

ActiveX specifies how objects should interact with each other. Applying ActiveX principles to Web browsers, such as Microsoft Internet Explorer, allows ActiveX controls to run within Web pages. The applications described in this section use ActiveX controls to bring extra functionality to Web pages.

Chapter 17 explains how a program can include ActiveX controls in a Web page. It shows how to build a Web page that displays data using the histogram control described in Chapter 16.

Most Web pages take data from a server and send it to a Web user. The WebSurvey application described in Chapter 18 does the opposite: It takes input from a Web user and sends it to a remote server computer.

Chapter 19 finishes the discussion of ActiveX on the Web by explaining the SiteMapper application. This application retrieves documents from a server so it can map out the pages at a Web site.

Chapter 17

ActiveX Controls on the Web

A control that follows the ActiveX specification allows itself to be manipulated by other objects. An application can create an instance of the control, examine and change its property values, invoke its methods, and respond to events it generates.

One of the more interesting ways in which an object can manipulate an ActiveX control is over a network. A Web page designer can place ActiveX controls directly on a Web page. When a user with an ActiveX-enabled browser such as Microsoft Internet Explorer visits the page, the control is downloaded to the user's machine. It can then run locally on the user's computer rather than remotely on the Web page server. The control can run much faster locally than it can remotely.

This chapter explains how a Web page can use ActiveX controls. The first section, "Using ActiveX Controls on Web Pages," shows several Web pages from the user's point of view. These pages use ActiveX controls to display data and interact with the user.

The "Key Techniques" section briefly lists the most important techniques used to place ActiveX controls on Web pages. The rest of the chapter explains those techniques in detail.

Using ActiveX Controls on Web Pages

The Ch17 directory on the compact disk contains four Web documents that include ActiveX controls served by a computer named Beauty. You need to edit these Web pages so they can find the controls on your network before you can test them. The two sections, "Displaying Active Controls" and "Learning Class Ids," explain how you can make the necessary changes.

The document Colors.HTM uses the WebLabel control described later in this chapter to display a set of sample colors. It is shown in Figure 17.1.

The document Gauge.HTM shown in Figure 17.2 uses the WebLabel control and the Bar-Gauge control described in Chapter 15. When the user changes the value of a BarGauge, VBScript code in the document changes the caption of the corresponding label.

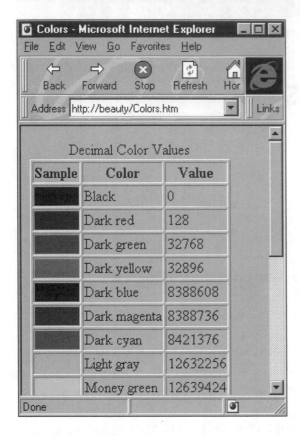

FIGURE 17.1 Internet Explorer displaying Colors.HTM.

Histgram.HTM, shown in Figure 17.3, uses the histogram control explained in Chapter 16 to display 100 data values using 10 bar gauges. Using the scroll bar, the user can examine different parts of the data just as if the histogram were running in a Visual Basic application.

Finally, the document PickClr.HTM shown in Figure 17.4 allows the user to experiment with colors displayed by a Web browser. As the user adjusts the red, green, and blue scroll bars, VBScript code computes and displays the selected color value. In Figure 17.4, for example, the colors selected red, green, and blue components are 128, 128, and 255, respectively. The color value RGB(128, 128, 255) has numeric value 16744576 and is pale blue when seen in color.

Key Techniques

Some of the following sections are very different from those presented in earlier chapters. Most of the applications discussed so far reside on a single computer. Even the client/server applications in Chapters 11, 12, and 13 are designed to run on a small number of computers. Placing controls on a public network such as the Internet creates new problems and requires extra work to ensure that the controls are used safely.

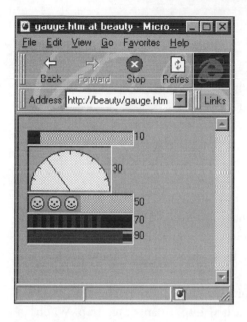

FIGURE 17.2 Internet Explorer displaying Gauge.HTM.

The following list briefly describes the new concepts covered in this chapter. The rest of the chapter explains these concepts in greater detail.

- **Ensuring Safe Use**. A Web page designer may use an ActiveX control's properties and methods in ways the control author never intended. This section describes issues the control designer must consider to ensure that the control is used safely.

- **Displaying ActiveX Controls**. Displaying ActiveX controls on a Web page is fairly simple using the HTML (hypertext markup language) OBJECT command. This section explains this command and describes some of the Web pages shown in Figures 17.1 through 17.4.

- **Learning Class IDs**. To use an ActiveX control, a Web page must include the control's class ID as recorded in the registry. This section tells how to determine the class ID and how to arrange for the control to be downloaded to the user's computer when necessary.

- **Updating Labels**. HTML does not provide updateable labels. This section describes a simple WebLabel ActiveX control that can be updated by VBScript code in a Web page.

- **Selecting Colors**. Passing color parameters to ActiveX controls is not easy since they must be decimal values. This section explains the documents Colors.HTM and PickClr.HTM that can make color selection easier.

- **Loading Data Asynchronously**. The World Wide Web is designed to load documents asynchronously. This section shows how an ActiveX control can use the AsyncRead method to read its own data asynchronously.

Ensuring Safe Use

If an ActiveX control is placed on a public Web page, some Web user will eventually find the control and use it to create other Web pages. The control's original author cannot know how that other person will use the control. If the control is used indiscreetly, it might damage the computer of an innocent person viewing those other Web pages.

For example, suppose a control generates and displays a large amount of data. The control's Num-Points property determines how many data points it creates. To save time, the control stores intermediate data values in a temporary file named DATA.TMP. When the control is finished creating the data, it removes the file.

Next, suppose someone takes a copy of the control from the Web and adds it to a new Web page. Suppose further that this page initializes the control's NumPoints property to 1 billion. If an innocent bystander views this page, the control will try to create 1 billion data values. It will write each value into the file DATA.TMP on the bystander's computer, taking up a huge amount of space and possibly filling the hard disk completely.

This control is not *safe for initialization*. Because it was initialized with a property value that was not anticipated by the original control designer, the control turned into a dangerous trap. When an ActiveX control is placed in a public place such as a Web page, it should be as safe as possible.

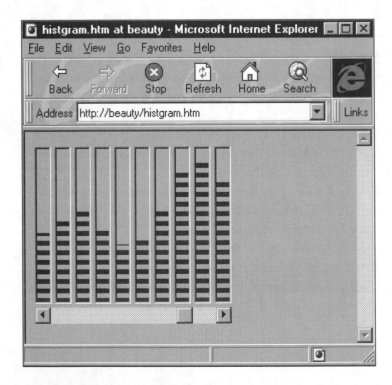

FIGURE 17.3 Internet Explorer displaying Histgram.HTM.

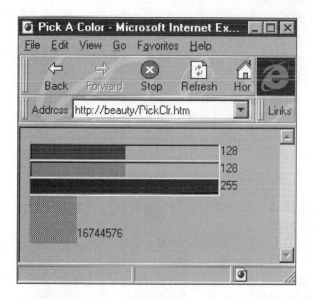

FIGURE 17.4 Internet Explorer displaying PickClr.HTM.

Just as a control developer cannot always anticipate how another Web page author will initialize a control's properties, there is no way to be certain its methods will be used correctly. If a control provides a CreateTempFile method that takes as a parameter the name or size of a file to create, that method can be abused. By specifying a particular file name, an ill-intentioned Web page could make the control write over files on the user's computer. By specifying a large temporary file size, a Web page could use up all of the available space on the user's hard disk.

Once a control is initialized, its methods can be invoked by a Web page scripting language such as VBScript. If a control's methods can be abused by the script, the control is not *safe for scripting*.

To prevent a control from being abused, it should check data values in its property procedures to see if they make sense. The control should ensure that values do not force it to access array entries that do not exist. It should place reasonable restrictions on the allowed values. The earlier example, where NumPoints was set to 1 billion, is dangerous because it allows the property to be set to a ridiculously large value. Setting an upper limit of 100 or 1000 points should provide enough space under most circumstances.

The following actions may also be dangerous when they take input from a control's properties or when values are specified by parameters to a method:

- Reading, writing, or deleting a file with a name supplied by a property or parameter
- Using a disk drive with a name supplied by a property or parameter
- Inserting, updating, or retrieving information in the Windows Registry using a value supplied by a property or parameter

- Executing an API function using a value supplied by a property or parameter
- Referencing array entries with indexes given by properties or parameters
- Creating data values or other objects with the number given by a property

When creating a control's Internet distribution package, as described in the following sections, the developer can specify whether the control should claim to be safe for initialization, safe for scripting, or both. These flags should be set only if the control has been thoroughly tested and if it really is safe. When a control is flagged as safe, the developer promises that no harm will come to the user from the control.

Certificate Authorities

Even with all these precautions, the eventual viewers of the control have little reason to believe a control is safe. After all, they do not know the developer personally.

One way to provide some sense of security is to use a *certificate authority*. A certificate authority is some trusted organization that keeps a record of the control. Using digital signature techniques, the authority marks the control with information that allows a browser to verify that the control has not been modified since it was originally published. When a browser downloads the control, it checks to see if the control has been modified. If it has been, it warns the user that the control may no longer be safe.

Even with a certificate authority, the control developer is still responsible for the behavior of the control. If the control is damaging, the user can consult the authority to learn who published it. The authority cannot prevent damage, but it can help hold the control designer responsible when damage occurs.

Displaying ActiveX Controls

Displaying an ActiveX control on a Web page is not too difficult using the HTML OBJECT statement. This statement creates the control and initializes its width, height, and other properties.

The OBJECT Statement

The OBJECT command takes several parameters. WIDTH and HEIGHT indicate the size the object should have on the Web page. CLASSID gives a class identification string for the control. This rather bizarre string is the class ID used by the Windows registry to identify the control. An easy way to determine a control's class ID is described in the next section.

The CODEBASE parameter tells where the Web browser can find a copy of the control if it is not already located on the user's computer. It also includes the control's version number. If the control is not registered on the user's machine or if the version number in the OBJECT statement disagrees with the registered control's version number, the browser automatically loads the new version.

After the OBJECT statement specifies this basic information, PARAM statements can initialize the control's properties. When the page has given values for all desired parameters, an </OBJECT> statement ends the object definition.

The following HTML code shows how a histogram control might be created on a Web page. The control's cabinet file is named Histgram.CAB and is located in the /Histgram directory on the server www.mysite.com. The cabinet file tells browsers where the control's .OCX file is located and what other controls might be needed to run the control. In this example, the control's BarForeColor property is initialized to 16711680.

```
<OBJECT ID="Histogram1" WIDTH=200 HEIGHT=184
CLASSID="CLSID:75CDDDBA-9A2A-11D0-AA34-0000E8167669"
CODEBASE="http://www.mysite.com/Histgram/Histgram.CAB#version-1,0,0,0">
    <PARAM NAME="BarForeColor" VALUE="16711680">
</OBJECT>
```

Learning Class IDs

The easiest way to learn a control's class ID is to use the Setup Kit Wizard included with Visual Basic 5 to create an Internet distribution kit for the control. The Setup Wizard's first screen asks for the project's name and setup options. To prepare the control for downloading to Web clients, the Create Internet Download Setup option should be selected, as shown in Figure 17.5.

When the Wizard asks for the distribution location, the directory where the downloadable files will be placed should be specified. The directory must be one that is accessible to Web clients. Otherwise, users trying to view Web pages that contain the control will be unable to download it.

The Wizard asks for packaging instructions, as shown in Figure 17.6. The Safety button displays a dialog where the control can be flagged as safe for initialization or safe for scripting.

When the Wizard finishes, it creates several distribution support files, including the control's .CAB file, in the directory specified earlier. One of the other support files is named after the control but with an .HTM extension. For example, when building an installation kit for the histogram control Histgram.OCX, the Wizard also creates Histgram.HTM. This file contains a short example Web page that includes the class ID for the control. This value can be copied into other Web pages that use the control.

An Example Page

The following HTML code is in the file Histgram.HTM in the compact disk's Ch17 subdirectory. Before you can use this page, you will need to modify the code to fit your system. First, use the Setup Wizard to create an Internet distribution package for the Histgram.VBP project contained in the Ch16 subdirectory. Examine the resulting .HTM file to find the control's class ID. Update the file Histgram.HTM so that it uses this class ID.

Next, change the file's CODEBASE parameter so that it indicates the location of the Histgram.OCX file produced by the Wizard. This step is not really necessary as long as you run the Web page on the computer you used to create the distribution package. That computer already knows where to find a copy of the control. It is necessary, however, if another computer will load the control.

This Web page displays a histogram control. First it uses the OBJECT command to create and initialize the control. It uses the PARAM statement to make the control's tic marks blue.

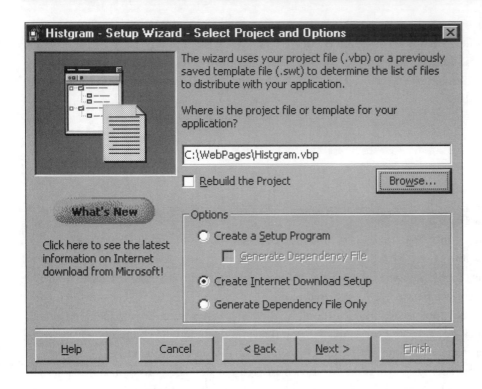

FIGURE 17.5 Selecting Setup Wizard options.

Next, the document uses VBScript code. Not all browsers understand VBScript and those that do not can fail in a couple of different ways. Netscape Navigator 2.02 realizes that it does not understand VBScript and quietly ignores everything it finds between the <SCRIPT LANGUAGE="VBScript"> statement and the closing </SCRIPT>.

SPRY Mosaic version 03.0A.08.19, however, displays all of the VBScript code as if it were normal output text. To reduce the amount of garbage output, Histgram.HTM begins its VBScript code with the normal HTML comment delimiter "<!--". This command is not recognized by VBScript so the document comments this delimiter out using the standard VBScript comment character ' (apostrophe). The end of the script code includes the closing HTML comment delimiter "-->" again commented out by the VBScript comment character.

With this arrangement, VBScript-enabled browsers execute the VBScript code as usual. Netscape Navigator ignores all of the VBScript code including the comment delimiters. SPRY Mosaic displays an apostrophe but then ignores the bulk of the script code because it lies between the "<!--" and the "-->" delimiters.

Within the VBScript code, the Window_OnLoad routine initializes the histogram control. This routine is executed by the browser after the window has loaded.

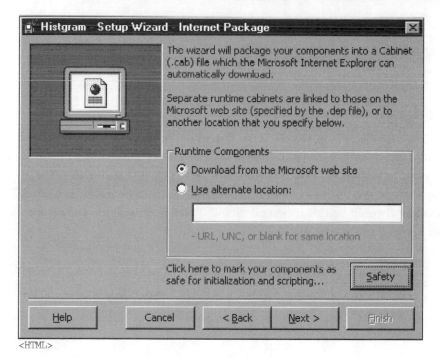

FIGURE 17.6 Specifying Internet packaging options.

```
<OBJECT ID="Histogram1" WIDTH=200 HEIGHT=184
CLASSID="CLSID:75CDDDBA-9A2A-11D0-AA34-0000E8167669"
CODEBASE="http://beauty/histgram/Histgram.CAB#version=1,0,0,0">
    <PARAM NAME="BarForeColor" VALUE="16711680">
</OBJECT>

<SCRIPT LANGUAGE="VBScript">
' <!--

Sub Window_OnLoad
Dim pi
Dim i

    Histogram1.NumBars = 10
    Histogram1.NumValues = 100
    pi = 3.14159265
    For i = 1 to 100
        Histogram1.Value(CInt(i)) = CLng(50 + 50 * _
            Sin(PI * i / 10) * _
            Sin(PI * i / 15) * _
            Cos(PI * i / 5))
    Next
End Sub
```

```
'  -->

</SCRIPT>

</HTML>
```

Updating Labels

VBScript allows a Web page to perform all sorts of calculations. The example in the previous section uses VBScript to initialize the data displayed by a histogram control.

VBScript also allows a Web page to respond to events generated by the controls it contains. These events have names very similar to those used by Visual Basic. For example, the Scroll event generated by a bar gauge control named Gauge1 would be called Gauge1_Scroll. The following code shows how a Web page can use VBScript to respond to this event.

```
<HTML>

<!-- Create controls with OBJECT statements, etc. -->
    :
<SCRIPT LANGUAGE="VBScript">
'  <!--
Sub Gauge1_Scroll
    '  Do something here.
End Sub
'  -->
</SCRIPT>
</HTML>
```

One of the more obvious actions to take in this sort of event handler would be to update a label control to reflect the gauge's newly selected value. Unfortunately, HTML was not designed with updateable labels in mind. HTML was originally intended to allow the downloading of static documents. If something on the document needed to be updated, a revised version of the document would be downloaded.

Fortunately, creating an ActiveX label control is easy. The Ch17\WebLabel subdirectory on the compact disk defines a simple label control suitable for use on Web pages. It uses two Visual Basic label controls, one with Appearance property set to 0 - Flat and the other set to 1 - 3D. The control uses these labels to display itself with either a two- or three-dimensional appearance.

The control also supports BackColor, BorderStyle, ForeColor, and Caption properties. It delegates these properties to the label controls.

The HTML code contained in Gauge.HTM in the Ch17 subdirectory uses WebLabel controls to respond to events generated by gauge controls. The code creates five gauge controls—one of each of the styles: bar gauge, dial, picture gauge, tic gauge, and wide gauge.

For each gauge the document creates a WebLabel control. VBScript code updates the labels when the corresponding gauges' Scroll and Change events occur. The following code fragment shows how Gauge.HTM handles the bar gauge control and its associated label:

```
<HTML>

<!-- Create the bar gauge -->
<OBJECT ID="Gauge0" WIDTH=126 HEIGHT=18
CLASSID="CLSID:1AC27B55-9A55-11D0-AA35-0000E8167669"
CODEBASE="http://beauty/Gauge/Gauge.CAB#version=1,0,0,0">
    <PARAM NAME="ForeColor" VALUE="16711680">
    <PARAM NAME="BackColor" VALUE="8454016">
    <PARAM NAME="Value" VALUE="10">
    <PARAM NAME="Style" VALUE="0">
</OBJECT>

<!-- Create the bar gauge's label -->
<OBJECT ID="WebLabel0" WIDTH=50 HEIGHT=18
CLASSID="CLSID:1AC27CA9-9A55-11D0-AA35-0000E8167669"
CODEBASE="http://beauty/WebLabel/WebLabel.CAB#version=1,0,0,0">
    <PARAM NAME="ForeColor" VALUE="0">
</OBJECT>
<BR>
    :
<!-- Create the other gauges and their labels -->
    :
<SCRIPT LANGUAGE="VBScript">
' <!--

' Bar gauge events
Sub Gauge0_Scroll
    WebLabel0.Caption = Gauge0.Value
End Sub
Sub Gauge0_Change
    WebLabel0.Caption = Gauge0.Value
End Sub
    :
' Events for the other gauges.
    :
' Set the initial label values when we load.
Sub Window_OnLoad
    Gauge0_Change
    Gauge1_Change
    Gauge2_Change
    Gauge3_Change
    Gauge4_Change
End Sub

' -->
</SCRIPT>
</HTML>
```

Selecting Colors

When the controls in the previous examples are created, PARAM statements specify their foreground and background colors. For instance, colors for the bar gauge created in Gauge.HTM are set by the following lines.

```
<PARAM NAME="ForeColor" VALUE="16711680">
<PARAM NAME="BackColor" VALUE="8454016">
```

The values 16711680 and 8454016 are the long integer representations for the colors blue and light green, respectively. You can calculate other color values by writing a Visual Basic program to display them. You can also execute statements such as ?RGB(0, 0, 255) in Visual Basic's Immediate Window to calculate color values.

Table 17.1 lists the decimal values of some useful colors. These colors are standard system colors so they should be available on most computers.

The Web page Colors.HTM in the Ch17 subdirectory displays the colors listed in Table 17.1. It creates a table that displays a sample of each of the colors, together with its name and decimal value. The page uses the BackColor properties of WebLabel controls to display the color samples. As with other Web pages, you will need to change the class ID and CODEBASE values used by this page before you can display it on your system.

TABLE 17.1 Decimal Representations of Useful Color Values

Color	Value
Black	0
Dark red	128
Dark green	32768
Dark yellow	32896
Dark blue	8388608
Dark magenta	8388736
Dark cyan	8421376
Light gray	12632256
Money green	12639424
Sky blue	15780518
Cream	15793151

TABLE 17.1 *Continued*

Color	Value
Medium gray	10789024
Dark gray	8421504
Red	255
Green	65280
Yellow	65535
Blue	16711680
Magenta	16711935
Cyan	16776960
White	16777215

The following code shows the table row entry Colors.HTM used to display the color sky blue. The <TR> and </TR> tags delimit a table row. Within a row the <TD> and </TD> tags delimit the table data entries. Each of the entries is placed in a separate column in the row.

```
<TR>
<TD>
<OBJECT WIDTH=50 HEIGHT=20
CLASSID="CLSID:1AC27CA9-9A55-11D0-AA35-0000E8167669"
CODEBASE="http://beauty/WebLabel/WebLabel.CAB#version=1,0,0,0">
    <PARAM NAME="BackColor" VALUE="15780518">
</OBJECT>
</TD>
<TD>Sky blue</TD>
<TD>15780518</TD>
</TR>
```

The HTML code in PickClr.HTM in the Ch17 subdirectory is also useful for selecting colors. It creates a bar gauge control and a label control for each of the colors red, green, and blue. It then creates two labels named ColorSwatch and ColorLabel.

Using the bar gauges, the user can adjust the amount of red, green, and blue that should be combined to form a new color. When the user changes a gauge's value, a VBScript event handler updates the gauge's corresponding label to show the amount of the color selected on a 0 to 255 scale. It then calculates the new color value using the specified amounts of red, green, and blue. It sets the BackColor property of the ColorSwatch label to this value so the user can see a sample of the color. It also updates the ColorLabel control's Caption property so the user can see the color's decimal value.

The following code shows the portions of PickClr.HTM that deal with the red color component. The code that handles the green and blue colors is very similar.

```html
<HTML>
    :
<!-- Red gauge -->
<OBJECT ID="RedGauge" WIDTH=200 HEIGHT=18
CLASSID="CLSID:1AC27B55-9A55-11D0-AA35-0000E8167669"
CODEBASE="http://beauty/Gauge/Gauge.CAB#version=1,0,0,0">
    <PARAM NAME="ForeColor" VALUE="255">
    <PARAM NAME="BackColor" VALUE="12632256">
    <PARAM NAME="Min" VALUE="0">
    <PARAM NAME="Max" VALUE="255">
    <PARAM NAME="Value" VALUE="128">
    <PARAM NAME="Style" VALUE="0">
</OBJECT>

<!-- Red gauge's label -->
<OBJECT ID="RedLabel" WIDTH=50 HEIGHT=18
CLASSID="CLSID:1AC27CA9-9A55-11D0-AA35-0000E8167669"
CODEBASE="http://beauty/WebLabel/WebLabel.CAB#version=1,0,0,0">
    <PARAM NAME="ForeColor" VALUE="0">
</OBJECT>
<BR>
    :
<!-- Create gauges and labels for green and blue similarly -->
    :
<!-- Labels to display the selected color -->
<OBJECT ID="ColorSwatch" WIDTH=50 HEIGHT=50
CLASSID="CLSID:1AC27CA9-9A55-11D0-AA35-0000E8167669"
CODEBASE="http://beauty/WebLabel/WebLabel.CAB#version=1,0,0,0">
</OBJECT>

<OBJECT ID="ColorLabel" WIDTH=50 HEIGHT=18
CLASSID="CLSID:1AC27CA9-9A55-11D0-AA35-0000E8167669"
CODEBASE="http://beauty/WebLabel/WebLabel.CAB#version=1,0,0,0">
</OBJECT>
<BR>

<SCRIPT LANGUAGE="VBScript">
' <!--

' Red events
Sub RedGauge_Scroll
    RedLabel.Caption = RedGauge.Value
    ShowColor
End Sub
Sub RedGauge_Change
    RedLabel.Caption = RedGauge.Value
    ShowColor
End Sub
```

```
' The green and blue events are similar.
    :
' Set the initial label values when we load.
Sub Window_OnLoad
    RedGauge_Change
    GreenGauge_Change
    BlueGauge_Change
End Sub

' Update the color swatch and label
Sub ShowColor
Dim val

    val = ((BlueGauge.Value * 256) + _
            GreenGauge.Value) * 256 + RedGauge.Value
    ColorLabel.Caption = val
    ColorSwatch.BackColor = val
End Sub

' -->
</SCRIPT>
</BODY>
</HTML>
```

Once again, you need to modify the code to set the correct class IDs and CODEBASE values before you can run this page on your computer.

Loading Data Asynchronously

When an HTML document creates an ActiveX control using the OBJECT statement, it can use PARAM clauses to specify the control's properties. Script code can also set control properties. These methods are fine for setting control properties that are integers, strings, Booleans, and other simple data types. They do not work, however, for pictures. An HTML document cannot set the VALUE field in a PARAM statement to point to a picture file.

Even if this was possible, this sort of property assignment would violate one of the goals of HTML. HTML documents are designed to be loaded in pieces asynchronously. A document may contain references to pictures and other resources located on the Web. After the main document has been loaded, the browser loads the references and places them where they belong in the document. This allows the user to see the bulk of the document while larger items such as pictures are downloaded.

Setting a control's picture property using a PARAM statement would slow the entire process. The browser would be forced to wait until the picture was loaded before it could continue displaying the main document.

Loading Asynchronous Data

ActiveX controls can provide their own asynchronous features using the UserControl object's Async-Read subroutine. AsyncRead takes three parameters. The first is the location of the resource to be loaded. This can be a path if the data is located on the local computer, or it can be a URL (Uniform Resource Locator) if the data should be loaded across the network.

AsyncRead's second parameter indicates how the data should be returned to the ActiveX control. This parameter can have one of the following values:

- **vbAsyncTypeFile**. The data is placed in a file.
- **vbAsyncTypeByteArray**. The data is returned in a byte array. The control must know how to handle the data.
- **vbAsyncTypePicture**. The data is placed in a Picture object.

AsyncRead's final parameter is the name of the object being loaded asynchronously. This can be any string value defined by the control code.

When the data has been loaded, the UserControl object's AsyncReadComplete event handler is executed. This routine receives as a parameter an object of type AsyncProperty. This object contains three properties of its own: AsyncType, PropertyName, and Value. AsyncType and PropertyName are the same as the second and third parameters passed to the AsyncRead method. PropertyName is particularly useful if the control loads several data items asynchronously. The event handler can check the value of PropertyName to determine which value has been returned.

The AsyncProperty object's Value property is a variant containing the actual data.

Loading Pictures on the Web

The gauge control in the Ch15\Combined subdirectory defines five different styles of gauge control. A gauge with the picture style displays its values by filling its control area with a picture. The picture is specified by the control's FillPicture property. As is mentioned in the previous section, HTML code cannot set the values of picture properties directly.

To allow HTML code to specify a fill picture, the control can provide an alternative property named FillPictureURL. This property is initialized, saved, and retrieved just like any other string property by the UserControl's InitProperties, ReadProperties, and WriteProperties event handlers.

The FillPictureURL property let procedure stores the property's new value. It then checks to see if the control is running in user mode rather than in design mode. If it is, and if the FillPictureURL property is nonblank, the control uses the AsyncRead method to begin reading the picture specified by the property value.

```
Public Property Let FillPictureURL(url As String)
    fill_picture_url = url

    ' If it's run time start the read.
    If Ambient.UserMode And url <> "" Then
        AsyncRead url, vbAsyncTypePicture, _
            "FillPictureURL"
    End If

    PropertyChanged "FillPictureURL" ' Tell VB.
```

```
    ' The gauge is repainted when the read
    ' finshes.
End Property
```

When the picture has been loaded, the AsyncReadComplete event handler executes. This routine checks the name of the returned data. If the name is "FillPictureURL," the routine sets the FillPicture property to the data retrieved.

AsyncReadComplete uses the On Error GoTo statement to protect itself against errors. There are many ways in which an error can occur while downloading data across a network. All AsyncReadComplete event handlers must be prepared to handle errors gracefully.

```
Private Sub UserControl_AsyncReadComplete(AsyncProp As AsyncProperty)
    On Error GoTo AsyncReadError

    If AsyncProp.PropertyName = "FillPictureURL" Then
        Set FillPicture = AsyncProp.Value
    End If

AsyncReadError:
End Sub
```

The HTML code in Gauge.HTM specifies the picture gauge's FillPictureURL property using the following PARAM statement. The control asynchronously loads the bitmap file Gauge/Smile.bmp and uses it for the FillPicture property.

```
<PARAM NAME="FillPictureURL" VALUE="Gauge/Smile.bmp">
```

Summary

Adding an ActiveX control to a Web page is relatively easy using the Setup Kit Wizard. The Wizard builds the control's .OCX and cabinet files, and creates a small sample Web document that invokes the control. This document includes a reference to the control's class ID. Using this ID, it is easy to use the HTML OBJECT statement to add new instances of the control to other Web pages.

ActiveX controls are extremely flexible. They can contain standard controls as well as other ActiveX controls. In fact, an ActiveX control that contains enough constituent controls can practically implement a complete application. Placing such a control on a Web page allows a designer to bring nearly all of the features of Visual Basic to the Web.

Chapter 18

WebSurvey

By automatically downloading ActiveX controls when they are needed, browsers implicitly transfer data from a server to a client computer. The UserControl object's AsyncRead method allows ActiveX controls to explicitly retrieve data from a server. Neither of these methods allows a Web client computer to send information back to the server.

This chapter explains how an ActiveX control on a Web page can send data from the client computer back to the server. Using the Microsoft Internet Transfer Control, the chapter builds a survey form that takes information from a Web page user and stores it in a file on a server computer.

The chapter's first section, "Using WebSurvey," describes the WebSurvey application from the end user's point of view. It explains how the user enters data using the HTML objects provided by the survey Web page.

The next section, "Key Techniques," briefly lists the most important programming methods used to implement WebSurvey. The rest of the chapter describes those methods in detail.

Using WebSurvey

To the end user, WebSurvey is just another Web page. It contains radio buttons (similar to option buttons in Visual Basic), select boxes (similar to combo boxes and lists), text areas, and a check box so that the user can respond to a brief series of questions. After entering the requested values, the user clicks the Send Data button to transmit the information to a server computer. There a program takes the data and appends it to a text file.

If the user checks the "Send a copy of the survey results" check box, the Web page requires an e-mail address. If the user checks the box but does not fill in an e-mail address, the page presents an error message.

Figures 18.1 and 18.2 show the top and bottom halves of the survey Web page. The following text shows the data that was stored in the server computer's data file by the entries shown in these figures.

```
Received: 3/12/97 6:49:09 AM
    QAlgs:    Daily
    QGraphic: Often
    QWeb:     Occasionally
    Access:   Only Phone Line
    MainLang: VB
    Name:     Rod Stephens
    Street:   1234 Bug Ave
    City:     Programmer City
    State:    CO
    Zip:      11235
    Email:    RodStephens@CompuServe.com
    SendCopy: True
    Comments: This survey is extremely contrived!
It should certainly be longer.
```

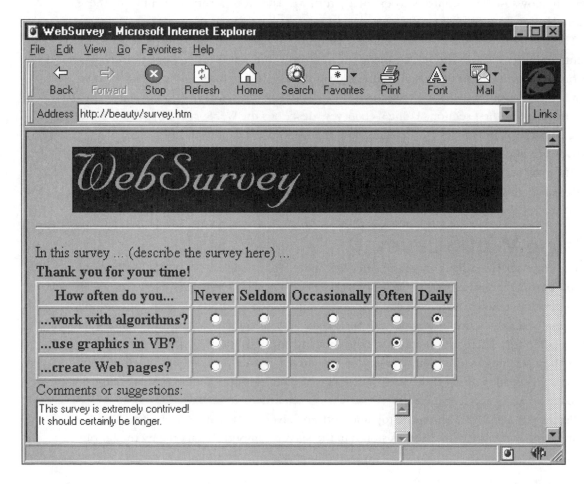

FIGURE 18.1 The top half of WebSurvey.

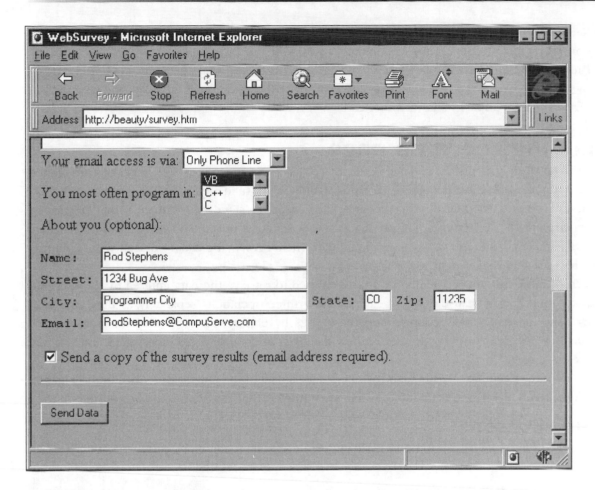

FIGURE 18.2 The bottom half of WebSurvey.

Key Techniques

A survey such as this has two parts: the Web page that takes information from the user and the server program that receives and processes the information. Both of the parts that make up the WebSurvey application are described in this chapter.

The following list briefly describes new techniques used to implement WebSurvey. The rest of the chapter explains these features in greater detail.

- **Building the Web Page**. The WebSurvey application was contrived to demonstrate the most important HTML data entry objects. This section describes the radio buttons, select boxes, text areas, and check boxes used by WebSurvey.
- **Sending Data across the Web**. The InetXfer ActiveX control sends data across a network. This section explains how the InetXfer control works.

- **Receiving Data across the Web**. The InetXfer control sends data to a server application. This section shows how the server application receives the data.
- **Packing and Unpacking Data**. Before sending data across the network, the InetXfer control packs the data so it will arrive safely. This section explains how InetXfer packs the data and how the server program unpacks it at the other end.

Building the Web page

Like most HTML documents, the complete code for WebSurvey is fairly long so only pieces of it are printed here. You can see the whole document Survey.HTM in the Ch18 subdirectory on the compact disk.

Survey.HTM is divided into two main parts. The first part is standard HTML code that creates the objects displayed by the browser. The second part, VBScript code, uses the objects to prepare and send the data entered by the user to the server computer. Then it resets the data to default values and presents the user with a success message.

Each of the HTML objects is first created, then used to retrieve the data entered by the user, and finally cleared. Rather than describing each of these three operations separately, as they appear in Survey.HTM, the following sections group these tasks by object. The section about radio buttons explains how the radio buttons are created, how the VBScript code accesses their values, and how the code resets them.

It is important to note that not all browsers understand all of the objects described in this chapter. These objects are described as they function in Microsoft Internet Explorer.

Radio Buttons

HTML radio buttons are similar to Visual Basic option buttons. They allow the user to select one of a set of options.

Creating Radio Buttons Like other HTML objects that take input from the user, radio buttons are created using an INPUT statement. Setting the TYPE parameter to Radio creates a radio button.

In HTML, radio buttons are grouped together by giving them a common NAME parameter. Only one of the buttons that share a name can be selected at one time. If the user clicks on another button, the currently selected button with the same name is deselected.

Radio buttons can optionally have a VALUE parameter indicating a value to be associated with the button. Assigning a value to each button makes it easier to remember the meaning of the button later.

Finally, the optional CHECKED parameter indicates that the button should initially be selected.

The following code creates three radio buttons, all named HowOften. The first button is initially selected. Quotes around the VALUE parameter of the second allow it to contain spaces. The result is shown in Figure 18.3.

Notice that each of these INPUT statements is followed by a text string describing the radio button. This is the text that is visible to the user. If this text is not included, the user will see only a button with no label.

```
<INPUT TYPE=Radio NAME=HowOften VALUE=Never CHECKED>Never
<INPUT TYPE=Radio NAME=HowOften VALUE="Once in a while">Once in a while
<INPUT TYPE=Radio NAME=HowOften VALUE=Always>Always
```

Survey.HTM uses similar code to create each of its 15 radio buttons. The way they are placed in a table is described later in this chapter.

Getting Radio Button Values Figuring out which radio button in a group is currently selected is a bit difficult. Because there is no single object that manages all the buttons, there is no central object to ask for the selected value.

When an HTML document creates radio buttons with the same name, the buttons are added to a collection. The previous code, for example, would have created a three-entry collection of buttons named HowOften.

VBScript code can access collections much as Visual Basic can. Survey.HTM uses the following code to figure out which of a set of radio buttons is selected. It looks through the collection until it finds the button with the Checked property set to true. It then returns that button's Value property.

```
Function RadioValue(btn)
Dim i
Dim max_btn

    max_btn = btn.Count - 1
    For i = 0 to max_btn
        If btn(i).Checked Then Exit For
    Next
    RadioValue = btn(i).Value
End Function
```

Survey.HTM uses function RadioValue to pass values to the InetXfer1 control's AddData method. For example, the following code sends the value of the currently selected button named QGraphic to AddData.

```
InetXfer1.AddData "QGraphic", RadioValue(QGraphic)
```

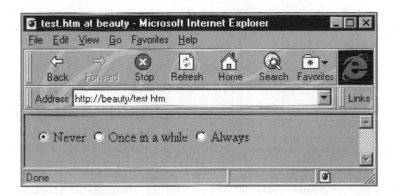

FIGURE 18.3 Radio buttons.

Resetting Radio Buttons   To reset a group of radio buttons to a given value, the Web page should set the Checked property for one of the buttons to true. The previously selected button is automatically deselected.

Survey.HTM uses the following code to reset the QGraphic radio buttons. This code selects QGraphic button number two. Because the button collection starts with index zero, this is the third button in the group. In Survey.HTM this is the button corresponding to the answer Occasionally.

```
QGraphic(2).Checked = True
```

Tables

HTML tables arrange objects in rows and columns much as grid controls do in Visual Basic. The syntax for creating a table is quite complicated so only some of the table functionality is described here.

A table begins with a <TABLE> tag. This statement can take an optional parameter BORDER to indicate the table should display visible borders. The table ends with the tag </TABLE>.

A table can contain a CAPTION statement. This is one of the few simple parts of a table. The CAPTION statement can include an ALIGN argument to indicate whether the caption belongs at the top or bottom of the table. The following statement adds a caption to the bottom of the table:

```
<CAPTION ALIGN=BOTTOM>This caption is on the bottom</CAPTION>
```

Rows in a table are delimited by <TR> and </TR> tags. Each row can contain header entries and data entries. Header entries are delimited by <TH> and </TH>. The table displays headers in a bold style. Table data entries are delimited by <TD> and </TD>.

Both table header and data entries can take an optional ALIGN parameter to indicate how the item should be aligned within its cell in the table. This parameter can have the values Left, Right, or Center. For example, the following statement centers the word "Middle" in its cell.

```
<TD ALIGN=Center>Middle</TD>
```

Similarly, the VALIGN statement determines the vertical alignment of an entry. This is useful if the items in one row are of different heights. VALIGN can take the values Top, Center, and Bottom.

A document can use the ALIGN and VALIGN statements in a TR statement to set the alignment for all the entries in that row. The row settings can still be overridden in the individual table header or data entries.

The last table options described here are ROWSPAN and COLSPAN. These commands make a table header or data entry span more than one row or column, respectively. These commands can be very confusing, particularly when used in the middle of the table. The following statement creates a table header entry that is two columns wide:

```
<TH COLSPAN=2>Double wide header</TH>
```

Survey.HTM uses the following HTML code to create its table of radio buttons. Only the code creating the first two rows of the table is listed here. The third and fourth rows are very similar to the second.

```
<TABLE BORDER>
<TR>
```

```
<TH>How often do you...</TH>
<TH>Never</TH>
<TH>Seldom</TH>
<TH>Occasionally</TH>
<TH>Often</TH>
<TH>Daily</TH>
</TR>
<TR ALIGN=Center>
<TH ALIGN=Left>...work with algorithms?</TH>
<TD><INPUT TYPE="Radio" NAME="QAlgs" VALUE="Never"></TD>
<TD><INPUT TYPE="Radio" NAME="QAlgs" VALUE="Seldom"></TD>
<TD><INPUT TYPE="Radio" NAME="QAlgs" VALUE="Occasionally" CHECKED></TD>
<TD><INPUT TYPE="Radio" NAME="QAlgs" VALUE="Often"></TD>
<TD><INPUT TYPE="Radio" NAME="QAlgs" VALUE="Daily"></TD>
</TR>
      :
<!-- Similar code for the third and fourth rows -->
      :
</TABLE>
```

Select Controls

A select control is similar to a Visual Basic combo box or list control, depending on the control's SIZE parameter. A select control allows the user to select one string from a list of options.

Creating Select Controls A select control starts with a SELECT statement that should give the control's name. The optional SIZE parameter tells how many of the control's options should be visible at one time. If SIZE is omitted or 1, the control is similar to a combo box. If SIZE is greater than 1, the control is similar to a Visual Basic list.

After the SELECT statement, OPTION commands define the select control's choices. The SELECTED parameter indicates the option that is initially chosen.

The following code shows how Survey.HTM creates two select controls. The first lists user Internet access types and uses a combo box style. The second allows the user to select a programming language. This control's SIZE parameter is 3 so it displays three choices at a time. The code includes text after each OPTION statement. This is the text displayed by the select control. If this text were not included, the control would display a series of blank choices.

```
Your email access is via:
<SELECT NAME="Access">
    <OPTION VALUE="Only Phone Line" SELECTED>Only Phone Line
    <OPTION VALUE="Second Phone Line">Second Phone Line
    <OPTION VALUE="Direct Connection">Direct Connection
</SELECT>
<BR>
You most often program in:
<SELECT NAME="MainLang" SIZE=3>
    <OPTION VALUE="VB" SELECTED>VB
    <OPTION VALUE="C++">C++
    <OPTION VALUE="C">C
```

```
    <OPTION VALUE="Delphi">Delphi
    <OPTION VALUE="Fortran">Fortran
    <OPTION VALUE="Pascal">Pascal
    <OPTION VALUE="Assembly">Assembly
    <OPTION VALUE="Other">Other
</SELECT>
```

Getting Select Control Values Radio buttons are related only through their names, but a select control's options are part of the control. This makes it a little easier to work with select controls. The control's SelectedIndex property gives the index of the currently selected option.

The control's Options property is an array containing the option objects. These have Value properties that hold the option VALUE, if any, assigned in the OPTION statement.

Using these properties, VBScript code can refer to the value of the selected option directly. The following code sets the variable choice equal to the value of the MainLang control's selected option:

```
choice = MainLang.Options(MainLang.SelectedIndex).Value
```

Resetting Select Controls To select a particular choice for a select control, the HTML code assigns a new value to the control's SelectedIndex property. The following code selects the MainLang control's first (index zero) option:

```
MainLang.SelectedIndex = 0
```

Text Areas

Text areas are similar to multiline text boxes in Visual Basic. They automatically provide vertical scroll bars when necessary. If the user enters a line of text that will not fit on the current line, the control automatically wraps the text to the next line.

Because the control displays a large amount of text and automatically provides scroll bars, users may enter a lot of text into a text area. A program that processes text area data should be prepared to handle very long strings.

Creating Text Areas A text area begins with a TEXTAREA statement. This statement should include ROWS and COLS parameters to indicate the number of rows and columns the text area should display. ROWS and COLS areas are specified using a fixed-width font, but the control will probably not use a fixed-width font when it is displayed. This means the actual number of rows and columns visible may not match the values of ROWS and COLS.

After the end of the TEXTAREA statement, the HTML code can supply text to be initially displayed within the control. The control ends with the </TEXTAREA> tag.

The following code creates a text area that initially contains one sentence of text. Because the text area is defined on three lines, the default text actually occupies three lines. There is one carriage return after the TEXTAREA statement and another after the initial sentence.

```
<TEXTAREA NAME="CommentText" COLS="80" ROWS="2">
This is a line of default text.
</TEXTAREA>
```

Getting Text Area Values A text area control's Value property holds the contents of the control. The following statement copies the value of the CommentText control into the variable cmt:

```
cmt = CommentText.Value
```

Resetting Text Areas To reset a text area's value, HTML code assigns the new value to the control's Value property. This line blanks the CommentText control.

```
CommentText.Value = ""
```

Text Boxes

HTML text boxes are similar to single-line text boxes in Visual Basic. They allow the user to enter a single line of text.

Creating Text Boxes A text box is created using an INPUT statement with TYPE parameter set to Text. The SIZE parameter indicates the number of characters that should be visible at one time in the field. Like the text area control's ROWS and COLS properties, SIZE is specified in a fixed-width font that may not be used by the control. That means the actual number of characters visible may not match SIZE.

The SIZE parameter does not prevent the user from entering more than the specified number of characters. If the user enters more characters than will fit within the control, the text is scrolled to the left.

The INPUT statement's optional VALUE property indicates the initial value the text box should display.

The following code creates a text box named NameText. Initially the control displays the string "(Your name here)."

```
<INPUT TYPE="Text" NAME="NameText" SIZE="30" VALUE="(Your name here)">
```

Getting Text Box Values As is the case for text area controls, the value for a text box is given by its Value property. The following VBScript code displays a message box showing the text entered in the NameText control surrounded by quotation marks.

```
MsgBox "The name is: """ & NameText.Value & """"
```

Resetting Text Boxes Setting a text box's value is also similar to setting the value of a text area. The following code clears the NameText control:

```
NameText.Value = ""
```

Check Boxes

HTML check boxes are similar to check boxes in Visual Basic. They allow the user to toggle a value on or off.

Creating Check Boxes Check boxes are created using the INPUT statement with the TYPE parameter set to Checkbox. The optional VALUE parameter associates a value with the check box for later use. The optional CHECKED parameter indicates the box should initially be checked.

The following code shows how Survey.HTM creates its single check box. This code displays text that indicates the meaning of the check box. If this text were omitted, the browser would display only the check box.

```
<INPUT TYPE="CheckBox" NAME="SendCopy">
Send a copy of the survey results (email address required).
```

Getting Check Box Values A check box's Checked property is a Boolean value that indicates whether the box is checked. VBScript code can use this value directly. The following code displays a message indicating whether the SendCopy check box is checked. For instance, if the button is not checked, the message will read "SendCopy = False."

```
Msgbox "SendCopy = " & SendCopy.Checked & "."
```

Script code can also use a check box's Checked property to decide which action to take. The following code presents a message only if the Checked property is true:

```
If SendCopy.Checked Then Msgbox "Send a copy."
```

Resetting Check Boxes To set a check box's value, HTML code sets its Checked property to either true or false. The following code unchecks the SendCopy check box:

```
SendCopy.Checked = False
```

Sending Data across the Web

Normally when an HTML document sends data to a program on a remote server computer, the server program must read the data through standard input. The program is expected to write a reply to standard output. Standard input and output are data streams similar to files that text-only applications use for input and output. In a DOS application, whatever the user types at the keyboard is standard input. The text displayed by the program on the screen is standard output.

Visual Basic does not include the concepts of standard input and output. Data enters the program through events when the user interacts with user interface elements such as command buttons and text boxes. The program displays information by modifying the user interface elements. This makes transferring data to a Visual Basic program difficult using only HTML.

The Internet transfer control does not have these problems. It can send data to a remote program through environment variables rather than standard input, and it does not expect to receive a response through standard output.

Using the control's Execute method, a program can fetch or execute files on a remote system. The following Visual Basic code shows how a program can use the control Inet1 to invoke the SaveData.EXE program located at http://www.myserver.com:

```
Inet1.Execute "http://www.myserver.com/SaveData.EXE?testdata"
```

Web addresses that include a question mark are designed for sending queries to remote programs. The text that comes after the question mark is passed to the program in the environment variable

QUERY_STRING. In this example, QUERY_STRING would be set to the value "testdata." The remote program SaveData.EXE can read this variable to find out what data has been sent. This process is discussed in more detail in the later section "Receiving Data Across the Web."

Unfortunately, certain characters have special meanings to the HTTP protocol. Space and carriage return characters can cause the data to be broken. That means a program cannot safely include text that contains these characters. If a program included the text "here is some text with spaces," it would arrive at the server application truncated to "here."

By convention, a program should convert spaces into plus signs (+) before sending the data. The program at the other end can then convert the plus signs back into spaces. The InetXfer ActiveX control performs this and a few other translations to safely package the data before sending it to the server.

InetXfer

The InetXfer ActiveX control provides no properties and is not visible at run time. It provides only three methods: ClearData, AddData, and SendData. An application can use these methods to package data for transport across the Internet.

ClearData ClearData empties the control's data buffer. The data is stored in the module-level string variable out_data. An application should invoke ClearData before it starts adding data to the transfer buffer.

```
Private out_data As String

Public Sub ClearData()
    out_data = ""
End Sub
```

AddData The AddData method takes as parameters the name of a data item and its value. It uses the AppendSegment subroutine to add the name and value to the out_data buffer.

AppendSegment protects special characters such as spaces and carriage returns in the string. It then appends the result to out_data. AppendSegment, its inverse function RemoveSegment, and their support routines are described later in the section "Packing and Unpacking Data."

```
Public Sub AddData(ByVal name As String, ByVal value As String)
    AppendSegment out_data, Trim$(name)
    AppendSegment out_data, Trim$(value)
End Sub
```

SendData The SendData method actually sends the data to a remote program using an Internet transfer control. SendData takes as a parameter the URL of the program that should receive the data. It combines the URL with the information in out_data, separated by a question mark. It then uses the Internet transfer control's Execute method to send the data.

```
Public Sub SendData(url As String)
    Inet1.Execute url & "?" & out_data
End Sub
```

Because it takes the URL as a parameter, one might think the SendData method was not safe for scripting. After all, a script could use any value for the URL and make SendData transfer data to any location. This is nothing a script cannot do anyway. Using HTML code, a script can invoke a command that contains a URL followed by a question mark and a string of data in any case. SendData does not greatly increase the danger of the control.

Sending Data in Survey.HTM When the user clicks WebSurvey's Send Data button, the VBScript event handler SendButton_OnClick sends the data. First, it uses the InetXfer control's ClearData method to empty the data buffer. Next, it uses the AddData method to place data items in the data buffer. It then invokes the InetXfer control's SendData method to transfer the data to the server program http://Beauty/Scripts/SaveData.EXE. You will need to change the location of the server before you can run the code on your computer. Finally, the event handler clears the form and presents a message to the user saying the data has been sent.

```
Sub SendButton_OnClick
    ' Empty the data buffer.
    InetXfer1.ClearData

    ' Build up the data to send.
    InetXfer1.AddData "QAlgs",    RadioValue(QAlgs)
    InetXfer1.AddData "QGraphic", RadioValue(QGraphic)
    InetXfer1.AddData "QWeb",     RadioValue(QWeb)
    InetXfer1.AddData "Access", _
        Access.Options(Access.SelectedIndex).Value
    InetXfer1.AddData "MainLang", _
        MainLang.Options(MainLang.SelectedIndex).Value
    InetXfer1.AddData "Name",     NameText.Value
    InetXfer1.AddData "Email",    EmailText.Value
    InetXfer1.AddData "Street",   StreetText.Value
    InetXfer1.AddData "City",     CityText.Value
    InetXfer1.AddData "State",    StateText.Value
    InetXfer1.AddData "Zip",      ZipText.Value
    InetXfer1.AddData "Phone",    PhoneText.Value
    InetXfer1.AddData "SendCopy", SendCopy.Checked
    InetXfer1.AddData "Comments", CommentText.Value

    ' Send the data.
    InetXfer1.SendData "http://Beauty/Scripts/SaveData.exe"

    ' Clear the form.
    ClearForm

    ' Tell the user the data has been sent.
    MsgBox "The data has been sent. Thank you for your time!"
End Sub
```

Receiving Data across the Web

The SaveData program, included in the Ch18\SaveData subdirectory of the compact disk, receives the data sent by Survey.HTM. The program has no visible interface. It begins execution with the Main subroutine.

The program uses Visual Basic's Environ function to retrieve the value of the QUERY_STRING environment variable. This string contains the data that was packaged by the InetXfer control in Survey.HTM. The string contains field value names and data values separated by semi-colons. Special characters have been protected by converting them into some other character; for example, spaces have been replaced with plus signs. The following text shows a portion of what the data might look like at this point. The translation process is described further in the section "Packing and Unpacking Data."

```
Access;Only+Phone+Line;MainLang;VB;Name;Rod+Stephens;...
```

Once it has read the QUERY_STRING environment variable, the program opens the data file where it will store the data values.

SaveData then uses the RemoveSegment function to pull a piece of data out of the environment variable string. It truncates data field names to 8 characters and data values to 100 characters. This protects the program from accidental or intentional misuse. For instance, a user could enter the following URL into a browser to send the program a long string of garbage:

```
http://beauty/SaveData.exe?Name;An+extremely+long+piece+of+garbage...
```

Someone can still send the program bad data, but the damage will be minimal.

After truncating the data values, the program appends the data to the output file. It repeats the process of removing a data name and value from the environment string and adding the data to the file until there is no more information to read.

```
Option Explicit

Const FILE_NAME = "WebData.TXT"
Const MAX_FIELD = 8
Const MAX_VALUE = 100

Sub Main()
Dim txt As String
Dim fnum As Integer
Dim field_name As String
Dim field_value As String

    ' We cannot recover if something goes wrong.
    On Error GoTo Done

    ' Read the environment variable.
    txt = Environ("QUERY_STRING")

    ' Open the file.
    fnum = FreeFile
```

```
Open FILE_NAME For Append As #fnum
On Error GoTo CloseFile
Print #fnum, "Received: " & Format$(Now)

    ' Write the segments to the file.
    Do While txt <> ""
        ' Get the next field name.
        field_name = RemoveSegment(txt)
        field_value = RemoveSegment(txt)

        ' Make sure they are not too long.
        field_name = Left$(field_name, MAX_FIELD)
        field_value = Left$(field_value, MAX_VALUE)

        ' Save the data.
        field_name = "    " & field_name & ":"
        Print #fnum, Format$(field_name, _
            "!@@@@@@@@@@@@@@") & field_value
    Loop

CloseFile:
    Close #fnum

Done:

End Sub
```

Packing and Unpacking Data

The InetXfer ActiveX control uses subroutine AppendSegment to fill a buffer string with data before sending it across the network. Before it adds new data to the buffer, AppendSegment translates certain special characters to protect them during transit.

When the server program receives the data, it uses function RemoveSegment to pull data segments out of the data buffer. RemoveSegment reverses the translations performed by AppendSegment to restore the original data.

These routines and their helper subroutines are described in the following sections.

AppendSegment

To prevent spaces from truncating the data, AppendSegment converts them into plus signs. If the data already contains plus signs, this could be confusing. The receiving program would not be able to tell which plus signs were in the original data and which represented spaces.

To prevent this confusion AppendSegment converts plus signs into the string "\+". For example, the string "Conversion + Confusion" becomes "Conversion+\++Confusion".

Similarly, AppendSegment converts carriage returns into asterisks and asterisks into the string "*". It performs these conversions using subroutine ProtectChar. This routine converts one character (for example, space) into another (plus) while placing a back slash in front of the second character when it occurs in the original data (\+). This routine is described shortly.

After protecting spaces and carriage returns, AppendSegment uses the ConvertToken subroutine to change semi-colons in the data into the string "\;". ConvertToken, also described shortly, makes simple replacements of one string for another.

Finally, AppendSegment adds the converted data to the buffer string, separating it with a semi-colon. Replacing semi-colons with "\;" in the original data allows the receiving program to tell which semi-colons delimit data segments and which are part of the data.

```
Public Sub AppendSegment(txt As String, ByVal now_txt As String)
    ' Protect carriage returns.
    ProtectChar new_txt, vbCrLf, "*"

    ' Protect spaces.
    ProtectChar new_txt, " ", "+"

    ' Protect semi-colons.
    ConvertToken new_txt, ";", "\;"

    ' Concatenate the result.
    txt = txt & new_txt & ";"
End Sub
```

ProtectChar Subroutine ProtectChar converts one character (for example, space) into another (plus) while placing a back slash in front of the second character when it occurs in the original data (\+). It does this using the ConvertToken subroutine described in the next section. First it adds the back slashes. For example, it converts "+" into "\+". Then ProtectChar replaces the first character (space) with the second (plus).

```
Public Sub ProtectChar(txt As String, fr_ch As String, to_ch As String)
    ' Convert to_ch into \to_ch.
    ConvertToken txt, to_ch, "\" & to_ch

    ' Convert fr_ch into to_ch.
    ConvertToken txt, fr_ch, to_ch
End Sub
```

ConvertToken ConvertToken replaces one substring with another inside a larger string. The routine loops through the data string looking for occurrences of the first substring. When it finds one, it copies the text before the substring to the end of the output string. It adds the second substring to replace the first, skips over the first substring in the original data, and continues looking.

```
Public Sub ConvertToken(txt As String, from_str As String, _
    to_str As String)
Dim new_txt As String
Dim old_pos As Integer
```

```
Dim new_pos As Integer
Dim token As String
Dim txt_len As Integer
Dim from_len As Integer

    txt_len = Len(txt)
    from_len = Len(from_str)
    new_txt = ""
    old_pos = 1
    Do
        ' Find the next from_str.
        new_pos = InStr(old_pos, txt, from_str)
        If new_pos < 1 Then new_pos = txt_len + 1

        ' Add this piece to the new string.
        token = Mid$(txt, old_pos, new_pos - old_pos)
        new_txt = new_txt & token

        ' If we're beyond the end, we're done.
        If new_pos > txt_len Then Exit Do

        ' Add a space.
        new_txt = new_txt & to_str

        ' Move beyond the from_str.
        old_pos = new_pos + from_len
    Loop

    txt = new_txt
End Sub
```

RemoveSegment

After the data arrives at the server program, that program uses RemoveSegment to pull data segments out of the data buffer. RemoveSegment returns the next piece of data and shortens the data buffer so it no longer contains the removed segment.

RemoveSegment first searches the data for a semi-colon that is not preceded by a back slash. This marks the end of the next segment within the data. It creates a string that contains the segment and removes the segment from the data buffer.

Next the function uses ConvertToken to turn the "\;" combinations back into semi-colons. It uses UnprotectChar to convert plus signs into spaces and asterisks into carriage returns. UnprotectChar reverses the effects of subroutine ProtectChar. Finally, RemoveSegment returns the resulting string.

```
Public Function RemoveSegment(txt As String) As String
Dim pos As Integer
Dim txt_len As Integer
Dim token As String

    ' Find the first semi-colon not after "\".
    txt_len = Len(txt)
```

```
        pos = 1
        Do
            pos = InStr(pos, txt, ";")

            ' If it's not found, use all of txt.
            If pos = 0 Then
                pos = txt_len + 1
                Exit Do
            End If

            ' If the 1st character is ";", the
            ' segment is blank.
            If pos - 1 Then Exit Do

            ' If the previous character is not "\",
            ' this is a segment delimiter.
            If Mid$(txt, pos - 1, 1) <> "\" Then Exit Do

            ' Look for the next ";".
            pos = pos + 1
        Loop

        ' Break the token off.
        token = Left$(txt, pos - 1)
        If pos > txt_len Then
            txt = ""
        Else
            txt = Right$(txt, txt_len - pos)
        End If

        ' Restore hidden semi-colons.
        ConvertToken token, "\;", ";"

        ' Restore hidden spaces.
        UnprotectChar token, "+", " "

        ' Restore hidden carriage returns.
        UnprotectChar token, "*", vbCrLf

        ' Return the result.
        RemoveSegment = token
    End Function
```

UnprotectChar UnprotectChar reverses the effects of subroutine ProtectChar. For example, it converts the substring "\+" into a plus sign and other plus signs into spaces.

UnprotectChar uses InStr to locate the first occurrence of the character with the back slash (\+). Because it has found the first occurrence, any occurrence of the character (plus) within the first part of the string should be converted into the other character (space). The program uses ConvertToken to make that substitution. It then adds the first character (plus) without the slash and looks for more instances.

404   Part Six • Chapter 18

For example, consider the case of converting plus signs into spaces and suppose the data contains the following text:

```
She+sells+sea\+shells+down+by+the+sea\+shore
```

The first occurrence of "\+" lies just before the word "shells." That means any plus signs before that point should be converted into spaces. After making these substitutions and adding the plus character without a slash, the output string is:

```
She sells sea+
```

The program searches for the next occurrence of "\+" in the input text and repeats the substitution process to get:

```
She sells sea+shells down by the sea+
```

The routine finds no more "\+" substrings so the final result is:

```
She sells sea+shells down by the sea+shore
```

The following code shows subroutine UnprotectChar in its entirety:

```
Public Sub UnprotectChar(txt As String, fr_ch As String, _
    to_ch As String)
Dim fr_str As String
Dim new_txt As String
Dim old_pos As Integer
Dim new_pos As Integer
Dim token As String
Dim fr_len As Integer
Dim txt_len As Integer

    fr_str = "\" & fr_ch
    fr_len = Len(fr_str)
    txt_len = Len(txt)
    new_txt = ""
    old_pos = 1
    Do
        ' Find the next \fr_ch.
        new_pos = InStr(old_pos, txt, fr_str)
        If new_pos < 1 Then new_pos = txt_len + 1

        ' Convert fr_ch into to_ch in this part.
        token = Mid$(txt, old_pos, new_pos - old_pos)
        ConvertToken token, fr_ch, to_ch

        ' Add the result to the new string.
        new_txt = new_txt & token

        ' If we're beyond the end, we're done.
        If new_pos > txt_len Then Exit Do

        ' Add the fr_ch.
        new_txt = new_txt & fr_ch
```

```
        ' Move beyond the \fr_ch.
        old_pos = new_pos + fr_len
    Loop

    txt = new_txt
End Sub
```

Summary

Microsoft's Internet Transfer Control allows a Web page to retrieve or execute a file on a remote server. The InetXfer ActiveX control uses the Internet Transfer Control to send data to a remote program. InetXfer takes care of the special processing needed to keep the data safe during transit. ProgramSaveData.EXE, running on the server computer, unpacks the data sent by InetXfer and appends it to a file.

The WebSurvey application was kept simple intentionally so it would be easy to concentrate on the new tasks of sending and receiving data across a network. This application could be extended to provide much more elaborate surveys or other programs that would allow a Web user to interact with a program running on a remote server.

Chapter 19

SiteMapper

Microsoft's Internet transfer control allows programs to transfer data across the World Wide Web in several ways. Chapter 18 shows how to use this control to upload data from a Web page to a remote server computer.

The Internet transfer control's OpenURL method allows a program to copy information in the other direction—from a remote Web page to a local application. This chapter shows how a program can use this capability to search a group of Web pages automatically. The SiteMapper program begins by visiting a Web page. It searches that page for references to other Web pages that are located at the same site. It then visits those pages, looking for new Web addresses that it has not yet visited. It continues visiting new pages until it has visited every HTML document at the site that it can reach from the original document.

The following section, "Using SiteMapper," describes SiteMapper from the user's point of view. It explains how to enter a URL, select the types of files the program should locate, and interpret the results.

The "Key Techniques" section that follows lists the most important programming methods demonstrated by SiteMapper. The rest of the chapter describes those methods in detail.

Using SiteMapper

To run SiteMapper the user enters a Web address or URL (Universal Resource Locator) in the Start URL text box. At a minimum, the URL must contain the protocol http and a site name as in "http://www.mysite.com." Next the user selects the types of files SiteMapper should locate using the check boxes.

When the user clicks the Start button, SiteMapper loads the document at the specified start URL. It searches the document for file names that match the file types checked. SiteMapper is not very clever about how it searches for these file names. It simply searches for the appropriate file extensions and assumes that they are parts of file names. This means the program will report file names contained within an HTML comment and that it will treat other strings that contain the correct extensions as file names even if they make no sense.

For example, if the program found the text "Download .GIF or .JPG files," it would treat the strings ".GIF" and ".JPG" as file names.

After SiteMapper has identified the files referenced in the original document, it loads any that are HTML files located at the same Web site and searches them for more URLs. It continues searching the documents it finds until it has examined every file it can reach.

When it is finished, the program displays the results of its search. For each document visited, the program lists the file name matches it found in that document. Figure 19.1 shows SiteMapper after it has visited the address http://Beauty/Ch19/Mapper1.HTM. You can find copies of the Web pages it visited in the Ch19\Html directory on the compact disk.

The documents that SiteMapper visited to produce Figure 19.1 are related in the simple tree-like way shown in Figure 19.2. Arrows indicate links between the files. For example, the file Mapper2.HTM contains links to Mapper1.HTM, Mapper2a.HTM, and Mapper2b.HTM. These links are listed by SiteMapper in Figure 19.1. The Ch19\Home directory on the compact disk contains a more complicated example.

Key Techniques

This program's use of the Internet transfer control is extremely simple. The parts of the application that use the data retrieved by the control are more complicated.

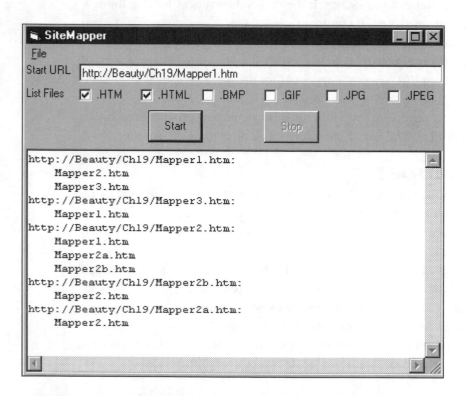

FIGURE 19.1 SiteMapper mapping http://Beauty/Ch19/Mapper1.HTM.

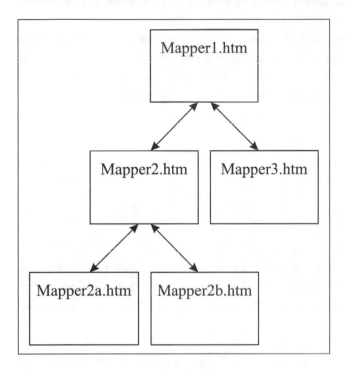

FIGURE 19.2 The relationships among the HTML documents that produced Figure 19.1.

The following list briefly describes the techniques used by SiteMapper. The rest of the chapter explains these techniques in detail.

- **Retrieving Web Documents**. The Internet transfer control's OpenURL method retrieves a document from the Web. This section explains how a program can use the OpenURL method.
- **Parsing URLs**. SiteMapper must parse each URL so it can determine if it is within the same site as the original document. This section shows how to parse URLs.
- **Expanding URLs**. Many Web documents contain partial URLs. This section tells how SiteMapper expands partial URLs into complete addresses.
- **Mapping Web Sites**. SiteMapper uses a depth-first search to examine a Web site. This section explains how SiteMapper avoids visiting a Web document more than once.
- **Modifying SiteMapper**. SiteMapper searches a Web site for certain kinds of files. This section suggests changes to SiteMapper to make it perform other, similar tasks.

Retrieving Web Documents

Retrieving a document from the Web is easy using the Internet Transfer Control's OpenURL method. This method takes as its only parameter the Web address of the document it should open.

If the address indicates a directory on an FTP server, OpenURL returns a listing of the directory. Otherwise, if the address leads to a file, OpenURL returns the contents of the file.

SiteMapper uses the following code to fetch Web documents. It uses the On Error Resume Next statement to trap errors that may occur when OpenURL is running. If there is an error, the program adds an error message to its output text. A program can fail to retrieve a document over a network in many ways, so it is important that every network operation be protected with error-trapping code.

```
On Error Resume Next
txt = Inet1.OpenURL(the_url)
If Err.Number <> 0 Then
    Results = Results & "     Error" & _
        Str$(Err.Number) & " reading " & _
        the_url & vbCrLf & "     " & _
        Err.Description & vbCrLf
    Exit Sub
End If
On Error GoTo 0
```

SiteMapper opens only HTML documents. Because these are text files, OpenURL returns a string containing the contents of the files. This string is pure HTML text and is not interpreted in any way by the OpenURL method. A Web browser built using OpenURL would parse the raw HTML code and decide what to display.

SiteMapper's needs are much simpler than those of a browser. When it retrieves a document, it searches for certain strings within the document. For instance, if the user checks the .GIF button, SiteMapper looks for the string ".GIF." This process is explained in more detail in the section "Mapping Web Sites."

Parsing URLs

SiteMapper must parse each URL it encounters for two reasons. First, it must decide if the new URL is within the site the program is visiting. Second, it must determine which parts of a possibly incomplete URL are present so it knows what pieces it must add to create a complete URL. The section "Expanding URLs" explains how SiteMapper fills in any missing pieces.

The following section briefly describes the pieces of a URL. The section after that explains how SiteMapper parses URLs to identify their pieces.

Understanding URLs

As far as SiteMapper is concerned, a URL has four pieces:

```
protocol://site/path/file
```

The pieces are described in the following list:

- **protocol**. The protocol tells Web browsers what methods to use when manipulating the file. This can be http, ftp, gopher, nntp, and so on.
- **site**. This is the name of the Web site that holds the document. In general, a URL may contain other information here including a user name and password or a port number. For example, in

"rod:let_me_in@www.mysite.com:80" the user name is "rod," the password is "let_me_in," and the Web site uses port number 80. SiteMapper treats all of these components as part of the site name.

- **path**. This is the directory path to the file on the Web site. A complete URL always contains a path, even if it is just "/" indicating the document is in the site's root directory.
- **file**. This is the name of the document. The name may include a marker within the document. For example, the address "File1.HTM#marker" indicates the Web browser should jump to the location "marker" within the file File1.HTM. The marker is defined in the document with the following HTML code:

```
<A NAME="marker">Text displayed at this point</A>
```

SiteMapper ignores markers because it does not matter what part of a document the program visits. When the program opens a document, it reads the entire file including all of the marked locations.

Many documents contain partial URLs. Missing pieces of the URL are filled in using the components of the current document's URL. For instance, suppose the document located at http://www.mysite .com/Public/Index.HTM contains the following reference:

```
<A HREF="Details.HTM">Jump to details page.</A>
```

The URL Details.HTM does not contain a protocol, site, or path. They are filled in using the values given by the current document. The complete URL is http://www.mysite.com/Public/Details.HTM.

Table 19.1 shows some partial URLs and their corresponding complete URLs. The table assumes the URLs are being read from the file http://site/dir1/dir2/File1.HTM. SiteMapper must be able to parse each of these different kinds of URLs correctly.

ParseURL

SiteMapper uses the ParseURL subroutine to separate URLs into their pieces. ParseURL begins by removing markers from the URL. It does this by stripping out any text that comes after a number sign. If the

TABLE 19.1 Partial and Complete URLs

Location of file	Partial URL	Complete URL
Same directory	File2.HTM	http://site/dir1/dir2/File2.HTM
Subdirectory	subdir/File2.HTM	http://site/dir1/dir2/subdir/File2.HTM
Root directory	/File2.HTM	http://site/File2.HTM
Another directory	/path2/File2.HTM	http://site/path2/File2.HTM
Parent directory	../File2.HTM	http://site/dir1/File2.HTM
Subdirectory of the parent directory	../subdir/File2.HTM	http://site/dir1/subdir/File2.HTM

original URL was http://www.mysite.com/dir1/dir2/File.HTM#marker, the address becomes http://www.mysite.com/dir1/dir2/File.HTM.

Next, ParseURL locates the address's protocol. The routine assumes the protocol is followed by the string ":/ /." After recording the protocol, ParseURL removes it from the URL string. The example URL becomes www.mysite.com/dir1/dir2/File.HTM.

If the protocol is not present, the URL is a partial URL that should not include a site either. Otherwise, the site name includes the text up to the next slash. The routine saves the site name and removes it from the URL, giving /dir1/dir2/File.HTM.

ParseURL then locates the file name in the URL by finding the rightmost slash. Whatever text comes after this slash must be the file name. If this text includes a period as in File.HTM, ParseURL records the file name and removes it from the URL. Otherwise, the subroutine assumes this text is a subdirectory name and there is no file name in the URL. For example, the URL /dir1/dir2 contains no period after the rightmost slash so ParseURL assumes dir2 is a directory name.

Whatever remains of the text is the path. If ParseURL found a site name, then the path must be absolutely not relative. In this case, ParseURL makes sure the path begins with a slash. The subroutine also makes sure the path includes a trailing slash whether this is an absolute path or not.

```
Sub ParseURL(ByVal the_url As String, the_protocol As String, _
    the_site As String, the_path As String, the_file As String)
Dim pos As Integer
Dim got_site As Boolean

    the_url = Trim$(the_url)

    ' Remove any reference to a marker.
    pos = InStr(the_url, "#")
    If pos > 0 Then
        the_url = Left$(the_url, pos - 1)
    End If

    ' Find the protocol.
    pos = InStr(the_url, "://")
    If pos = 0 Then
        ' There is no protocol or site.
        the_protocol = NO_PROTOCOL
        the_site = NO_SITE
        got_site = False
    Else
        ' Record the protocol.
        the_protocol = Left$(the_url, pos - 1)

        ' Remove the protocol from the URL.
        the_url = Right$(the_url, Len(the_url) - pos - 2)

        ' Find the site.
        If the_url = "" Then
            ' There is no site.
```

```
            the_site = NO_SITE
            got_site = False
        Else
            pos = InStr(the_url, "/")
            If pos = 0 Then pos = Len(the_url) + 1
            the_site = Left$(the_url, pos - 1)
            got_site = True

                ' Remove the site from the URL.
            the_url = Right$(the_url, Len(the_url) - pos + 1)

                ' If there's nothing left, use the
                ' root path.
            If the_url = "" Then the_url = "/"
        End If
    End If

    ' Find the file.
    If the_url = "" Then
            ' There is no file.
        the_file = NO_FILE
    Else
            ' Find the last "/".
        pos = 1
        Do While InStr(pos, the_url, "/") > 0
            pos = InStr(pos, the_url, "/") + 1
        Loop
        If pos > Len(the_url) Then
                ' The url ends with a "/". No file.
            the_file = NO_FILE
        Else
                ' See if the "file" has a "." in it.
            If InStr(pos, the_url, ".") > 0 Then
                    ' It does. This is the file.
                the_file = Right$(the_url, _
                    Len(the_url) - pos + 1)

                    ' Remove the file from the URL.
                the_url = Left$(the_url, pos - 1)
            Else
                    ' No ".". There is no file.
                the_file = NO_FILE
            End If
        End If
    End If

    ' Whatever is left is the path.
    If the_url = "" Then
            ' There is no path.
        the_path = NO_PATH
    Else
```

```
        the_path = the_url

        ' If we got a site, make sure there's
        ' a leading slash.
        If got_site And Left$(the_path, 1) <> "/" Then
            the_path = "/" & the_path
        End If

        ' Make sure there's a trailing slash.
        If Right$(the_path, 1) <> "/" Then
            the_path = the_path & "/"
        End If
    End If
End Sub
```

Expanding URLs

When SiteMapper encounters a partial URL, it must convert it into an absolute URL for two reasons. First, SiteMapper uses complete URLs so that it can correctly identify different documents. Suppose one document refers to a file using a partial URL and another document refers to the same file using a complete URL. SiteMapper uses the complete URL to determine that the two refer to the same file. This allows the program to visit each file only once.

The second reason SiteMapper uses complete URLs is that OpenURL does not understand partial URLs. It has no concept of a current document, so it does not have values it can use for missing portions of a partial URL. For that reason, SiteMapper needs a complete URL whenever it invokes OpenURL.

The starting URL entered by the user must include a protocol and site. Initially SiteMapper has not visited any document so it cannot use the current document's protocol and site to fill in missing values. If the user does not provide a protocol and site, SiteMapper presents an error message.

If the URL does not contain a file name, the Web page server at the site decides which file it will return to OpenURL. Some servers return Index.HTM; others return Home.HTM if those files exist in the directory specified by the URL. If the appropriate file is not present, and if the site's directory permissions allow it, the server may return an index of the directory. This will include a list of every document in that directory—it will give SiteMapper lots of URLs to explore.

In these cases, SiteMapper does not know whether it received Index.HTM, Home.HTM, or a directory listing. Later, if it encounters a document that contains a reference to this file, SiteMapper will not realize that the files are the same. This will make the program visit the file again.

For example, suppose the user enters "http://Beast/Home" as the starting URL. This does not include a file name, so the server running on Beast decides to return the file Index.HTM. Now suppose one of the files referenced in Index.HTM refers back to Index.HTM. SiteMapper will not realize it has already visited Index.HTM, and it will visit it again.

Once SiteMapper begins, it knows the site and path of the current document. It stores these values in the global variables CurrentSite and CurrentPath and uses them to fill in missing parts of any relative URLs it encounters.

Subroutine CompleteURL performs this task. It begins by checking the parsed URL for a site name. If no site is present, the subroutine uses the value CurrentSite. At that point, if the path is an absolute path (starting with a slash), the URL is complete.

If the site is not present and the path is a relative path (not starting with a slash), CompleteURL has more work to do. The routine determines whether the new path begins with "../" indicating an upward movement through the site's directory structure. If so, the routine removes the "../" characters from the new path and removes the rightmost directory from CurrentPath. It repeats this process until the new path does not begin with "../."

For example, suppose CurrentPath is "/dir1/dir2/dir3/" and the new path is "../../subdir/." Then these paths would undergo the following series of transformations:

```
/dir1/dir2/dir3/  ../../subdir/
/dir1/dir2/       ../subdir/
/dir1/   subdir/
```

At this point CompleteURL combines CurrentPath and the remainder of the new path to find the new absolute path. In the previous example, the new absolute path would be /dir1/subdir/.

```
' The URL components currently in use.
Private CurrentSite As String
Private CurrentPath As String
Private CurrentFile As String


Private Sub CompleteURL(the_site As String, the_path As String)
Dim i As Integer

    ' If no site is specified, use CurrentSite
    ' and check for a relative path.
    If the_site = NO_SITE Then
        ' No site. Use CurrentSite.
        the_site = CurrentSite

        ' If the_path is an absolute path, it's
        ' already set. Look for a relative path.
        If Left$(the_path, 1) <> "/" Then
            ' It's a relative path.

            ' Check for ".." in the path.
            Do While Left$(the_path, 3) = "../"
                ' Remove the last directory
                ' from CurrentPath.
                For i = Len(CurrentPath) - 1 To 1 Step -1
                    If Mid$(CurrentPath, i, 1) = "/" Then Exit For
                Next i
                If i <= 1 Then
                    CurrentPath = "/"
                Else
                    CurrentPath = Left$(CurrentPath, i)
                End If
```

```
             ' Remove the "../" from the_path.
                the_path = Right$(the_path, Len(the_path) - 3)
            Loop

            ' The ".."s are gone. Add the_path
            ' to CurrentPath.
            the_path = CurrentPath & the_path
        End If
    End If
End Sub
```

Mapping Web Sites

SiteMapper performs a depth-first traversal of the documents it can reach from the initial URL without leaving the initial site. The process is controlled by four collections: GotoSite, GotoPath, GotoFile, and BeenThere. The Goto collections store the sites, paths, and files of documents the program has not yet visited. BeenThere stores the complete URLs of documents that the program has already visited. Before visiting a document, SiteMapper checks BeenThere to make sure it has not already visited the document.

The document traversal begins with subroutine ReadSite. This subroutine uses ParseURL to break the initial URL into its components. It adds the URL's site, path, and file name to the Goto collections. Then it repeatedly invokes the VisitURL subroutine until there are no more URLs to visit.

```
Private Sub ReadSite()
Dim the_protocol As String
Dim the_site As String
Dim the_path As String
Dim the_file As String

    ' Start with no results.
    ResultText.Text = ""
    Results = ""

    ' Parse the URL.
    ParseURL Trim$(URLText.Text), the_protocol, _
        the_site, the_path, the_file

    ' Make sure we have a site name.
    If the_site = NO_SITE Then
        Beep
        MsgBox "The URL must include a site name.", _
            vbOKOnly + vbInformation, _
            "Site Required"
        URLText.SetFocus
        Exit Sub
    End If

    ' Allocate empty collections.
    Set GotoSite = New Collection
```

```
Set GotoPath = New Collection
Set GotoFile = New Collection
Set BeenThere = New Collection

    ' Put the URL in the list of URLs to visit.
    GotoSite.Add the_site
    GotoPath.Add the_path
    GotoFile.Add the_file
    NumUrls = 1

    ' Repeatedly loop until we have visited all
    ' the URLs or we're told to stop.
    ContinueReading = True
    Do
        ' Visit a URL.
        VisitURL

        ' Process events (including the Stop
        ' button press).
        DoEvents
    Loop While ContinueReading And NumUrls > 0

    ' Display the results.
    ResultText.Text = Results

    ' Free the collections.
    Set GotoSite = Nothing
    Set GotoPath = Nothing
    Set GotoFile = Nothing
    Set BeenThere = Nothing
End Sub
```

Subroutine VisitURL fetches one of the documents with site, path, and file name stored in the Goto-Site, GotoPath, and GotoFile collections. The routine begins by reading the next site, path, and file name from the Goto collections. It builds the document's complete URL and checks to see if the URL appears in the BeenThere collection. If so, the document has already been visited so VisitURL is done.

VisitURL then uses the Internet transfer control's OpenURL method to fetch the document. It passes the returned text to the ExamineDocument subroutine to perform the actual processing of the file.

```
Private Sub VisitURL()
Dim the_url As String
Dim txt As String
Dim been_there As String

    ' Fetch the next URL in the list.
    CurrentSite = GotoSite(NumUrls)
    CurrentPath = GotoPath(NumUrls)
    CurrentFile = GotoFile(NumUrls)
    GotoSite.Remove NumUrls
    GotoPath.Remove NumUrls
```

```
GotoFile.Remove NumUrls
NumUrls = NumUrls - 1

    ' Build the URL.
    the_url = "http://" & CurrentSite & _
        CurrentPath & CurrentFile

    ' See if we have already visited it.
    been_there = ""
    On Error Resume Next
    been_there = BeenThere(the_url)
    On Error GoTo 0

    ' If we've already visited it, quit.
    If been_there <> "" Then Exit Sub

    'Add it to the list of visited URLs.
    BeenThere.Add "X", the_url

    ' Try to open the URL.
    On Error Resume Next
    txt = Inet1.OpenURL(the_url)
    If Err.Number <> 0 Then
        Results = Results & "    Error" & _
            Str$(Err.Number) & " reading " & _
            the_url & vbCrLf & "        " & _
            Err.Description & vbCrLf
        Exit Sub
    End If
    On Error GoTo 0

    ' Read the document looking for links.
    ExamineDocument the_url, txt
End Sub
```

Subroutine ExamineDocument searches the returned file for certain key values selected by the user. It begins by checking to see if the document contains the string "Object Not Found." If OpenURL tries to open a file that does not exist on a Web site, the server will return a valid HTML document that says "Object Not Found." Normally a Web browser would simply display this document. SitcMapper adds an error message to its result string.

Next, ExamineDocument looks for the names of files with the types selected by the user. When it finds an appropriate file extension, it uses the FindFileType function to find the complete file name within the document. SiteMapper does not actually parse the entire HTML document. It merely searches for appropriate file extensions.

When it finds a file, ExamineDocument adds its name to the Results string. If the file extension is .HTM or .HTML, ExamineDocument also calls the AddURL subroutine. AddURL verifies that the new URL is within the same site and adds it to the list of URLs to visit later.

```
Private Sub ExamineDocument(the_url As String, txt As String)
Dim i As Integer
Dim pos As Integer
Dim file_name As String

    Results = Results & the_url & ":" & vbCrLf

        ' See if it says "Object not found" and
        ' not much else.
    If InStr(1, txt, "Object Not Found", INSENSITIVE) _
        > 0 And Len(txt) < 80 _
    Then
        Results = Results & _
            "      Object Not Found" & vbCrLf
        Exit Sub
    End If

        ' Look for each of the selected file types.
    For i = 0 To MAX_FILE_TYPE
        ' See if we should visit it.
        If FileTypeCheck(i).Value = vbChecked Then
            ' Find the first file of this type.
            pos = 1
            file_name = FindFileType(txt, pos, FileType(i))
            Do While pos > 0
                ' Display it.
                Results = Results & "      " & _
                    file_name & vbCrLf

                ' If it's an HTM or HTML file
                ' and it's in this site,
                ' add it to the list of URLs
                ' to visit.
                If i = 0 Or i = 1 Then _
                    AddUrl file_name

                ' Find the next file of this type.
                file_name = FindFileType(txt, pos, FileType(i))
            Loop
        End If
    Next i
End Sub
```

Function FindFileType takes as parameters an HTML document, a position at which to start searching the document, and a file's extension. It searches the document from the indicated point looking for the extension.

If it finds the extension, FindFileType uses the NameStart and NameEnd functions to locate the beginning and end of the file name that contains the extension.

NameStart searches the document backwards from the extension looking for the beginning of the file name. It stops when it reaches a nonprintable character (space, tab), an equals sign, a single or double quote, or an angled bracket. This covers the following situations:

```
<A HREF="File.HTM">...
<A HREF='File.HTM'>...
<A HREF=File.HTM>...
<A HREF = File.HTM>...
```

NameEnd searches the document forward from the extension looking for the end of the file name. It stops when it reaches a nonprintable character, an equals sign, a single or double quote, or an angled bracket. It also stops at a number sign so URL markers are not considered part of the file name.

These rules for finding file names are not perfect, but they work in the majority of cases. For instance, the HTML code <A HREF="File Name With Spaces.HTM"> references a file name that is valid in some operating systems, including Windows 95 and Windows NT. File names that contain spaces are not guaranteed to transmit safely across the Web, however, so they are rare in Web pages.

```
Private Function FindFileType(txt As String, pos As Integer, _
    ext As String) As String
Dim pos1 As Integer
Dim pos2 As Integer
Dim pos3 As Integer

    ' Find the extension.
    pos2 = InStr(pos, txt, ext, INSENSITIVE)
    If pos2 = 0 Then
        pos = 0
        FindFileType = ""
        Exit Function
    End If

    ' Find the beginning of the file name.
    pos1 = NameStart(txt, pos2 - 1)

    ' Find the end of the file name.
    pos3 = NameEnd(txt, pos2 + Len(ext))

    ' Get the resulting file name.
    FindFileType = Mid$(txt, pos1, pos3 - pos1 + 1)

    ' Move pos after the name.
    pos = pos3 + 1
End Function

Private Function NameStart(txt As String, pos2 As Integer) As Integer
Dim i As Integer
Dim ch As String

    ' Look for a stopping character.
    For i = pos2 To 1 Step -1
```

```
            ch = Mid$(txt, i, 1)

            If ch <= " " Or ch > "~" Or _
                ch = """" Or ch = "'" Or _
                ch = "<" Or ch = ">" Or ch = "=" _
                Then Exit For

            If ch <= " " Or ch > "~" Or _
                ch = """" Or ch = "'" _
                Then Exit For
        Next i
        NameStart = i + 1
End Function

Private Function NameEnd(txt As String, pos2 As Integer) As Integer
Dim txt_len As Integer
Dim i As Integer
Dim ch As String

        txt_len = Len(txt)

        ' Look for a stopping character.
        For i = pos2 To txt_len
            ch = Mid$(txt, i, 1)
            If ch <= " " Or ch > "~" Or _
                ch = """" Or ch = "'" Or _
                ch = "<" Or ch = ">" Or ch = "#" _
                Then Exit For
        Next i
        NameEnd = i - 1
End Function
```

Subroutine AddURL is the last major piece of SiteMapper. It begins by using ParseURL to separate the URL's pieces. It compares the URL's site to the variable CurrentSite to ensure that the URL is within the current site.

AddURL then uses CompleteURL to convert a partial URL into an absolute URL. It adds the completed site, path, and file names to the GotoSite, GotoPath, and GotoFile collections. Later the VisitURL subroutine will retrieve these values and visit the document if it has not already been visited.

```
Private Sub AddUrl(ByVal the_url As String)
Dim the_protocol As String
Dim the_site As String
Dim the_path As String
Dim the_file As String

        ' Parse the URL.
        ParseURL the_url, the_protocol, _
            the_site, the_path, the_file

        ' Make sure it's in the same site.
        If the_site <> "" And _
```

```
        the_site <> CurrentSite Then Exit Sub

    ' Complete the URL to give it a site and
    ' absolute path.
    CompleteURL the_site, the_path

    ' Add the URL components to the list.
    GotoSite.Add the_site
    GotoPath.Add the_path
    GotoFile.Add the_file
    NumUrls = NumUrls + 1
End Sub
```

Modifying SiteMapper

SiteMapper searches documents at a Web site that are related to an initial URL. It presents a list of the files referenced in those documents. In addition to describing the layout of the site, this provides useful Web debugging information. In one test on my home page, SiteMapper discovered that one of the connected documents referred to the file AnoutRod.HTM. This was a typographical error—the file's name should have been AboutRod.HTM. When SiteMapper tried to visit the nonexistent AnoutRod.HTM, it presented an error message indicating that the file did not exist. This made it easy to find and correct the problem.

SiteMapper could be enhanced to provide even more file validation. For example, it could attempt to open each of the .GIF, .JPG, and .JPEG files it encountered. If a file could not be opened, SiteMapper would present an error message.

SiteMapper currently searches documents for file name extensions. It could be easily modified to search for keywords as well. SiteMapper could traverse Web documents and present a list of the documents that contained certain words or phrases.

The program could also traverse documents in more than one Web site. In that case, it would need some method for deciding which sites to visit. Without some direction the program would attempt to traverse the entire World Wide Web. Assuming the computer had enough disk space and memory, such an unrestricted search would take an extremely long time.

Instead of running unchecked for weeks, the program could ask the user for permission to visit each new site it encountered. Alternatively, it could keep track of the number of intermediate sites between the starting URL and new documents. The program would not visit sites where the number of intermediate sites exceeded some limit.

Some search engines use an unrestricted Web search to gather data. These Web crawlers, spiders, and worms traverse sites all over the Web, looking for interesting information and adding it to their databases. Users can later search the databases for keywords to obtain a list of the URLs that might be interesting.

Summary

SiteMapper only hints at the possibilities available to an automated Web client program. Such a program can be used to map and debug a Web site, list all of the files available at a site, or search for specific keywords and phrases. The program can even use artificial intelligence methods to identify pages containing information related to certain topics of interest. Using search techniques, it can venture out onto the larger Web and examine many sites to achieve its goal.

What's on the CD-ROM

The CD-ROM contains Visual Basic source code for all of the applications described in this book. The files on the compact disk are separated by chapter. Code for the PeopleWatcher application described in Chapter 8, for example, is stored in the Ch8 subdirectory. Some chapter directories contain subdirectories that hold data or different programs described within the chapter. The contents of the directories are listed in table A.1.

TABLE A.1 CD-ROM Contents

Directory	Application	Purpose
Ch1	ExpenseReporter	Create and print expense reports.
Ch2		(There is no Ch2 directory.)
Ch3	AppointmentBook	Manage appointments,
Ch4	PropertySetter	Add-in to examine and set control properties at design time.
Ch5	Aligner	Add-in to align controls at run time.
Ch6	Scroller	Add-in to create scrolled windows.
Ch7	AddInMaker	Add-in to create other add-ins.
Ch8	PeopleWatcher	Customized personnel database system.
Ch9	Query	Ad hoc database query tool.
Ch10	PeopleWatcher Remote	Personnel system distributed across a network.

Continued

TABLE A.1 *Continued*

Directory	Application	Purpose
Ch11	TimeSync	Client/server that synchronizes the clocks on two computers.
Ch12	QueryServer	Client/server database reporting application.
Ch13	AsyncServer	Asynchronous client/server database reporting application.
Ch14	Alarm	Alarm custom control.
Ch15	BarGauge	Bar gauge custom control.
Ch16	Histogram	Histogram custom control.
Ch17		Using ActiveX controls on Web pages.
Ch18	WebSurvey	Web survey form processing.
Ch19	SiteMapper	Web site mapping.

Hardware Requirements

To run and modify the example applications, you need a computer that is reasonably able to run Visual Basic 5.0. You will also need a compact disk drive to load the programs from the accompanying compact disk.

The client/server applications described in Chapters 10 through 13 use more advanced networking and OLE server techniques that work only in the Visual Basic Enterprise Edition under Windows 95 and Windows NT. The ActiveX applications presented in Chapters 14 through 19 use features introduced in Visual Basic 5.

If you do not have the Enterprise Edition, or you are running an older version of Windows, some of these applications will not run as they are presented in the book. You can still read the chapters and learn valuable lessons about the application architectures, however. Using the fundamental architectures and some file management tricks, you can even implement similar applications without using OLE servers. This is a hard route to follow, however, and you may be better off if you upgrade your software and save a lot of time and trouble.

All of the applications on the compact disk have been tested in Visual Basic 5.0 under Windows 95 and Windows NT. The programs explained in Chapters 1, 2, and 4 through 13 were also tested using Visual Basic 4.0. Though the programs may look slightly different in the two environments, they will perform in roughly the same manner. The applications described in the Chapters 3 and 14 through 19 use features introduced by Visual Basic 5.0 so they will not run with earlier versions of Visual Basic.

The applications will run at different speeds on different computers with different configurations, but they will all work. If you own a 200 megahertz Pentium with 64MB of memory, applications will run much faster than they would if you owned a 486-based computer with 8MB of memory. Both machines will be able to run the applications, but at different speeds. You will quickly learn the limits of your hardware.

Installing the Software

You can load the example programs into the Visual Basic development environment using the Open Project command in the File menu. You can select the files directly from the compact disk, or you can copy them onto your hard disk first. Note that files on a compact disk are always marked read-only since you cannot save files to a compact disk. If you copy files onto your hard disk, the copies are also marked as read-only. If you want to modify these files, you must give yourself write permission for them.

You can do this with the Windows Explorer. First, copy the files you want onto your hard disk. Then select the files and invoke the Properties command in the Explorer's File menu. Uncheck the Read Only check box and press the Ok button. At this point you can make changes to the copied application and save the changes to your hard disk. Do not worry about making careless changes to the copy and accidentally breaking the application. You can always copy the files again later from the compact disk.

User Assistance and Information

The software accompanying this book is being provided as is without warranty or support of any kind. Should you require basic installation assistance, or if your media is defective, please call our product support number at (212) 850-6194 weekdays between 9 A.M. and 4 P.M. Eastern Standard Time. Or, we can be reached via e-mail at: wprtusw@wiley.com. You can also send comments or questions to the author at: RodStephens@compuserve.com.

To place additional orders or to request information about other Wiley products, please call (800) 879-4539.

Index

Using the Software

This software contains files to help you utilize the models described in the accompanying book. By opening the package, you are agreeing to be bound by the following agreement: